Through the Dark Labyrinth

Also by Gordon Bowker

Pursued by Furies: A Life of Malcolm Lowry
Malcolm Lowry Remembered (*ed*)

GORDON BOWKER

Through the Dark Labyrinth

A Biography of Lawrence Durrell

St. Martin's Press
New York

THROUGH THE DARK LABYRINTH. Copyright © 1997 by
Gordon Bowker. All rights reserved. Printed in the United
States of America. No part of this book may be used or
reproduced in any manner whatsoever without written
permission except in the case of brief quotations embodied in critical articles or reviews. For information, address
St. Martin's Press, 175 Fifth Avenue, New York, N.Y.
10010.

ISBN 0-312-17225-7

Library of Congress Cataloging-in-Publication Data

Bowker, Gordon.
    Through the dark labyrinth : a biography of Lawrence
Durrell / Gordon Bowker.
        p.   cm.
    Includes bibliographical references and index.
    ISBN 0-312-17225-7 (cloth)
    1. Durrell, Lawrence--Biography. 2. Authors, English--
20th century--Biography.   I. Title.
PR6007.U76Z525 1997
828'.91209--dc21   97-5672

                                              CIP

Designed by Intype London Ltd.

First edition: April 1997

10 9 8 7 6 5 4 3 2 1

To Ramdei, Catherine and Gordon – my Muses

Contents

List of Illustrations

Section 1

A Family of Empire (*Margaret Durrell*, Whatever Happened to Margo?, *André Deutsch*)
St Saviour's and St Olave's Grammar School (*The Headmaster, St Saviour's and St Olave's Grammar School*)
St Edmund's School, Canterbury (*The Headmaster, St Edmund's School, Canterbury*)
G.P. Hollingworth (*The Headmaster, St Edmund's School, Canterbury*)
Richard Aldington (*Catherine Aldington, with thanks to Rosica Colin Ltd*)
The Queen's Hotel (*GB*)
John Gawsworth (*John Cromer Braun*)
The Durrells in Corfu, c. 1937 (*Alan Thomas*)
The White House, Corfu (*GB*)
18 Villa Seurat, Paris (*GB*)
Dylan Thomas (*British Council*)
Tambimuttu (*British Council*)
David Gascoyne (*British Council*)
Henry Miller, 1933 (*Peter Owen Ltd*)
Anaïs Nin, 1933 (*Peter Owen Ltd*)
Robin Fedden (*Frances Fedden*)
Durrell's official pass for the Alexandria docks, c. 1943
Bernard Spencer (*British Council*)
Eve Cohen Durrell, 1947 (*Mary Hadkinson (Mollo)*)
Lawrence Durrell, 1947 (*Sir Bernard Burrows*)
Anaïs Nin with the Durrells, 1958 (*Peter Owen Ltd*)

Section 2

Durrell with Penelope, 1960 (*Loomis Dean/Life Magazine,*
© *Time Warner Inc/Katz*)
Durrell, Claude and Sappho, 1962 (*Hulton Deutsch*)
Gerry, Margo, Louisa and Larry at the zoo, 1960
(*Loomis Dean/Life Magazine,* © *Time Warner Inc/Katz*)
Durrell and Claude, 1961 (*Cecily Mackworth*)
15 Route de Saussines (*GB*)
Henry Miller and Durrell, Edinburgh, 1962 (*David Sim,
The Observer*)
G.S. Fraser (*John Cromer Braun*)
Durrell concealing his nose with hats (*Ghislaine de Boysson*)
Durrell with Ghislaine and Jacquie at 15 Route de Saussines
  (*Ghislaine de Boysson*)
Durrell in London, 1985 (*Neil Libbert, The Observer*)
St Julien de Salinelles, near Sommières (*GB*)

Preface

> I write like other people make love; it's a
> vice.
>
> Lawrence Durrell

Lawrence Durrell is undoubtedly one of the most important and fascinating writers Britain has produced this century. Often he is linked with two other writers of the same generation, Malcolm Lowry and William Golding, as producing experimental fiction of great power and originality outside the mainstream of English fiction, with its often parochial obsessions. Durrell was certainly the most prolific of the three. He published eighteen novels (to Golding's ten and Lowry's four), numerous volumes of poetry, three plays, six travel books, three books of humorous anecdotes, four volumes of letters and essays, many prefaces, and several screenplays. He also had a modest success in France as a painter under an assumed name. By any standard he is a writer of considerable power and importance. Many thought he should have won the Nobel Prize for *The Alexandria Quartet*, still undoubtedly one of the greatest achievements of any postwar novelist. Like Proust, another writer with whom he is often compared, he chose a wide canvas and saw all his fiction as interconnected, so that, in his late five-part *Avignon Quintet*, characters from his earlier novels put in appearances. He wrote with a painter's eye, and it is this, plus his subtle attempts to explore modern love in all its aspects, that has won him a vast readership throughout the world.

Durrell's life is fascinating and controversial – a complex

enigma, a dark labyrinth into which, it seems, he deliberately plunged in pursuit of hidden knowledge and self-enlighten-ment. He married four times, once to a girl twenty–five years his junior, and was accused after his death of having had an incestuous relationship with his daughter, who committed suicide in 1985. He went wherever his adventurous mind took him, often into murky regions of the unconscious, in trying to uncover the sources of human creativity and happiness. Exploring these hidden territories of the mind, he sought in eastern philosophy and modern psychology means of harnessing his own obsession with sex to a powerful drive for creativity. From early on he was fascinated by sexual deviation, especially by bisexuality in the animal world and its manifestation among humans. His curiosity about sex led him to read the Marquis de Sade, and his friends attest to the strange streak of cruelty which underlay the cheerful, humorous, humane and happy-go-lucky exterior. It was prob-ably this obsessive interest in sex and cruelty which led him to involve the women in his life in his fantasies, so that love was something he sought and yet seemed ever ready to destroy.

Following the trail into the dark labyrinth of Durrell's mind is to venture deep into the creative subconscious. His was a mind which gave birth to some of the most lyrical poetry of the century and some of the most exquisitely composed and conceived fiction of our time, but a mind which at the same time dwelt amongst the cruel and violent fantasies of de Sade. He was, as he confessed, completely amoral where sex was concerned – anything went, and along with his friend and mentor Henry Miller he set out to change western conscious-ness in a more sexually liberated direction.

His amorality probably stemmed from his sense of disloc-ation from English society and the freedom which comes from his kind of expatriation. But he sought to justify himself through eastern religions, especially Buddhism, and argued that life is just a dream and that reality is glimpsed only when our dreams are disrupted. Eighteen months before he died at the age of seventy-eight, he told an interviewer:

I must confess I have enjoyed nothing in my life. I've been bored ever since I crawled out of my mother's womb and never found anything that really pleased me... I've always been conscious of being... stillborn... and I feel always very posthumous...[1]

Now that he is dead, Durrell will, I believe, continue to leave his mark on modern literature, and on the lives of the many who fell under his spell.

Insofar as all lives are fictions – something Durrell recognized in his subtly compelling novels – any account of a life can be no more than a version of that life. This version of Durrell's life is offered in homage to a writer who has impressed and excited me ever since I first read his poetry as a teenager. I first discovered Durrell while serving at a desert outpost in Egypt in 1953, when I came across a volume containing some of his poems. Later I spend six months in Cyprus while he was Director of Information there (though I was unaware of it at the time), and when I read *Bitter Lemons* it seemed to me the perfect account of that lovely island at a tragic and explosive period of its history, and one of the best sustained pieces of poetic prose I had then read. When *Justine* appeared shortly afterwards, I was hooked on Lawrence Durrell, and have remained so ever since, though not everything he wrote afterwards recaptured the magic of those earlier works. When I set out on this enterprise, I was unable to get the support of the Lawrence Durrell Estate because an 'official' biography was in train, so instead I thought to write a book on the general theme of literary exile, with Durrell as one of a number of writers illustrating that subject. However, as I learned more and more about him, the old obsession reasserted itself and my interest in the general theme and the other writers gradually waned. What I had written about Durrell had expanded to book size, and the thought of having to cut it down was too much to bear. So it seemed that all I could do was to produce a full-blown biography, and that is what I have tried to do. I have, however, been unable to quote from Durrell's works, published or unpublished, except occasionally and briefly for purposes of literary explanation or critical comment.

*

The following people who knew Durrell have been most helpful to me and I would like to thank them all: Françoise Kestsman; Mary (Mollo) Hadkinson; Ghislaine de Boysson; Sir Steven Runciman; Sir Bernard and Lady Burrows; Richard Lumley, Lord Scarborough; Beatrice Dennis; Alan Ross; Hamish Henderson; Penelope Tremayne; Cecily Mackworth; Mrs. Noel Anan; Maria Pera; Diane Deriaz; Victor Selwyn; John Cromer Braun; Mursi Saad El Din; Henry Woolf; Miguel Alfredo Olivera; Professor Patrick O. Dudgeon; John Craxton; Desmond Hawkins; Alan Seabrook; Guy Wilkinson; Mary Fedden; George Lassalle.

I also owe grateful thanks to the following who have helped me: Shelley Cox and staff at the Morris Library, Southern Illinois University at Carbondale; T.W. Tuey, University of Victoria; Lorna Knight, National Library of Canada; Robert A. McCown, Head of Special Collections at Iowa University; Sue Presnell, Indiana University Libraries; Steven Tomlinson, Western Manuscripts, Bodleian Library; Anne Aldridge and staff, Goldsmiths' College Library; Dorothy B. Johnstone, Keeper of Manuscripts, University of Nottingham; Neil Sommerville, BBC Written Archives; staff at University College Library, London; the Brotherton Library, Leeds; The National Library of Scotland; Kings College Library, Cambridge; Senate House Library, London; Southwark Local History Library; Westminster Local History Library; Holborn Local History Library; Croydon Local History Library; Norwood Local History Library; Public Record Office, Kew; India House; St. Catherine's House; Somerset House; The British Library; The London Library; The National Sound Archives; Royal Geographical Society; Slade School of Art; the Royal British Legion; Queen's Hotel, Crystal Palace; F.D. Coulson, Headmaster, and Miss Rhoda Edwards, Archivist, St Olave's and St. Saviour's Grammar School; Mr. J.J. Astbury-Bailey and Miss Catherine Davis of St. Edmund's School; T.J. Walsh, Dulwich College; Elizabeth Hughes, Royal Society of Literature; Fr. G.E. Leclaire, S.J., St. Joseph's College, Darjeeling; Tasso Anastasiou, Corfu; Frances Fedden; Suzanne Lowry, Paris correspondent of the *Daily Telegraph*; Robert Fraser; Eddie Linden; James McKay; R.J. Collinson; Bryan Hayes; George Woodcock; Julian

Symons; Neville Braybrooke; Michael Holroyd; Elisabeth Barillé; James and Margaret Hepburn; Matina Raymond; Mr. and Mrs. David Petford, Oxford; Martin Durrant; Denise Hooker.

All biographers can benefit from the scrupulous scholarship of academics, and in the process of interpreting the life and work of Durrell I have been much influenced by reading the advanced research of the following: Patrick Von Richtofen, Emmanuel-Gabriel Georginis, A.F. Hassan and Donald P. Kaczvinsky, to whom I therefore owe a debt of gratitude.

I am grateful to the Estates of Robin Fedden and Dylan Thomas for permission to quote from their writings. I am also grateful to Valerie Eliot for permission to quote from the published work of T. S. Eliot.

Extracts from *Stephen Spender: Journals 1939–1983* reprinted by kind permission of the Estate of the Late Sir Stephen Spender. Copyright © 1986 by Stephen Spender. Extracts from the works of Anaïs Nin reprinted by permission of Gunther Stuhlmann for the Estate of Anaïs Nin. Extracts from works by Arthur Luce Klein, David Gascoyne, Charles Foley, Desmond Hawkins, Anne Ridler, Patrick Leigh Fermor and G. S. Fraser are reprinted with permission.

All students of Durrell and Miller owe a debt to the universities where the bulk of their letters and manuscripts are held. Although many of their letters are published in *The Durrell–Miller Letters 1935–80*, most of these are held in collections at the Universities of California in Los Angeles and in the Morris Library of Southern Illinois University at Carbondale.

Extracts from the *New York Times*, Copyright © 1957, 58, 59, 60, 63, 68, 70, 88, are reprinted with permission. Also extracts from *The Times, Times Literary Supplement, New Statesman, Spectator, Sunday Times, Daily Express, L'Express, Sunday Telegraph, Liverpool Daily Post, Boston Globe, New Republic, Independent, Listener, Scotsman, Nation, Figaro Littéraire, London Review of Books, Magazine Littéraire, Esquire, Evening Standard, Vogue, Time/Life, Washington Post, Radio Times, Paris Review,* BBC Written Archives, *Yale Review, Guardian* and *Observer* are included with permission. Extracts from the *New York*

Review of Books reprinted with permission from *New York Review of Books*, copyright © 1970 Nyrev, Inc.

The review of the *Booster* by George Orwell is reprinted by permission of the Estate of the Late Sonia Brownell Orwell and Secker & Warburg Ltd. Material from *Shenandoah* is reprinted with permission of the Editor of *Shenandoah*, the Washington and Lee University Review.

Every effort has been made by the author to trace all copyright holders, but if any have been inadvertently overlooked, the author will be pleased to make the necessary arrangements at the first opportunity.

CHAPTER I

Shangri-la (1912–1923)

But, you know, that's my life! I was born
a stranger already in India.

Lawrence Durrell

When Lawrence Durrell was six his father went to work as
chief engineer on the Darjeeling and Himalaya Railway on the
Indian–Tibet border. The family lived in Kurseong, where
the company has its headquarters, but Durrell was sent up the
mountain line to school in Darjeeling to the Jesuit College of
St Joseph's at North Point. There, from his dormitory window,
he could see the Himalayas, and on a clear day Mount Everest
itself. From there, too, he could see Tibetan monks with their
twirling prayer-wheels passing to and fro across the border
with India, *en route* to the cities of the plains and back again.
This vision remained with him till his death, for what he saw
were the monks passing through a mirror from one reality to
another.

He claimed in later life that he lived in a Tibet of the mind.
Moving through the mirror from his earthbound reality to the
reality of his fiction perhaps accounts for why he thought (or
so he said) that the life we call reality was a dream.[1] And to
and fro, across the Tibetan border of his mind, trekked the
caravan of characters who inhabited the dreamworld of his
fiction – the magus figures, the *femmes fatales*, the comic
officials, the omniscient, godlike writers, the menacing
brothers, the good-hearted whores and the redeeming female
artists.

From his obscure beginnings in India, Durrell was destined

himself to become a part of the almost forgotten world of the British Empire, with his name duly inscribed on the Foreign Office List; but he was also to become the caricaturist and chronicler of its decline.

From the vantage-point of the expatriate he was to peer down from snowcapped heights into the caves and labyrinths of the dark Victorian subconscious with its lurking Minotaurs – for there, under the polished exterior of respectability, he was to discover the muddy well-springs of his fiction. The brilliant expanse of sky and mountains in northern India, the colourful pageant which a teeming subcontinent of religions, nations and languages offered to the servants of Empire, contrasted dramatically with the gloomy, repressed and shadowy world of gaslit London to which Durrell was brutally transferred as a small boy. The response to his 'abandonment' was to be dark and violent, in both the fiction he wrote and the fiction he lived. For life, after all, was for him but a dreamlike fiction. As Shakespeare reminded us, we are all confined in our own ways inside Prospero's cell, bewitched by one dream or another. That was the dreamworld which Durrell made his own empire, over which he came to hold sway, over whose inhabitants he was to have the power of life and death. The true artist, after all, as he and his friend Henry Miller agreed, was a god. Men of genius were assigned a power which was not subject to the same rules and restraints as circumscribed the ordinary person, members of the mere mob whose lives were meaninglessly endured until death removed them from the scene.

Two striking images of death haunted Lawrence Durrell from childhood, so much so that he often said that he had been born dead.[2] He was a sickly child who might not have been expected to live, and who was always undersized. He claimed that Indian servants, believing him to be near death, fed him the blood of a freshly killed chicken each morning – a horrible experience for a small child, which never left him. He told, too, of being taken for a walk one afternoon by a large frigid English nanny, Miss Farrell, who inadvertently found herself and the child passing through a Parsee graveyard. Bodies were being cut up and hung on trees for the vultures to feed upon, others were being burned. There were the relics of bodies – arms and legs, strewn about, half buried or half burned in a smouldering fire. Recognizing too late what had happened, the near-hysterical Miss Farrell raced the young Durrell straight home. But the image had photographed itself on his memory and would never be erased, not least the shocked behaviour of the horrified nanny.[3] There was something profoundly wrong with the western approach to death, he later decided.

Durrell was always very vague about his ancestors and seems to have been uninterested in disinterring them, except as vaguely romantic figures – a heroine of the Indian Mutiny, a big-game hunting judge, perhaps even a general, conjured from a fertile imagination. He almost never dated letters and was cavalier about the timing of events, even events in his own life, which he considered more a source for his fiction than a piece of historical narrative requiring verification. Nevertheless, he was acutely interested in the nature of biography, and his most celebrated achievement, *The Alexandria Quartet*, is a sustained reflection on the way in which life stories are created and continually recreated.

The Lawrence Durrell story (real and fictional) has a Kipling-esque beginning, and the book with which the young Durrell came to identify was *Kim*. The parallels with his own life must have made it seem as though Kipling had written the book with him especially in mind. Kim is the son of Irish parents, whose father works on the Indian railways and who is born close to where Durrell himself was born, Jullundur. He is greatly influenced by an encounter with a Buddhist lama, with whom he sets off in search of the healing waters of the sacred River of the Arrow.[4] Durrell's feeling of affinity with the children of Kipling's Indian romances was constantly emphas-ized by Durrell himself – as a child, he said, Kim lived at the end of his garden. They were not just friends; they were doppelgängers. In a late autobiographical memoir, Durrell views the world from the vantage-point of an elephant's back – the elephant he remembered learning to ride as a young boy in the Indian jungle – and so he could claim some affinity with

another Kipling character, the Elephant Boy. Perhaps the image
became, in some unconscious way, built into his inner being,
so that later his friend Alfred Perlès could say that the small
but sturdy Durrell always reminded him of nothing less than
an amiable pachyderm.[5]

His Indian childhood was profoundly important to him, just
as it had been to Kipling, and to numerous other writers who
were born into that fabulous world and then abruptly transferred to the grey mists of cold English mornings, and the
sad, threadbare life which the English have been so good at
cultivating. The rich and exotic setting – the jungle, the teeming
wildlife, the multifarious people and religions and languages,
the dry hot plains and the spreading Himalayas – gave Durrell
a sense of space and timelessness which remained an essential
part of his mental landscape, even though, after the age of
eleven, he never returned to it.

He was born in Bengal, into a family which was frequently
on the move – a gypsy life, he called it – in a line of doughty
Kiplingesque colonials (English *pied noir*, he liked to say, three
generations of whom had never seen England), servants of the
Crown since before the Indian Mutiny, who carried the white
man's burden with pride, and to whom India was 'home' as
much as the Mother Country.[6] He liked to tell of a grandmother
who sat on her veranda during the Mutiny armed with a
shotgun, a sight which sent a mutinous crowd fleeing in terror
– an unlikely tale since the eldest of his grandmothers would
have been little more than a child at the time. Perhaps he meant
great-grandmother.[7]

His grandfather, Samuel Amos Durrell (born in Suffolk) was
a bombardier in the Royal Artillery in Allahabad when he and
his wife Emma produced their first child, Emma Agnes, in
1876. William Amos followed a year later, when the bombardier was attached to the 11th Brigade in Ranikhet. Emma, it
seems, died a few years afterwards, and with the second Mrs
Durrell, Dora Maria, Samuel Amos produced a second son,
Lawrence Samuel, on 23 September 1884. Lawrence Samuel
Durrell was destined to become the father of Lawrence George,
the elephant-loving, Kim-like boy who decided at eight that he
wanted to be a poet. By the time of Lawrence Samuel's birth,

Samuel Amos had risen to the position of conductor of ordnance at Fatelihgarh, and when another child, Margaret
Dorothy, followed a year later he had moved to a similar post
at Ishapur. He was destined to rise through the ranks to major
by the time Lawrence Samuel married in 1910.

Samuel Amos and Dora produced two more children – Jesse
Mahahal, in 1892 when Samuel was conductor of ordnance at
Ferozepore, and Enid Nell, who was born in 1900 and died of
diphtheria in 1912. Samuel rose to the rank of major and
ended his career as commissioner at the small-arms factory at
Dum-Dum where the sinister and terrible flat-nosed bullet was
first produced.

The early life of Lawrence Samuel is somewhat obscure. His
poetic son called him 'a failed BA of Benares University' – an
old colonial joke, for from 'BA Benares University' came the
acronym 'babu', the colonists' term for an educated Indian. He
turned up in 1908, aged twenty-four, as a lowly overseer in
the employ of the North-West Railway in Lahore, the provincial capital of the Punjab. At Lahore there was also a
North-West Railway Night and Day School for Europeans and
Eurasians, and it seems likely that Lawrence Samuel graduated
here.

By 1909 he was overseer at Sutlej Bridge, close to the station
town of Jullundur, not far from Lahore. In the following year,
at the age of twenty-five, he went, it seems, to study at the
celebrated Thompson Engineering College at Roorkee in the
Sarahanpur district of the North-West Provinces, the town
where he met the woman he was destined to marry. Perhaps
with matrimony in mind, and in search of a better salary, he
abandoned his railway career to become engineer to the District
Board of Karnal, just north of Delhi. His choice of bride was
the twenty-four-year-old Louisa Florence Dixie, daughter of
George Dixie, an Irish Protestant, previously head clerk and
accountant at the Ganges Canal Foundry and Workshop in
Roorkee.

The wedding took place at the St John the Baptist Church
in Roorkee on 23 November 1910. Her own father being dead,
Louisa was given away by her brother William, a sergeant in
the Supply and Transport Corps in Lahore. They appear to

have been a fairly conventional Edwardian couple. In their wedding photograph Lawrence Samuel looks earnest, sober-suited and moustachioed, Louisa Florence innocent and demure. They settled in Jullundur.

The Dixies are said to have come from Cork, the marriage of Louisa's grandparents uniting the Dixies with the O'Briens.[8] This inherited 'Irishness' was something which became important to Lawrence Durrell, and he often played up his Irish roots, though he visited Ireland only once, and confessed in old age that it was really an act – he was no more than 'a stage Irishman', he said.

Being Irish provided a wonderful defence, he told Malcolm Muggeridge, if one was mentally lazy or intolerant of logic. It was an alibi for him to hide behind. In truth, he was unsure of exactly how Irish he was, but on his mother's side they were certainly pure Irish, and he felt that from this ancestry he inherited his expressive personality and mental cast – his gift of the gab and Irish slant of mind.[9]

Along with the Irishness of his family, however, went an oppressive form of Protestantism which he found suffocating. It was Dora Durrell, Lawrence Samuel's mother, to whom Durrell referred as 'Big Granny', who provided him with the model for Dulcie Clifton, an overweight matriarch and Christian fundamentalist, whom Walsh Clifton, the hero of his first novel *Pied Piper of Lovers*, finds utterly repellent. She was apt to corner young Clifton, grip him powerfully by the arm, and moan in the most depressing way, about the impermanence of life and the menacing presence of death – her own in particular, which seemed to terrify her and which she seemed to expect at any moment.[10] The real Dora did not expire until 1943; her husband, Major Samuel, however, passed away from the official record without trace, and Durrell probably knew little of his grandfather. Nevertheless, there was a family legend that there had been a general among their immediate ancestors, and a uniform and medals were carefully preserved in a trunk when the family finally moved to England.[11] After Major Samuel's death, Big Granny seems to have circulated around the family, staying for a time with this one and for a time with another. If young Clifton is anything to go by, young Lawrence looked upon her intermittent appearances with a creeping horror.

Nevertheless, he retained a sneaking admiration for his *pied noir* family (middle-brow and bourgeois, he rated it). It spread its branches, or so he claimed, throughout imperial India – its industrious members working for the railways, the postal service, the police, the military and the civil service. An uncle, he maintained, was a magistrate in Bihar (also a big-game hunter), though there is no magistrate called Durrell or Dixie listed in *Thacker's Indian Directory* for that period, so perhaps this uncle was simply married to a Durrell or a Dixie. On the maternal side, there was a series of formidable aunts, with names such as Nora, Fan, Prudence and Patience, whose presence, in real or imagined form, would also bring out the rebel in Durrell,[12] and who were, in turn, to be depicted as mild figures of fun by the younger writers in the family, Gerald and Margo.[13]

The Edwardian twilight of the Victorian age finally expired with the death of Edward VII. The old world in which the British Empire was so firmly rooted, and inside which the Durrell–Dixies had so devotedly served, moved silently on to the skids. When George V was crowned in June 1911, Louisa must already have known that she was pregnant with her first child, and when a son was born at home in Jullundur at 1 a.m. on Tuesday, 27 February 1912, what more appropriate names to give him than that of his father Lawrence, and that of the new king, George. His initials, L.G., gave Lawrence George Durrell his school nickname, Algy, though Larry was the name by which he came to be known within his own family and the one which he preferred.

The time of his birth meant a lot to Durrell in later life. He was a Piscean, and water was not just his sign, but in some ways his element: he was never entirely happy when too far away from the sea on which to sail or in which to swim, as he did, like a dolphin. He took astrology seriously, having several horoscopes drawn up (as Kim has *his* read by the holy man Sarsut Brahmin), and so put great store in being born a Pisces (with Jupiter rising). Tuesday was also important, because, as he wrote gleefully in the *Avignon Quintet*, Muslims believe that nothing good was created on a Tuesday, an idea which seems to have pleased him a great deal, though he disliked Islam as much as he did those other great monotheistic religions, Christianity and Judaism.

By the time of Durrell's birth, his father had gone back to work for the railways, in the exalted position of executive engineer on the Jullundur–Doab Railway at a salary of 600 rupees (£48) a month. When his first child was just six months old, Lawrence Samuel drew up his will, making Louisa Florence sole executrix and beneficiary of his estate. He was, according to his son, a serious, good, but unimaginative man, an Edwardian whose values were rooted deep in the nineteenth-century belief in the irrefutable power of science. His was a practical world in which most problems had been solved by science, and those left unsolved would not be so for very long. He was not a cultured man in the way his son would have liked, but an empire-builder in the grand spirit, and a character of great determination. Durrell later recalled him thumping the dining-room table and exclaiming, 'My God! We must drive ahead! We must drive ahead and *win*!'[14] No doubt this was just the spirit to inspire exhausted construction workers hacking a railway track up the slopes of the southern Himalayas. But perhaps, after a while, it could become wearing at home. Every morning all over India, according to Durrell, colonials shaved in mirrors on which was pasted on a vellum sheet the words of Kipling's 'If', for the Kipling of *Kim* and *The Barrack Room Ballads* was *their* mouthpiece, spoke *their* sentiments, reminded them of the white man's burden.[15] But L. S. Durrell was not a conventional member of the Raj in that sense – Durrell said that they lived not like the British, but like Anglo-Indians. On one occasion, or so Durrell claimed, his father was blackballed from his club for proposing for membership an Indian doctor just back from Oxford. This doctor had saved his son Lawrence's life, from a disease called rue – in one version of this story, it was the doctor who prescribed the daily dose of fresh chicken blood.

Of his mother, whom his brother Gerald depicts as an endearing, somewhat bewildered woman in *My Family and*

Other Animals,[16] Larry rarely spoke, but, pressurized on television by Malcolm Muggeridge, he said that he felt strongly
repressed on the subject. He admitted, however, that she was
the dominant influence in his life, though how much of an
influence he could not say. Once asked to write a truthful
account of her – not like Gerald's, which was correct but
superficial – he found her impossible to describe. She was
extremely shy and withdrawn, but there was a great deal underneath, and he did not dare look into that.[17] Certainly his later
obsession with the Oedipus Complex suggests an unusually
intense, perhaps even unhealthy, relationship, one engendered
no doubt by the proximity and dangers of their isolated life at
the time. Louisa Durrell was, according to Durrell's daughter
Sappho, extremely close to her children, and so possessive of
them that she would never stay to the end of parties or recep-
tions, hurrying home to make sure they were all right.[18] As
Durrell admitted later, he was dreadfully spoiled in India,
spoiled on the one hand by indulgent ayahs, and on the other
by a mother who lavished him with affection. If this caused
tension between the Durrell parents, Lawrence Samuel could
sublimate his feelings in his empire-building, and Louisa
could immerse herself in the home and children. Perhaps it was
she who provided Durrell with what he thought of (no doubt
thinking of his poetic gift) as 'a pre-Raphaelite sensibility'.[19]
He was, he said, brought up strictly but not oppressively, and
was taught to revere girls, perhaps rather too much, he felt.

He had started out as a sickly infant (he liked to claim that
he was stillborn). Over thirty years later, he warned Henry
Miller against taking his youngsters to India – remembering
that his own parents had had to slave to keep him free of the
ever-present amoebic dysentery and typhoid.[20] In *Pied Piper of
Lovers*, there is a vivid image of the way death stalked through
Durrell's youth, when young Walsh Clifton is isolated because
of a cholera epidemic, and watches from his bedroom window
the endless processions of Indians, dead of the disease, being
wheeled past his house towards the burial grounds.[21] There
was also the threat from snakes, scorpions and other wildlife,
of which his protective mother must have been particularly
conscious, and with which all children of the Raj had to learn

to deal. From a very young age Lawrence was taught to observe very closely the flora and fauna around him – a skill he was to find invaluable as a writer.

On the social side, of course, the India into which he had been born was, for a young Englishman of his class, a world of servants and large houses and privilege, as well as a world of responsibilities and duties. It was, thought Durrell, a queer world left over from the past haunted by the shades of Sir Henry Newbolt and G. A. Henty, Edwardian patriotism and the Gatling gun. And although the Empire fell out of favour later on, the colonials who sweated away there believed in it absolutely.[22]

The First World War did not immediately affect the young Durrell family. By November 1915 when a daughter, Margery Ruth, was born to them, they were settled in Mymensingh, and in June 1916 Lawrence Samuel is listed in *Thacker's* as executive engineer of the Mymensingh Bhairals Bazar Railway on a salary of 800 rupees (£64) a month. But Margery Ruth died in infancy of diphtheria, probably the event which made Louisa so excessively cautious about the health of her children. By now, too, her husband bore after his name the proud letters AMICE (Associate Member of the Institute of Civil Engineers), which may account for one of the two years 1914–15 when he is absent from the official records – he was perhaps away studying, probably at the Thompson College in Roorkee again.

Just after he was five, Lawrence George was joined by a new brother. Leslie Stewart Durrell was born on 10 March 1917 – small and dark where Lawrence was small and blond. Lawrence's education at this stage had consisted of little more than learning to read at home and being casually tutored. If the early life of Walsh Clifton, the hero of *Pied Piper of Lovers*, is anything to go by (and Durrell claimed that it was),[23] then he broke free from his cautious mother enough to wander freely through the village markets, like his youthful hero Kim, and even to stray along the edges of the jungle with his friends. Durrell may have learned something about natural history from someone similar to Mr Sowerby, the amateur lepidopterist in his novel. When Clifton brings him a lovely butterfly he has caught, he calls for his killing bottle and they watch together while the beautiful thing gradually suffocates to death. Then Sowerby carefully pins the dead creature down among his collection. The call for the lepidopterist's pins and killing bottle recurs as a motif in Durrell's later notebooks, and as he grew into old age he became more and more obsessed about his breathing and developed a fear of suffocation. It can only have enhanced his youthful sense of the tenuous quality of existence, the ease with which life can be snuffed out of a living creature – himself included.

He also seems to have remembered vividly the casual acts of cruelty or inexplicable skill of which people were capable. The boy in *Pied Piper* who fed pebbles to a lizard so that it was incapable of moving rings very true, and the boy who could silently approach and catch a green lizard without its shedding its tail later provided him with an apt metaphor for writing a poem – a knack which was difficult to explain. He also recalled the India of the rope trick and hypnotic Indian conjurors, of playful monkeys pelting him with nuts and stones as they swung from trees overhead, making him thank God that he was wearing his father's pith helmet, and he recalled, in true *Jungle Book* fashion, seeing a fight between a cobra and a mongoose.[24]

Another picture of India which must have come to haunt Durrell was the array of deformities and disfigurements found among the beggars of the subcontinent. There is hardly a book of his in which there is not a character who is one-eyed, wall-eyed, blind, disfigured by smallpox or Lupus, minus a nose, a hand or a pair of legs. And a major and recurring theme is death in its many and most grotesque and brutal forms. The Indians saw it all around them, the British shielded their eyes from it. But Durrell would serve it up to them in shovelfuls.

But the days of running wild were drawing to a close. In the second half of 1918, when Lawrence George was six, Lawrence Samuel, then thirty-four, became resident engineer of the Darjeeling–Himalayan Railway in Kurseong, 370 miles north of Calcutta, at a salary of 750 rupees a month. Why he chose to move so far and take such a drop in salary (From 1050 rupees at Mymensingh) must be left to conjecture. But the

growing unrest among the Indian masses which followed
the First World War may have had something to do with it.
Mymensingh was not far from Amritsar, where, in April 1919,
Brigadier General Dyer notoriously ordered troops to open fire
on a crowd. Perhaps Durrell's father carried his wife and
children off to the Himalayas to be out of harm's way. He took
a large old house in Kurseong called Everleas Lodge. On 30
July 1919, Margaret Isabel Durrell (know in the family as
Margo) was born.

Larry was packed off to the Jesuit-run College of St Joseph
at North Point in Darjeeling, and for the first time came under
the disciplined eye of dedicated teachers. But the loss of
freedom and partial separation from home were compensated
for in several ways. The Jesuits of North Point were not
the martinets under whom James Joyce suffered. They were
tolerant men, mostly Belgians, who accepted children of
many faiths. Durrell recalled there being Hindus, Buddhists,
Taoists, Sufis and Protestants like himself, as well as Catholics,
at the College, which was set among tea plantations on the
Himalayan slopes, with Everest on the distant horizon. The
open prospect to the north was gloriously spectacular, and
there were occasional trips along the Nepal-Bhutan border.
The vista across which young Walsh Clifton looked in *Pied
Piper* was so well observed that it must have come from the
sensitive visual memory which, Durrell found, could photograph and retain the smallest detail of landscape and of flora
and fauna. The move seems to have suited his 'Pre-Raphaelite
sensibility' in another way. He began as early as six, he said,
to scribble little bits of things.[25] Durrell also found teachers
who took a liking to him (a short, sparky, mischievous, if
sometimes dreamy, boy) and encouraged him with his writing
and reading. Kipling had now been supplemented with Henty,
Ballantyne, Rider Haggard and John Buchan, all with their
own tales of imperial daring-do to tell the impressionable
young colonial. One master he remembered in particular.
Father J. de Gheldere (the College's rector and prefect of
studies), whom he once heard reading poetry, inspired in him
the wish to be a poet. And it was probably with Kipling, poet
and storyteller, in mind that at the age of eight he told his

father that he wanted to be a writer, an idea which de Gheldere
had encouraged in him.

Whatever fine ambitions Lawrence Samuel had for his eldest
boy (Oxford and the Colonial Service probably), he took this
announcement with equanimity. The family, Durrell often
said, was completely philistine – there were no books in the
house at all. But, on his eighth birthday, 27 February 1920, an
ox-cart drew up outside Everleas Lodge with a present for
him – a huge parcel of books. His father had bought him a
complete set of Dickens which had belonged to a recently
expired tea-planter. Durrell claimed later that he never got
beyond *The Pickwick Papers* (sometimes he said that he
got through about ten of them), but Dickens gave him a vision
of Merrie England – what most colonials referred to as 'home'
– supplemented later by reading Thackeray and R. S. Surtees.
In Surtees's convivial tales of the hunting, shooting, sporting
Mr Jorrocks and his pursuitful adventures, there was something
ruddy, jolly and rumbustious which appealed to the perky
youngster. Although he made little headway into Dickens's
world of tragic-comic grotesques, he would, in his own good
time, people his own world with figures of strange and unusual
shape and stature. His first prose model, he wrote later, was
Frank Richards' stories of Billy Bunter. It was such wonderful
figures from the carnival of literature who first beckoned him
towards writing.[26] Meanwhile, the young poet took Kipling as
his guiding star, and it was simple Kiplingesque doggerel that
he first began to write.[27]

Although he liked the Darjeeling Jesuits, and in later years
kept in touch with them, he knew little of their Catholic
religion, perhaps because they were scrupulous in creating
an atmosphere of tolerance among the community of pupils
from so many faiths. The forty or so Protestants at the school
worshipped at the Church of England chapel in the town.
However, he recalled straying into the College chapel one day
and there finding on a crucifix the figure of a bleeding, suffering
Christ, which to him was so brutal and horrifying[28] that he
reacted strongly against a faith which worshipped and (at mass)
consumed the body and blood of a dying man. Yet, however
powerful a sense of sickness then consumed him, it was

repressed until much later when he discovered Freud and trawled through his past for traumas. Many were shocking images of death – half-consumed bodies in graveyards, processions of corpses during cholera epidemics, skewered and suffocating butterflies, and crucified, bleeding effigies of a dying man. This theme of death was to consume him and, along with sexual love in its many forms and contortions, permeate his work as a writer.

But another important theme for him was the sense of place which he felt so strongly among the mountains at Darjeeling – the towering peaks, the snow-capped roof of the world, the spectacular vista and the almost permanently blue skies. And how different the mountain people were from the people of the plains, the teeming market places and the jungles! Place and character appeared somehow to go together – a belief which his later travels only seemed to confirm. Human character and culture were somehow the result of what he called 'the spirit of place'. Darjeeling, perched close to the border of Sikkim between Nepal and Bhutan, he associated mostly with the smiling Buddhist lamas, who he recalled flocking back and forth like birds, heading south or back home to the north, along the road through Darjeeling which ran beside the College playing field. Sixty years later he could recall the sound of their whirring brass prayer-wheels, and see them strolling, as it seemed, through the chapters of his favourite book, *Kim*.[29] It was their spirit with which he identified the place. And Buddhism was a far greater influence on him than the Jesuits. Five of his fellow students, he recalled, were Chinese Taoists, and at home his father practised yoga, not from any religious motive, but simply because he found it a good way to relax. He began to recognize these childhood influences in the 1930s, when he met people such as Henry Miller, for whom Buddhism represented the philosophy of quietism, sought as an escape from politically inspired art.

Darjeeling was the Provincial Government's summer residence, and here were to be seen the men of Empire in all their imperial splendour and oddity. Durrell recalled being taken by his father to the Planter's Club in Darjeeling where the talk was frequently and intensely about cricket, and especially about

how to lay a suitably fine turf to make a good playing pitch –
the local grass was too rough in texture. Imported grass from
England had failed and matting had to be used. Many Indians
found these strange governess-obsessed servants of the King
Emperor incomprehensibly bizarre. Of course, when they
finally got round to playing the game the Indians were often
better than the British, for whom it became a sort of religion.
Durrell was to find such eccentrics a continuous source of fun.
As an adult, he knew them well enough to play the part and
join in; but he felt sufficiently apart from them, too, to regard
them as likeable buffoons. Antrobus, his comic diplomat, may
well have been born in the Planter's Club in Darjeeling.

Some time in 1920, Durrell's father left the Darjeeling Himalaya Railway and moved with his young family to Jamshedpur
in Bihar Province. At that time, Jamshedpur was something of
a boom town, in fact a company town, planned and built by
the Tata Iron and Steel Company (a 'Garden City', they proudly
announced), and in good imperial tradition it had one section
for Europeans and better-paid Indians, one for Anglo-Indians
and a new section for the manual workers. Lawrence Samuel's
house, called Beldi, stood in the European sector. There he also
set up Durrell and Company, launching himself into business
as an independent civil engineer. His son Lawrence George
liked to claim later that his father constructed the Tata Iron
and Steel Works in Jamshedpur, but the works and the company
town long predated the arrival of L.S. Durrell, and he is not
listed among the company's engineering contractors. More
likely, he worked for Tata on an occasional contractual basis,
as apparently he did in helping to build a local hospital. But
he was also contracted to build railways and this is what seems
to have taken him to Burma, then a part of imperial India.
  Young Lawrence, however, continued at school in Darjeeling,
and joined the family during the holidays. Once he was sent
by his father to spend a vacation with the magistrate uncle,
who lived in a large house in Ranchi, not very far from Jamshedpur. The uncle (claimed Durrell) had command of fourteen
Indian dialects, translated Hindu poetry and was close to Indian
culture.[30] He was a gun-enthusiast and big-game hunter, and

his house was a menagerie of trophies. The heads of tiger, elephant, water buffalo adorned the walls of his study, and the young Durrell was encouraged to pick up a gun and join in the sport. The fascination with hunting remained with him, and in many of his novels there is a hunting scene – most memorably, perhaps, the duck-shoot on Lake Mareotis in *Justine*. Guns were, after all, something of a family tradition, thanks to Major Samuel, the one-time commissioner of small arms at Dum-Dum. At Ranchi, too, the diminutive Durrell made friends with a young elephant, and learned a new perspective on life from riding on its back. The image of the view from the back of an elephant was an apt one for the lofty perspective of the later author, and he was not slow to employ it.[31]

India was a movable feast of colour and smells and visions and characters, of beauty and death, and as close to untamed nature as one could hope to be, something which left its mark on him. In his 1943 poem, 'Cities, Plains and People', written at a time when he was radically reassessing his life, he reminds us how his Indian childhood haunted him, and how he saw it as having helped make him what he became.

He often spoke about times spent by his family under canvas in Burma. His father kept horses, so he learned to ride, and this gave his childhood a further dimension of freedom, though also the threat of danger from the lurking panther, scorpion or snake.[32] Walsh Clifton in *Pied Piper* tells how his father has taught him how to deal with a king cobra if faced with one in deadly mood – the secret was always to avoid its hypnotic gaze.[33]

His family were always on the move, following his father through the jungle as he oversaw the railway construction work, and it was the first time he had lived in an entirely Buddhist society, which only confirmed his fascination with the religion.[34] This life of camping in the jungle is the reason he gave for his later ability to move about and live anywhere. They lived the gypsy life and were perfectly at home in any dilapidated house they moved into. But he later told Henry Miller that he was actually born in Burma, which suggests that geography, not to mention literature was one of those areas in which that sloppy 'Irish' cast of mind was at work.

In the more settled atmosphere of St Joseph's, back in Darjeeling, Durrell was regarded as one of their best young pupils. When he was ten, and 'a sturdy young scamp', according to the College Annual Report, he was chosen to read a eulogy 'from the boys of the South Dorm' on the occasion of the presentation of the Kaiser-i-Hind Medal, for services in India, to Edward Fitzgerald, head of St Joseph's Primary Division. The ceremony took place at the College on 19 October 1922, and the printed extract of Durrell's little hymn of praise to 'Sir' is suitably shot through with ringing imperial sentiments about the King–Emperor and cloying phrases about the man about to be honoured. 'Sir' was being given the King–Emperor's medal because of his goodness and because he meant so much to the boys and always cared for them. And when the boys told their daddies, they replied with a smile that they had said just the same to their fathers a quarter of a century before.[35] If this was the sturdy young scamp's own composition, then it was undoubtedly his first published work, and, as it was to turn out, a sad speech of farewell to India, for Lawrence Samuel was about to announce his plans for his two sons – Lawrence and Leslie were to be sent to public school in England. What to Durrell was a life of carefree innocence was about to end.

He later claimed that his father had come to terms with his desire to become a writer, and had told him that he was sending him to England to get the very best education that a writer required. However, elsewhere he suggested that Lawrence Samuel had a career mapped out for him in the Indian Civil Service and wanted him to go to public school 'to get the ball-mark'.[36] In any event, the parental foot had come heavily down.

Lawrence Samuel's decision precipitated a bitter quarrel between himself and Louisa, who appears not to have been previously consulted on the matter. She became distraught at the prospect of losing her two young sons. Durrell said that it was the first time he had ever seen his parents quarrel, or his mother cry. He hated the idea of leaving India and leaving his family. Being sent to England was like being given a prison sentence, and only served to heighten his Oedipal feelings about his parents. He felt that his father now had the highest expectations of him, expectations he could never hope to fulfil, and hinted at a lifelong sense that he had never succeeded in gaining his father's approval.[37]

However, Louisa was not entirely defeated. The price for her agreement to her husband's plan was that if Larry and Leslie were to be sent to England then she would at least accompany them on the journey, taking the two-and-a-half-year-old Margaret with her. In that way the separation might be eased. The fact that his parents had quarrelled so loudly and openly left a deep impression on Larry (and no doubt on Leslie, too) and made the break with India that much more traumatic.

On 18 March 1923, barely three weeks after young Larry's eleventh and a week after Leslie's sixth birthday, Louisa and her two boys and the young Margo sailed first class from Calcutta on the Ellerman Line ship, SS *City of London*, bound for London. Before he left, if *Mountolive* is a guide, his father, unable to show emotion, gave him a celluloid toy aeroplane. As the *City of London* steamed down the Ganges, the image that remained with young Larry was of corpses floating downstream and out to sea – just as *he* was floating away from his Shangri-la.[38] The young colonials were returning 'home', but also setting off into exile.

The loss of India, the loss of the vision of the pristine mountain peaks, the colourful simplicity of life, the gentle lamas, was somehow to be part of a vision of lost innocence and the search for wholeness which was to infuse his later thinking.

CHAPTER 2

Torn Up by the Roots

(1923–1930)

People talk of the mysterious East, but
the West is also mysterious.

E. M. Forster, *Notes on English Character*

An Elephant's Child . . . full of 'satiable
curtiosity'.

Kipling, *Just-so Stories*

The six-week voyage to England took Louisa and the three
children across the Indian Ocean and through the Suez Canal
to Port Said, where, for the first time, young Lawrence got a
sight of Egypt, and the Mediterranean, which was to become
the emotional and aesthetic focus of his later years. In *Pied
Piper of Lovers*, sighting Dover, Walsh Clifton sees the white
cliffs as not white at all, but as pearly grey – compared with
what is truly white, the snow-capped peaks of the Himalayas.[1]
Whiteness, to Durrell, came to symbolize wholeness and the
image of snow-clad Tibet, and was already a recurrent motif
in the poems he started to write a few years later,[2] and in his
most experimental early writing over a decade later.[3]

Disembarking at Tilbury on 27 April 1923, they stayed for
a while at a London hotel, then found lodgings in Dulwich, at
36 Hillsborough Road, a large suburban house, backing on to
the playing fields of Alleyn's School (the preparatory school for
Dulwich College). The house may well have been that of a
relative of R. C. Dyson, Lawrence Samuel's former supervisor
on the NW Railway. Edith Dyson became their landlady, and,

when Louisa returned to India, she became the guardian of the
two boys. This was very much Kipling's experience at the age
of six.[4] If Durrell did not know about that then, he was to
claim later that it gave him an affinity with his childhood
literary hero.

England was a painful experience for the young Larry. He
told Malcolm Muggeridge that being transported from the
Indian jungle to a tidy suburb in East Dulwich had really
staggered him – a paralysing trauma.[5] To have exchanged the
rich pageant of exotic cultures, the dazzling scenery and sense
of freedom and privilege which he had enjoyed in India for
cold, grey, gloomy London, where everyone seemed miserable,
was a shock to the system. On an imaginative level, too, the
disappointment was made worse by the discovery that this was
not the jolly roistering England of Surtees's Mr Jorrocks. He
never forgave his father for sending him there, and he later
attacked England, he said, because he identified it with his
father.

During that first year in England, the lugubrious Dora
Durrell (Big Granny) came from India to join them – something
which Durrell hated, she being the one thing he was glad to
have left behind in India. Although she was only sixty-one at
the time, to young Larry she seemed ancient. He wrote of her
layers of fat, the unpleasantness of her touch, her constant self-
pitying whines to 'the Lord'. Early in 1924, Louisa returned
to India with young Margo, leaving him and Leslie in the care
of Big Granny, which cannot have made matters any better.
Durrell later hinted that he thought that Margo was the family
favourite. His mother's departure left a deep scar, and might
explain his attitude towards his wives, whom he always feared
would leave him in the same way. He coped with this, it was
said, by being unfaithful to them, and thus getting in the first
strike, as it were.[6]

Whatever schooling the two boys had for their first year in
England it could not have amounted to much, possibly a local
day school in Dulwich or some tutoring at home, though he
remembered his guardian Mrs Dyson as kind but ignorant.
After a year came liberation of sorts. Leslie was sent to the
Caldicott, the Wesleyan Methodist preparatory school in

Hitchen, where Malcolm Lowry had been until the previous year; Lawrence was sent, perhaps with his interest in Shakespeare in mind, to St Olave's and St Saviour's Grammar School in Tooley Street, Bermondsey (popularly known as 'St Oggs'), on the south bank of the Thames, next to Tower Bridge. The school dated back to Elizabethan times, and drew boys from all over London, but especially bright youngsters from the city's East End. One of Durrell's fellow pupils was Abba Eban, later to become the Foreign Minister of Israel. Durrell commuted every day from Dulwich to London Bridge by the Southern Railway, a journey which on cold winter mornings often meant having to grope along the fog-bound banks of the Thames down Tooley Street to the school. One can well imagine how grim and gloomy Durrell's London must have seemed, with its river fogs and hooting grey barges looming and then sliding away like spectres along the shrouded Thames. It cannot have done anything to heighten his love for his 'home' country. However, this little riverside grammar school was intended only as a temporary measure, while he waited for a place at a public school, where entry was at fourteen.[7]

In October 1924, shortly after the boys had been settled in their new schools, Dora Durrell returned to India. Perhaps the boys' dislike of her had finally got her down, or perhaps she simply missed colonial India with its superior climate and the privileged status she enjoyed as a *memsahib*. In England, as Durrell himself discovered, 'colonials' tended to be snubbed, and had no clear place in highly structured English society, with its subtle gradations and petty snobberies. Another reason for Dora's return was probably the news that Louisa was again pregnant and she wanted to be there to take care of her daughter-in-law during her confinement.

Now Durrell was quite alone, and this he believed was what his father intended – a very English thing, meant to toughen him up, a Roman philosophy good for civil servants perhaps, but with a personal price to be paid, in hang-ups, loneliness and lack of true feelings. E. M. Forster made the same point well: 'It is not that the Englishman can't feel. He has been taught at his public school that feeling is bad form . . .'[8] It took garlic, wine and Mediterranean bathing, Durrell said, to rid him of this baggage and turn him into a truly free writer.[9]

At twelve, Durrell was an undersized, backward child. In school photographs he looks perky and puckish enough, neck crammed into an Eton collar and a shock of blond hair standing bolt upright above mischievous blue eyes and a snub nose. But the jolly exterior concealed a deeply unhappy child who felt deserted and betrayed. Even so, according to his old school-mates and school reports, he did not appear to be particularly miserable and was not at all badly behaved. Although he was poor academically (except for Scripture – thanks perhaps to the Jesuits and to Granny's unremitting stream of Biblical quotations) he was always thought to have potential. 'Could do better' was, in his case, more than just a trite comment by a master unable to think of anything constructive to say about a pupil.

If the gloomy suburbs of south London caused him to feel depressed, then the squalid inner suburbs around Bermondsey only intensified the feeling, which is reflected in the early novels based on his youthful life in London. In *Pied Piper of Lovers* the scene is evoked with deathly conviction, as it is in the later *Panic Spring* and *The Black Book*. It was that horrid Dickensian world of shadows which was suffocating his pre-Raphaelite sensibility. And Dickens himself was not far away from Tooley Street, for Mr Sam Weller had first presented himself to the Pickwickians at the White Hart Inn in Borough High Street, just a short jaunt away from his new school.

A few hundred yards from the school stood Southwark Cathedral, which he discovered soon after arriving at St Oggs. There he found, to his delight, a touch of the Merrie England. For there was the tomb of the fourteenth-century Southwark poet John Gower, contemporary and friend of Chaucer, and there, too, was the burial place of Shakespeare's actor brother, Edmund, and a monument to the great Bard himself. And the brightly decorated tombs reminded him hauntingly of India.[10] The aspiring young poet found himself, he said, at the hub of Shakespeare's London. Indeed the Southwark bank of the Thames was the very site of Shakespeare's own theatre, the

Globe, which had stood in nearby Park Street alongside other Elizabethan theatres – the Hope, the Swan and the Rose. Inside the cathedral one could also find medieval gargoyles, coats of arms and other heraldic devices, and Durrell's later attachment to heraldry no doubt dates from his discovery of this treasure trove of emblems and escutcheons. He realized that he was, as it were, wandering around the world of Shakespeare's plays. He already knew them fairly well, but now he took them to re-read on the very site where they had been performed in Shakespeare's day. Exploring that whole area around Tower Bridge and the theatre sites, he envisioned more clearly the Elizabethan world, which was to fascinate him throughout his life.[11]

He also developed a taste for first-class cricket, claiming to have seen the great Jack Hobbs hit his 100th century at the Oval, not far from his school, and to have witnessed the delirium which greeted it. He also claimed to have seen Harold Larwood, one of the fastest fast bowlers ever, bowling 'body-line' against the Australians.[12] But since Hobbs hit his 100th century at Bath and Larwood bowled 'bodyline' in Australia in 1933, he probably saw both players at the Oval, but on less significant occasions. (He later ascribed this sort of exaggeration to his 'Irishness'.) In imitation of their heroes, Durrell and his schoolfriends played 'backstreet' cricket on asphalt in the purlieus of Southwark, and 'proper' cricket on the lovely green playing-fields of Alleyn's School, just behind his own lodgings in East Dulwich.[13]

At St Oggs, because of his small size and general backwardness, Durrell was placed in a form for boys eighteen months his junior. Although twelve, at just four foot four he was only as tall as the average ten-year-old. With the advantage of age, at the end of his first term he was placed fifth in a class of twenty pupils. He was a punctual boy, according to his report, and a good attender; his health was judged good, and his conduct 'Very Good'. He came fourth in Scripture, English, History and Geography, fifth in Nature Study, but a sad sixteenth in Arithmetic. He was, however, judged 'Excellent' at Repetition and Recitation, and, concluded his form master, 'He worked well and with much intelligence. He is always attentive.

He has a genuine taste for English Literature, and reads much on his own account.'[14] His progress had been such that for the following term he was promoted from Class II to Class III, where the others were only a year younger than him.

In 1925, Durrell acquired a new brother. Gerald Malcolm was born on 7 January at Jamshedpur. This was the brother to whom he would be closest throughout most of his adult life, but he was not destined to see him for more than a year after he was born. Leslie, who had inherited the family fascination with guns, and whose interest in literature reached little further than Westerns, he saw in the school holidays in Dulwich.

In his first term in Class III, Durrell turned in an 'average' performance, coming eleventh in a class of thirty-three. His report stated: 'His attention is not yet capable of long sustained effort, and he does not settle down well to *grapple* with any difficulties such as those of French Grammar. His bad place in Geography is due to mere lack of *application*.'[15] By the end of that school year, in June, he had sunk to twenty-first in the class, and even in English, his best school subject, he could only scrape into seventeenth place. His master, the 'strict' and 'not very fatherly' 'Larry' Hampshire,[16] wrote a remarkably perceptive report on the embryonic author of the whimsical Antrobus stories and the deceptively elusive *Alexandria Quartet*:

> He is too frivolous; and even when he is, comparatively, sedate, his attention is only superficial. He *very* frequently answers 'the question that was *not* asked', in his eagerness to produce an impression of willingness. This 'slap-dash' habit will make him a mine of misinformation, for he seldom gets hold of what was really said just before he sprang back to attention.

His poor performance led to him being moved to the Shell Class under F. G. 'Jammy' Firth, 'a strong disciplinarian' though a more 'fatherly figure' than Hampshire.[17] The boys were still on average a year younger than Durrell, and he teamed up with one of them, Guy Wilkinson, to produce a class magazine to which Durrell must have contributed his first published piece of fiction. Recalled Wilkinson: 'We called [the magazine] the *Shell Ragbag*, and I remember that even in those early days he had a flair for writing and a sense of humour. I cannot remember his story, but it was about an Arab called "Yuswi hafno Ben Anas".'[18]

The frivolous manner that 'Larry' Hampshire had noticed was something new. One of Durrell's responses to England was to acquire an 'English' refinement in speech and manner, tempered by a wickedly 'Irish' conviviality. It equipped him splendidly for the subversive role he was later to adopt. 'My identity was foxed all the time by counter-identities,' he said. 'I wasn't an Indian, but I wasn't English either. I'm not real. I was a series of afterthoughts, which is a terrible thing to be. I'm a complete fake really!' But he also hinted at where he had found this particular 'afterthought' identity – the 'fake' English humorist – from another favourite author. He told Michael Dibdin, 'If P. G. Wodehouse had never existed, neither would I.'[19] The frivolous manner which his teacher frowned upon was probably that of Bertie Wooster.

Another source for this act was more direct. An actor called Ridley came to the school to give elocution lessons, and it was probably from Ridley that he acquired the refined, Wodehouse-ish tones which readers can detect in his Antrobus stories, in some of his poetry and in certain passages of his fiction. Ridley made the boys perform poetry with actions, and Durrell was a star turn. Wilkinson remembered how '[He] kept us in fits of laughter with his exaggerated actions to "I wandered lonely as a cloud" '[20] – very appropriate, one might think, for a future editor of Wordsworth. The school also had a Literary Society where, in his first term, he could have heard lectures on Swinburne and Oscar Wilde, poets probably new to the young Kiplingesque poet from India.

Durrell complained about being beaten at school, but his friend Wilkinson could not recall him having been punished in that way. 'Not that he was a paragon of virtue, but he could talk himself out of anything.' Despite the increasingly refined English accent, the Irish blarney was proving just as valuable. Wilkinson and Durrell became quite close because of the class magazine, and on school days the two boys would always walk to London Bridge Station, where Durrell caught his train back to Dulwich.

The school had a vigorous Debating Society. At the beginning of his second school year, in November 1925, probably prompted by form master 'Jammy' Firth, Durrell took part in a debate on the winning side, opposing the motion 'That the Lord Mayor's Show is a futile and expensive anachronism and ought to be abolished'. The school magazine, the *Olavian*, reported that 'The Chairman with Wright and Durrell joined in bemoaning the gradual loss of a romantic existence and asked that the last link with the past should not be snapped.'[21] The young poet and creator-in-waiting of Justine, Balthazar, Mountolive and Clea, and a host of other romantic figures, was already acting in character, dreaming wistfully of a lost reality and incidentally fathering the creative man.

That term, too, he met a real poet for the first time. Walter de la Mare visited the school to talk about technical aspects of poetry such as metre and rhyme, and read some of his own shorter poems to illustrate what the *Olavian* called 'the magic of words which he had described in his lecture'.[22] Durrell was certainly entranced by the magic of words, but the techniques which de la Mare employed he would shrug off as too cramping.

At Christmas 1925, Durrell was bumping around at the bottom of the Shell form. It may have been Larry's poor performance which prompted his father to agree to Louisa's returning to England with the six-year-old Margo and the one-year-old Gerry in tow, the cheerless Dora acting as chaperone. The parting from her two eldest boys must still have been painful, and the tension between her and her husband must have remained, especially if letters from young Lawrence told of the suffering solitude he later recalled. Then Lawrence Samuel himself had ideas about living in England, and so agreed to send Louisa to England to find a house to which he might one day retire, just as in *The Alexandria Quartet* the father of Mountolive sends his wife and child back to Blighty with much the same commission.[23] The unrest, which led to massive rioting in Calcutta and the imposition of martial law there in early April, may also have made England seem a safer place in which to bring up a young family. Louisa, the children and her mother-in-law left Bombay on the P & O ship SS *Ranchi* on 11 March. She gave her English address as c/o Grindlay's Bank, the bank used by most India hands, and later Durrell's own bank, too. Her future country of residence she gave as England. She had left India behind and would never return there.

Louisa was handicapped in her house-hunting by the General Strike, which broke out on 5 May. In the end, she bought a house at 43 Alleyn Park, a short walk from Hillsborough Road, where Lawrence and Leslie were boarded. It was a substantial detached three-storey property with a large garden, a suitably splendid home for an ex-colonial servant to retire to, though perhaps not as grand as the sort of house he could have afforded in India.

When Larry finally left St Oggs he was fourteen and a half. He stood four feet seven inches high and weighed a mere six stone three pounds. He was still a year behind other boys and his final place for the last term was thirtieth out of a class of thirty-four. His poor school reports must have injured his sense of himself; certainly they stayed with him, and in *The Avignon Quintet* he has ex-public schoolboy Felix Chatto, English Consul in Avignon, remembering words that could have come straight from the pen of 'Jammy' Firth – about doing better and dreaming less.[24] Chatto also remembers the schoolboy jokes of that period, doubtless exchanged while playing 'back-street' cricket on the asphalt wickets of Southwark, such as the well-known 'A net is a hole tied together by string.'[25]

The school his father most preferred was Dulwich College (P. G. Wodehouse's old school), close by the new house in Alleyn Park, but Larry's poor academic record may have precluded his acceptance there. Instead he was offered a place at St Edmund's in Canterbury, a Clergy Orphan School, which no longer catered solely for the orphaned offspring of Anglican clergymen.

In September 1926, with little Latin and less Greek, he was sent off to St Edmund's, housed in a fine-looking building set on a hill. It was no doubt a healthier environment than the foggy south bank of the Thames in Bermondsey, but took him away from the roots of his Elizabethan inspiration – from Shakespeare's South Bank theatre world. Now he was 'buried in the country', and only fractionally closer to the world of the sporting Mr Jorrocks.[26] Fortunately, however, the lovely town of Canterbury had its own Elizabethan hero. Christopher Marlowe, the son of a Canterbury shoemaker, was educated at the other public school in the town, King's School, and a statue to him, unveiled in 1893 by Sir Henry Irving, was there to remind Larry of the Merrie England he had hoped to find on his arrival from India. And Larry, though separated by over three centuries, came within an hour of sharing the great Elizabethan dramatist's birthday, 26 February (1564).

He regarded the school buildings as beautiful in their own right, as if Ruskin and William Morris had got together and cooked them up between them. The playing-field with its pagoda-like pavilion, was a memory he also cherished. He said that listening to the crack of cricket bat on ball while lying in the long grass eating cherries and reading Donne's love poems was the sweetest music in the world. Cricket was like a Roman rite of spring.[27] And one of the reasons he took to Corfu was the fact that, thanks to its having been a British possession until 1864, the Corfiots played an almost perfect replica of English cricket on a pitch down by Corfu harbour.

Now with boys of his own age, he was back at the bottom of the class. Although he was not unhappy, he found the new school's regime considerably harder, and punishments more severe. None of his schoolmates could remember his having been beaten, but he later complained about the oppressiveness of the English public schools, which took ages to work out of the system. And he told Marc Alyn that despite the Dickensian atmosphere and character-moulding, he had learned one lesson which had saved his life more than once – always to retain his sang-froid.[28]

The Dickensian atmosphere extended to the dormitories, lit in those days by flickering gaslight. Durrell slept at the top of Watson House and, in winter, snow would blow under the eaves into the unheated dorm. By mimicking his father's yoga exercises he was able to withstand the cold as he huddled under the rough school blankets. But it was not just cold weather he could not escape at bedtime; there were hearty bullies to cope with, too, and he recalled pillow fights after lights-out, a memory which he passed on to his consul, Felix Chatto, in *Livia*.[29] Sleep, if achieved, was dispelled each morning by having to swim a length of the school swimmingpool, often at near-freezing temperatures. And doubtless it was a memory of endless dreary school meals in that stodgy Dickensian atmosphere which led him to refer to England as 'Pudding Island' (too much treacle tart and spotted dick, he hinted in *Livia*).

Despite his sense of oppression, he did conform. Unlike St Joseph's in Darjeeling, St Edmund's was a single-faith school and the prevailing theology was Anglican. He was duly instructed, and on 3 December 1926 was confirmed with twenty other boys by the Archbishop of Canterbury in the school chapel. On a more expressive level, he continued to consume poetry, and took music lessons. By the end of his first term he had passed the preparatory examination for the piano (the school was linked to the Royal College of Music, which examined the pupils there). He was to become a quite accomplished pianist, though he later rebelled against classicism and turned to jazz.

But, for a poetry-reading, poetry writing schoolboy who played the piano, life in an English public school could be rough. He claimed that if he had not got his house colours for boxing, he would have been unable to choose to play the piano rather than rugby on Wednesday afternoons. Such free time had to be earned if one was not going to be picked on as a 'swot'.[30] There were no boxing colours to be won at St Edmund's, however. If he did learn to box there, it was from his House Master, W. 'Steve' Stephen-Jones, a charismatic figure, sportsman and naturalist, who may well have taken him into the gym and given him a few pointers on how to use his fists. To Durrell, 'Steve' was a school hero, the man who taught him all he knew about cricket and boxing.[31]

Apart from learning how to stand up for himself, he learned to keep his distance, by developing a kind of reserve and following his own distinctive interests. He felt he had to pretend to be like the other boys, but in secret he raided the school

library and read voraciously. This did not go entirely unnoticed.
One school friend, Alan Seabrook, remembered:

> He was a bit of a loner, friendly without *close* friends (or enemies)
> as far as I can remember. He was known as 'Tubby' for obvious
> reasons or Algy because of his initials ... I can clearly recollect
> being puzzled when his name first became famous because none of
> us had been conscious of any great latent literary talent. I do recall,
> however, that he spent a lot of time sitting at a bench near the door
> of the big schoolroom or hall that Wagner & Watson [Houses]
> shared as a common room. Usually he was alone & often writing,
> [or] either reading or cutting out pictures of scantily dressed ladies
> from glossy magazines, such as the 'Tatler' while others of us would
> be drooling over the latest design of Bentley, Lagonda, etc. as
> depicted in the latest 'Autocar'. I would not like to give the
> impression that he was in any way isolated. He participated in all
> normal school activities but he did not belong to any group of close
> friends or cliques.[32]

Being more interested in scantily clad females would not necessarily go down well in those days with the cold-shower and
games-playing Christians among whom he found himself. They
became his lifelong enemy.

In 1926, Lawrence Samuel Durrell made the pilgrimage to
Mother England,[33] to inspect the house which his wife had
chosen for his retirement, and to visit his sons at their English
schools. He had abandoned his career as a contractor to
become executive engineer of the B & N Railway in
Jamshedpur. Before returning to India, he had decided that his
backward son Larry might need special coaching to make it to
the university.

Louisa had her hands full with her family at Alleyn Park.
Gerry was still only two in 1927 and Margo ten. When Leslie
and Larry returned from the school holidays the house must
have been in pandemonium. However timid and solitary he
was at school, with his own family Larry could let himself go
– knocking out jazz on the piano, declaiming his latest poem,
practising his newly learned craft of boxing. He claimed to
have sharpened up his boxing with the family butler, Stone –
no doubt beginning to turn that snub nose of his into the

W. C. Fields proboscis it finally became. However, although the electoral register shows no one called Stone living at 43 Alleyn Park at that time, there was a Reginald James Horace Wood. It would have been perfectly in character for Lawrence Durrell, the mischievous alchemist, to have jokingly turned Wood into Stone.

By the end of his first year at St Edmund's, Durrell, still in the Lower Fourth, had struggled up from fourteenth to twelfth out of sixteen boys. French, history, divinity and English were his best subjects, Greek, Latin and maths his worst. In September he was moved to the Upper Fourth, where he came under the wing of the master who made the greatest impression on him at the school. 'Holly' Hollingworth was a lover of French literature, who spent all his spare time in Paris. Detecting a liking for French in the young Durrell, he encouraged him by supplying him regularly with the literary pages of *Le Monde*. From then on Durrell became hooked on French literature and the French way of life – there was even something about the smell of a French newspaper, he said, that spoke of an exotic culture.[34] This gave him an entirely new attitude to studying; now that he had a focus of approval for his wide reading, he consumed anything in French hungrily.

In the Christmas exams of 1927 Durrell's results show a remarkable improvement, and he came second in the class. He was first in French, second in Greek and was commended in both; he also came second in Divinity, English and Science. This dramatic progress may not have been entirely due to a sudden intellectual blossoming. An epidemic of chickenpox in November had reduced his class by half (the rest were isolated in sick-bay), so there was less competition and more personal attention from masters. He also hinted to Henry Miller in 1937 that he had been asked to assist with the mimeographing of the examination papers, and had been placed on his honour not to look at them. However, he was, he told Miller, a very smart young boy . . .[35]

In any event, the new shining star of the Upper Fourth was soon to shoot off. His father had made his plans; in December Durrell left St Edmund's to go to an army crammer, a year before he would have entered for School Certificate. Presumably

Lawrence Samuel was impatient to see his eldest boy achieve university entrance. Larry spent his last term at St Edmund's, no doubt at his father's insistence, as a member of the school's Officer Training Corps.

When he left Canterbury at the end of the autumn term in 1927, his friends thought he was moving back home to Dulwich. But, in January 1928, he was sent to a 'College' at West Wratting Park in Cambridgeshire. Run by a W. L. B. Hayter and a Major H. Charlewood Turner, and with five resident tutors, it prepared boys for army, air force, navy and all university entrance examinations. 'All candidates', boasted the prospectus, 'receive individual attention.'

It was in his first year at West Wratting that Durrell settled down to writing seriously, perhaps in reaction to the grind of studying. He was a lazy student, but the poetry he wrote at the crammer made up the first slight collection of poetry he published[36] – now included in his *Collected Poems*. It was while there, too, that he started work on his first novel, heavily based on the experience of coming to England from India – the novel which emerged some years later as *Pied Piper of Lovers*.[37] All this coincided with the sudden disappearance of the source of his fiercest inhibitions.

Just seven months after Durrell started at West Wratting, on 16 April 1928, his father died aged forty-three of a brain haemorrhage at the Civil Hospital at Dalhousie, and was buried the following day in Dacca. For Louisa there was no time to return to India for the funeral, and it seems that she never went back, but settled instead into a prolonged widowhood, an exile from what she regarded as her home, devoting herself to her growing and ever more boisterous family. The absence of a father, even a remote figure who could be evoked as a source of authority, left the rather indulgent Louisa vulnerable to her children's increasingly undisciplined behaviour. Durrell hinted later that, while Margo was the family favourite, Leslie was the most resentful of his father. *He* liked to act tough and indulge his obsession with firearms and the Wild West; Margo complained persistently about school. Lawrence, meantime, was turning Bohemian. He was certainly not the servant of Empire his father had in mind. Lawrence Samuel was no longer there, but he was still a weighty invisible presence, a key psychological factor in the making of Larry's complex feelings of guilt and anger.[38]

In July, Lawrence Samuel's will was granted probate. Louisa was left 246, 217 rupees – the tidy sum of £18,500 at the 1928 exchange rate. Durrell said he received a legacy of £150 a year from his father, but since Louisa was the sole beneficiary of the will this must have been arranged for his education by his father before he died and continued by her afterwards.

For almost three years at West Wratting he continued to fail his Cambridge Entrance (Little-Go) examinations. He said that he would like to have passed to please his father, but, after reading Freud, he thought that probably he had failed purposely out of 'subconscious resentment' at being sent to England – it was his own Oedipal crisis which he had to resolve.[39] But it was the Maths paper that kept flooring him. By now, at seventeen or eighteen, he said, he was 'anti-everything'.[40] He implied later, to Richard Aldington, that a sense of being unloved had provoked his bad behaviour, to draw attention to himself. However, he continued to live 'a perfectly stupid puppy-clubman life',[41] on the money that was set aside for him, developing a passion for nightclubs and fast cars, and visiting London as often as he could.

In his last year at the crammer, he made one of the most significant discoveries of his life – 'abroad':

> the first breath of Europe I got was when on a reading party for one final cram for something – I think it was for Cambridge again, which I must have tried about eight times, I suppose. Mathematics – three, two, one, nought – it was always this damn thing. I was taken to Switzerland, you see, which gave me a glimpse of Paris on the way, and I went to do a reading party which was conducted by a very deaf old scholar, and instead of reading I suddenly had a look at Lausanne, Vevey and the lakes there, and on the way back managed to get three days in Paris which converted me to Europe as such. And then after this whole question of being educated failed and faded out, I made my way immediately for Paris.[42]

Playing hookey from his studies and touring through Switzerland and on to Paris was like rediscovering his happy past.

The Swiss mountains evoked the Himalayas of his childhood, France was everything England was not, open, sensuous, relaxed and exciting.

The Continent became a second home to him, and he quickly came to consider himself a European rather than either English or British, except in a residual sense. He was born a foundling without roots, he once said. His fidelity to England was more to a language than to a place.[43] He now visited 'abroad' as often as he could – especially Paris. In Amsterdam in 1930 he composed one of his most successful early poems, 'Happy Vagabond', in which he presents not just himself as a vagrant, but his heart too. The memory of friendly, white-capped mountains gladdens him, as do sunset and moon and overarching skies. But there are also memories which evoke anguish and terror, and there is even mention of the blessing of 'rebirth'.[44]

Paris seems finally to have done for Durrell, the would-be Cambridge student. He had already fallen in love with France and French culture at school, but now he learned at first hand how different life could be from that in Pudding Island. Some experiences transformed him. In his last book, *Caesar's Vast Ghost*, he tells of being picked up by a young French student, Gabrielle, in the Luxembourg Gardens and taken back to her seedy attic room, where she cooked him an unforgettable *croque-monsieur* with red wine before seducing him. Afterwards they talked about food and her passion for watercolours. How unlike the girls he had met in London – the progeny of Canute, he called them.[45] Whether he was required to pay the poor student he doesn't say, but he retained a predilection and affection for the whores of Paris throughout his life, and wrote a sad elegy when the French brothels were closed by a puritan French government just after the Second World War.[46] What he came to call with such contempt the 'English Death' related as much to the frigidity of its men and women as to its exhausted cultural and spiritual atmosphere.

Durrell's initiation into the paradise garden of sexual delights was clearly a major turning-point in his life. He later told a friend that he could not consider himself mature until he had notched up some sexual experience.[47] Sexuality became Durrell's chosen realm, and in it he was to encounter philosophers of the erotic arts (from Plato to de Sade, Rabelais to Henry Miller), poets and writers from both occident and orient, as well as large numbers of the opposite sex. It was here, too, that he would set much of his poetry and most of his fiction. Now the young Durrell began to challenge the basis of his education and religion. His 'anti-everything' extended itself to the basic values of his upbringing. His education, he thought, had made him a determinist and Aristotelian – perfect for a civil administrator, but not for the kind of poet and lover he wished to become.[48] And gradually he came to reject the religion he had so publicly embraced at his confirmation at St Edmund's. If he did not rush from the arms of one Christian sect to those of another, it was probably because he associated Christianity with everything he was then rejecting, especially the suffocating prudery which characterized much of English life in the 1930s. And he felt that he had already been touched by something greater, by contact with the Himalayan Buddhist lamas who had always had a strong grip on his imagination.

The fresh-sounding work of the War generation, which began to appear in the late 1920s and early 1930s, provided him with important models. Huxley, Wells and Aldington (especially *Death of a Hero*) were rapidly digested; his poetic models were Edith Sitwell, Aldington, Nichols, Sassoon and Graves (in the cheap Benn's Sixpenny Poets editions), to be followed by the more lasting influences of Eliot and D. H. Lawrence. (He added Roy Campbell later.) They provided a perspective and, in Larry's case, a voice, which echoed his own feelings and thoughts. He read an essay by Lawrence in which he showed how England treated its writers. That, he said, made him decide 'to swim against the current'.[49] He lapped up those French writers who kicked against the conventions – Rabelais, Villon, Baudelaire, Rimbaud. And, like any bright young intellectual of his day, he was greatly influenced by Freud and writers on sex, such as Havelock Ellis and Norman Haire, who had taken their cue from Freud's liberating initiative.

Towards the end of 1929, Louisa sold 43 Alleyn Park. She had found it too expensive to keep up, and had decided to realize some capital from the house sale and move into rented quarters. However, she lost money on the move, and was

unable to continue supporting her playboy son at West Wratting. Durrell was probably not unhappy to leave, though it
meant the end of a leisurely life on £150 a year; he was happy
enough finally to give up pretending to try for university, and
to abandon his father's compromise with public service. Now
he could commit himself to the more detached, alienated role
of poet. From this point onwards, his university was to be
wherever he located himself, and like a mendicant friar or
scholar gypsy he sought the places and books which stimulated
his mind and imagination. Oxbridge would probably have
proved too restrictive for him, and he would have left after a
short time, like Christopher Isherwood and Dylan Thomas's
friend, Vernon Watkins. He was, however, always conscious of
never having 'made it' to university ('the gateway to the world'
he called it),[50] and this seems to have led him to pursue ever
more esoteric knowledge – as many autodidactic writers have
done, like his part-Irish contemporary George Barker, and like
Henry Miller.

By the beginning of 1930, the family had moved from
Dulwich into a spacious apartment at 10 Queen's Court, an
annexe of the rambling Queen's Hotel in Church Road, West
Norwood, where lived Louisa's sister, the formidable Aunt Fan
(Fanny Louisa Prudence Minnie Hughes). The hotel, a
Victorian monstrosity stuck like a stranded whale in Church
Road, in suburban West Norwood, was famous in a small way
for having given sanctuary to Emile Zola after the Dreyfus
Affair in 1888. Perhaps Louisa found this old pile reminiscent
of the wedding-cake hotels which littered the landscape of
British India. If she had been feeling homesick for the Raj, the
Queen's offered her some sense of comforting familiarity. It
was built no doubt to cater for visitors to the Crystal Palace,
and combined a pretentious nineteenth-century grandeur with,
by 1930, an air of faded gentility. The Queen's Court annexe
and the hotel had become the home of the widows of Indian
civil servants, maiden ladies and retired army officers. For
Louisa it would have seemed a home from home, but to the
Durrell children it was far too cramped and stuffy, with few
other children to play with, and a battalion of disapproving
old ladies whenever they got boisterous.

And for Lawrence, such disapproving respectability must have been as suffocating as his rumbustious sense of humour was embarrassing. So he would disappear off into London in search of a more congenial climate, where you could stay up all night, sing and strum your guitar as loud as you liked, get drunk and fornicate to your heart's content, and with no Aunt Fan or Prudence to regard you disapprovingly through their pince-nez. In *The Black Book*, he wreaked his revenge on the Queen's, portraying it as the Regina Hotel, the very epitome of the English Death, and filling it with eccentric degenerates and dissipated perverts. The disapproving maiden aunts and frosty widows got their deserts in the form of the wrathful Mrs Juniper, for whom there must have been many a model in the Queen's.

Although freed from the tyranny of his father's ambition, Larry was on a reduced stipend, and, now spending more and more time around London's Bohemia, he needed to supplement his meagre income. He said he tried for the Jamaican Police but failed (on the grounds of height, no doubt); he also tried rent collecting for an estate agent in Leytonstone, but was too often bitten by dogs. He had developed a passion for Bach, but, deciding he lacked the talent for a concert pianist, turned instead to jazz, which suited more his rebellious nature, and found work playing jazz piano in London nightclubs. Dancing, too, became a craze for him. Much later in life, he astonished his children by demonstrating the Charleston with his third wife, Claude. And, looking back on that time, he wondered at his own suppleness.[51] The mild-mannered, dreamy, rather solitary little schoolboy had emerged now as a lively extrovert with an infectious laugh and a great gusto for living. As a friend who knew him during the war in Egypt said of him, 'When he came into the room it was as though someone had uncorked a bottle of vintage champagne.'[52]

He had grown to only five foot two, and would not grow much more, but his mischievous sense of humour, his readiness to attack and mock, and his remarkable 'Irish' wit and charm now provided him with a formidably dynamic personality. All this was combined with an apparently inexhaustible supply of energy, a gritty determination and a capacity for hard work which he generously ascribed to his father's example. The mischievous streak, however, could sometimes be hurtful. Gerry said of him, 'He was designed by providence to go through life exploding ideas in other people's minds and then curling up with cat-like unctuousness and refusing to take responsibility for the consequences.'[53] As a poet he could justify being self-absorbed at times, though he blamed his narcissism on lack of paternal approval as a child.[54] Writing itself can be seen as a search for approval, and Durrell made no secret of the pleasure he got from admiring reviews. He would also search more and more for approval and love from women. Along with the role of inspired poet, which he cultivated, went the role of romantic lover. He was to achieve technical mastery of both of these arts, and sometimes an astonishing degree of inspiration.

To the young Gerry his eldest brother was, perhaps naturally, something of a hero, and he recalled him returning home in the early hours from playing his jazz, sitting on his mother's bed smoking a cigarette and telling grossly exaggerated versions of his latest adventures or reading something he had just written. Sleeping in the same room as his mother, young Gerald found all this spellbinding and his brother's way with words wondrous. Larry was like a magician to his young brother, encouraging him to read extensively, explaining difficult bits to him. Gerry felt he owed his lifelong delight in the English language to the infectious enthusiasm of his older brother.[55]

Larry was obviously fascinated by London night-life, especially life out on the gaslit streets – the world of the prostitutes, the pedlars, the night cafés, and the dark handsome Jewish women around Soho and Red Lion Square. He tried his hand at song-writing and ventured into the shadowy world of London's Tin Pan Alley. There he came into contact with Jews working in the music business, and, either because of some hard business dealing or because of his own lack of success, picked up the anti-semitism current among the smart set he was trying to emulate. After all, even the great Eliot's *Waste Land* made sly digs at the Jew as a symbol of ruthless self-interest. Durrell seems to have been both attracted and repelled by Jews, and, from his reading, began to regard the influence of Jewish thought, especially in introducing monotheism to the world (resulting, as he saw it, in determinism and materialism), as the source of most of modern mankind's woes. Jesus, Freud and Marx, he came to think, had much to answer for.

The wider purlieus of south London were, perhaps, a good enough urban desert against which the inspired soul of a young poet could healthily rebel, especially one who had tasted the joys of European travel and the sensual pleasures of gay Paree. And always etched in his memory were the sweeping vistas of the Himalayas seen from his dormitory at St Joseph's, and the mystic memory of Tibetan lamas, clutching their prayer-wheels, journeying to the land forbidden to strangers. Against such a magnificent backdrop, West Norwood, despite the Crystal Palace and the crumbling majesty of the Queen's Hotel, could not compare.

Leslie was still away at Caldicott School and Margo was at Malvern Girl's College, while Gerald remained at home, and during the holidays they must have made up an unruly brigade among the retired worthies of the old hotel. The noisy, irresponsible, gregarious Durrell children must have all too often scandalized their prim neighbours, greatly embarrassing their mother. Perhaps this was what finally prompted her to leave the teeming capital and try for a more settled life well away from London. If Durrell had thought that East Dulwich was a centre of the English Death, Louisa's next port of call would be, for him, just another part of the suburban wasteland.

CHAPTER 3

Pudding Island and the English Death (1931–1935)

I cannot enter society except as a vagabond.

> James Joyce to Nora Barnacle, 1904

I was born with a typewriter in my mouth.

> Lawrence Durrell

In 1931, the family moved to Berridge House, a large detached house at 6 Spur Hill in Parkstone, near Bournemouth. For a while the nineteen-year-old Durrell worked as a porter at Bournemouth station, and his wild behaviour must have been some compensation for the drudgery of portering, but his extravagances again embarrassed his mother in front of her sedate neighbours. At that time he sported a black bowtie in homage to Lautréamont, took up absinthe *à la* Baudelaire, and only started writing after midnight.[1] (In fact he claimed that between seventeen and twenty-four he never slept, and that that probably shortened his life.) Finally, Louisa delivered an ultimatum: if he wanted to be a Bohemian, he could be one somewhere else. He did not need much persuading – he was eager to find somewhere to live in the great metropolis, and there to make his name as a poet, away from what he saw as a dreary parochial seaside resort.

Bournemouth became a base for the Durrells, the place to which family members retired, including all those strange aunts who figure in their nephews' and niece's writings. There seems

always to have been a formidable aunt to poke her nose into
the books which the clever Durrell children published – aunts
Fan and Nora, Patience and Prudence among them. For Lawrence they represented not the dottily comical members of the
older generation, as Margo and Gerald portrayed them, so
much as heraldic figures to be mercilessly satirized.[2]

Although he appears to have loathed suburban life, Bournemouth, West Norwood and the Crystal Palace recur in his
novels, not just the early ones which deal with the pre-war
England he detested, but also in his later, more highly wrought
fiction, where they appear as fleeting memories in the complex
minds of his characters[3]. The young man who escaped the
suburbs is shown in photographs of that time as a small, highly
attractive, sturdy young man, with a snub nose, a fine head of
flaxen hair and clear blue, fiercely determined eyes. Over the
next decade that fierce determination would take him away
from obscurity to the very brink of success.

He found himself bedsitting-rooms in London. One, in
Howland Street off Tottenham Court Road, he claimed was
the room in which Rimbaud had assaulted Verlaine with a
dead fish. As he began to circulate around the capital's
Bohemian scene (singing and sinning around the capital,' he
said), mostly in Soho and the streets radiating off Charlotte
Street and around the British Museum, he was keenly aware
of his lack of university education. But he read voraciously and
scribbled like a good poet should, continued writing songs,
and added the guitar to his musical repertoire.

London's Bohemia gave Durrell as free an element in which
to swim as any to be found in pre-war England, whose moral
claustrophobia and restrictive censorship laws had driven his
hero Lawrence out of the country. In this artistic underworld,
the left-over conventions of post-Victorian British society were
happily overturned, and mild perversion and gentle debauchery
were *de rigueur*. Heavy drinking was the main form of anti-
social gesture, and the pubs in and around Soho, the Marquis
of Granby at Cambridge Circus and the Fitzroy Tavern in
Charlotte Street, became, in the 1930s, the haunts of such
creative deviants as Malcolm Lowry, Dylan Thomas and Nina
Hamnet. Sex and drugs were also freely indulged in, though

the drugs were mostly confined to cannabis and occasionally opium. Alcohol and sex were Durrell's favoured indulgences. Sex, he believed, was a direct route to maturity. Deprived of sex one could only remain a narrow-minded innocent. From the outset, sex for Durrell was not just a physical act, but part of the process of enlightenment essential to his artistic development. It was certainly a more pleasurable route to knowledge than the university.

The opportunity to break into print came when a friend, Cecil Jeffries, bought a hand press and asked Durrell for poems to practise on; printing poetry, he thought, would be simpler than printing prose. He gave him the notebook containing all the poems he had written since the age of sixteen. Using the imprint 'Cecil Press', Jeffries set up the poems under the title *Quaint Fragment*. The poet claimed that only a couple of copies were ever produced before the type was broken up, but three or four are said to have turned up in book sales, especially after Durrell's success gave his early work a high value on the second-hand book market.[4] *Quaint Fragment*, dedicated to his mother, appeared in 1931, and most of the poems are included in his *Collected Poems 1931–1974*. They are almost all lyrical evocations of youthful emotion, and 'the pangs of dispriz'd love', not to say lust. He was probably close now to what young Walsh Clifton became by the end of *Pied Piper of Lovers* – a nihilistic sensualist. He saw himself, in retrospect, as having been a kind of cultural terrorist, a 'pre-Beatnik Beatnik', out to destroy certain cultural ikons and demolish certain taboos.

In September 1931, Durrell's younger brother Leslie, now fourteen, and as much a Tom Thumb as Lawrence, left Caldicott to go to Dulwich College. His father would have been proud of him. But the tiny Leslie had 'a rough time' at his new school, suffering a great deal from bullying.[5] He would rebel in his own way, becoming in due course an irresponsible, gun-obsessed wastrel – no doubt with much the same people in his sights that his older brother was happy to mow down with words.

Early in 1932, Larry met Nancy Myers, who was to become his first wife. He later claimed that he met her on her doorstep when selling vacuum cleaners, and he did resort to such jobs when the demand for jazz pianists fell off. Nancy Isabel Myers was two months younger than Durrell, a very tall, pale, blonde, blue-eyed art student who greatly resembled Greta Garbo.[6] So tall was she beside the diminutive Durrell that he christened her 'The Lamp Post'. She was born in Eastbourne, grew up in Gainsborough, Lincolnshire, and was educated at the Westminster Art School. She was studying at the Slade School and living in Robert Street, close to Regent's Park. In those days the main influence at the Slade was Augustus John, and in *The Avignon Quintet* Durrell makes his beautiful, doomed, anti-heroine Livia a Slade student of the same epoch.[7] They were quite poor and had their share of Bohemian squalor, though they never actually starved. There are powerful evocations of their life in bedsit land in *Panic Spring*, Durrell's second novel, where the character of Ruth, the artist, bears more than a trace of Nancy Myers, and Reuben, the would-be composer, more than a trace of Lawrence Durrell.[8] Nancy had a small annuity of about £50 a year; she and Larry supplemented their joint income, however, by taking occasional jobs.

Shortly after meeting Nancy, Durrell was playing jazz piano in the Blue Peter Nightclub in Upper St Martin's Lane, where he first met the young actor, Peter Bull. Late one night, there was a police raid. Thanks to his small size, Durrell was able to slip out through a lavatory window and escape down a drainpipe. Nancy had been working late, acting in a theatre, and that night at 3 a.m. they were drinking coffee at the Windmill Café in Windmill Street when Durrell noticed a young man busily correcting galley proofs. He was duly impressed, and so struck up a conversation. As the young man, who was called John Gawsworth, began to talk, Durrell became even more impressed. Here was a poet who had met Yeats and Hardy, had exchanged letters with de la Mare and Drinkwater, and was writing an essay on Wyndham Lewis, whom he knew. He was an acquaintance of Havelock Ellis, the high priest of sexual psychology, and had once even caught a glimpse of T. S. Eliot.

They adjourned to Gawsworth's attic in Denmark Street, where the poet kept a treasure-trove of first editions, manuscripts, letters from celebrated poets and many literary and historical curios – Dickens's skull cap, Thackeray's pen, Emma Hamilton's ring (which Durrell later lost).[9] He seemed to know everywhere in London with literary associations, and every literary date that mattered – and yet he was only Durrell's age. Because of his championing of neo-Georgians against modern verse, influential old poets such as A. C. Squire and Lascelles Abercrombie had got him elected a fellow of the Royal Society of Literature, and, amazingly, he had also been made a Freeman of the City of London. One older writer who greatly favoured him was the novelist M. P. Shiel, the 'King of Redonda'. Redonda was a Caribbean island which, on a cruise, Shiel's wealthy Irish father had claimed in the name of his small son, who was crowned King by the Archbishop of Antigua. Queen Victoria had revoked this title, but Shiel still claimed his kingdom and had named Gawsworth, who was his bibliographer, his eventual heir.[10] Gawsworth was breathtakingly prolific, publishing great amounts of his pedestrian verse, mostly through small presses. He was said to be directly descended from Shakespeare's Dark Lady of the Sonnets, Mary Fytton.

Durrell thought highly of Gawsworth (christened Terence Fytton Armstrong), admiring him for his wide literary contacts and experience as a published poet and bibliographer. But George Woodcock, who met Gawsworth at Charles Lahr's bookshop in Red Lion Square, a rendezvous for young writers such as Liam O'Flaherty and H. E. Bates, thought Gawsworth 'a wretched poet and one of the most rat-like human beings I have ever known, full of grievance and always ready to bite'.[11] Dylan Thomas also had a low opinion of him. Such people, he wrote, 'were not poets at all but just bearded boils in the dead armpit of the nineties'.[12] But, to Durrell, Gawsworth was a contact man, someone who knew his way around the back-alleys of literary London, and, he thought, an expert on printers and publishers' contracts.

Larry decided that the best alternative to a university was the British Museum, and he became a lifelong devotee, obtaining a reader's ticket at the end of 1932. He was riveted by the *Encyclopaedia Britannica*, which he found ready to hand in the great oval Reading Room, the magnificent eleventh edition of 1911 as well as the new fourteenth published in 1929. He managed to buy his own copy and from time to time resolved to read the entire thing. A cynic might conclude, from his work, that Durrell spent a long time dawdling over Anatomy, Elizabethans, Empire and (reading the spine-chillingly detailed accounts in *Panic Spring* and *Nunquam*) Embalming, which later led him to *The Egyptian Book of the Dead*. And entries for de Sade and Freud, he would certainly have read diligently.

This process of self-education was an extension of what he had begun at school, reading outside and beyond the set books, and in the North Library at the Museum he got to the special collection of banned books, with which he became very familiar. Cruising around the outer fringes of learning, he found himself delving into exotic territory. Now holding Christianity in contempt, exploring alternative religions and metaphysical systems became second nature to him. His quick, retentive mind soon enabled him to achieve a degree of erudition which distinguished him from those educated in the prescribed fashion along routes mapped out in universities.

Two topics in particular were a focus of his enthusiasm – the lives of Elizabethan writers and medicine. To study medicine became an unfulfilled ambition; discovering medical texts and journals in the British Museum, he became addicted to them, often citing obscure cases from the *British Medical Journal*. A fascination with disfiguring illnesses is evident from his fiction, and, as the dark side of the human body began to obsess him, so did the dark side of the human psyche. A keen interest in madness, alchemy, necromancy, astrology and the black arts, hinted at in *The Alexandria Quartet*, becomes more evident in later novels. The benign mage, Balthazar, in the *Quartet*, is succeeded by Julian, the cruel enigmatic master of the Firm in *Tunc–Nunquam*, an evil Frankenstein, using modern science to resurrect the dead, and by Akkad in *Monsieur*, who is all but on speaking terms with the Prince of Darkness. It was in the North Library of the British Museum, too, that he first read the Marquis de Sade, whose influence runs through his work, giving an edge of cruel sophistication to his otherwise infectious good humour and increasingly polished wit.

It was probably at Charlie Lahr's bookshop that Durrell met other 'characters' to add to his collection of eccentric friends – Raj Mulk Anand (the Indian novelist), young George Barker and Count Potocki of Montalk. The Count, pretender to the throne of Poland, was a familiar exhibitionist on London's Bohemian fringes. Geoffrey Potocki and his younger brother Cedric, were born in New Zealand of Polish descent, and, according to George Woodcock, had as good a claim to the Polish throne as any other Pole, since it was elective. He was a genuine count, spoke with an Antipodean twang, wore a long purple robe and a pie-shaped hat, and grew his hair down to his shoulders. He was loudly anti-semitic, and, although people called him a fascist, in Woodcock's opinion 'he was really an old-style authoritarian reactionary'.[13] However, he later ran a periodical, the *Right Review,* in reaction to the socialist *Left Review,* and his admiration for Hitler did bring him into close alliance with fascists. According to Durrell, he was obsessed with sex and had an entourage of Bloomsbury typists and casual pickups. On more than one occasion, Potocki embarrassed Durrell in the Reading Room of the British Museum by loudly recounting his latest sexual escapade.

Nancy had left the Slade in the summer of 1932, and from then on she and Larry were inseparable. At his Guilford Street bedsitter, they would settle down, he with his guitar or type-writer (he often worked straight on to it) and Nancy with her paints. And here they could entertain friends such as Gawsworth and Potocki, Peter Bull and his friend George Wilkinson. Wilkinson was tall and thin with a brown beard, son of the owner of the Curwen Press, heir to a title and a member of the First Edition Club in Pall Mall, and he was to play a very important part in Durrell's life over the next three or four years. At the Guilford Street lodgings, according to Gawsworth, 'we all boiled kippers in a saucepan and read Aldington aloud',[14] and no doubt drank the foul-tasting pre-war coffee called Camp, recalled by Durrell in *The Avignon Quintet.*[15] For a while, Gawsworth became a serious rival for Nancy's affections, even publishing a poem to her, but his friendship

with Durrell survived this probably uneven combat. Gawsworth retreated unhurt, it seems, and by 1933 was married to
(or cohabiting with) a woman called Barbara who worked for
the *Daily Express*.

A snapshot of the disorganized life which Durrell lived in
London can be found in *Pied Piper of Lovers*, where the squalid
bedsitter is the centre from which his young Bohemian hero,
Walsh Clifton, sallies forth to sample the sex and drugs and
world of young would-be artists. The talk is of Freud and
Havelock Ellis, of Lawrence and Rémy de Gourmont, whose
Natural Philosophy of Love Durrell had read in the British
Museum library. Freud, Ellis and Lawrence had provided a
generation with a new religion of licensed sensuality as a road
to mental health which found young Durrell a ready disciple.
His poetry more and more reflected a keen awareness of bodily
pleasure, pleasure which he was adept at rendering into the
subtlest language.

Durrell said that he took Nancy to Paris at this time, though
he did not say whether he told her about Gabrielle. They stayed
in Montparnasse, at the Royale, a hotel in Boulevard Raspail,
just around the corner from the Café Dôme. Durrell claimed
that all the rooms in the hotel had even numbers, and he
persuaded the manager to create a Room 13. Thereafter,
throughout his life, when he visited Paris he always stayed in
Room 13 at the Royale.

He was now keen to launch his literary career; if publishers
failed to recognize his 'genius', he would publish his own work,
much as Gawsworth did. Through George Wilkinson and his
fiancée, Pamela Black (pretty and blonde, and, like Nancy, also
an artist), Durrell found J. A. Allen, who ran a bookshop
in Grenville Street, Bloomsbury, and was ready to publish
his second book of poems, simply called *Ten Poems*, under
the imprint of the Caduceus Press. It bore an epigraph from
Massinger, 'Angels desire an alms', was dedicated to Nancy,
who designed the cover, and appeared in a limited deluxe
edition (twelve copies in buckram), sold at a shilling each. The
caduceus, a rod entwined by serpents, is the symbol of power
attributed to the god Mercury, also a healing symbol associated

with medicine. It was re-echoed in the serpent-worship and serpent-imagery in Durrell's last cycle of novels, *The Avignon Quintet*.[16]

Ten Poems still bears the plaintive note of the love-lorn, with faint echoes of the Elizabethan lyricists and Shakespeare's sonnets. Larry was fortunate enough to have *Ten Poems* reviewed in the *Times Literary Supplement*. 'Mr Durrell's verses,' said the nameless reviewer, 'have a careful distinction of style, although he occasionally indulges in such phrases as "the old magnificence and peace," which suggest more of poetic grandeur than of original necessity. Indeed, his verse as a whole is rather too mannered.' And 'although his theme is that of the sweet bitterness of love and his art is restrained and his feeling never facile or expansive, he seldom quite convinces us that the need for expression is more urgent in him than the taste for experiment.'[17]

Durrell's and Nancy's Christmas card for 1932, designed by Nancy, is today a collector's item. Lawrence's satirical verse about the cost of the joyful season caught his disenchantment with religions and their festivals. The mood of penny-pinching gloom chimes with that of the Depression, just then gathering force. It had been a year of rising unemployment and cuts in wages and welfare. A coalition government in London was threatened with collapse, and, by the end of the year, Hitler was poised to become Chancellor of Germany. The year's literary highlights had been the publication of Huxley's *Brave New World* and Waugh's *Black Mischief*; while *Stamboul Express* launched the career of the young novelist Graham Greene. 1932 had also seen the death of the century's subtlest iconoclast, Lytton Strachey; and the world's highest literary honour, the Nobel Prize for Literature, went to an Englishman – the popular, but hardly electrifying, John Galsworthy.

The same year had seen Michael Roberts's *New Signatures* anthology launch the decade's most celebrated literary triumvirate of Auden, Spender and Day Lewis, later joined by Louis MacNeice. These innovatory left-leaning young writers, who incorporated what was modern into sharp, intelligent, experimental verse, had provoked the displeasure of conservative critics such as Gawsworth and his neo-Georgian cronies.

Gawsworth countered with his own anthology, *Known Signatures*, which made no impact whatever. Durrell saw that Gawsworth and company were wrong to dismiss Auden and his friends, and saw, too, that Gawsworth was merely trying to resurrect the 1890s, an enterprise which he felt was pointless and unimaginative. To him the poetry of the neo-Georgians such as W. H. Davies and Masefield had for years said very little, even though they said it exquisitely. Only a genius like Yeats could rise above the limitations of traditional verse.[18] But Durrell liked Gawsworth and regarded his antics with amused tolerance. Another opponent of the new poets, the right-wing Roy Campbell, who dubbed them 'MacSpaunday', won his admiration because what *he* hated was that some of the Auden group were barely concealed homosexuals and were soon to be elevated into a new establishment. The pugnacious young Durrell was 'against everything'. He saw himself as something of a ruffian and disturber of the bourgeois peace, and gradually his contempt for Pudding Island and the English Death would drive him to seek an alternative life elsewhere. As to his own poetry, he believed that he had found the point at which his material and sensual world were fused – the procreative act – and in expressing this lay the shock effect of his verse.[19]

Lawrence celebrated his twenty-first birthday on 27 February 1933, and Nancy celebrated hers a few weeks later, on 8 May. On that day, Nancy came into a strange inheritance. Eighteen years earlier, the author E. Fielding-Hall, author of *Burma: The Soul of a People*, dined with her parents, and so took to their young daughter that he decided to leave her his entire literary estate. This windfall, plus a small income of her own, enabled the couple to survive without having to moonlight.

Durrell was still working on that first novel, producing poems and turning out a few satires, which he had no success in placing. But he did arrange for one little squib to be published by J. A. Allen, again from the Caduceus Press and under a pseudonym. This was an odd piece called *Bromo Bombastes*, subtitled 'A Fragment from a Laconic Poem by Gaffer Peeslake, which same being a brief extract from his Compendium of Lisson Devices'. This 'fragment' was a parody of George Bernard Shaw's *Black Girl in Search of a God*, and gave him the opportunity to poke gentle fun at Christianity. It was his first piece of published drama.

In mid-1933, he and Nancy set up a business to capitalize on her talent as a photographer. They took a top floor over Dora Stephens's Dairy in Millman Street, between Southampton Row and Gray's Inn Road, turning it into a photographic studio called Witch Photos. Their plan was to lure writers to be photographed. Those who posed for them included George Wilkinson's friend A. J. A. Symons, bibliophile founder and secretary of the First Edition Club, then in the throes of writing his masterpiece of biographical detection, *The Quest for Corvo*. The urbane, witty Symons was probably the Durrells' biggest catch, but even he, a generous and reliable man, did not consider prompt payment a matter of good breeding. Witch Photos foundered because the writers photographed did not settle their bills.

Durrell continued to trust Gawsworth as a judge of literature, sending him not only his poems but also his satires and stories. One four-part poem, called 'Faces', is about deceptive masks treated as grotesque flaps of flesh and membrane behind which puppets enact a meaningless charade.[20] It hints at a future fascination with deceptive human connections masquerading as love, the theme of *The Alexandria Quartet* over twenty years later. He showed a taste for free verse in the Elizabethan dramatic mode, reflecting his continuing interest in the sixteenth century, the only previous age in England, he thought, when writers were free to express themselves with uninhibited gusto.

If his poems were all modelled closely on the work of one or two favourite poets, so was his autobiographical novel, which slowly grew in size. Among the influences were Kipling, Huxley, Wells and Aldington. According to Durrell, he would change styles from page to page, so that the novel, as it grew, became a patchwork of pastiches.[21] Sometimes, to get away from their cramped London lodgings, he and Nancy escaped to the country, still, in the early 1930s, not too far removed from that of Mr Jorrocks. But a love of the English countryside was no compensation for the feeling that England was

collapsing culturally. George Wilkinson lent them a cottage at
Loxwood in Sussex, the county once beloved of his childhood
hero, Kipling, and here Durrell did most of his work on *Pied
Piper of Lovers*, determined to stay away from London until
he had something to show for his labours – a finished novel at
least. Even so, it was not all hard work at Loxwood, and
sometimes the four friends, Larry, George, Nancy and Pamela,
would while the night away with long meaningful discussions,
and listen to records of Beethoven and Bach, and songs sung
to Larry's guitar.

Durrell and Nancy became regular browsers at H. G.
Commin's bookshop in Bournemouth, and they became very
friendly with one of the assistants, Alan Thomas, who was
invited to the Durrell home in nearby Parkstone, where they
engaged in endless discussions about the nature of art and
artifice.[22] Thomas found the members of the family remarkable
in their own right, but especially when they all interacted
together: the shared Rabelaisian humour provoking storms of
laughter, Larry singing his compositions at the piano or to the
guitar, arguments, vigorous conversations lasting late into
the night. For the small-town bookseller, the household of this
colourful family buzzed: Larry scribbling, Nancy at her paints,
Leslie fussing over his illegal gun collection, Gerry filling the
wash basins with newts and tadpoles. Margaret, meanwhile,
fed up with school, had persuaded her mother to let her stay
at home.[23]

Thomas was astonished by Larry's gusto, his verbal pyro-
technics, his bawdy humour and warm friendship. Larry
composed jazz songs in the hope of making his fortune: 'Love's
Just a Noose Round Your Neck', 'First Love Must Die', 'When
You Go I Know That It's Paradise Lost, Dear'. When some
were rejected by a Soho song-publisher on the ground that
they were too highbrow, Larry sent in a waltz called 'Three
Pawnbroker's Balls' with a note indicating that if the others
were highbrow this one was an affliction.[24]

George Wilkinson and Pamela Black were planning to move
abroad, possibly to Greece. George was keen to write travel
books, and Pamela to find exotic places to paint. Before he
left, George tried to place a novel he had written, but it was

rejected by one publisher after another, which was not very encouraging for Durrell. Obviously, they told each other, there were certain swine determined to keep them down. George and Pamela married on 31 May 1934, at Kensington registry office, with Peter Bull as best man. A poem of Durrell's called 'Gifts' reads like a wedding present, and is about the sacred tenderness of the gift of love which woman offers to man. Its burning Lawrentian imagery is darkened by references to 'betrayal' and 'Sappho' – a theme which came back to haunt him in *Livia*. Almost immediately the Wilkinsons left for Corfu, where the living was cheap and the climate attractive.

Durrell was still slaving over his novel, hoping to achieve something in literary London before making any sort of move, and by the middle of 1934 he had finished *Pied Piper of Lovers*. He began to send it to publishers. Towards the end of the year, after several rejections, he handed it over to Curtis Brown, the literary agent, aware however that stylistically it was rather derivative. As he said:

> I pinched effects, I was learning the game. Like an actor will study a senior character and learn an effect of make-up or a particular slouchy walk for a role he's not thought of himself. He doesn't regard that as being particularly influenced by the actor, but as a trick of the trade which he owes it to himself to pick up.[25]

Later he listed his main influences, describing how he interwove them to disguise the effects of imitation: Aldington, Graves, Huxley, Huxley, Lawrence, Aldington, Graves, Sitwell. He considered himself quite competent at this.[26] Although he had leaned heavily on others, *Pied Piper of Lovers* does show flashes of the unique author to come. And the experience on which it is based is no one else's – an Indian childhood, being sent to England, life in Bohemian London, coming to maturity though sexual liberation.

After this first novel, Durrell never again dealt with his Indian childhood, though he alluded to it from time to time, most notably in Mountolive's story. He explores squalid Bohemian London again in *Panic Spring* and uses it to great symbolic effect in *The Black Book*. It is evident that he had acquired a great eye for detail, and noted down whenever possible characteristics of people and places, salting them away for future use. The structure within *Pied Piper* of three books and an epilogue prefigures future two-, four- and five-decker works. The story, however, follows a straightforward chronological sequence and employs a conventional narrative. The theme of the journey westward from one reality to another also prefigures future switches between London and Greece, Egypt and Switzerland and Occupied France in the Second World War. Durrell had discovered the dramatic force which the journey between cultures can provide to a writer. There is also some switching of viewpoints here, which was a technique he developed in a far more ambitious and crucial manner when he came to write his *Alexandria Quartet*, as he did with 'the letter within the novel'. And his predilection for bringing characters from one book into another can already be found here: the doctor who attends at Clifton's birth turns up at the bedside of the dying Ruth.

Waiting for news of his novel was painful, as were the seductive letters which Wilkinson now wrote him from Corfu, full of sunshine and blue water. Durrell had returned to poetry, and Wilkinson received a new verse with every letter from him. Durrell now had enough new poems for a third slim volume, *Transition*, again published by the Caduceus Press, with Allen distributing it from his bookshop in Grenville Street. He had to wait till December for the *TLS* to notice it. The most apt criticisms of his verses, said the reviewer, were to be found in his own lines, which were 'certainly ingeniously and often tortuously his own but for the most part thin and brittle through excess of cerebration'. To such a consciousness, men were inevitably reduced to puppets manipulated by impulse. 'His verse leaves the same impression except when "some imp of the spontaneous moment" breaks through the web of wires.'[27] This review only added to Durrell's sense of being frustrated by moaning and mindless critics and pedantic scribblers who were ever ready to crush aspiring talent.[28] Yet his problem as a poet was that for poems about love, as most of them were, there was a remarkable absence of feeling.

Durrell's studies at the British Museum turned even further towards the Elizabethans. He took in Sidney, Marlowe, Nashe,

Greene, Peel and Tourneur, as well as Shakespeare, and began to build up a personal library which included facsimiles of early folios. Not that he hankered after the scholarly life, he told Wilkinson unconvincingly, but such studies helped him to concentrate, and he would love to write a textbook on Elizabethan writers. He was also interesting himself in poets such as Keats, Fitzgerald and Yeats, and in European painters such as Cézanne, Gauguin, Van Gogh, Monet and Picasso. And he consumed works of western philosophy, from Rousseau to Wyndham Lewis. All this he added to his diet of sexology – Freud, Rémy de Gourmont, de Sade and Krafft-Ebing. And with the Mediterranean in mind, he read D. H. Lawrence's *Sea and Sardinia* and Norman Douglas's *South Wind*. Douglas would help supply him with a vision and a language with which he could turn his own experiences of that blue sea of islands into literature. Douglas's voice can also be detected in pages of *The Alexandria Quartet*.

Slowly the idea of joining the Wilkinsons in Corfu began to grow. His mother was having money problems, and he got down to persuading her that life in Corfu was cheap and pleasant, and that they would enjoy themselves much as they had in India, living an independent life among friendly peasants. She was not difficult to persuade; she was, said Durrell, a very sweet person who hated to say no. Nor did Nancy need much convincing. The idea of exploring what remained of early Byzantine paintings along the Greek coast excited her greatly, and Durrell was keen to explore Minoan civilization, having discovered, he thought, that on average the Minoans were about his own height and were both strong and lusty. He was hoping to discover that their undoubtedly healthy private members were suitably ornamented.[29] With an eye to the coming migration, he was assembling as large a library of Elizabethan material as he could, and considered taking his own *Encyclopaedia Britannica* with him as well as books of philosophy, lots of poetry and Nancy's art books.

In preparation for their move, Mrs Durrell sold the house in Parkstone and took a flat in Bournemouth. In the meantime, Durrell asked Wilkinson to scout Corfu for a house for them, and he soon found a villa next to his own place in Perama, not far from Corfu town. He had a few misgivings about emigrating, wondering, for instance where his loyalties would lie in the event of war. However, the marriage of George, Duke of Kent, and Princess Marina of Greece in December seemed a good omen.

With his bookshop friend Alan Thomas, Durrell decided to explore some of the lovelier parts of England, the parts evoking a past with which he could identify through history and literature. Thomas, sad at the prospect of losing his brilliant friend, hoped to captivate him with England's essential beauty. More than once he took him up on to the roof of Christchurch Priory out on the leads. The view from the priory roof over watermeadows and marshes down to Christchurch harbour was breathtaking, and the image left an imprint on Durrell. This was the scene he recaptured in *The Black Book*. He no doubt realized that leaving England, much as he hated its deathly gloom, would be a turning-point. Perhaps with this in mind, he told Wilkinson, at Christmas, that he was cooking up something gigantic – something on a heroic scale.[30] At Christmas time, too, he sent friends his *Mass for the Old Year*, a poem regretting the passing of the selves they had been in 1934, a lyrical dirge, suitably decorated by Nancy – herself on the front cover passing under a lighted lamp-post, and on the back a Picasso-esque block of a guitarist and what looks like the shadow of the prow of a Greek ship.

Early in 1935, Durrell told Thomas that he and Nancy were getting married, but in secret. Thomas was puzzled, because he thought that Louisa Durrell would be only too delighted. Perhaps Nancy's parents, the Myers, objected to the rather raffish Larry Durrell marrying their beautiful daughter, and in any case the idea of a secret marriage would have appealed greatly to Durrell's sense of mystery and intrigue. So neither set of parents was aware of the wedding, which took place at Bournemouth registry office on 22 January 1935. Thomas and Nancy, being so much taller than Durrell, feared that the registrar would marry *them* by mistake, so they approached two midgets in a local freak-show and asked them to be witnesses, but their employer refused to allow it. Instead, Thomas and one of his bookshop colleagues stood in. On their wedding certificate Nancy wrote that she had no profession, while Durrell is down as 'Private Secretary' – a good (perhaps Freudian) joke, because if Durrell was anyone's private secretary he was his own, Lawrence the secretary of Durrell. 'There is somebody who is living my life,' wrote Luigi Pirandello, the new Nobel Laureate. 'And I know nothing about him.'

By getting married, Durrell ensured that there was no objection from Nancy's family to her going with him to Corfu. Louisa, it seems, had made him an allowance dating from his twenty-first birthday. Thomas puts it at £150 a year;[31] Durrell put it at ten pounds a month for three years.[32] This, together with Nancy's annual £50, gave them an income of £4 a week. They could have scraped by well enough on this in England; in Corfu, thanks to the exchange rate, they would enjoy a life of easeful comfort.

Having been exiled from India against his will, Durrell was now deliberately exiling himself from England. He would slip into the role of expatriate with the ease of one born to live on society's margins – a gypsy, he called himself – and from the margins he would be better placed than many to draw on a wider world of ideas, a wider spectrum of colours, historical associations and heraldic representations. The aspiring poet and embryonic novelist was highly conscious of following a very English tradition of literary exile – from Byron and Shelley to Norman Douglas, from D.H. Lawrence and Richard Aldington to Robert Graves. All had left England and found inspiration abroad. But Durrell still had no offer to publish his first-born novel. He may have set off in a spirit of high romanticism, but he made sure that he left behind a bank account at the Whitehall Branch of his father's old bank, Grindlay's, into which his small monthly stipend was paid. Even gypsy poets have need of a reliable postal address and the wherewithal to subsist.

CHAPTER 4

In Prospero's Cell (1935–1937)

I count religion but a childish toy,
And hold there is no sin but ignorance

Marlowe, *The Jew of Malta*

There is heavenly freedom and infernal
freedom.

Emanuel Swedenborg, *Heaven and Hell*

The newly spliced Mr and Mrs Lawrence Durrell, with the
fifteen-year-old Margo in tow, set sail on the SS *Oronsay* from
Tilbury for Naples *en route* for Corfu on 2 March 1935. To
the P & O Steamship Company Larry gave his occupation as
'Sanitary Engineer'. It may also have been playfulness which
made him give his future country of residence as Italy. (Mr
Durrell, the sanitary engineer, about to make his mark on the
alimentary canal of Europe's spine.)

A stormy passage through the Bay of Biscay produced several
poems about sea gulls and upset stomachs, sent back in letters
to Thomas. The sensuously rich culture and topography
resonant with classical associations of the Mediterranean, the
cradle of western civilization, was about to transform his eager
young mind. Greece in particular would draw him under its
spell, offering him the challenge of self-discovery.

Plans to cross from Brindisi to Corfu, a mere 130 miles
across the Strait of Otranto and the Ionian Sea, were frustrated
by an attempted *coup d'état* against the restoration of the
Greek monarchy. Sea traffic to Greece and the islands had been
disrupted. Stuck in Brindisi, Durrell could still only dream of
Corfu. The joke about Italy as a future place of residence

threatened to become self-fulfilling. He did not find Italy to his taste – a country of waiters, he thought. Yet some aspects of the place appealed to him – unbowdlerized editions of *Lady Chatterley's Lover* on sale for a mere fourteen lire a copy (some five English shillings) and legalized brothels. The other local entertainments he found appallingly bad and his suffering was only alleviated, he told Thomas, by being constrained to consume the local vino, which was giving him a belly-bulge[1] Luckily, in a bar, he found a Greek ship's captain willing to take them to Corfu, even though it meant arriving there in the middle of the night. (In his second novel, *Panic Spring*, he gives this boat the improbable name *Bumtrinket*, the name of a farting maid in Thomas Dekker's *Shoemakers' Holiday* – a name which had touched Durrell's Falstaffian funny-bone.)

Sailing to Corfu, Durrell passed back through the mirror, like his Tibetan lamas, from one reality to another. He found himself warming to the ship's Greek crew, and caught something in their speech of the classical Greek he had begun to grasp as a schoolboy in Canterbury. Even their looks – swarthy skin, dark eyes, curly hair and aquiline profiles – helped his feeling of sailing back into the ancient Greek past.[2] He saw it as a profoundly sensual transition, and marked the point of passage most memorably in *Prospero's Cell*, as falling somewhere between Calabria and Corfu – the point, he wrote, 'at which the blue begins'.[3]

The Corfu of the 1930s was still an ancient land of myths and legends, largely untouched by modernity, whose visitors were mostly archaeologists, painters and writers. It had passed under the rule of Rome, Venice, Italy, France and Britain, before achieving *Enosis*, union with Greece, in 1864. The Venetians left the impressive fortress which stands guard over Corfu Harbour, the French lined the front with an elegant arcade built in imitation of the Rue du Rivoli, and the British left a few imposing structures, a road system, a reliable postal service, and cricket played every summer on the green sward of the Spianada (Esplanade) beside the old Venetian fort. Behind the Spianada and the arcades on Capodistria Street, lay the old Venetian town itself, strangely and delightfully intact. Edward

Lear had stayed in Corfu, and left behind notes and drawings which captured the spirit of Corfiot peasant life in the mid-nineteenth century. The Victorian attitudes introduced by the British, Durrell decided, made the place rather more civilized than the rest of Greece. 'Compared to Athens,' he said, 'Corfu was like . . . Florence.'[4]

Nancy, Larry and Margo booked into the Pensione Suisse, close to the harbour, where they would be on hand to greet the rest of the family when they arrived. While the ancient fourteenth-century town and the haunted island awaited him, Durrell was thinking mostly of his belongings and of his novel. Their baggage had not arrived, but he had no news from either Curtis or Brown, he complained to Thomas. But he had already bought notebooks for his next novel at a shop which sold them by weight – they were placed on a great luggage-scale. Two books laden with dust cost him twenty-four drachmas, or one shilling.[5]

On their first Sunday there they went to church and were bowled over by the grandeur of the Orthodox-style contrapuntal singing, and took in the cathedral to St Spiridion, the island's patron saint, whose mummified remains are paraded solemnly through the town every saint's day. There was also a fine archaeological museum with relics of the lives of the ancient Greeks, and an impressive library of some 40,000 books.

Louisa, Leslie and Gerald arrived about two weeks after Larry, Nancy and Margo. They turned up unexpectedly, surprising the newly weds in bed, but brought news that the British Consul had a letter for Larry from Thomas with news from Curtis Brown. Cassell had accepted his book, and were offering a £50 advance. Durrell wrote back via Thomas, who was acting as a go-between, accepting the offer. Cassell also wanted an option on his three next novels, and he was ecstatic. Now he felt like a real writer, even toying with the idea that he could write best-sellers and solve all money problems while doing what he enjoyed. He relayed the exciting news to Gawsworth, adding that he was now writing some good poetry and some not so good short stories. With the offer of that £50 advance, Durrell shelved the idea of the gigantic work and decided to write something quickly – more romantic, more popular and even more lucrative than his first.

The Wilkinsons had arranged for the Durrells to rent a small villa next to theirs at Perama, the Villa Agazini, overlooking the sea and the famous Mouse Island (Pondikonisi), a tiny rock with nothing but a monastery perched upon it. With the family ensconced, with young Gerry quickly beginning to amass strange specimens of local wildlife in the bathroom, and with Leslie, who had the new habit of farting aloud as an act of self-assertion, Durrell christened the house Agabumtrinket – after the 'privy fault' of the servant in Dekker's play. In *My Family and Other Animals*, Gerald Durrell referred to the Villa Agazini as the 'Strawberry Pink Villa', the first stop-over for the gypsy Durrells on Corfu. Because the house was cramped, Durrell and Nancy sometimes booked into the Pension Suisse to be alone, and have the peace in which to work.

With the Wilkinsons they carried on much as they had done when they shared the house in Sussex – talking through the night, listening to Beethoven, and exploring the countryside. Their friends introduced them to a tall, bearded Greek doctor, Theodore Stephanides, who was a radiologist and a natural scientist of amazing erudition, and was to make a huge impression on both Larry and young Gerald. Stephanides was almost forty, and had been born in India. He spoke fluent English and seemed to know every species of wildlife on the island, as well as most other things known to science. He knew about the folklore and festivals of Corfu, and about Greek heroes such as Karaghiosis, the cunning Rabelaisian character who, in one guise or other, appeared in puppet shows all over the Middle East. He also wrote poetry, and introduced Durrell to modern Greek poets such as Palamas and C. P. Cavafy (Kavaphis). Himself a commanding presence, he was instantly taken with the jaunty, self-confident, energetic young Larry, so effervescent with bright ideas.[6]

Larry, in turn, was struck by the Greek's shining integrity, his modesty and great nobility of character. Stephanides became the first of five 'uncles' he was to acquire over the next two or three years. Committed as he was now to the life of the senses, Corfu (or Kerkyra or Corcyra, as he sometimes preferred) brought a range of experiences he had not encountered since leaving India. He drank in the light, the sounds and the smells, and the many striking images – the cypresses stroked by the sirocco, the blue of the sea curving round the coast to the south with the solitary sailboat painted on it, the colourful vivacity of the peasants in scarves and headdresses passing by on their donkeys, the mysterious close presence of Albania, squatting on the horizon, and the islands to the south, shrouded in secret mists. Everything seemed to be given heraldic significance by the magical beliefs of the peasants and the ghostly presence of Homeric heroes – Ulysses had landed, according to legend, at Paleocastrizza on the west coast of the island, close to where Odysseus and Nausicaa are said to have met.[7] All these impressions and associations invaded his poet's senses, and he was enchanted.

Servants were cheap and amenable, and in some ways the Durrells, by moving to Corfu, had reverted to the colonial role. They enjoyed a privileged standard of living. They soon acquired friends among the locals, and Dr Stephanides became young Gerry's mentor, boosting his emerging passion for wild-life.[8] Louisa also found a protector-cum-majordomo in the local taxi-driver, Spyros Chalikiopoulos, 'Spiro Americanus' of *My Family and Other Animals*, a likeable though bombastic and slightly dubious character who drove an old Dodge tourer, and seems to have taken over as her personal chauffeur. (Larry claimed that Spyros overcharged the gullible Louisa for provisions and services, but to Gerry he was a figure tailor-made for the amusing account of his chaotic family on Prospero's island.)[9]

Slowly, Larry became aware of the range of subtle pleasures which the island afforded. Thanks to the failed coup, the exchange rate had tipped in their favour. Food was cheap (a splendid meal of red mullet cost a mere tenpence), though drinking inexpensive local wine was, he thought, like drinking chilled blood. The sun shone endlessly, and they swam every day from Wilkinson's sailboat. The sensual delights to which as a poet Larry had tuned himself before coming to Greece, seem here to have overwhelmed him, but having a line about going with a strange woman cut from his book by his publisher brought him down to earth. 'My God', he complained to Thomas.[10] England, as ever, was like a cold shower to him.

But the new book was taking shape. It was based on present experience, though facets of himself were dispersed through a group of characters who come to a Greek island and pass through the mirror into another reality just as he and Nancy had. He toyed with possible titles – 'Music in Limbo' and 'Phoenix and Nightingale' – before settling on *Panic Spring*. This was his first, but not his last book with an island setting. The device of characters retiring to islands to reflect on their past lives was to be repeated in *The Black Book* and *The Alexandria Quartet*. By mid-June the novel was half completed. He was greatly cheered by reviews and comments about *Transition*, which saw something very distinctive in his poetry, marking him out as a poet with a future. He was always ready to defend the free verse of the *New Signatures* poets, whom Gawsworth despised, regarding the new tradition of free verse as directly descended from the Elizabethans. Meanwhile, with Nancy teaching him to observe more closely the visual subtleties around them, his verse began to reflect the colour and light of Greek landscape in a way that few other English poets had achieved.[11]

Two events occurred in the late summer. The family uprooted and moved to Sotiriotissa, a few kilometres north of the town, to a larger house, the Villa Anemoyanni – Gerald's 'Daffodil-yellow Villa' – set in wild, untended grounds where cypress and olive trees sat in undergrowth which had run riot. Nancy and Larry had a large room there in which they soon spread themselves – books, files, manuscripts, typewriters – and on the lawn visitors were dragged into riotous games by the rumbustious Durrells – nature-obsessed Gerry, gun-obsessed Leslie, boy-obsessed Margo, word-obsessed Larry, and their fathomlessly tolerant mother who could not say no to anything. Here young Gerry was subjected to a series of tutors, including George Wilkinson, and later Patrick Evans, a friend of Larry's on vacation from Oxford. Brother Lawrence liked to encourage him to write poetry, and Gerry in turn found his older brother fascinated by some of his entomological specimens – especially those which were self-inseminating or which coupled incestuously.[12]

The second thing that happened was more earth-shaking for Larry. Barclay Hudson, an American living near by, lent him a new novel to read. It was published in Paris by the Obelisk Press, a publisher specializing mostly in pornography in English for visiting tourists, and in books banned elsewhere. The novel Hudson lent him was the recently published *Tropic of Cancer* by Henry Miller. The impact was immediate, and Durrell read it straight through twice, urging his friend Thomas to get copies into England and read it himself as soon as possible. It was, he thought, the most important book of modern times, the book his generation had been waiting for. He admitted later that initially it had repelled him, but he realized that this arose from factors in his own upbringing, and his ability to turn his feelings over and accept and grasp Miller was, he thought, a measure of his spiritual advance into adulthood.[13]

The author of this transformatory work was a forty-three year-old German–American. Miller, a self-proclaimed enemy of society, had left America for Paris in 1930, hoping never to return to what he thought was a decayed and collapsing civilization. In America he had had any number of jobs, including typist, dishwasher, plantation worker, messenger-boy, grave-digger, bill-sticker, book salesman, bartender, librarian, garbage collector and personnel manager for the Western Union. In Paris he committed himself to writing, and starved rather than do anything else. He shared Durrell's belief that Anglo-Saxon bourgeois culture was inimical to the creative artist, and *Tropic of Cancer*, his first published, autobiographical novel, was a cry of outrage against the grim reality of life and against bourgeois culture, which through various subtle forms of censorship tried to conceal that grimness from us.

The vigour of Miller's prose and his crudely frank descriptions of sex among characters living on the margins of Parisian society were balanced by passages of philosophical reflection and disquisitions on art. It shows us the mind of a writer, delirious with ideas, drunk on language and imbued with a wry bawdy humour, whose eccentric creations come and go while he ruminates on the human condition, expounds metaphysical dogmas and meditates continually on a doomed civilization. At the same time, throughout this apocalyptic book he sounds the trumpet for total freedom of expression. Question everything was his motto. He was, he wrote, an agent from the world of the liberated here to induce dread and confusion.[14] It was a radical book, striking at the heart of bourgeois, and especially literary, values. Yet despite his squalid and promiscuous lifestyle, those who knew him thought that he himself was, deep down, both bourgeois and puritanical. Since the publication of *Tropic*, he had been ensconced by his mistress, Anaïs Nin, in a fine modern Paris studio at 18 Villa Seurat in the 14th arrondissement near Parc Montsouris. The thirty-four-year-old Nin (of Cuban–Danish–French origin) was the wife of an American banker, Hugh Guiler (also called 'Hugo', and 'Ian Hugo', artist). She was a beautiful, slight, exotic creature, a newly published writer herself, whose main preoccupation was a huge diary, which she had kept since the age of eleven.

To Durrell, reading Miller's book was a 'Road to Damascus' experience. What he had so far written now seemed to him derivative and contrived compared with this untrammelled flow of raw experience. Excitedly he wrote to Miller, congratulating him on the first and only truly adult work of the century. He had gone well beyond Joyce's *Ulysses*, Lawrence's *Chatterley* and Wyndham Lewis's *Tarr*, he said: it was the model which writers of his generation had been waiting to follow.[15] He had recognized something of himself, the rebel, the literary hooligan, in Miller's book. It was, he said later, 'like a volcanic eruption; verbal larva'.[16] He not only admired Miller as a great literary revolutionary, and chose him as his exemplar, but came to judge his life against Miller's, believing that by doing work other than writing he had compromised himself as an artist. Miller was prepared to starve rather than stop writing, and Durrell blamed himself for cowardice in this.[17]

The great impact and 'justified infatuation', as he might have called it,[18] was strange to him because in some ways he and his hero were very different. They disagreed about almost everything from a literary point of view, admiring different authors. *Tropic of Cancer*, however, had woken Durrell up, and even the obscene passages seemed salutary. No one had made him laugh so much before, except Rabelais – another purveyor of joyful obscenities. Miller's book had changed his outlook so that he no longer regarded such things as furtive and salacious and it enabled him, by sheer chance, to find himself.[19]

At the end of the summer, he and Nancy went north to visit the Barclay Hudsons and fell in love with the rocky, and to him masculine, country. This, they thought, would be the perfect place to live. The idea of getting away from the noisy family (especially from young Gerry and his marauding speci- mens – some of his leeches had attacked Larry in bed one night)[20] and finding the peace and quiet in which to write and paint was very tempting.

Miller responded to Durrell's fan letter on 1 September, clearly flattered. He was rather an anglophobe, so was sur- prised and delighted by what he saw as a highly intelligent letter from an Englishman, a letter he himself might have written as a reader rather than author of the book. He was especially struck by Durrell's calling *Tropic* the book his generation was waiting for. That was exactly it, he declared; the world was waiting for change, but only some great upheaval, like a war, would wake it up to the fact. Was Durrell a writer, he wondered, and how had he got hold of the book – through his friend Barclay Hudson, by any chance?[21] With Miller's reply began a correspondence, which cemented a lifelong friendship as well as a mutual admiration society.

Durrell told Miller that if D. H. Lawrence had been alive to read *Tropic* he would have yelled with joy, though he also thought that, while Joyce and Lawrence had gone down into the pit, only Miller had emerged from it smiling and guiltless. Although Miller had caught the spirit of the Elizabethans, he thought they were too constrained by stylistic conventions to have produced anything so freewheeling. Ben Jonson might have condemned him as wanting art, but François Villon would have recognized *Tropic* as the kind of thing he himself was attempting to write in his own style and time.[22]

Pied Piper of Lovers was published in London in September,

with a cover-design by Nancy, and Durrell asked Alan Thomas
to send him only the good reviews. He said that at least the
book was proof to his family that he was a writer, not just of
naive poems published by his friends, but of something that
actually made money. The cheque, he said, convinced them.[23]
However, Thomas was not put to much trouble collecting press
cuttings, as the reviews were few and poor and far between. A
belated notice in the *TLS* was about the best. Although mostly
a summary of the plot, it concluded, 'This novel, though it is
often adolescent in tone and outlook, has a genuinely sincere
intention which finds expression in the author–hero's somewhat vague dissatisfaction with himself and the society in
which he moves.'[24] That feeling of dissatisfaction was what
sent Durrell abroad while many of his contemporaries, equally
unhappy with the state of England, such as Auden, Spender
and Orwell, chose to try changing it through political action.

Pied Piper sold badly and remaining stock was destroyed
during the London Blitz. The final nail was put into the coffin
of the book by friends of Durrell's in London. Reginald Hutchings and John Mair ran a short-lived literary magazine, *Janus*,
with contributions from Dylan Thomas, Auden and Gertrude
Stein. Mair, a lofty and caustic critic, wrote a review of *Pied
Piper* which never once mentioned the book or its author,
but sneered at autobiographical first novels about dull young
geniuses seeking their true selves through school beatings,
boxing with bullies, drinking neat gin and engaging in mass
copulations under divans. It was meant to be satirically funny,
but succeeded only in being gratuitously cruel.[25] Durrell was
wounded by this review and never forgot it. He sent a limerick
to Thomas, attacking the magazine, in which he angrily rhymed
'Janus' with 'anus'.[26] Nevertheless, he was soon referring to
Pied Piper in excremental terms and dismissing it as 'wretched'
and 'snivelling'.[27]

Around October, he and Nancy moved north to rent a
fisherman's house perched on a big white rock on Kalami Bay.
Their landlord, Anastasius Athanaios, a small, dark, modest
man, moved his wife Eleni and his two daughters into one
room and let the Durrells have the remaining two, plus use of
the kitchen and dining room. The house (known as the White

House) was a single-storey whitewashed cottage, with (rare then in rural Corfu) a working toilet. The view over the encircling bay towards Albania was idyllic, and at high tide the water lapped right up to their windows. Cypresses lined the coastline, and around it grew the olive trees from which most of the peasants made their living. The Venetians had subsidized the planting of olive trees and the Corfiots had added lemon, orange, peach and pear trees. Kalami was remote and difficult to reach by road, especially in the rainy season, so communication with Corfu town was mainly by the twice-weekly caique, which deposited their possessions at the White House shortly after their arrival.

Life at Kalami, where only Greek was spoken, meant learning the language fast in order to be able to shop for food. After their near-poverty in England, living like Greek fishermen they were comparatively well off. Their joint income was £16 a month. Their spacious rooms with a view of the sea cost them a mere £1 a month, and a full-time live-in servant cost ten shillings. They could afford no luxuries like spirits but there was wine and food aplenty.[28]

The primitive life – cooking on a primus or over a charcoal fire, woodfires and candlelight in the evenings – gave Durrell practice at living frugally and precariously, which would stand him in good stead later on. The rhythm of the fisherman's life became his own rhythm, and he discovered that it was easier to work in the early morning than right through the night, which had been his habit in London. From that time onwards he always tried to be up before sunrise and to write steadily until mid-morning.[29]

It was their first close contact with Greek peasants, and they found the Athenaios family delightful. Durrell described them with great affection in *Prospero's Cell*, a book which brought the island alive through the eyes of a poet for whom it was an Heraldic Universe, one rich with symbolic reference. They were taught Greek in return for English lessons for the landlord and his children. Durrell was taken fishing for octopuses at night with the traditional fisherman's trident. He and Nancy found a cove with a fisherman's shrine to St Arsenius where they could bathe naked and dive into clear water from the rocks.

They met Nicholas the schoolmaster, who also fished, and Father Nicholas the priest. They found remnants of Corfu's old Venetian aristocracy; the Count D. in *Prospero's Cell* is fictitious (based on a doctor they knew), but the Countess Theokati was the genuine article. Meanwhile, Nancy painted and took photographs, while Larry stored all experiences away for future use, and worked to finish *Panic Spring*.

The impact of Miller's *Tropic* was not yet absorbed, and his second novel bears little trace of its influence. But the feeling of dissatisfaction with himself as a writer which it had prompted is evident in his letters. If Miller could produce such a first published book, his own efforts looked very puny by comparison. He decided he was going to try leaving Cassell – they had censored some amusing filth and a hint of lesbianism from his first poor novel so as to render it unrecognizable. If they asked for cuts in *Panic Spring*, which he felt sure they would, he could then shrug them off. When it was finished in December, he sent it first to his meticulous friend Thomas to correct and to have a fair-copy typed for Curtis Brown. He hoped never to clap eyes on it again and decided that from then on what he wrote would get better and better until he was properly acknowledged as a writer.[30]

Cassell were not unhappy to lose him, and Curtis Brown obtained another deal with a three-novel option from Faber & Faber, but on condition that the author of the unsuccessful *Pied Piper of Lovers* wrote for them under a pseudonym. Durrell agreed and chose the name Charles Norden, the Charles from Dickens perhaps, and the surname from Van Norden, the sex-obsessed buffoon in *Tropic of Cancer* – a suitably ironic combination. But he was still worried that his new publisher would excise the few four-letter words he had included.

In his first two novels his characters were all romantic constructions, but only after reading Miller's book did he realize that he also had in store a whole cast of grotesques known from first-hand experience. His characters were never entirely imaginary, and certainly not in *Panic Spring*. There, five people converge on a little-known Ionian island owned by Rumanades, a Greek arms-dealer, a lonely man, pining over a wife who has left him. Two of these characters were originally in *Pied Piper*

– Gordon, a self-confessed 'loafer', and Walsh, who lives by turning Elizabethan lyrics into pop-songs. Other familar Durrell characters are a demoralized schoolteacher, Marlowe, and a beautiful woman artist, Francis, also trying to recover from a lost love. Fonvisin, a sinister Russian doctor, is the sort of grotesque Durrell was later to enjoy portraying in his novels – this one a self-confessed murderer with a morbid fascination with death and embalming. Nothing much happens in the way of plot, except that by the end Rumanades is dead and each of the characters has been able to reflect upon and reassess his or her life, and can leave the island refreshed. Recollecting and reconstructing the past from the tranquillity of a remote Greek island is a theme which was to recur in Durrell's work, notably in *The Alexandria Quartet*. The closing scene, a festive wake in honour of Rumanades, offers a foretaste of what was to become a mark of Durrell's fiction, the beautiful set-piece description – image built upon image to produce a cumulative effect of poetic grandeur.

Other features which recur in later novels are already to be seen in *Panic Spring*: death in many forms; burial alive; mummification; breathing diseases; lesbianism; medical and surgical detail; transvestism; women's bodies; passivity in the face of destiny; Christian cannibalism; and, perhaps most importantly, the spirit of place and its manifestations.[31] The narrative pace is unhurried. One chapter describes a gramophone concert of Beethoven's Fourth Piano Concerto, Durrell's great passion at the time. The romance is a romance of exile, a major Durrell theme, exploring the foreigners' reactions to an exotic culture. It gave him his first opportunity to write in his own lyrical way about the beauties of Greek landscape, an important focus also for his poetry. Stylistically there is as yet no evident influence from Miller, but more his 'patchwork anthology' of authors imitated – Graves, Huxley, Lawrence, Aldington. But his new hero does get a passing mention when a country parson is scorned for never having heard of, among others, Henry Miller.[32] Representatives of the Christian Church were fair game to him – all antediluvian dullards. He thought of the book as an experiment working on two planes – the presents and pasts of the various characters – and one which did not progress as a novel normally did, but spread its feelers sideways, leaving the body at rest. At the end of it he felt poised on the brink of writing something important.[33]

Miller, now working on *Black Spring* (and *Scenario*, a filmscript of Anaïs Nin's unpublished *House of Incest*), had sent *Tropic of Cancer* to T. S. Eliot at Faber, who judged it a 'a very remarkable' book with more insight than *Lady Chatterley*. But elsewhere *Tropic of Cancer* excited just as much hostility as *Lady Chatterley*. Durrell promised to send a copy to the Bishop of London, who he placed on the summit of the English moral dung-heap, and to whom, he said, he sent insulting messages regularly. The Bishop was one of D. H. Lawrence's major persecutors, and had thereby helped bring him to public attention; he could do an equally good job on *Tropic*. But one of his friends (possibly Thomas, who stood to take over Commin's Bookshop in Bournemouth, and was nervous about handling banned books) had written saying that *Tropic* made even dirt cheaper,[34] so he must have realized that getting such a book more widely accepted would be an uphill struggle.

With his book banned in the US and Britain, Miller decided to send out copies of the letters of praise which he had received from prominent writers, such as Eliot, Shaw, Pound and Huxley. Durrell wondered if his circle of admirers included 'real men' such as the ballsy Roy Campbell, Wyndham Lewis and Richard Aldington,[35] and Miller was keen to hear more suggestions for his list. However, the good opinion of one writer, George Orwell (whose *Down and Out in Paris and London* he admired), he had no need to solicit. Orwell liked *Tropic*, and had given it a sympathetic notice,[36] as had Cyril Connolly, who later went to Paris to see Miller and had his own book published by the Obelisk Press.

Durrell was about to embark on the sort of colossal book he had announced before he left England – something so Milleresque as to be startlingly different from what he had done before. But writing it was to be a very disturbing experience for him. Even the title kept changing, from 'Lover Anubis' to 'Anubis' to 'Anabasis' and lastly to *The Black Book*.[37] He would erase the past and begin again, even though his rebirth would constitute his own 'Book of the Dead'. He would dig deeper into himself with this novel than with his first two. Joyce, Lawrence and Miller had given him his lead in embarking on what amounted to a ruthless essay in self-exploration.[38] The writing of the book would become a form of self-therapy, but would, at the same time, release impulses in him which in the long run were probably inimical as well as beneficial.

But first he felt he had to prepare himself. He plunged into his *Encyclopaedia Britannica*, attacking what he thought were the major subjects – from Biology to Surgery. When he began the new book it was in a mood of despondency, fearful of what deformed monster he might bring forth.[39]

At the same time there was the lure of the island, and, to enjoy it further, he and Nancy dug into their reserves and bought a twenty-foot Bermuda-rigged cutter which they named the *Van Norden*. Now they could swim, fish, circumnavigate the island, sail across to Albania, explore the savage north with its isolated bays and coves, explore other islands and, when Leslie showed up, go shooting. On a previous expedition they had discovered lakes in the north where wildlife had been undisturbed for centuries. The brothers took their guns back there and indulged in their very own duck-massacre, though Larry banned their shooting herons on the ground that they were so heraldic. The ducks, which were not, were duly blasted. It was the jolly Mr Jorrocks, armed with a twelve-bore, fowling around the Ionian. The set-piece shooting party crops up in more than one Durrell novel.

Having read *Tropic*, he thought that important things must be happening in Paris, and wanted to belong to this fraternity of free spirits.[40] Unable to afford the trip to France, he invited Miller to Corfu, despite his fears of the Italians invading once they had conquered Ethiopia. But he had his escape plans worked out – a fishing boat to Epirus and thence to Athens.[41] But with spring under way and nude bathing possible on their deserted stretch of coast (to the strains of Beethoven on the gramophone), such worries were easily forgotten. And while he made a tentative start on *The Black Book*, he was also writing poems, short stories and bits of plays, which he sent to Thomas for comment and to Gawsworth, hoping to get them published.[42] He talked of starting a literary magazine, and of writing a detective story for the money. He planned to send Nancy's photographs of Corfu to the *Geographical Magazine* in London. Then he thought of doing a travel book in the form of a series of letters – the first hint of his writing a prose work about the island, which he finally accomplished nine years later with *Prospero's Cell*.[43] Whether these were attempts to put off getting to grips with his novel or were simply manifestations of a prolific multiple talent is difficult to gauge.

Miller sent him his second novel, *Black Spring*, which only whetted his appetite for more of the same. His American friend, he concluded, understood exile better than anyone, and his work was a blast against the low-life of the English literary establishment. And he was intrigued by Miller's interest in Lao Tse. He reached Demonology in his *Encyclopaedia*, and decided that this was perhaps the most exact of the sciences, for that is what science had become in the twentieth century. Cheap Victorian scientific certainties had been swept away, and we could offer ourselves up entirely again to the unknown.[44] One of the mysteries he described in loving detail in a letter to Thomas was the death-throes of the speared octopus, especially the strange colours it emitted when it is stabbed while dying, and how it behaved if you cut the chords over first its right and then its left eyes, so that it died in two halves. Very funny, he thought.[45]

Miller promised to mention *The Black Book* to Jack Kahane, who ran the Obelisk Press. He suggested that it might be a piece of English surrealism, but Durrell demurred. He thought the leaders of the surrealist movement too conscious and deliberate in their claims for it, which was destructive of their work; Miller said that surrealism was much older than was supposed, and cited Swift, Rabelais, Lewis Carroll and at times Shakespeare. Some of his own work turned out surrealistic, though not consciously intended to be. Perhaps it was due to his obsession with China. He urged Durrell not to compromise. The critics would dump on him of course, as on everyone, so he might as well get in the first word. And he needn't use obscenity, but be himself in his own way.[46]

Breton's Surrealist Manifestos Durrell considered to be promoting a trade union for writers – too Marxist, wanting to make art easy, to produce mediocre art. Genius would get through despite all; he had no interest in the artist being able to change the world. Great figures put through the social wringer were what was required to produce art, which now *had* to be true prophecy. His intention was to create his Heraldic Universe single-handedly. This he was already achieving by systematically, though not consciously, eliminating time. The idea of duration, he realized, was false; there was nothing but space, which meant abolishing memory. Surrealism comprised little more than memory, whereas true art was timeless. The war that mattered to artists was not political but personal. His Heraldic Universe would be the only place to live, his own individual territory, not a place for movements and agreements. The writer must feel free to write as he damn well pleased and not be dictated to by cliques.[47] Those who focused on the author's role in society had cut man off from his spiritual sources, offering explanation in place of experience in art. The world, he thought, was accessible not only to science and the critical method, but also to mysticism, and psychology now supported people such as him and Miller in believing this. He had created the timeless mental world of his Heraldic Universe for himself to work in – at least that was the idea. He thought that *Hamlet*, about which Miller was corresponding with Michael Fraenkel, the death philosopher, was heraldic; the play had no secrets even though we constantly search it for them. He would love to be part of a movement, but, being argumentative and having fallen out with so many contemporary writers, all he had ended up becoming was a passionate 'Durrealist'.[48]

In November 1936, Durrell sent Miller a long letter about *Hamlet*. It was a picture, he thought, of a man trying to be his own self but pressurized into being a prince; it was the Shakespearean epoch's own tragedy – one which foisted the humanities on its youth while lacking all humanity itself – much the same as 1930s England, where this was found in a more extreme, decayed form. Hamlet personified the country's madness. This was the question, long posed, which Lawrence had answered in a new way. *Tropic* was an even more devastating answer – one which no Englishman could possibly have given; it took a true exile to accomplish something so great. Shakespeare almost succeeded but not quite. Whatever their national anthem said, the English had always been slaves. None but Chaucer, Skelton and one or two others were primitive enough to achieve freedom. Eliot had said that *Hamlet* was an 'artistic failure', which convinced him of its greatness. Durrell promised Miller that an essay on all this would follow.[49] Miller was so impressed with this letter that he sent copies of it immediately to Philip Mairet, editor of *New English Weekly* and to his friend Fraenkel, with a view to incorporating it into a book of their own Hamlet letters.

Progress on *The Black Book* was intermittent – some wonderful bits, Durrell thought, but it just fell short of being literature. However, there was hope for him in the fact that he was no Englishman but an Ango-Indian which meant that one day he would produce something to amuse the reader.[50] That autumn, as the weather began to turn, Larry and Nancy moved back into Corfu, staying again at a hotel just across from the Ionian Bank in the old town's centre. Miller's help had borne fruit, and Mairet asked Larry for an article for the *New English Weekly* on his Hamlet theme. Larry had read Otto Rank's *The Trauma of Birth*, commending it to Miller, unaware that he and Anaïs Nin both knew Rank intimately, and had even practised Rankean therapy while visiting America.

Faber were considering a selection of his latest poems as well as *Panic Spring*. Larry felt that what he had written six months earlier bore no comparison to what he was writing now. But, to be a poet published by Faber – publishers of Pound, Eliot, Auden, Spender and Day Lewis – would be to 'arrive' in a very special way. By December, he was claiming a rebirth, having destroyed the literary Durrell he had almost become (with those first two novels), and was urging on Miller a book which was helping his intellectual transformation – *Time and Western Man* by Wyndham Lewis. Miller in turn sent his suggestions for reading – Lao Tse, Lin Yutang, Keyserling, Krishnamurti,

Cocteau and Saroyan. He also commended a young American, James Laughlin IV, who edited a yearly anthology, *New Directions*, and who he was sure would be interested in his work.

A new force had entered Durrell's life in Corfu: Constant Zarian, the Armenian poet, whom he had met at a party given by an American painter, and who now became another surrogate uncle. With Theodore Stephanides they met on a regular basis at a restaurant in Corfu town where they had created a kind of club. There Zarian expounded the huge Armenian trilogy he was writing, and Durrell no doubt talked about his Heraldic Universe of one, while Dr Stephanides spoke only when he had something pertinent to say. There was also Max Nimiec, a wealthy Polish poet, exile and fatalist.[51] The wine and conversation flowed, Zarian read out letters from Unamuno and Céline, and preposterous projects were hatched – one being to compose a new Bible, with several contributors, and with annual celebrations and meetings to consider progress. At least these expansive deliberations provided Durrell with an opportunity to be blasphemous in convivial company, a company which also agreed that Corfu was decidedly the island in Shakespeare's *Tempest*.[52]

The proofs of *Panic Spring* (by Charles Norden) arrived just as Durrell was nearing the end of the first draft of *The Black Book*. To his dismay Faber asked him to rewrite part of it. He felt he was no longer that kind of writer, and it was galling that Faber had turned down his poems. He was envious of Miller, who he pictured sitting at the Villa Seurat in the middle of a gigantic Hollywood workshop with massed typewriters tapping out his Hamlet article.[53]

By 19 December, the first draft of *The Black Book* was finished and Durrell was thrilled with it. After months of cogitation and slog (amid the diversions of family and drinking friends), he had finally produced a book which he felt would establish him as an important writer. The effort had taken a great toll on his nervous system, and at times he had come close to breakdown. He had turned himself inside out, using the book to destroy his old self in the hope of becoming someone new. It was, he told Richard Aldington later, like a captive octopus chewing off its own tentacles.[54] It brought home to him the sense of loneliness which had haunted him since childhood, and which, despite his infectious good humour, would continue to plague him and threaten his sanity. The after-effects of his ruthless self-analysis showed themselves in what he now began to write and in his occasional bad-tempered treatment of Nancy. He was aware that he had already made her miserable while writing his novel. She, being somewhat placid and retiring, responded slowly to these provocations, which were later to blow up into open fights which horrified Miller when he finally met them.

Although there would be revisions of *The Black Book* – mostly suggestions from Miller and Nin – the book published later was mostly there. It was subtitled 'A Chronicle of the English Death', and was a combative, revolutionary critique of what Durrell, like D.H. Lawrence, considered a moribund culture. The message, as he stated in *Key to Modern Poetry*, was that we are dying without having lived.[55] But here also, as in later work, the medium carried an important message; the style and structure were statements about the nature of reality. Here was not the usual linear narrative told by a omniscient author; rather it was laid out spatially, and the story unfolds through a series of framed realities, rather as a Chinese box unfolded, slowly revealing its contents. This enabled Durrell to obliterate time, as he had set out to do, and reflected the ideas about time and space he had imbibed from Wyndham Lewis.

The Black Book was Durrell's *Portrait of the Artist as an Angry Young Man* – the cause of his anger being, the English Death which threatened to strangle his youthful romantic soul. The book's language, shot through with obscenities, embodies that anger and desire to shock. The novel chronicles the struggle of Durrell's *alter ego* to break free from the suffocating clutches of a decaying England (symbolized by the mice-ridden Regina Hotel, where most of the story is set), with its joyless and inhibiting values, and escape to a climate where his budding genius might thrive. One escape route is sex, the other is exile. While all Durrell's characters are contending with this English Death in their own way (often through sexual excess or deviation), only the narrator achieves wholeness by moving to Greece, to a place where the spirit is more in tune with his own artistic and philosophical intentions.

Throughout the book runs a dialogue between two voices, the dead and the living voices of the author himself. On the one hand stands the Durrell who is tempted (like Christ in the wilderness) by an idea of England (Christian England buttressed by medieval tradition), and on the other stands the one who is repelled from it into exile. The dead Durrell (Death Gregory, diarist and composer of the Black Book) passes away to be superseded by the living Durrell (Lawrence Lucifer, teacher, autobiographer and orchestrator of voices), and the English Death is replaced by another, better reality, the remote Greek island from which Lucifer can view the hell through which he has passed to achieve his heaven.

Of all the characters, only Lawrence Lucifer is able to react against the cold English Death. The others conform in one way or another (Gregory by succumbing to deathly English culture), although many of the women (two of them prostitutes) become sick or die. Lucifer alone achieves wholeness by moving to sunny and 'pagan' Greece, to a place where the spirit is more in tune with his own artistic and philosophical intentions. If there is progress here from the nihilism of *Panic Spring*, it is towards Epicureanism – the pursuit of pleasure through the senses – which Durrell considered one of the few worthwhile western alternatives to Christianity, as mystical as Buddhism and based on sincerity, honesty and engagement.[56]

The book is closer to being a *roman à clef* than anything else Durrell wrote, probably because the experience on which he drew was not fully digested. The Regina Hotel is obviously the Queen's. Lawrence Lucifer was his self-confessed *alter ego*, the 'you' in the book is Nancy (a published extract from the end was subtitled 'Coda for Nancy'), Alan Thomas makes an appearance, tempting him from the roof of Christchurch Priory with the prospect of a place in the scheme of medieval England, if only he would conform. Death Gregory, the literary man with a taste for prostitutes (a vision perhaps of what Durrell saw he might have become), was probably based on Gawsworth, and there are passing references to Zarian, to Patrick Evans, to someone called Durrell, and to a gun-toting brother. If the others had some reality, it may never be known, but Durrell's choice of names for his characters is fascinating. Gregory, Hilda (a prostitute) and Clare (a gigolo) have saint's names, while Grace (his other prostitute) is Bunyanesque. Chamberlain, a Lawrentian idealist advocating free-love, is ironically named after an English politician who was a by-word for bourgeois respectability. There is also a sensuous widow called Connie (fat and diseased, a grotesque distortion of Lawrence's Connie Chatterley).

Although Durrell claimed that he had left artifice behind and found art with *The Black Book*, the novel is by no means devoid of contrivance. In it he employs every lyrical device in his armoury, even the rhythms of his prose being consciously ornate and contrived to achieve (so G. S. Fraser argues) something like a new *Euphues*.[57] And despite its not being as derivative as his earlier novels, it has its influences – Lawrence, Huxley, Lewis, Aldington, Norman Douglas, Walter Pater, Tourneur and Marston. But, as many of its critics have pointed out, the most important influence on the book is Eliot's *The Waste Land*, for it is that underworld of unfulfilled grotesques, of coarse and sterile sex and of implied violence in a misty and mythical London which Durrell's characters inhabit.

Through *The Black Book* flit the shades of the Bohemians Durrell recalled from his Soho and south London years, and here too lurk embryos of future characters: Tarquin, the mincing, made-up homosexual, is an ancestor of the redoubtable Scobie; Gracie, the warm-hearted whore who dies of tuberculosis, foreshadows Melissa; and Lawrence Lucifer on his Greek island is certainly the father of L. G. Darley. There are also references to the author's literary influences at the time of writing – Rémy de Gourmont, Stendhal, Petronius, Norman Douglas – and there is much Elizabethan allusion, Euphuistic flourish, rambunctiousness, raw language and a wild disregard for social niceties. Also there are some characteristic Durrellian features: the fragmentary style, the diary, the switching of registers, perspectives and locations, the surrealistic dream-sequence, and set-pieces built from one image piled upon another. Some critics seen misogyny, and the use of obscure words to mystify and impress – a compensation for that lost

university education. Here and there he has a joyful prod at
some pet hate or other – the pretentious literary frumps of
Fitzrovia, genteel Sitwellian prose, impotent Lawrentians. And
above all there is the obsession with death.

In mid-December George Orwell, bound for the Spanish Civil
War, which had broken out that July, visited Miller at the Villa
Seurat. Orwell saw in Miller someone who could articulate the
worldview of not just the man in the street but the man in
the gutter, and they had in common the experience of working
as *plongeurs* in the kitchens of expensive Paris hotels.[58] But,
whereas Orwell was a social revolutionary, Miller was a
fatalist, ready to accept what history dished out to him. It
was Miller's quietism which Orwell would later discuss in his
celebrated essay 'Inside the Whale', an expression which Miller
had coined to describe the remote standpoint from which he
thought the artist should view life.[59] He thought Orwell's going
off to fight in Spain was utterly pointless; Orwell saw Miller
as blind to the political threats in Europe. Even so, this incon-
gruous pair – Miller, bald, extrovert and sometimes wild, and
Orwell, tall, thin, serious and shy – always remained on good
terms.

Although he said he did not much care for Greek civilization,
Miller promised Durrell he would visit Corfu before travelling
on to see places which interested him – Lesbos, Corinth and
Crete, and the labyrinth at Knossos. Durrell was delighted. He
and Nancy were paying to have an extra storey built on to the
White House (it cost £40), so there would be plenty of space
for another writer to move in with them. Miller had sent them
House of Incest, which they both enjoyed, Durrell judging it
the first pure dream he had read that was living, like tears that
suddenly dazzle. They were curious about its author; Anaïs
Nin sounded oriental. Was she a sleek, black Cleopatra, Durrell
wondered?[60] In his turn, he sent Miller a 'Christmas Carol'
(dedicated to him), a skit, he said, which had occurred to him
one night. He never made carbon copies so asked Miller to
return it if it wasn't his thing. He needn't have worried. Miller
and Nin thought it a work of genius, and it came to be regarded
as one of Durrell's most important early works.[61] It reflects the

feeling of liberation he had after finishing *The Black Book*, for it is as freewheelingly imaginative a work as he ever wrote.

CHAPTER 5

Up and Running in Paris and London (1937–1938)

> I am bewitched by the rogue's company:
> If the rascal have not given me medicines
> to make me love him, I'll be hanged.
>
> Shakespeare, *Henry VI*

When Miller read Durrell's 'Christmas Carol' he announced himself flabbergasted. He was filled with envy, it was so perfect, and outdid anything done by André Breton or Dylan Thomas. He suggested a change of title (Durrell renamed it 'Asylum in the Snow'),[1] wrote to Laughlin suggesting it for his next *New Departures* anthology, promised to try to interest French and Scandinavian editors in it, and even suggested that he and Anaïs might bring it out themselves in mimeographed form.[2]

If *The Black Book* is about revolt, and the death and rebirth of the self, 'Asylum in the Snow' is about madness and the prospect of cure. It is an extended prose poem, freed from even the ingenious but formal structures of *The Black Book*. It is a disturbed dream, a journey through a darkened subconscious still reeling under the effects of a creative brainstorm. The asylum in the snow is the subconscious of the mad fugitive from a lavatorial society. It is a madhouse but one helpful to the writer in search of wholeness and repose through art. (The whiteness of snow brought memories of peaceful, magical childhood days in the Himalayas.) References to 'the dancer' suggest Nijinsky, whose schizophrenic diary of life and death it in part echoes, with its strange, impassive, staccato rhythms.

'Asylum in the Snow' gives us a glimpse into the unreal world of dream or hallucination into which Durrell's later novels sometimes stray, when lyrical madness takes the reader beyond established 'reality'.

Doubtless, reading the phantasmic *House of Incest* had influenced him in writing his 'Carol', which prompted an even more lyrical response than Miller's from Anaïs Nin, who found its enigmatic and dreamlike quality and its air of enchantment astonishing. He had, she told him, penetrated to an atmosphere so rarefied, to a climate so elusive – into a dreamlike state achieved through the senses, the air of pure imagination, of mystic ethereal words, written from inside the very carapace of mystery. It was what she had attempted to achieve in *House of Incest*, she said, and it made her want to throw her novel straight into the Seine.[3]

Basking in the warmth of all this praise from Paris, Durrell said he had no idea what he wrote when he wrote his 'Carol', but that it made him glow for a day afterwards.[4] Having read some of Miller's correspondence with Fraenkel about Hamlet he told him that he (Miller) had fulfilled himself as a man; now, in fulfilling himself as an artist, he was on the way to realizing himself as God. Modestly, Durrell was content to tell himself that *he* was no more than a man. He asked for a full-faced photograph of 'the man he would make God'. Having read Kretschmer's book on physical types, he wanted to see which of these Miller resembled – pyknik or leptosome.[5]

His essay, 'The Prince and Hamlet: A Diagnosis' appeared in *New English Weekly* on 14 January 1937. The critics, he argued, were unable to penetrate to the inner world of the artist, a private realm which could not be explained, only experienced. By equating the outer drama of *Hamlet* with the inner drama, they had missed the truth of the play. The play of the Folio is where the drama of *Hamlet* is to be found; the better known Quarto version is the Prince without Hamlet.[6] This assertion of the greater significance of the artist's inner reality compared to the outer reality of everyone else was to evolve and persist with him, as was the notion of multiple personalities.

Miller sent a series of manuscripts to Corfu, including one of *Max and the White Phagocytes* (with its unsympathetic portrait of Max, the Jew). This prolific burst by Miller impressed Durrell greatly, though Nin thought he was wrongly dispersing his energies on such grandiloquent fragments. But Miller believed he was at last in a position to make people sit up and listen, and was going to have his say, come what may. He was hatching ideas at a great speed, writing obsessively, as if doomed to do so forever. And he predicted great things for Durrell. He had been intrigued to hear that he was from India, and thinking that he might have Indian blood said that he believed in all that stuff about a collective unconscious. He horrified his Jewish friend Fraenkel, in letters about *Hamlet*, by referring to the role of the Jew as 'microbe', and wrote, too, about the need for a new man – one who could fulfil his potential – which made him sound suspiciously in tune with extreme right-wing opinions of the period.

Thinking to have a horoscope of Durrell drawn up, he asked for details of his birth. Told that he had lived on the borders of Tibet, close to the Forbidden Land, he was thrilled, he said, because he himself was a Chinese at heart. Miller's interest took Durrell back to his childhood in Darjeeling, and, soon after, he discovered *My Journey to Lhasa* by Alexandra David-Neal, who had gone on foot to Lhasa in 1923. It confirmed his Tibetan 'ancestry' and he began to cultivate his 'Tibetan' side, claiming that he lived in a sort of Tibet of the mind. If Miller was a Chinaman, then he himself was a Tibetan.

The horoscope (cast by Miller's sinister friend Conrad Moricand) was strangely prophetic. Moricand found Durrell highly complex – both deceptive and self-deceptive. Influenced by Jupiter, he would fall on his feet, come what may. Jupiter 'penetrates all things; he is the "protean" god of a thousand metamorphoses, who assumes all shapes to impregnate all goddesses'. The influence of Sagittarius represented 'a musketeer, looter of works of art, on a galloping horse', indicating 'religious feelings in a rebellious heart'. He was fiery with a taste for danger but with a cheerful, laughing, self-assured aspect. There was 'a rather aggressive critical attitude' and there could be 'disorder and anarchy in the mind . . . encouraging the subject to spread himself across many areas, and often in vain quests'.[7]

Larry was still revising *The Black Book*, unwilling to let go of the child he had laboured so long to produce. However, in February he told Faber he had produced something out of the ordinary, not the 'cheap romance' they might have expected from Charles Norden. It might be unprintable in England, he warned them, but they reminded him that they had first refusal of his next two novels. He would not let them cut it. Even so, he was having doubts about his heraldic idea. Having read a book on the anatomy of the brain he wondered whether the whole problem of reason versus unreason might not be centred in some cerebral dysfunction, and had written to two brain specialists for their reaction to his theory. Studying medicine was a long-standing ambition for him, and it was not too late even now to start. Meantime, applying Kretschmer to Miller's photograph he judged him a pyknic, the type characteristic of all great artists, and declared his frontal lobes positively Shakespearean.[8]

With summer approaching, plans had to be made. Miller had half promised to visit, and Alan Thomas was coming in May, so there was the prospect of convivial times ahead. They planned to rent a villa at Paleocastrizza, on the west coast of the island, and entertain their friends there. They could sail on the *Van Norden* to lovely isolated beaches, and planned trips to Zante and Kythera, and to Ithaca, the island of Odysseus, where Heinrich Schliemann had begun his archaeological career and which Byron had loved so much he wanted to buy it. Durrell, like Cavafy, loved Ithaca, too, and it gave him one of his best poems, 'On Ithaca Standing', a hymn of praise to the island. To stand on Ithaca, he declared, was to stand 'on miracle ground'.[9]

He continued to agonize over his novel, feeling that it was too Millerish. His friend Patrick Evans had spotted some passages of pseudo-Miller and, despite having rewritten the thing four times, Larry sat down promptly to de-Millerize the affected parts. Zarian reassured him. Everyone imitated *him* in Armenia, so he simply changed his style from time to time. Meantime, Durrell wrote a second 'Carol', called 'Zero', which he dedicated to Anaïs Nin.[10] It begins with a quotation from the mad Nietzsche, and is a celebration of illogicality, a kind of nightmare dream sequence. In this surrealist flow, Durrell seems to want to forge a new idiom, to capture what can barely be captured by language – a modern reality where all the old certainties are gone. But what cannot be grasped can sometimes be portrayed, and this piece has an impact simply as a powerful flow of inspired writing – verbal action painting in sinuous, colourful prose. It was close to what he thought his Heraldic Universe meant – in Buddhist terms, it was the state of perception which went beyond mere cognition. He referred to 'Zero' and 'Asylum' as his 'bughouse' stories.

At the beginning of March, Durrell finally despatched his only (beautifully bound) copy of *The Black Book* to Miller. He said later that he told Miller that if he did not like it he was to pitch it into the Seine – echoing what Nin had said she felt like doing with *House of Incest* after reading his 'Carol'. Miller began reading it slowly, savouring each word, and wrote to say that he was overawed by the book, and liked in particular the Tibetan dimension, to which he attributed its originality, and was struck by his harping on the theme of loneliness. It was something forbidden that he had risked himself in writing. The result was overwhelming and stunning. He would give him an unbiased verdict after he had finished it, but for now it was simply shattering.[11] No English or American publisher would dare bring it out, certainly not Faber. Miller promised to forward it to them, but, alarmed that this was Durrell's only copy, said he would pay to get copies typed. (He and Anaïs did the work and with a few friends proofread the copies.) Having now crossed the line, he told Durrell, he could no longer do the sort of book Faber would like from him. He truly was England's leading writer, outstripping Lawrence and the rest. Miller would also approach Jack Kahane, his publisher, a man he needed but despised (because he was a Manchester Jew, and wrote bad pornography).

Not only did Durrell feel proud of Miller's reaction, but so did Nancy, since the book was dedicated to her. Working on *The Black Book* had left Larry in a state of wild exhaustion and so uncertain about his creative powers that he even contemplated having hypnosis. But Miller, already hypnotized by the novel, wrote to say that it had caused a stir at the Villa Seurat; Anaïs and his friend David Edgar had read and discussed it and its author until after midnight. There were phenomenal passages, and some far too spicy to be digested rapidly. He recognized the poetic and symbolic nature of the book and its great theme of death and rebirth – the theme of the future. The death–rebirth theme coincided with his own ideas (taken largely from Fraenkel), that it was necessary to kill the old self in order to emerge into a new life on a new plane of abstract existence – achieving the liberation, in which we passively live out our destiny.

Miller seemed uncertain about coming to Corfu that summer, so Durrell vowed that he and Nancy would visit him in Paris the following winter *en route* for England. If Miller was broke, he would send him money, once he had paid off his builders and bought an engine for the *Van Norden*.[12] Nin wrote saying that although they were all drunk on his book, and recognized its great power and savage mystery, she thought he had opened a pandora's box that had best been kept shut.[13] When she sent him her own unpublished novel, including a passage about her own pregnancy, Durrell told her that she was the greatest woman writer he had read. Others took men as their standard; she had created a new Art. And when Miller said that he felt some of the language of Durrell's book was unbelievably obscure, Larry assured him that all the words he complained of were real, mostly gleaned from his extensive reading of medical texts; but he accepted Miller's suggestions for revision.

Out of gratitude for his help and encouragement, Durrell sent Miller lists of writers who might support him in getting *Tropic of Cancer* unbanned in Britain and America. For himself, Durrell planned a summer of abstinence – boxing, diving, swimming and decidedly no cigarettes. The old self was giving place to a new. The summer would complete the purification, and he would sail off, leaving literature well in his wake. But already he had ideas for further novels – a three-fold plan, of which *The Black Book* was the first part, the agon. Then would come a pathos (The Book of Miracles) followed by an anagnorisis (The Book of the Dead). (He had been reading, and been much impressed by, *The Egyptian Book of the Dead*.)[14]

When Alan Pringle, of Faber, enquired about *The Black Book*, Durrell quoted words of praise from Miller, and modestly differentiated himself from Joyce. He offered himself as Miller's manager (he thought he could do the job as well as any Jew – a sidelong reference to Kahane). He was ready to take up the *general* cause of free speech with the censor, by taking up the *specific* case of Henry Miller – circulating petitions on his behalf.

Durrell's natural ebullience and boundless energy had lurched into overactiveness, easy enough for him to sustain, but exhausting for others. He was not only an active campaigner for Miller, but an unrelenting organizer of exhausting summer schedules for Nancy and his friends. He knew that others sometimes found him impossible – intellectually arrogant and overbearing – and tried to compensate for this with his fertile sense of humour and his conviviality. Amid all this hectic activity, his friend Dr Stephanides wondered how Durrell got any work done at all.[15]

Miller was equally energetic. He had sent a copy of *The Black Book*, as Durrell requested, to Eliot via Curtis Brown in London, but suggested further cuts, and felt there was still a strained quality in the book; the man who wrote to him from Corfu was quite different, he said. Anaïs thought that perhaps Corfu was nearer to his 'climactic source' – an idea which accorded with his own belief in the spirit of place, and its effects on human personality. Miller told Durrell that he thought Anaïs's diary (fifty-two volumes of it already) phenomenal and he could not quite believe that she, nothing but a woman, was writing constantly, as if forever knitting.[16] (His view of women was primitive, to say the least; he told Durrell that a woman was merely 'an aperture'.) When Nin sent Durrell a volume of her diary to read he was bowled over.

In April, Charles Norden's *Panic Spring* came out, dedicated to Thomas, in a gesture of farewell to 'sentiment'. Durrell merely reported to Miller that his 'shit book' had appeared. However, it attracted some favourable attention, – from *The Times* ('exceedingly promising'), the TLS ('bright, cynical, hyper-sophisticated and inordinately clever') and *The Spectator* ('highly entertaining'). Sending these notices to Miller, Durrell joked (prophetically) that he would find him in the Book of the Month lists yet.

Miller sent Durrell a large watercolour called *The Ego and its Yid*, and a 'Tibetan' one, and reported that he had just proofread the latest version of *The Black Book*. This delighted Durrell, who did not believe in correcting proofs – that, he thought, was what the printer's devil was paid to do. But he enjoyed campaigning against censorship, and wrote to the US Censor, Huntington Cairns, who, as it happened, was personally well disposed towards Miller. He was also ready to smuggle copies of *Tropic* into Britain via Alan Thomas, or via Grindlay's Bank, to be held in his mother's name. Louisa was a Miller 'fan', but having read thirty pages of *Tropic* said she preferred her imaginary Miller to the reality she had discovered there. Durrell also sent Miller one of his own watercolours, which he said had made Nancy, the real artist, sick.

For the summer, the Durrells moved to Paleocastrizza, leaving the black-painted *Van Norden* at anchor in the bay. Alan Thomas arrived on 27 May, and was amazed especially by Leslie, who had blossomed in the sun and become a thoroughly Rabelaisian character, drinking and fighting with the Greek peasants at every opportunity. They all swam, sailed, explored, took tea at the local monastery, talked about war with Dr Stephanides, watched the local militia's uncoordinated drill and discussed art and life late into the night.[17] Durrell concluded that Thomas was very uptight about literature, failing to understand what he and Miller were about. He was also annoyed that he was too scared to smuggle Miller's book into England.

News came that *Panic Spring* had been accepted in America by publishers Covici-Friede. Notebooks Durrell had begun keeping were already bulging, and he felt that something big awaited him. His next book would be dedicated to his Villa

Seurat friends – perhaps a vast autobiography, or a small book of *pensées*.

Durrell was still writing poetry, mostly of the sensual kind, and still taking in the history, culture, scenery and flora and fauna of the island. The dates in Durrell's lyrical book about Corfu, *Prospero's Cell*, are invented, so are not much help biographically. But there we meet a memorable list of his friends in Corfu, some real characters – Zarian, The Count D., not a real Count, Theodore Stephanides, and Max Nimiec. N. is Nancy and Spiro is Spyro Americanus. There is swimming at the shrine of St Arsenius (where fishermen kept a flame burning), octopus fishing with Anastasius, endearing memories of Father Nicholas, and all the fun of the island festivities – dancing, courtship and marriages. And there are endless meals of bread, olives and good island wine, and even more endless discussions about art and the art of living. Durrell was absorbing Greece through his pores, as if recapturing something of his lost childhood, claiming that the ancient Greek philosophers had learned their philosophy at Benares University in India, a tenuous claim but one which suited his need for metaphysical roots.

The question of what Faber would do about *The Black Book* was answered when, on 28 June, Eliot wrote that he was greatly impressed by it and that it had accomplishment and potential. He thought the book ought to be published, he said, but Durrell should go on from it to something even better. The formal structure of the book made him optimistic for Durrell's future, but, as it stood, it could not be published in England, and so the question was how Durrell felt about altering it in order to reach an English readership. He understood that any writer worth his salt wanted to produce at least one book without considering whether it was practical or not, but such freedom could be a form of servitude. He would see what could be done to publish the book in England; failing that he would be only too happy to see it published abroad.[18]

Durrell thought Miller was right in warning him not to try too hard, and was quite willing to admit that the book's imperfections were his own. He indicated to Eliot that if a Faber expurgated edition did not preclude an unexpurgated

Paris edition he would be pleased enough. He confided to Miller that if Kahane's Obelisk Press would publish the book he would keep Charles Norden for lesser work. If not, he would save up and publish the book himself. His horoscope said that he was destined for more than a sufficiency of money and love, so things seemed set fair for him.

Miller, however, was against the idea of an expurgated edition with Faber. That way, he thought, lay disaster. An expurgated book might be in Faber's interests but it was not in Durrell's. He could not look in two directions at once, but had to take responsibility for his own work.[19]

Somewhat shamed by Miller's directness and honesty, Durrell decided that he did not care how the book came out, but he felt very isolated, and believed that he needed Norden in order to keep in touch with the real world. The books he wanted to do took so much out of him, he could only work at full blast every few years. Consequently he needed Norden for minor works of non-fiction, and lighter novels. Writing at the intensity of *The Black Book* had been a violent experience for him. He could not do this without isolating himself altogether and at his young age he was scared that isolation would send him mad. In any case no one could alter the fact that he had written the book. His Heraldic Universe came around only periodically: outside of it he was Jekyll, inside it he was Hyde. While trying to puzzle out this problem of identity he told Anaïs Nin that he had fallen in love with an innocent seventeen-year-old on the island, though whether that was as Jekyll or as Hyde he did not say.[20]

Miller urged him not to take the path of the split personality. He had everything – youth, a happy marriage, health, a rising reputation, a little money, friends, and a boat, as well as the wide Ionian. He must stand up as Lawrence Durrell or fall apart. He needed more faith in himself. Miller admired men who stood firm, like Mussolini – despite his policies. It was there in the Tao, the only choice – the true and honest course.[21] He mentioned a scheme he had brewing with a friend, Alfred Perlès (Carl in *Tropic* and author of a novel, *Sentiments Limitrophes*), who had been asked by the president of the American Country Club of France, Elmer S. Prather, to take over the Club magazine, the *Booster*, and make it something like the *New Yorker*. The advertising money was good, and provided they devoted two pages to Club activities they could do with it as they liked. They already had a few crazy ideas which they could talk about when he got to Paris.

When Larry and Nancy arrived at the Gare du Nord on 12 August 1937, Durrell recalled, Henry and Anaïs were waiting for them at the station, with a gift for him, a copy of Otto Rank's *Art and Artists*. Anaïs has them meeting first at Miller's studio. In any event, it was a historic meeting – the bald, bespectacled American; the fragile, beautiful Nin; the tall, blonde Nancy; and the short, merry Durrell. A strange company, but they would affect one another's lives forever.

The Villa Seurat, a pretty cul-de-sac of exclusive modern studios, was just off the Rue de la Tombe-Issoire, close to Place Alèsia, the Parc Montsouris and St Anne's mental hospital. Here lived mostly artist and writers – Miller, Chaim Soutine and until recently Antonin Artaud at number 18, and Salvador Dali briefly in the studio on the corner. After flea-bag hotels, this, for Miller, was heaven, and it had soon become a maelstrom of activity centred on him – poets, painters, astrologers, philosophers and hangers-on of various kinds came there for talk, food, drink and handouts. Miller was immensely tolerant of intrusions, and able to work at his typewriter amid all sorts of noise and confusion. The studio was once in the hands of his friend Walter Lowenfels (Cronstadt in *Tropic of Cancer*); now Anaïs Nin paid his rent.

The Durrells moved into a flat on the ground floor, normally occupied by a young American artist, Betty Ryan, with whom Miller was secretly in love. She had gone abroad trying to avoid her father who was visiting Paris. The Durrells were pitched right in among Miller's circle. Larry's arrival electrified them all. Perlès was bowled over, struck, even before they first met in Miller's studio, by his loud infectious laughter. There was a party in progress, the air was thick with cigarette smoke, the floor strewn with bottles, glasses, half-eaten food, books, papers; Nancy was cooking steak in the studio kitchenette. Perlès found Larry sitting cross-legged on the floor, looking youthful and angelic, with a round face, shining eyes and long hair bleached almost white by the sun. To Perlès he looked like a cherub from an Italian fresco. Miller was obviously fascinated by this dynamic newcomer, and awestruck by the brilliant, tumbling flow of words that came from Durrell and which at times moved Miller to tears. At this stage of their friendship, Miller tended to revere this *wunderkind* and hold him in rare affection.

While the world was hurtling towards war, the ethos at the Villa Seurat was one of 'optimism and good cheer', only added to by the sparkling little Englishman with his well-modulated accent and Falstaffian bonhomie. Nancy, beside the nut-brown Larry, had 'a delicate pale pink complexion, very English ... something about her ... suggested an elegant flamingo'.[22] But she was all too often banished to the kitchen while the men made history. The only one there who seemed conscious of what was happening in Europe was Nin, who through a lover, Gonzalo Doré, was aiding Republican Spain.

Talk, endless talk into the early hours, oiled by good food and copious wine, became the order of the day. Walks around the *quartier*, meals at Zeyer's Café at Alèsia, or at one of the many bistros around the Parc Montsouris, trips to the cinema (*Lost Horizons*, about the lost land of Shangri-la, became an ikon for Miller and Durrell, who saw it ten times together). Miller also gave Durrell some hints on painting learned from Hans Reichel – most memorably, to run his watercolours under the bath-tap after finishing them.

Nin was impressed by Durrell.

> What struck me first of all were his eyes of a Mediterranean blue, keen, sparkling, seer, child and old man ... He is short and stocky with soft contours like a Hindu ... He is a faun, a swimmer ... Nancy, his wife, is a long-waisted gamin with beautiful long slanting eyes. With Durrell I had instant communication. We skipped the ordinary stages of friendship at one bound, with hardly a need to talk.[23]

There were visits to Nin's seventh-floor apartment at 30 Quai de Passy, beside the Seine, where she learned that she and Larry were both Pisceans, and felt even more drawn to him. They went to the Paris Exhibition, where Durrell acted like a small boy, wanting to ride the roller-coaster and the miniature train. They explored his Heraldic Universe together one night, she said, and achieved it – a healing experience – though she was not quite sure what it was. She noted how he admired Miller's ruthlessly cold dissecting of people, considering it objective and truthful. And although he played the objective observer himself, as a poet and a romantic he had what Miller lacked – sensitivity. But Durrell in turn lacked empathy and, while he would never cut people open as Miller did, he would never get into their feelings as she thought *she* did. He confessed that often he felt contempt for people, which he felt was wrong, and thought he might go mad if he kept on writing.[24] She thought he seemed overwhelmed by his 'monstrous', extraordinary talent, which spoke through his every gesture, the tumbling flow of words and the fine shades and nuances of his language. But he and Henry attacked her for personalizing everything she wrote, lacking their objectivity and always retreating back into the womb.

Among this self-obsessed trio, Nancy was rather sidelined. Nin, however, admired her 'eloquent silences',[25] and sympathized with her faltering efforts to articulate her feelings. When Durrell told her to shut up, a strong female bond sprang up between them. *She* would never shut up, she vowed, but would speak out always on behalf of women as a whole.[26] Miller too was upset by Durrell's treatment of Nancy, and wrote of (perhaps metaphoric) 'black eyes' at breakfast-time. He could not understand why two such beautiful, talented youngsters were so often at war with each other.[27] Nin felt that they were fearful of Paris, and wanted to escape from it, and offered help. 'I conjured up the demons and we exorcised them. We had a moment of wholeness, of repose, of Oriental serenity.'[28] Perhaps Miller was one of those demons. He took Durrell with him to brothels, to enjoy the company of the Paris whores, without necessarily sleeping with them – and Durrell became quite attached to these places.

The *Booster* was poised for publication, and Nancy was persuaded to design the cover. Perlès was down as managing editor, Durrell, Miller and William Saroyan as literary editors.

The down-market Charles Norden was sports editor, Patrick Evans turf editor, Nancy art editor. The first issue was not much out of the ordinary, and concealed the editorial crew's intentions – to run the magazine into the ground in a Dadaist spirit of lunacy, to offend the sort of people who belonged to the American Country Club, and to buck the political trend of most serious literary magazines of the time. The main risk was that the lucrative advertising would drop away. According to the editorial the magazine would have no fixed policy, but be eclectic and alive – 'a contraceptive against the self-destructive spirit of the age'. Political, economic or social panaceas were out. Things were not as bad as they seemed; in fact it was a Golden Age, and everything was excellent – 'including the high-grade bombers with ice-boxes and what not'.[29] This was truly living 'inside the whale', if not inside the ostrich, head in sand. The fact that Perlès, an Austrian Jew, concurred with this shows how influential Miller was, with his a-historical philosophy of acceptance, based largely on his reading of Lao Tse. (The wise man, said the Chinese sage, goes with the flow.)

The first new *Booster* would include Charles Norden's sports column, Anaïs on a visit to St Anne's mental hospital, Miller's 'Benno, the Wild Man of Borneo', and Durrell's 'A Lyric for Nikh', a not untypically sensuous poem about soft 'belly pockets' and the 'knife-thrust' of desire – a taste of the mystical sexuality which later became an obsession with him. Norden was listed as author of *Panic Spring* and contributor to *Night and Day*, Durrell was down as 'a Tibetan writer now residing in Paris, author of *The Black Book* . . . now working on *The Book of the Dead*'. Nancy is described as 'wife of Charles Norden and Lawrence Durrell', working, among other things, on illustrating *The Book of the Dead*.[30]

After ten days in the hot-house atmosphere of the Villa Seurat, Larry and Nancy were ready to go on to England, as planned, though Miller and Perlès urged them to return and get involved in the future of the *Booster*. Durrell was certainly involved by now, and planned to gather as many subscriptions and offers of contributions as he could while in London. He was also eager to meet Eliot to ask for a blurb for *The Black Book* – soon, he hoped, to be published by Kahane. Anaïs suggested he contact Rebecca West, who might be helpful, and noted that for Miller the time since the Durrells arrived had been one of 'intoxication [and] sleeplessness . . . followed by depression'.[31] Their departure left a vacuum.

After a week in London Durrell sent Miller a letter full of news and complaints. The place was crawling with the English. However, Havelock Ellis had promised something in praise of Miller for the *Booster*, and he had procured a Hindi poem from Raj Mulk Anand, as well as an essay from Potocki demonstrating that Bach was a Potocki. He had got promises of subscriptions from Orwell and G. Wilson Knight, and had arranged a meeting with Eliot and Alan Pringle at Faber. The Durrells also met again Peter Bull and his friend, the diminutive film actor Desmond Tester, with whom he had worked in Hitchcock's film *Sabotage*. Durrell asked them both, plus Tester's sister Veronica, out to Corfu. He corrected proofs of articles to be published, worked at the British Museum, and visited the Café Royal, only to have his low opinion of English writers reinforced. He felt strongly what he was to feel throughout his life, that in Anglo-Saxon society it was the artist who was the true foreigner. And he was aware of another difference in him, that exiles like him tended to be more British than the British.[32] He made his feelings for the English very clear. 'Fuck Them!' he told Miller.[33]

Meanwhile, the *Booster* was launched, followed on 4 September by publication of a piece by Charles Norden in *Time and Tide*. 'Ionian Profile' (dedicated to Theodore Stephanides) is a charming portrait of Father Nicholas, the Corfiot priest, and the scene describing an island dance festival would reappear years later, barely altered, in *Prospero's Cell*.

When he met Eliot, Durrell was charmed, and his earlier opinion of *The Waste Land*'s author as a 'dried up' poet turned a complete somersault. The great man actually offered to help Miller, though he considered it too soon to provoke a test-case over *Tropic of Cancer*, since losing at this stage would put the cause back, not further it. Through Eliot he met W. T. Symons, who ran his own magazine, *Purpose*, advocating the Social Credit philosophy of Major Douglas, but with an independent literary section. He also met Herbert Read and André Breton. And his friend Norden published again, this time a story in *Night and Day*. 'Obituary Notice: A Tragedy' is a sub-Wodehousean comic sketch, illustrated by 'Nancy Norden', and is really early Antrobus – the story of an old colonial brigadier agonizing over a zebra wearing his old school colours when unentitled to do so. It ends with an appropriately comic shooting accident. The interest of this story, apart from its foreshadowing Antrobus, is its author's intimate knowledge of firearms – the Brig's favourite shotgun is a Double Express, and his favourite shot is Kynock Smokeless. Major Sam Durrell, commissioner of ordnance at Dum-Dum, would have been proud of his inky-fingered grandson.

In September, too, *Panic Spring* appeared in America, billed as 'The delightful adventures of five people on a Greek island'. It seems to have made little impact, and if the novel he liked to refer to in excremental terms disappeared without trace, the last to mourn its passing was Charles Norden, who would soon become Lawrence Durrell again. And it was to Durrell that Eliot wrote on the 9th, wishing him well with *The Black Book*, agreeing to do a blurb for it, and inviting him to lunch when next he visited London.[34] From then on, Eliot took a great interest in him, as he did in many other young Faber writers. Durrell had found yet another uncle to add to his literary family. His visits to Faber paid off in another way when he discovered publishers' blank dummies stored in their cellars, and never thereafter visited the office without pinching half a dozen to use as notebooks.[35]

By late September, the Durrells were back in Paris and flat broke. No doubt Larry could stomach the English for only so long, and the ferment around the Villa Seurat was difficult to resist. He found waiting a letter from Bernard Shaw, to whom he had sent a copy of *Tropic of Cancer*, asking support for its beleaguered author. Shaw said that, although Miller could write, his work lacked artistic value, his straight reporting of bad language was nothing more than recording, and tasteless recording at that – filth for its own sake. He should not be so damned foolish, and he warned that while being found guilty of obscenity was a great disadvantage to an author, to peddle obscenity was a devilish business. They were obviously young and foolish and had better do what he told them.[36] Durrell told Miller that he thought Shaw's letter impudent. Nevertheless he readily bowdlerized a passage from *The Black Book* to make it more acceptable for the next *Booster*.

Miller and Perlès were selling copies of the *Booster* around the cafés and promptly boozing the money away, which was all in the spirit of the thing. Fortunately, President Prather of the American Country Club, unaware of what was about to happen to the magazine, merely remarked on how amusingly 'roguish' it was, and so the advertising held up. However, the magazine was not selling well. Alan Thomas was unable to sell any at his shop in Bournemouth, nor, it seems, was Sylvia Beech at her Shakespeare & Company in Paris.

Betty Ryan having returned, the Durrells moved to an apartment beside the Parc Montsouris at 21 Rue Gazin, just ten minutes from the Villa Seurat. They made new friends – the young, attractive poets Cecily Mackworth and Audrey Beecham, Betty Ryan herself, 'small, pretty and talkative',[37] and the tall, thin, sinister Moricand, who had done Durrell's horoscope. And there was the remarkable twenty-one-year-old poet David Gascoyne, who had come to Paris at sixteen, and had written the first English book on surrealism. He was slender and beautiful, and Anaïs was very drawn to him. Durrell lent him *The Black Book* to read and it left him shaken and filled with admiration. What Miller had done for Europe and America and what Céline had done for France, Durrell had now done for 'the particular English horror'.[38] In turn, he lent Larry his diary, but when Durrell wrote a poem, 'Paris Journal', mocking it, he was rather hurt, feeling that his privacy had been betrayed; however, their relationship survived. For a while in October, the starving poet became a daily visitor to 21 Rue Gazin, where Nancy fed him.

Mackworth thought Durrell a kind of electric force who worked too hard and drank too much. And, to her, Nancy seemed very young and school-girlish, especially in the way she sat, legs splayed, in a manner typical of young English girls. She disliked Miller, who she thought a dirty old man, and liked Alf Perlès, the self-proclaimed 'renegade', though she thought he always look haunted by some unspecified panic.[39] Perlès, born in Vienna, a conscript in the Austro-Hungarian army in the First World War, had been condemned to the firing-squad for refusing to order his men to advance on the enemy. Bought a reprieve by his rich parents, he spent the rest of the war in an asylum, then travelled Europe as a penniless vagabond before settling in Paris and meeting the equally indigent Miller. The two became inseparable, enjoying a life of self-indulgence and debauchery during their quiet days together in Clichy. When Anaïs Nin set Miller up at the Villa Seurat, Perlès had to fend for himself, but the two men remained close. They had an endearing way of calling one another 'Joey'.

Miller was aware of Durrell's hero-worship and so felt occasionally free to attack him, once snapping at him, 'If you don't understand Picasso there is a limitation in you.'[40] Nin felt less inclined to argue with the young man with whom she felt so *en rapport*. She told him that she had long decided that he was a man, but inside him perhaps there was a Peter Pan which they could always reserve for their game.[41] He maintained they were never lovers, but her flirtatious letters to him indicate that they stretched the meaning of 'platonic' to the very limit. She called him 'dear limpet' and he addressed her as 'the Whale'. He told her that after being with her he returned to Nancy with a hatchet.[42] So as he drew nearer to Anaïs he seemed to draw further away from Nancy.

The October *Booster* (edited by Perlès) featured Charles Norden on boxing, a weird piece by Gerald Durrell about an operation, an extract from *Tropic of Capricorn* and 'A Boost for the Black Book' from Miller. The consciousness of its author, born close to the Tibetan frontier, wrote Miller, was soaked in its magic and mystery, held hovering by counter-vailing currents, and created a new soil, a new creative life-form. It was a book for those who sought a fertile world in which to be inventive.[43] This was followed by the conclusion of *The Black Book* (clinically expurgated), subtitled 'Coda for Nancy' and bearing a black border, heralding, one supposes, the English Death as much as signalling that its author had sub-mitted to self-censorship.

Miller also announced somewhat hopefully the coming publication of volume one of Nin's diary, 'Booster Broadsides' (including Durrell's 'Asylum in the Snow'), and twelve-year-old Gerald Durrell's modestly titled 'Flora and Fauna of the World'. One amusing item was 'Nukarpiartekak', an Eskimo tale about the passion of an old bachelor for a young girl. As he makes love to her he thrusts himself so far into her that he disappears completely. When she leaves her tent next day to urinate, out comes Nukarpiartekak's skeleton. Despite all the other items which might have caused offence, this one brought a swift reaction from the American Country Club: President Elmer S. Prather wrote dissociating the Club from the magazine. Before long the advertising would began to melt away.

A review of the *Booster* by George Orwell in *New English Weekly* in October, prompted the wrath of the editorial team. Orwell could not believe that, with monsters like Hitler and Stalin on the rampage, anyone should produce a magazine as futile and meaningless as the *Booster*, without intending it as a subtle gesture against them – which he had discovered it was not. 'All you get is a perfectly ordinary, damn-silly magazine of the pseudo-artistic type that used to appear and die with the rapidity of May flies in Montparnasse in the twenties.' Its advertisers also seem to have been caught hopping. For the *Booster*'s sake he hoped they paid cash in advance. The only reason worth buying it, he concluded, was that it might one day have scarcity value.[44] Durrell replied anonymously in scathing tones, quoting himself from the next issue's editorial, a piece of good contradictory Durrellian nonsense, and adding a piece of his own Freudian doggerel – something at which he was to become a minor master. He accused Orwell of being muddled, and in any case an unworthy opponent. There was hardly any point burning the bed because they had found a flea in it.[45] Being described as a flea, replied Orwell, was a neat enough blow against him, but the length of the complaining letter suggested that some of his bites had had their effect. He was obviously wrong about the *Booster*, which he had taken to be a deliberately bad joke. Now it turned out to have a serious and deep meaning which had escaped him completely. He thought someone more qualified to review it should be given the job.[46]

The *Booster*, freed from the Country Club, was now geared up for self-destruction, and the November issue, edited by Durrell, was called 'The Tri-Lingual Womb Number'. Although listed as associate editor, Nin did not approve of the magazine, considering it far too frivolous for her serious purposes, and she rebelled against Miller's continual 'begging, stealing, cajoling, school-boy pranks, slap-stick humor, burlesque'.[47] Nancy disappeared as art editor, but brother Gerald's poem, 'Death', strongly influenced by brother Larry, was included. There were contributions from William Saroyan and Raymond Queneau, and the epilogue from Miller's *Black Spring*, a horrific vision of impending destruction. On the back cover Durrell placed what was his then favourite comic couplet:

> Out of the gorse
> Came a homosexual horse.

After the American Country Club's outrage at the Eskimo story, Miller said that if vaginas offended members of that Club they could have vaginas aplenty, so the December *Booster* was christened 'The Air-Conditioned Womb Number'. It would be the last of the series, the advertisements having all but dried up, and the number of pages halved. In preparation for this last fling, everyone was encouraged to read Otto Rank's *Trauma of Birth*. The idea was that the artist must serve not man but God – He being the ultimate point of self-fulfilment of the artist. Overcoming the trauma of birth was a major obstacle to this, and how to reproduce the womb for creative purposes was the artist's major problem. Miller's offering was 'The Enormous Womb', Durrell's was 'Down the Styx in an Air-Conditioned Canoe'. And despite her dismissal of the *Booster*, Nin contributed an essay, 'The Paper Womb', about the womb of words she had created in writing her diary.

Nin and Perlès disliked one another, but her affair with Miller continued, if now more on an intellectual and literary level. She had come to despise his crude anarchistic streak and his attitude towards women, and thought he misused his talent. Eliot said much the same thing to Durrell when he submitted an essay on poetry to him for the *Criterion*. He said he would prefer something creative from him, like a passage from *The*

Black Book.[48] Perhaps Durrell should have offered him 'Down the Styx' rather than put it into the *Booster*. It is a small *tour de force*, a stunning story in the same vein as his 'bughouse' stories, but also a brilliant if cruel joke. It takes the form of a letter to his aunt Prudence, conducting her on a fantastical last journey from Bournemouth to the Beyond on Charon's ferry through a horrifying surrealist world of diseased human orifices and passages, of labyrinthine tunnels, and disgusting alimentary tributaries – most probably her own. Signed 'your affectionate nephew', it leaves the distinct impression of being written to exact a deliciously disgusting revenge on an excruciatingly self-righteous prig. Anaïs found it haunting – further proof of Durrell's genius. It reminded her, she said, of a Jules Verne story where a group of people make a subterranean journey through volcanic caverns, hoping to emerge at the other end. The idea may have stayed with him, for some seven or eight years later he wrote such a story himself – a novel called *Cefalû* or *The Dark Labyrinth*.

With so much publishing and optimism in the air, Miller, Nin and the Durrells decided to establish their own imprint, and so the Villa Seurat Series was created. Nancy agreed to invest some of her capital (mostly money from the Fielding Hall Literary Estate) in the first three titles – *The Black Book*, *Max and the White Phagocytes* and Nin's novel, *Winter of Artifice*. Kahane would publicize and distribute the books through the Obelisk Press, retaining 20 per cent of returns on sales.[49] Durrell decided to go briefly to England to set the thing up, but Nancy went skiing in the Alps.

Meanwhile, Durrell was immersed in Beethoven, and writing an important long poem – the best since *The Waste Land*, he told Miller. This was 'The Death of General Uncebunke', which he regarded as being both ironic and compassionate, written, apparently, with Aunt Prudence's late husband in mind – fourteen carols plus five soliloquys on the Tomb of Uncebunke. The tomb is a little anomalous since Uncebunke, says the author in a short preface, was cremated and his ashes scattered in the Channel. Uncebunke, a traveller, author of *Roughing It in Tibet*, and a Tory MP since 1925, although deranged for the last seven years of his life, remained an MP till his death in 1937. The General represents perhaps the old generation of self-confident imperialists, but the mock-heroics of the poem inject the requisite Durrellian note of irony. His uncle sleeps only 'in the image of death'. He has departed 'beyond astronomy'. His world will never return.[50]

The plan was to make the next *Booster* a poetry number, which Gascoyne and Andrey Beecham would edit. Durrell would seek contributions from poets in London, where he would stay at the flat of Hugh Guiler (Nin's husband, who worked there for an American bank) in Notting Hill Gate. When he travelled there in mid-December, he took along David Edgar and Buffie Johnson, who thought his marriage was already on the rocks. In England, she found him less ebullient than usual, and even more disparaging. For him it was a return to the English Death, for her it was all jolly fun. They visited Potocki, who showed them his plans to carve up Poland, and then Gawsworth, who had now been made Regent of Redonda by M. P. Shiel, giving him the power to confer honours on all those who promised to aid Shiel in the recovery of his island from the usurping British. All three were duly invested, Johnson being dubbed Duchess de la Nera Castilla de Redonda and Durrell becoming Don Cervantes Pequèna (the Little Duke).[51] They joined a select band, which was to include Roy Campbell, G. S. Fraser and even Victor Gollancz.

On a visit to the poet Anna Wickham, said to have an unpublishable diary which interested Miller (a false lead). Durrell met the young Dylan Thomas, looking slim and neat and well turned out. Thomas told him he greatly admired Miller, and the two shared a bus ride back to Notting Hill. On the way, Durrell got him to promise to send something for the poetry *Booster*. He tried to persuade him to visit Corfu, but Thomas actually liked Pudding Island. 'I think England is the very place for a fluent and fiery writer. The highest hymns of the sun are written in the dark. I like the grey country. A bucket of Greek sun would drown one in colour, the crowds of colours I like trying to mix for myself out of grey, flat, insular mud. If I went to the sun I'd just sit in the sun; that would be very pleasant but I'm not doing it . . .'[52] While in London Durrell also met George Reavey, Oswell Blakeston and Hugh Gordon Porteus – all potential contributors to the *Booster*, though he found the broad opinion of it to be that the fooling about was tasteless, the serious bits incomprehensible.[53]

Miller saw Nancy off on the train to the Alps, thinking it strange to see them go off in different directions.[54] Larry may have planned to reunite with Nancy in Paris for the New Year, but a couple of days before Christmas he left London suddenly and headed for Austria. Possibly she had sent him an ultimatum about their marriage: either he join her for Christmas or else . . . In any case, he made for Innsbruck without knowing precisely where she was staying, and having to borrow the money for the trip from Hugh Guiler. His dash across Europe was dramatic – a hair-raising trek across the Alps and over the Italian border through the Brenner Pass in a skidding car with luggage hauled behind it on a sled. He arrived at Innsbruck, complete with Christmas present, but had to ask around the hotels before finding her. He joined her in bed on Christmas Eve, just as she was waking up. After Christmas, they went off to ski at Gris, staying at the Goldener Adler Hotel, from which they sent out New Year's greetings.

Miller, delighted to hear they were reunited, urged Nancy to send the money for spring publication of *The Black Book*, which he thought needed no further alteration. He asked Durrell for a blurb for it, 500 balanced and weighty words, as the Villa Seurat Series was about to be advertised.[55] He sent Kahane's contract, which Durrell posted on to Gawsworth for his 'expert' opinion. Although it looked as if *The Black Book*, with Nancy's help, might soon be out, things were not going well with the poetry *Booster*. Audrey Beecham had landed it all in Gascoyne's lap, and he (inundated with poems which Durrell thought should go in) withdrew, consigning the job to Durrell. Miller thought the *Booster* would have to come out on an irregular basis in future; Durrell was amazed that it was still alive, and both of them found Perlès's lack of enthusiasm frustrating.

By mid-January 1938 the Durrells were back at 21 Rue Gazin. *The Book of the Dead* was still incubating, 'Uncebunke' was finished, as was a nine-part poem called 'Themes Heraldic'.

He had also written another long poem, 'Solange', about the life and death of a young Paris prostitute, which may have been based on first-hand research. Eliot, as good as his word, wrote on 18 February, enclosing a blurb for *The Black Book*, which was not just a generous act in itself, but risky to his own reputation, remembering Shaw's warning about peddling pornography. "Lawrence Durrell's *The Black Book*," he wrote

> is the first piece of work by a new English writer to give me any hope for the future of prose fiction . . . One test of the book's quality, for me, is the way in which reminiscences of it keep turning up in my mind: evocations of South London or of the Adriatic, or of individual characters. What is still more unusual is the sense of pattern and of organisation of moods which emerge gradually during the reading, and remain in the mind afterwards. *The Black Book* is not a scrap-book, but a carefully executed whole. There is nothing of the second-hand literary about the material; but what is most unusual is the structure which the author has made of it.

In late February, Anaïs moved on to a houseboat, *La Belle Aurore*, moored in the Seine on the Quai des Tuileries. It had, she told Durrell, a 'Down the Styx' feel about it.[56] It would prove a suitable place for her to carry on her extra-marital liaisons. The world, she told Durrell, was teeming with men she could eat.[57] In mid-March Hitler invaded Austria. There was a lunch at the apartment where Miller declared that in any coming war Durrell was so favoured by fortune that he would always survive; Gascoyne, by contrast, had 'a future of darkness and gloom'. He told Gascoyne, 'You ask for trouble; your destiny can only be a tragic one.'[58] It proved to be prophetic.

In April there appeared the first poetry *Booster*, rechristened *Delta* and edited by Durrell. It included Durrell's 'Poem to Gerald', about the death of their father, and part of 'Themes Heraldic', Dylan Thomas's 'Poem for Caitlin', a flat piece of doggerel from Gawsworth, and poems by Antonia White, David Gascoyne, Theodore Stephanides and the Swedish poet Artur Lundkvist. Unlike most of the poetry magazines of the time, Durrell's *Delta* was both international and a-political. It carried only three advertisements.

Just before the issue of *Delta* appeared, the Durrells did a moonlight flit from their Paris apartment and returned hot-foot to Greece. Nin and Miller saw them off at the station, slightly shocked. They rushed round to the Rue Gazin, assured the concierge that the Durrells were returning, and removed as many books as they could, plus a painting by Cézanne. Why Durrell bolted, risking the loss of his possessions, is difficult to understand. Perhaps it was the lure of the sun, and the fact that his marriage was going through a sad patch, as well the imminence of war.

Miller thought that the last days in Paris had seen Nancy really coming out of her shell, and it may have been Durrell alone who was tensed up. It was he who complained of feeling burned out as a writer, and in need of regeneration – back in the place where his spirit was most in tune. The Paris and London literary worlds had come to seem unreal to him, and he told Anaïs that he felt his marriage was preventing him being fully himself as a writer. But she told him that only *he* could unleash the 'mythical being' who spoke from inside him, and that Nancy had nothing to do with it.[59] In May he told Miller he was seriously considering returning to England to study medicine; it would fill in several years of his life ahead and remove him from the obligation to write books for Faber to hawk like sides of beef or legs of lamb.[60] It would also, he thought, put him back in touch with reality, from which literature had seemingly detached him.

It was the end of an epoch. Europe was hurtling towards the abyss, and Paris of the 1930s would survive for him only as a fond memory, impossible to recreate.

CHAPTER 6

The End of the Idyll

(1938–1941)

The isles of Greece, the isles of Greece!
Where burning Sappho loved and sung,
Where grew the arts of war and peace...

Byron, *Don Juan*

Nancy's New Year cards, which the Durrells sent out at the end of 1937, depicted a lion and a unicorn which had been fighting around the town, and so were late for the feast. The sense that life in Paris had been stringing them out too much drew them back to Corfu and the healing rays of the sun. Although Larry was feeling frustrated with his writing and they were all but broke, they left for a week in Ithaca,[1] back once again 'on miracle ground'.

Nin and Miller were still trying to placate the Durrells' Paris landlord, who could not relet their apartment until they formally relinquished their lease. They would be responsible for his loss of rent, and he could make it difficult for them to re-enter France if he took action through the Service des Etrangers Bureau. Nin and Miller finally shamed the delinquent young Durrell into paying up and sending the required letter to the landlord.

The extra floor to the White House was completed, and Larry and Nancy returned to Kalami; they now had plenty of room for visitors. Nancy was truly blossoming as an artist, thanks to Miller's encouragement in Paris. Larry was hoping that studying medicine would give him a greater sense of reality, and an extra string to his bow. However, Anaïs told him that the only reality medicine would show him was cripples, and the impersonal role of doctor was not for him.[2] He told Miller to sling *The Black Book* into the river and he would do something better for him next time. But Miller thought the novel magnificent and better at every reading, and he said that at last he realized who Gregory was – Durrell himself! But Durrell was amused at the idea that he might have portrayed himself as two selves, both narrator (Lucifer) and freak (Gregory). In fact, he intimated, Gregory was based on a friend he thought typified the English Death. What he did not say was that Gawsworth was the friend and he feared he might prosecute. But, in late June 1938, Audrey Beecham reported that Gawsworth seemed to be drinking himself to death, and the chances were that he would be dead before he had time to sue.[3]

Nicholas Moore's poetry magazine *Seven* published the 'womb' passage from *The Black Book* that summer. (It appeared as 'Ego', the only passage of the book to be published in England before 1973.) Durrell was slowly becoming known in England. The *Geographical Magazine* was prepared to take an article and photographs on Corfu, and Oswell Blakeston liked his 'Uncebunke' poem enough to put it in an anthology, called *Proems*, together with 'Themes Heraldic' – a poem shot through with images of sexual mysticism and allusions to Greek landscape.

Miller had one last fling with Delta, announcing that summer a blistering edition of the magazine to be called 'jitterbug shag', which would include Durrell's Hamlet letter – the greatest letter he had ever received in his life, he called it. He was also madly trying to finish *Tropic of Capricorn* before he hightailed out of Paris and headed for Corfu.[4] Excited at the news that Miller might be on his way, Durrell wrote to say that he was having the boats watched. On landing Miller should look out for the Falstaffian taxi-driver, Spyros, who Leslie was teaching to swear. He himself was struggling with a new book, *The Aquarians*, but getting nowhere. He also wrote to Anaïs. As there was a full moon that week, he said, he had ceased to be a doctor. His letters were again filled with haunting detail – the sea under moonlight, the little shrine to St Arsenius, pebbles and limestone through clear warm water, the hum of hornets, the aching heat. They planned a shrine to the nameless, mysterious god concealed inside us all.[5]

To get away from the distraction of visitors at the White House, Durrell went to Athens and made some new friends, including the giant poet, George Katsimbalis, whom Miller later immortalized as the Colossus of Maroussi. He found cafés around the Plaka (the Bohemian quarter of Athens), where he could carouse with friends and drink good wine. He thought of starting a verse play, feeling that he now knew what he wanted to say, and told Thomas that he was one of those to whom he wished to say it.[6] But he had a block over his new novel, *The Aquarians*, and found it easier just to go swimming or write poetry. He had adopted a rather unusual form for the novel, a proposition from Euclid and a correspondence between God and Durrell about it and its psychological implications. It was a complicated and he thought, petrifying attempt to discover himself.[7] Although their funds were rather depleted, Durrell began to toy with the idea of returning to London at the end of the summer. At least they had Hugh Guiler's flat rent free, and who knew what he might get published? Symons, it was true, had turned down an essay on Otto Rank for *Purpose*, but he could offer it to Eliot.

After many delays, *The Black Book* was published by Kahane in mid-August, greatly lifting Durrell's spirits. Kahane was optimistic, writing:

> I have no doubt that Durrell will go far indeed. He is very young and has not yet shaken off all the traces of the influences that have gone to form him, but to my mind he will in a very short time indeed be looked upon as one of the most important of living English writers, as Henry Miller is abundantly one of the most important of Americans.[8]

But this very young writer was irritated, first by two pages being wrongly arranged by an incompetent printer, and then by discovering, to his fury, that Kahane had held back proofs from which Eliot wanted to take an extract for the *Criterion* prior to publication. The money would have been extremely welcome and the man from Manchester was roundly cursed for his hopelessness.

Miller was quick to congratulate Durrell and send the latest news from Paris. Anaïs was revising her book *Chaotica* for the Villa Seurat Series, Hans Reichel was in St Anne's with the DTs, his friend the US Censor was organizing an exhibition of his watercolours in Washington, and he had finally finished *Capricorn*.[9] Durrell was as delighted about *Capricorn* as he was about *The Black Book*, but was feeling panicky and suicidal about his own new book. Nancy, however, having realized herself, was painting beautifully; only he, with his selfish demands, stood in her way.

The first English review of *The Black Book* came in *New English Weekly* from Hugh Gordon Porteus, who declared it 'one of the major books of our time'. It was Rabelaisian ('satiric–grotesque') in formula, 'romantic–naturalist' rather than 'realistic' (more Proust–Petronius than Dante–Shakespeare). It was 'poetic' in the way that Joyce and Eliot were poetic, and dramatic after Ford rather than Webster. He cited Freud and saw sections of the book as aspects of Ego and Id, and said that it could be regarded as an illuminating film scenario of the Tibetan *Book of the Dead*. He also detected the influence of Rank. 'Psychiatrists agree that most of their patients are seeking a way back to the womb: in Tibet the metaphor is believed literally, where contrariwise the physical world is regarded simply as illusory.' It compared favourably to *The Waste Land* and *Ulysses*, and there was the danger of the book becoming a cult, he said. 'But it stands a fair chance of teaching some people how to die and some how to love. It is the perfect Birthday present for the suicide.'[10] It was a remarkably insightful review. Durrell sent Porteus a thank-you card.

The threatened German invasion of Czechoslovakia caused Miller to panic. He fled Paris, heading for the south coast in order to be on the first US gunboat to leave. By 25 September, he was in Bordeaux, expecting war at any moment, and thinking only about staying alive. Having shut his eyes to events in Europe for so long, he now had the solution. If he could meet Hitler he would soon have him chuckling. People simply didn't understand this highly strung and sincere man. If no one could jolly him up then we were done for.[11] He was cured of Europe, he told Anaïs. He was Chinese at core, not Western.'[12] The day after he renounced Europe the Munich Agreement was signed, the crisis passed, and he promptly became a European again. But he was furious with the Germans; he would now work not only for Hitler's downfall but for the castration of all the Germans, he said.[13] Presumably he excluded himself and his German-American compatriots from this painful fate.

He was in Marseilles when Kahane published *Max and the White Phagocytes*. A 3,000-franc advance from Kahane and $200 from Laughlin for the US rights of all his past and future work enabled him to pay off his debts. But now he had no faith in the future of Europe; the Huns, he thought, would sweep all over it, even into Russia and China. He would head for the US and visit all those places he had long wanted to see – Mobile, New Orleans, Alabama, Mississippi, Nevada, Arizona. If war came he would not fight; the outcome was foregone.[14]

Durrell now saw that a European catastrophe was bound to come, but in the silent beauty of a Corfu night beside the dark sea his fear could, at least temporarily, rest easy. Veronica Tester was visiting and when she and Nancy went to Athens he found himself enjoying the solitude, and planned a camping trip on the Albania border with just a dictionary, a revolver and some rations for company. He had been reading Spengler's *Decline of the West*, sent by Miller, and felt that it was a strange mixture of large error and great veracity. Spengler was to be more of an influence on him than perhaps at the time he thought.[15]

When she returned from Athens, Nancy announced that she wanted a child – perhaps a last attempt to hold a fracturing marriage together. Durrell was unsympathetic. The times were uncertain and he was bored. He felt he should go to England to get involved, however briefly, in literary life. With the good reviews *The Black Book* had received he was something of a celebrity, and could only benefit from being in the place which his book attacked. However, he did not greatly relish returning to a country to which he was morbidly antipathetic, he told Desmond Hawkins, literary editor of *New English Weekly*, who wrote inviting him to contribute book reviews. He was eager to accept, however, assuring Hawkins that he planned to stay on in London longer this time than usual. When Hawkins asked what sort of books he would like to review, he listed Lao Tse, Chinese mathematics, anything on Tibet, histories of chess, algebra and the tarot, symbolism and religious love and even crude general histories like Spengler's. He said he thought he was what Wyndham Lewis called a 'time-mind'.[16]

Miller told Durrell that after the Munich Crisis he had lost faith in the future, but he was already planning his extra large issue of the new *Delta*,[17] and when Durrell sent him some watercolours he pronounced them masterpieces. If he had learned his technique from Nancy, he should stick to her. Things were looking up for him, he said. Laughlin was publishing him in the US and some of his work was coming out in French translation.[18] Laughlin, he added, was also interested in publishing *The Black Book*.[19]

American interest in Durrell had been heightened by a review of his novel in the *Nation* at the end of October, which named him leader of a new Paris movement pioneering the newest post-Kafka form of prose fiction, 'the dithyrambic novel'. Then, on 21 November, *Time* carried a lengthy spread on Laughlin, Miller and Durrell. A woman reporter had visited Miller and grilled him about himself and his books. Miller, wanting to help Durrell, had talked blithely about him, too. The piece was sparked off by Laughlin announcing that he was about to publish in the US *Tropic of Cancer*, which Edmund Wilson had declared 'The lowest book I can ever remember to have read'. The article said that what some called 'the dithyrambic novel' others would call "plain' old-fashioned pornography'. It noted that *The Black Book* followed Miller's pattern of 'realistic scenes giving way to tumultuous passages of invective and bitter rhapsody'. However, there was much 'incoherent prose' interspersed with 'passages of isolated brilliance', comprising 'a type of curdled romanticism... more brutal, less artful, pervaded by a sense of hopelessness and despair beside which Joyce at his most pessimistic seems blithe and full of spirit'.

Durrell was described as a twenty-seven-year-old Anglo-Irishman, born in Burma and raised on the Tibetan border, now working as a clerk at the Ionian Bank in Corfu – the source of this, no doubt, the address on his letters to Miller.[20] The article upset Durrell, who said it made him and Miller out to be nothing but merchants of smut.[21]

At the end of November, the Durrells came briefly to Paris *en route* for London. Durrell left some of *The Aquarians* (renamed *The Book of the Dead*) for Miller to read, and they collected Anaïs, who in London settled them into Hugh Guiler's flat at 140 Campden Hill Road, at Notting Hill Gate. (Durrell later wrote that Hugh had left six cases of good Bordeaux for them to enjoy, but Anaïs angrily complained that this was a gross exaggeration and that Hugh was merely a bank employee and by no means wealthy.) It was an unusually grim London that they found – sandbags and barbed wire everywhere and barrage balloons floating overhead. But Durrell was encouraged that the new issue of *Seven* contained 'Asylum in the Snow' and his 'Carol on Corfu', a poem to the solitary poetic self.[22]

He took Anaïs to Faber to see Alan Pringle, and left the introduction of his novel for Eliot, hoping he would print an extract in the *Criterion*. Then rumours of a general strike sent them all hurrying back to Paris, where Miller spoke extravagantly of *The Book of the Dead*, saying that at times it seemed to surpass Dostoevsky. His sole criticism was that Durrell sometimes cheapened what he said by bowing and smirking just before he said it.

The strike threat in England passed and the Durrells decided to return for an indefinite stay at 140 Campden Hill Road, despite Miller's offer of the Villa Seurat for the winter. Durrell said later that looking around at the faces in Paris he could see that in the event of a German invasion the French would quickly cave in.[23] On an impulse, he went to the Impasse Rouet, at Alèsia, to the squalid room where Alfred Perlès lived, and told him that he was coming with them to England. Not only that, but he, Durrell, would pay for his ticket.[24] The bemused Perlès went meekly along, was given half a crown by Durrell for pocket money, and then floor space at the Campden Hill

Road flat. Here Durrell planned to edit a poetry issue of *Delta*, and Perlès was expected to help. But the Austrian found England an alien place and was determined to return when he could to his rat-hole in the Impasse Rouet.

Durrell quickly picked up again with his old literary cronies, and invited Dylan Thomas to visit them. But Thomas, now living in Hampshire with his new wife Caitlin, said he was broke, and asked for a copy of *The Black Book* in exchange for everything he'd written. Durrell sent him a pound and told him to come to London at once. He also invited Miller over for Christmas, but Miller also declined pleading poverty. He had never spent a happy Christmas, he said. However, he was anxious to meet Veronica Tester and to wander around Covent Garden and into the Café Royal. Money was sent to him and just before Christmas he arrived in England.

On a previous visit he had been turned back at Newhaven, so was not very well disposed towards the country. However, Durrell had arranged for him to meet numerous writers, Thomas and Eliot included. He had brought copies of the second *Delta*, his jitterbug shag, which included Thomas's 'Prologue to an Adventure' and Durrell's *Hamlet* letter. There was also an extract from Anaïs's almost completed *Winter of Artifice*. She wrote to say that *The Black Book* was on prominent display in the Rue du Rivoli, and sent Durrell a letter for him to post in London to her father (with whom she had recently had an incestuous affair) to deceive him into thinking she was there and so could not join him for Christmas.

On 29 December, a gravely composed Eliot turned up for dinner. He and Miller had not met before, and were seemingly relieved to find how human the other was. The discussion at one point touched on metaphysics, and, said Durrell, E. Graham Howe's new book from Faber, *Time and the Child*, embodied all they had discussed with magnificent clarity.[25] Meetings were arranged for Miller with Howe, Havelock Ellis, W. T. Symons and M. J. ('Tambi') Tambimuttu, the Ceylonese poet (who Durrell regarded as quite batty), whose new magazine *Poetry London* was due to appear in the New Year, and who kept contributors' manuscripts in a huge Victorian chamber-pot under his bed.[26] Durrell entertained visitors by singing old ballads and his own poems to the guitar, including one dedicated to Tambi, who was greatly flattered.

When Dylan Thomas was finally persuaded to come up to London, he failed to show up at 140 Campden Hill Road as expected. Just as they had lost hope of him turning up, he phoned to say that he could not find the place and so was not coming. Asked where he was calling from he named the nearby pub, the Windsor Castle. Durrell immediately went and found him looking very dishevelled, scarf around neck and extremely nervous, vowing he could not leave the pub. They had a drink, and Durrell explained how Miller was pacing the apartment swearing at him. Finally, Thomas calmed down, went to the flat and behaved perfectly coolly, as if nothing untoward had happened. They drank Hugh Guiler's wine, Thomas read his poems and they talked the night away. Next day, they toured the Soho taverns, and Thomas took Miller off to savour British music hall at the Holborn Empire. Durrell presented Thomas with one of his watercolours, and Miller promised to visit him in Wales, where he had once visited John Cowper Powys. Thomas wrote just afterwards to Vernon Watkins:

> Last week I went up to London to meet Henry Miller who is a dear, mad, mild man, bald and fifty, with great enthusiasms for commonplaces. Also Lawrence Durrell. We spent 2 days together, and I returned a convinced wreck. We talked our way through the shabby saloons of nightmare London.[27]

Nancy meantime was taking her paintings around in the hope of selling them or getting an exhibition. But Durrell's attitude to her still upset Miller, who urged him not to squelch her, but to allow her plenty of space.[28]

There was a New Year's celebration at Gawsworth's place in St James Street, with Miller, Perlès, Desmond Tester, the Durrells and Audrey Beecham. Perlès, who had brought out his second novel, *Le Quatour en ré majeur*, had another finished, but neither Miller nor Durrell nor even Kahane thought it worthy of publishing as it contained too much gratuitous sex. However, Perlès made friends with W. T. Symons, claiming to have been converted to his Social Credit doctrine, and thought he could contribute to *Purpose* and other London magazines. 'Joey', said Durrell, was suddenly working like a stoat.[29] The survival instinct which had kept Perlès just out of the gutter in Paris seemed to have taken over again in London.

For Durrell, there was quite a lot to cheer with the dawn of 1939. *New Directions* was to include selections from *The Black Book*, the *Geographical Magazine* accepted his article on Corfu, and he had a poem and a review in the *New English Weekly*. Then, in the January *Criterion*, Desmond Hawkins gave his novel a most glowing review, which must have signified 'arrival' at last. Hawkins greeted *The Black Book* as 'an extended metaphor in poetic prose, keyed up to rhetorical pitch and focussed on the most exciting of objects – the *zeitgeist*. Because he brings to the novel that which it lacks, Mr Durrell is a very exciting newcomer.' Despite a few reservations, and thinking that it was Durrell's first novel, he concluded:

> *The Black Book* is liable to be as important for fiction as Auden's first poems were for verse. It challenges the kind of exacting scrutiny which very few first novels (or last ones, for that matter) could pretend to face. Its width of reference, its qualities of perception, and – above all – the fertility and brilliance of its idiom, give Mr Durrell an extremely formidable equipment. *The Black Book* is a limited, erratic and sometimes wayward achievement, but it is nevertheless an achievement of a high order – and something to be thankful for.[30]

After failing to get an extract from his book into Eliot's review, this was a great consolation. But even this was not enough; he wanted to be *drowned* in adoration he said.

Encouraged by all this, he sketched out 'A Cosmography of the Womb', which never got beyond a few tentative notes from his reading of Otto Rank, E. Graham Howe and other works of psychology, mathematics and the Tao. He was fascinated by ways of learning – cognition versus perception, the cause–effect method versus revelation, the life in the objective world of man versus life inside the womb, life according to western science and life according to the Tao. Cognitive thought moved in a straight line towards infinity, sensibility moved in a curve towards the completed circle, and he knew in which realm he thought the poet should dwell. If, as Rank claimed, the fundamental problem of art was one of *form*, then the straight line was the form of science, but the circle was the form of art. The realm of matter was the realm of death. The healing secret was balance. He quoted Hermes Trismegistus, 'If you would be born again you must cleanse yourself from the irrational torments of matter.' This further confirmed the Fraenkel–Miller philosophy that creativity must be preceded by the death of the artist. If Durrell was no longer a Christian, the metaphysical beliefs which attracted him were not, in some ways, so very different. In one sense his religious tendency is to be found in his belief in revelation and in the artist as healer. The search for wholeness was all.

Durrell made an important friend at this time, Anne Bradby, newly married to the artist Vivian Ridler. She was Eliot's secretary and met him through Faber. The Ridlers came to dinner at Campden Hill – a meal of red wine with risotto cooked by Nancy – where Durrell dazzled them with his brilliant talk, his humorous gossip about fellow poets such as Barker, Auden, Spender, MacNeice, and his hiliarous mimicry. His imitation of Tambimuttu, rendering one of his passionate love poems, Anne thought especially memorable. She found Larry deeply respectful of Eliot, once comparing him with Wyndham Lewis, whom he thought more brilliantly endowed as a poet, saying 'yet look how much further Eliot has got, with a plank and two bits of string'. What she found likeable in him was his lack of jealousy of other writers, and his readiness to help with encouragement and advice. But, as a religious woman, she was rather shocked by his vehement atheism; he could never refer to Christians without adding the adjective 'smelly'.[31] They all went to the cinema together and visited one another frequently. Durrell was greatly encouraging to Anne, sending her poems to editors who he thought would like them – Nicholas Moore, James Laughlin, Desmond Hawkins, and Tambimuttu.

The eccentric Hugh Gordon Porteus also became a friend. Porteus, who had trained as an artist, reviewed widely and lived in a Pimlico attic with a charming Jewish woman called Zenka. He was a close friend of Wyndham Lewis, and had written the first full-length study of him in 1932. He dressed like Lewis, wide-brimmed hat and all, and came to Campden Hill Road where the talk was of Graham Howe and Lao Tse. Durrell was thrilled that he read and spoke Chinese, and felt he could learn a lot from Porteus. He later told him that, apart from Eliot and Howe, he was the person whose spirit and sensibility he admired most.

Back in Paris, Miller felt warmed by his London visit, saying that it had helped change his whole outlook. He had decided no longer to diffuse his talent or engage in shameless self-promotion, and was abandoning the *Booster* and *Delta*. He was reading Balzac and found something deeply mystical in his work. *Tropic of Capricorn* appeared on 15 January, and he felt as if a definite period of his life had come to an end. Anaïs was now living in the Rue Cassini, where Balzac had once lived, and with her lover Gonzalo Moré was helping to shelter refugee Spanish Republicans being harassed by the right-wing Daladier government.[32]

Perhaps catching Miller's mood of renewal, Durrell had begun to dream again of Corfu and its welcoming landscape. Drinking a sad toast in a pub to the ghost of Yeats, who had died on 28 January, he felt depressed by the intellectual drabness of the young drinkers there, destroyed, he thought, by economics and labour laws.[33] The gloom was intensified when news came that Eliot was winding up the *Criterion*. Durrell was destined never to appear in its august columns.

Miller in his new serenity had decided that there would, after all, be no war and that he actually sympathized with Hitler and Mussolini. He thought that the western Europeans should hand over all their colonies, and Canada, Australia and Morocco, too. The French were now exploiting the refugees who had flocked to their country and were not worth fighting for. Anaïs called this new mood his mystic 'Chinese phase'. He spent time writing delightful little books for his friends in publishers' blank dummies.[34] Durrell's, which he called a Jupiter diary, was full of exquisite drawings and contained some thirty Zen quotations. Dylan Thomas, feeling less than mystical, wrote to say that he was 'all at sea on the B.B. . . . sickened and excited'. He offered a poem for the new *Delta*, his 'January 1939', and hoped that Durrell and Miller would come to Wales, as they had promised him they would.[35]

Durrell's obsession with Howe waned suddenly when, having read the essay which he had done for *Purpose*, the guru himself came to dinner at the Campden Hill Road flat and told him that he had totally misunderstood him. The Tao, he said, provided him with a usable system when linked to Einstein's theory of relativity, which so far had never been applied in metaphysics but had been regarded only as a theory of mechanics. He disappointed Durrell by appearing to look down on art. He disliked Durrell's essay, preferring a more mechanical approach, and said he was actually constructing a machine to illustrate Taoist theory. The man, thought Durrell, was fiendish and egotistical,[36] an uncouth, inhibited Englishman looking for disciples, who was concerned with mechanisms rather than sensibilities. But linking Einstein with metaphysics and then with creativity became a theme which he was to make his very own.

Tambimuttu's *Poetry London* was launched at the end of February. There were poems by Audrey Beecham, George Barker, Louis MacNeice, Stephen Spender, Dylan Thomas, Gawsworth and Durrell. Durrell's offerings were 'Epitaph' and 'Island Fugue', one a sad commemoration of a Corfiot drunk, the other expressing his continuing yearning for the island. Dylan Thomas congratulated Tambi on the first issue of his magazine but wondered why he had to publish Gawsworth – 'that leftover, yellow towelbrain of the nineties soaked in stale periods'.[37]

In March, the *Geographical Magazine* carried Durrell's article, 'Corfu: Isle of Legends', with Nancy's photographs,[38] showing how Larry had been accumulating details of the island's folklore as assiduously as Gerry had been collecting its flora and fauna. In both cases their chief mentor had been the encyclopaedic Dr Stephanides. But the article bore Durrell's own distinctive style, though it owed something to D. H. Lawrence and Norman Douglas. He first scanned the island geographically and historically, touching on its classical associations – the landing place of Ulysses, a temple to Artemis – before venturing into the shadowland of peasant superstition

– Turkish ghosts, a headless negro left by the Venetians, the miracles of St Spiridion, demonaic possession, appearances of the god Pan, sea sprites who bewitch sailors, protections against the Evil Eye. He was even able to insert a little Greek, ancient and demotic. Nancy's pictures captured an antique Corfu which post-war tourism would all but eliminate – donkeys, peasant costumes and heavily bewhiskered fishermen. It was yet another preview of the 'Ionian Diary' which was to become *Prospero's Cell*.

The first three authors in the Villa Seurat Series called themselves the Three Musketeers. But, if the series was to continue, they had to find suitable new books. Miller urged Durrell to look out in London for any undiscovered geniuses.[39] Kahane was now angry, feeling he had been conned into publishing Anaïs's book, which he clearly disliked, and Miller demoted him to the bottom step of the evolutionary ladder. Kahane had asked for one of his little painted books, but any book he wrote for Kahane, said Miller, would be a posthumous one.[40] Durrell agreed: Kahane was in the insect category.[41] He had conceived the Villa Seurat Series as a respectable platform on which to build up Miller's reputation, rather than to benefit Kahane, who was known in England mostly as a pornographer.

By March the new *Delta* had been sent off to the printers, 'Joey' Perlès was trying to write something for *Picture Post*, but asking Durrell to do it for him. Durrell, however, now felt there was nothing for him in England – it was like a fine but rotten oak, he thought, and he planned to return to Corfu in June. He thought of buying a yacht and sailing back there with Desmond Tester, taking a year and stopping off at ports where things were cheap. Tester, who had recently starred with Sabu in *The Drum*, a film set in the Himalayas – very much Durrell's mental territory – also wanted him to write a play for him, and Durrell had started work on a verse play. At the end of March the Durrells and Desmond and Veronica Tester went searching for a yacht along the south coast, but their scheme collapsed because the threat of war had brought in restrictions on cruising.

On 21 March, Eliot's *The Family Reunion* opened at the Westminster Theatre, and, after attending a first night with the Ridlers, Durrell reviewed it for *Poetry London*. It was a strange notice. He began by saying that Michael Redgrave was miscast in the central role, and ended by saying that, after a second visit to the play, he had changed his mind and that Redgrave was splendid. He then wrote what amounted to an essay on *Hamlet*, reiterating his theory that Hamlet was not mad but just an artist behaving normally. Only at the end did he mention the play, as one about suffering and escape, adding a short encomium on Eliot. Larry's talent lay elsewhere than in dramatic criticism. Even so, he was conscripted as drama critic of the short-lived *International Post*, for which he again reviewed the Eliot play.

He had reason to think well of Eliot, who had been considering his poems for Faber. Anne Ridler had kept an eye on things there, trying to ensure that the poems were given proper consideration. Eliot had been distracted by illness and the launch of his play but when he did get round to writing to Durrell about them he said that if they were to be published it should be by Faber. However, he saw them as the by-products of a prose-writer. He would prefer him to get out a significant work of prose in England first.[42] Fine, distinctive poet though Durrell was becoming, Eliot saw his strength as lying in the novel. This may have made Durrell wonder whether Miller had been right to persuade him to refuse an expurgated *Black Book* in England. Had he agreed, Eliot might then have been happy to publish his poems right away. However, what now interested Eliot was Durrell's *Book of the Dead*.

Durrell had six poems in the spring issue of *Seven*, and for *Delta* he chose a long poem, 'The Sonnet of Hamlet', for Anne Ridler, a sequence of fourteen sonnets, a conception which hints at the Shakespearean dimensions of his ambition. *Delta* appeared at Easter with poems by Ridler, Thomas, Gascoyne, Perlès, Audrey Beecham, Gawsworth, Tambimuttu and Elizabeth Smart. Shortly afterwards Durrell went to the Shakespeare festival at Stratford-upon-Avon to review performances of *Othello* and *The Comedy of Errors* for the *International Post*. But what struck him most forcefully was not what went on inside the theatre so much as Stratford itself and the Warwickshire countryside. He wrote such ecstatic,

124

lyrical letters to Miller and Anne Ridler about the lush greenery of the landscape and the haunting sense of being where Shakespeare was born and lived and died, that it sounded a million miles from Pudding Island, home of the English Death, that he had spent the previous fifteen years hating so much.

Back in London there were some memorable times around the pubs with the clownish Dylan Thomas, sometimes discussing poetry (he was more interested in sound than meaning) and at other times off on some mad escapade. One afternoon Durrell toured thirteen drinking-clubs with a barefoot Thomas, searching for the shoes he had lost, only to find at the end of a fruitless afternoon that he had left them at home.⁴³ What Durrell did not discover either, was that Thomas told John Davenport that Durrell was overrated, that his poetry was bad and that *The Black Book* was highly derivative of Miller. But he obviously liked Durrell, and in April, surprised to hear that he had not returned to the Greek sunshine, wrote asking, 'Why are you still in London, has somebody moved Corfu?'⁴⁴ However, Durrell was uncertain whether to remain or return to his island, and his work was in the doldrums. Miller wondered what had happened to *The Book of the Dead*. Did he first need to suffer more, he wondered? Durrell did one final trip into the English countryside in May when Anaïs and Hugh visited them in London and took them touring through Kipling's Sussex.

Miller's plan was to travel to everywhere he had ever wanted to visit, from Corfu to Cornwall, Mississippi to Darjeeling.⁴⁵ But Greece, he thought, was going to transform him. Meanwhile *Tropic of Capricorn* was due out any day, with an advance sale of 800 copies. But he had had a slight blow to his pride when his friend Blaise Cendrars, who had read it, said that the third which dealt with sex and adventure was fine, the rest bored the hell out of him. He left the Villa Seurat and checked into a hotel to plan his journey south.

On 22 May, the Durrells left for Greece, Larry with a commission to write a monthly letter from Athens for the *International Post*. Miller moved south in June, heading for Nice, hanging on Hitler's every word, which held the key to peace or war. He was obviously terrified of being caught up in a war, and furious with Hitler for threatening to destroy his world – and also, presumably, his cosy view of fate and the need to accept it.

In the event of a war, Durrell thought he would join the navy. He had sent his name in at the time of Munich, and hoped to be quickly called up if hostilities broke out. To get the lie of the land, he visited Athens, meeting again Max Nimiec, his old Corfu drinking friend, and Katsimbalis. He also met the poet Robin Fedden, who later recalled their first meeting:

> Knowing the poet and writer, I expected, in the person, unusual energy and an even more unusual approach to experience. In both, my expectation fell short of the reality. His exuberant vitality kept us talking on a bench in Syntagma Square until it grew cold and late, and then took us on to the Argentine Cabaret. There . . . we continued our discussion, going home at last through one of those rinsed and lucid Athenian dawns which so decisively start each day afresh. For me at any rate the experience was too good not to be repeated.[46]

Fedden was press attaché and translator at the British Legation in Athens, and this friendship was to stand Durrell in good stead a few months later.

Miller sailed from Marseilles on the good ship *Théophile Gautier* on 10 July, and arrived in Corfu on the 22nd. Larry and Leslie were there to greet him in Spyros's open tourer. Larry bought him a straw hat and then whisked him straight to Kalami and installed him in a cool upper room at the White House, the only room equipped with fly-screens. Miller was sorry to find Larry and Nancy still tearing into one another[47] but was ready to enjoy the hot days, cool nights and colourful peasant life. They were cut off from the world and its depressing flow of news, but in sight of the Albanian coast where the Italians had landed in April. There were secret coves for nude bathing, otherwise he wore his straw hat, khaki shorts and espadrilles. He let his beard grow and swam every day and began to feel a new man.

He started to learn some basic Greek himself, and was delighted by the Corfiot tendency to fabulate, circumambulating in the

historic present like true mythologists.⁴⁸ He went with the
Durrells for a week's camping, met a real Venetian countess
(Theotaki), talked and drank with priests, went fishing with
Nicholas the fisherman, and was urged by Durrell to read
Baron Corvo's *Hadrian VII*. He noted how Durrell spent time
every day on his balcony at the White House scribbling exercises to perfect his style, and he himself settled down to painting
watercolours. He was fascinated by Dr Stephanides' knowledge
of the stars and his talk of poets such as Seferis and Katsimbalis,
and made friends with the peasants, with whom he became
very popular.

When the war broke out in early September, the Greek King
left Corfu, where he had been staying, for Athens, and the
island became a hive of activity, the harbour crowded with
evacuees, troops drafted in from Crete, the navy planning to
mine Kalami Bay. Mrs Durrell had already removed herself
and the family back to England. Leslie and Larry parted on
bad terms, Leslie having made a local girl pregnant and having
then declined to marry her. They never again resumed their old
camaraderie. Larry and Nancy decided to make straight for
Athens, taking Miller with them. Larry wanted to join the
Greek army on the Albanian border, and, staying at a hotel in
Petras, Nancy and he had a terrific wrangle, according to
Miller, about his plan to fight for Greece rather than England.⁴⁹
   Durrell was eager for Miller to meet some of his Athenian
friends, especially Katsimbalis and the poet–diplomat George
Seferis, then press attaché at the Greek Ministry of Information.
It was a momentous encounter. Miller compared meeting Katsimbalis to meeting Durrell or Blaise Cendrars, all so exuberant
and enchanting.⁵⁰ Seferis said that Durrell and Miller were
among the earliest of his readers to understand what he was
doing in his poetry, saying to him: 'You know what [I] like
about you is that you turn things inside out. And . . . in the
good sense.'⁵¹ The two Greeks became, for Durrell, yet two
more uncles, and lifelong friends to Miller, too. There were
evenings of poetry and powerful *retsina* at Katsimbalis' house,
which they nicknamed Wuthering Heights, meetings in the
Plaka with others such as the poet Sikelianos, the novelist

Kazantzakis, the painter Ghika, the ailing Max Nimiac, and Theodore Stephanides visiting from Corfu. Afterwards, there were walks through the night to recover from all this junketing. With extraordinary timing, on 28 September, *New English Weekly* ran Durrell's and Stephanides' translation of Cavafy's 'Waiting for Them', that is, waiting for the barbarians.

The encounter between Miller and the British circle in Athens was not so happy; he considered them a farcical group of feeble pansies. He understood why Durrell preferred to fight with the Greeks.[52] His worst encounter seems to have been with the effete Fedden and the extravagantly camp Eddie Gathorne-Hardy, famous for London orgies with Guardsmen[53] and described by Xan Fielding as 'a large, lazy sponge'.[54] Fedden recalled their encounter:

> Durrell wanted the great man to meet a new and brilliant friend, Eddie Gathorne-Hardy. The four of us dined under the trees outside a quiet taverna. The setting and the food were right; the outcome was disaster. The chief guests took an immediate dislike to each other. Gathorne-Hardy, learned, incisive and witty, seemed to Miller effeminate and superficial. The latter struck Gathorne-Hardy as loud, imprecise, and overconfident. Dinner was a battle and Miller was the loser. At some point, provoked beyond endurance, Miller, striking his belly, shouted 'But I write my books here.' The sensible reply came in a flash. 'Do tell me *just* where, my dear.' Their host was pained.[55]

Miller decided that the British were all pretty much like Gathorne-Hardy, and, apart from Durrell (and W. T. Symons, a real gentleman, he thought), were not worth knowing. After ten days, he gave up on Athens, and returned alone to Corfu to reassume his Chinese meditation nude on a secluded beach.

As the navy was slow to take Durrell – he was hoping for an intelligence job – he thought he might find something useful to do in the capital. Being that rare bird, an Englishman who spoke Greek, he was found work by Fedden with the British Legation, gathering information about Greek opinion and feeding British propaganda to the Greek press. It involved eavesdropping on conversations at cafés, having clandestine meetings at street corners, and skulking in taxis. It was a job which fitted Durrell's sense of adventure perfectly, spying for his country in Athens, as Compton Mackenzie had done in the previous war. He thoroughly enjoyed it, but also got his first taste of stuffy British diplomatic life at which he poked so much pleasant fun later on.

But his 'spying' did not always provide the information he required, and he found having to write it up a bit of a grind, as Robin Fedden remembered:

> Durrell was responsible for putting out an information bulletin. It was not an enviable task. After a late night I met him despondent in the Press Attaché's office. 'Do tell me,' he said, 'what the Greeks are thinking. No one has any idea and I must say *something*.' I suspect the Greeks themselves did not know.[56]

As well as Greeks and propaganda colleagues, there was also, of course, the British expatriate community (like something out of Thomas Mann, he said) for the Durrells to meet, mostly attached to the Legation or to the British Council – Jock Jardine, Mary and David Abercrombie, Anna and Wallace Southam and Alexander (Xan) Fielding. Fielding was most struck by Durrell's virtuosity – poet, novelist, composer, jazz pianist, guitar-player, mime and actor.[57]

Durrell's reputation was both as author of the banned *Black Book* (and *Seven* had just published 'Zero') and as a dazzling conversationalist. Fedden recorded one of Durrell's enthusiastic metaphysical expositions delivered one evening at the Mykonos Taverna in Athens: 'One's aim is of no importance [he said], one's manner of progressing towards it is everything . . . The poison of life is the desire for a permanent synthesis . . . The problem of life is in the reconciliation of Time and Space' – words Fedden recalled especially after *The Alexandria Quartet* appeared.[58]

Max Nimiec, suffering from a bad heart, and shocked by the defeat of Poland after the German *Blitzkreig*, gave a huge party one evening in an expensive suite at the King George Hotel, to which seem to have been invited all the society ladies of Athens, bedecked in black satin and pearls. It was too much for Durrell, not a man to enjoy small talk. He soon disappeared, and Fedden discovered him later, 'alone, in the splendidly appointed bathroom declaiming verse on a black bidet with a glass of vodka in one hand'.[59] He later wrote a Pound-like poem of five lines about a black bidet, which Fedden is convinced was in memory of the bathroom at the King George.[60]

Shortly after the outbreak of war, Fedden, a pacifist, resigned, and by October a new man, Mackworth Brown, took over as director of publicity. He quickly decided that Durrell's section, Propaganda, was surplus to requirements and closed it down. Durrell was disgusted. Mackworth Brown, an old India hand, he decided, was the kind of short-sighted incompetent imperialist responsible for so much loss in the First World War. With this lack of imagination he did not see how the British could win the war, and, with the country's let-down of Poland, he had become less eager to fight, certainly in northern Europe. He trusted neither the purpose behind the fight nor those who championed it, he told Anne Ridler. On the other hand, he would be happy to fight in a naval unit in the Mediterranean.[61] In that way he could at least help in the defence of his new homeland, Greece.

Despite his own misgivings about how best to fight in the war, he had realized finally that Miller's outlook on world affairs was deeply flawed and myopic, and that it was all those despised left-wingers who had been right about Hitler. On the other hand, those same left-wingers were now thrown into utter confusion themselves because of the Hitler–Stalin Pact. His own Greek friends, however, Katsimbalis and Stephanides, were unambiguously ready to fight. The war and the job at the Legation opened his eyes to political reality, something which dramatically disrupted his own creative metaphysic of introspection. In a review for *New English Weekly*, he had to admit that neither Lao Tse nor even the sparkling comedian Chuang Tzu had anything to offer to the distressed peoples of Europe.[62] Unsure of where he would settle he sent his most valuable papers and books (including his collection of Elizabethan authors) to Bournemouth, where Alan Thomas carefully stored them for him. He felt angry, like Miller, that the war had cut him off from everything which so far had sustained him. He blamed intellectual cliques in Paris and London for the war (though whether that included the Villa Seurat group he did not say) and told Anaïs that this war was really Hugo's war – he being a banker.

His job at the Legation had brought him for the first time in his life a decent salary, and now he felt deprived. Fortunately, he had friends at the British Council, Abercrombie and Southam, and after being fired as a propagandist was offered a Council job teaching English to Greek students, so he was soon back among the salariat. The money was now important because Nancy was pregnant and due to give birth in the spring. He quite enjoyed teaching, but felt that he only ever reached a few bright sparks.

In November, Miller left his retreat in Corfu and returned to Athens, intending to see more of Greece. Having adopted the yogic state of mind of the Zen Buddhists, he was ready to write and have adventures again. He was embraced enthusiastically by Katsimbalis, with whom he soon left for Hydra and Nauplion, the start of a tour which took him to Epidaurus, Mycenae, Knossos and Phaestos. This adventure would be the making of Katsimbalis.

Anaïs was still in Paris, Perlès was in London compiling an astrology anthology, and Gascoyne had turned ever more mystic. However, Durrell said he was determined to stay in Greece as long as he could.[63] When Miller returned from his adventures the Durrells took him in Max Nimiec's little car for a tour of the Peloponnesus. Because of petrol rationing the roads were deserted and there was not a tourist in sight. Larry had however managed to wangle enough fuel for the trip. In spite of wretched weather, they toured all the sights – Mistra, Delphi, Corinth, Argos, Tripoli and Sparta – and he was up at dawn to greet the sun, madly crying 'Helios!' The Spartan countryside, which he thought so Tibetan, seemed a most suitable place to end his Greek visit.[64]

The Durrells said goodbye to their friend in the rain at Tripolis on Christmas Eve, then returned across the Argos Plain to Nauplion and Epidaurus, to Mycenae and Tiryns and to the Valley of Nemea. Afterwards Durrell wrote one of his most elegiac letters to Anne Ridler about this tour of the ancient sites of mainland Greece, enclosing a poem, 'Nemea', which caught something of his new mood of poignancy.[65] It heralded one of the finest bursts of lyrical landscape poetry by any English poet this century, a burst which he was to sustain for some years ahead. What haunted him was the silence in the great valley, the wide, snow-lined rocks, reminiscent of Tibet. It was an apt image for the pause before the storm about to overwhelm Europe, and also revealed a poet in Durrell which had been struggling to get out. The image of the remote plain, cut off in the mountains, recurs in his later novel *Cefalû*. Other poems of place date from this time, including 'In Arcadia',[66] 'At Epidaurus'[67] and 'In Corinth', dedicated to Vivian Ridler.[68] He had found his finest poetic voice, and this outpouring of poetry, he said later, was his way of disciplining the lava-flow of his creativity.[69] Poetic themes other than that of place did exercise Durrell – those of exile and loss, and personal ones about his relations with Nancy: 'In Crisis',[70] 'A Noctuary in Athens'[71] and 'Exile in Athens',[72] for example, in which the titles alone seem to speak for the man. And, despite the continuing personal nature of his poetry, it was always a response to a new set of circumstances in which he found himself or a new set of ideas which were engaging him.

Anaïs had left for America, like Miller, and in January 1940 Durrell wrote congratulating her on *Winter of Artifice*, which he had finally read.[73] Meanwhile, Miller, writing to her from sea *en route* for the States, declared himself transformed by his Greek experience. But living among Americans again, he said, was like living with the unborn, monstrosities escaped into the world too soon.[74]

Now the last link with the Villa Seurat and the Obelisk Press had been severed. Kahane had died the day before war broke out after taking to his bed and consuming a full bottle of French brandy.[75] The Manchester Jew whom Miller and Durrell so loved to hate was beyond their scorn, and beyond the reach of the threatening Nazis.

Still pining for Corfu, Durrell had applied for a British Council job there. In February, the poet Bernard Spencer and his wife Nora arrived to take up a British Council job in Salonika, and Durrell soon got to know him. The tall, good-looking, rather lugubrious Spencer, born in India, son of a

High Court judge in Madras, had been to Marlborough and Oxford, where he had known Spender and MacNeice, and had published mostly in Geoffrey Grigson's poetry magazine *New Verse*. Greece made a big impression on Spencer, greatly affecting his poetry, as it had Durrell's, and, although different in temperament, they became firm friends.

Nancy wanted to have her baby in England, so in early February she flew to London, and Durrell was left bemoaning his solitude. He hated living alone,[76] and at one point did not even have the prospect of that year's Athens carnival to distract him, the authorities having banned masks for fear of encouraging spies and general sedition. However, the ban was lifted, and Durrell's enthusiasm for carnival is evident in his celebrated set-pieces in *The Alexandria Quartet*. He managed to finish the first act of a play, but could not settle to work. The frustration was increased by the sudden realization of how to write his *Book of the Dead*. It was all simmering inside him but he could not get stuck into it until he was free.[77] He borrowed Max's car again and continued visiting the ancient world and soaking himself in the past civilization he loved – before the barbarians came.

Laughlin's *New Directions in Prose and Poetry 1939* appeared in March, with extracts from *The Black Book* and *Tropic of Cancer*. But Durrell was greatly upset by Laughlin's apparent refusal to consider his poems, and judged *New Directions* dull and mediocre; he also formed a low opinion of the editor's judgment. (Four of Durrell's poems later appeared in *New Directions in Prose and Poetry 1940*.) But his annoyance with Laughlin was tempered by a sudden reticence about publicity. When Miller told him he was working to get *The Black Book* published unexpurgated, Durrell urged him not to. He needed as much anonymity as possible. As he was about to become a parent and needed his British Council salary, and as he had enemies at the British Legation who would love to discredit him and have him fired, he dared not run the risk of bringing out something of a scandalous nature.[78] He also urged Miller not to send through the mail any questionable manuscripts, which might be opened and so get him into trouble. Circumstances had led him to embrace the very mores he had gone to Greece to escape. However, he was quietly planning his revenge on the inane diplomats who so hated the British Council people and were forever plotting their downfall. He was collecting comic stories about their idiocies, which he thought would make Waugh's *Black Mischief* look tame. And he was by now halfway through a book on Corfu, and had discovered a great deal of material for it in the Gennadion Library in Athens. This book he had decided to dedicate to Theodore Stephanides.

Nancy, fed up sitting around in the Phoney War, had decided to return after all to Athens to have her baby. She phoned with the news that Margaret had got married, Leslie giving the bride away. She had also heard that the British Council had confirmed Larry's assignment to Corfu for the following year, and that Theodore's wife (who had evacuated to England with the Durrell family) had quarrelled with Louisa and left with her daughter to find a place of her own to live. Sad news also came from Corfu. 'Spiro Americanus', the rambunctious taxi-driver, had died.

The Phoney War ended when the Germans attacked Norway and Denmark in April, and then France and the Low Countries in May. Early in June, after the evacuation at Dunkirk, Nancy returned to Athens, and Penelope Berengaria Nausicaa Durrell (pet name Ping-Kû, or Pinky), was born on the 18th. Durrell was delighted with her, but thought that cultivating the values of domesticity at a time of war was misplaced. Theodore, now an army officer, had passed through, and he more and more felt the need to get into uniform himself. His attitude to the war was slowly changing. People who had been at Dunkirk had told him of the ferocious bravery of the Guards and he thought some of their aggressive ardour was required if defeat was to be avoided.[79] Nor was he in the mood for defeatist talk; the outlook might be dismal, he told Miller, but the British were very obstinate.[80]

Nancy was lucky to get back. Spencer's wife had got home for a visit and been refused permission to return. Durrell, like many others, blamed the collapse in Europe on the craven-hearted mummies of the Chamberlain government in London, and by extension the useless English gentlemen of the

Diplomatic Corps in Athens who so despised the Greeks. There was talk of getting a job in Cyprus, of having to flee Greece in a small fishing boat and travel across Turkey, but when school had ended in May his money had stopped and he could not afford to leave. It was impossible to get money from London, so he cabled Miller for help, and his friend promptly sent him a sizeable sum, drummed up from among his New York contacts. If he got to Cyprus, he told Anne Ridler, he planned to publish his collected poems privately, using newsprint if necessary.[81]

He felt a strong bond with Council people who the hated Legation were constantly trying to get drafted into the war. When at the end of August he finally got his posting, to Kalamata (site of an old Frankish town in the southern Peloponnesus), he and Nancy found lodgings with another Council man. And when Miller sent him extracts from his new book about Greece, *The Colossus of Maroussi*, he was amused at some of his attacks on the British, especially those he had met in Athens, but thought he had been too hard on Byron. His long letters to Miller at this time seem to be an attempt to cling on to a world which was slipping away from him. Even so, he felt settled enough to ask Thomas to send back his books and papers.

In July he and Nancy spent a holiday with Bernard Spencer on the island of Mykonos in the Cyclades. On the boat Durrell wrote to Miller the story of Katsimbalis standing on the steps of the Acropolis one evening and crowing loudly to set all the cocks in Athens crowing too. This letter went into *The Colossus of Maroussi*, which was to make a legend of both Durrell and the Greek poet. The stay on Mykonos was a last summer interlude before the war finally swamped Greece, an interlude of poetry. Spencer was a slow and painstaking poet compared to the prolific Durrell, but he had already written a few Greek poems. Durrell's major composition on Mykonos was his important long poem, 'Fangbrand: A Biography', dedicated to its subject, Stephan Syriotis, and, unlike Spencer's poetry, carrying no direct reference to the war. If there is such commentary, it is at another level – the story of a man who, finding an island where he lives in loving harmony with the landscape, discovering himself in the process, is at last overtaken by the death which awaits us all. And yet in death there is life.[82]

It is not surprising that, with war so close, he should meditate on death; it had in any case fascinated him since he was a child in India, a fascination which grew with his reading of *The Egyptian Book of the Dead* and developed in discussions with Miller. Reviewing Rilke's *Duino Elegies* in *Poetry London* prompted in him the thought that poetry brings one's death alive in one, and he quoted Rilke's dying words when refusing morphia for the pain: 'I want to feel my death ripening in me.' Awareness of death, he now believed, brought awareness of existence, and Rilke's poems represented perhaps the first bridging of eastern and western philosophy in European literature. This idea would ripen in him and flower, especially in its Gnostic manifestation, in his final work of fiction *The Avignon Quintet*, where determining the moment of one's death is raised to the highest level of virtue.

Durrell had not been teaching in Kalamata for long when Greece was plunged into war. On 28 October Italian troops invaded. Britain immediately sent warships and offered to aid Greece. Kalamata was threatened by air-raids. Katsimbalis went off to the front with the artillery, and Durrell felt stirred enough to offer his services now to the RAF as well as the navy, specifying that he wished to fight in the Corfu area. He was told that the British were not operating there.[83] By 4 October the Greeks were repelling the Italians, who by the 22nd had been routed. The Greeks were more united than Durrell had ever known them and he was greatly impressed by their magnificent victories.

Spencer was transferred to Cairo, and in the New Year Max Nimiec finally expired at a cabaret, surrounded by blondes – his true field of combat, thought Durrell.[84] There was a sense of things coming to an end, a group of friends being dispersed by events. In the midst of all this, in February 1941, Durrell told Miller that his *Book of the Dead* was now laid out before him, a strangely exciting conception which would pay tribute to him and Anaïs and commemorate the Villa Seurat.[85] He had huge plans and his notebooks were bulging.

Miller, removed from the scene of battle, now felt detached from it, setting off on his American travels and even thinking of visiting India or Mexico. His earlier determination to exterminate the Germans had been replaced by a feeling of irritation that Hitler's adventures had disturbed his work. Neither side would win, he predicted.[86] Durrell thought that the real rats were the French, who would probably soon side with Germany, and curiously enough many of the French writers whom Miller admired, such as Céline, Giono and Blaise Cendrars, would end up doing something like that.

In April the storm broke. On the 6th, German troops invaded Greece and Yugoslavia. On the 17th, Yugoslavia fell, and on the 23rd King George and the Greek government left Athens for Crete. According to Durrell, when he asked the Council for instructions he received a cable simply saying, 'Carry on – Rule Britannia!'[87] However, he was too shrewd to obey orders, and he and Nancy decided to head for Crete themselves. They packed nappies and a little food, and left, with Durrell carrying his baby daughter in a wine basket. They had to travel light; most of his precious books and papers had to be left behind. They got down to Navarino beach at Pylos, where they managed to find a caique ready to run the gauntlet of German planes and submarines. The sea trip via the island of Antikythera across to Crete took them past Cape Matapan, the point from which Durrell was to recall his sense of loss of Greece in *Prospero's Cell*. The journey took several days, the caique hugging the shoreline because a poorly maintained diesel engine threw sparks into the sky, making them a perfect target for the marauding Stukas. A full moon made things even more hazardous and nerve-wracking, especially for Durrell, who had to wash baby napkins all the way.[88] They had escaped from the Peleponnesus just one day ahead of the invading Germans.

When they arrived at Chania, on the north-west coast of Crete, they were starving. The island was under constant attack from Stukas and it became more and more imperative to leave. They hung around in Crete for some six weeks, and Durrell managed to see enough of the place to set a novel there four years later.

Finally, they scrambled on to one of the last passenger

steamers to leave Crete for Egypt, commandeered, he said later, by drunken Australian soldiers.[89] When they said they were short of food for the baby, the Australians broke into a shop and stole enough canned Carnation milk to feed her for several weeks.[90] Around 25 April, a couple of days before Greece fell, they arrived in Alexandria. It was the end of an era, but the beginning of an experience which finally would bring Durrell the celebrity for which he thirsted. He later recalled knowing that he would end up in Egypt, because a fortune-teller in Salonika had read it in his coffee grounds. She had told him that he would pass over water and be very fearful and would be stripped of all his worldly possessions. He would arrive in a country which would make him miserable and which would leave a lasting mark on him, but once he had left, its significance to him would soon become apparent.[91]

CHAPTER 7

The Great Cultural Hinge: Cairo and Alexandria

(1941–1945)

My body I shall give to pleasure,
To the imagined delights,
To the most daring erotic desires,
To the sensual impulses of my blood,
Without fear . . .

                    C. P. Cavafy

Let there be no doubt about it: it was in
the countries which first recognized gods
that the novel originated; and, to be more
specific, in Egypt, the cradle of all divine
worship.

                    Marquis de Sade,
            Reflections on the Novel

Durrell's Egyptian war was to transform him, for both better
and worse.

The impact of Egypt and its strange mix of cultures, the
unreal life lived by Europeans there during the war, the new
literary friendships and tastes he developed, and the changes
in his own personal circumstances, all helped to induce a
ferment of ideas and a more exotic moral outlook than hitherto. It was, as Ruth Speirs said to him, a world of its own,
like spending four years at a unique university. His *Book of
the Dead*, which had been richly simmering in Corfu, London
and Paris, would have added to it even richer ingredients than
before, to make what would probably have been a fine book

into something far more subtle and complex – a dish for the epicure. In *Clea*, Durrell's *alter ego* Darley, escaping the war in Greece, arrives in Alexandria in a caique from an island in the Cyclades during an air-raid. For Darley, it was a return to a *past* which both haunted and inspired him. Durrell arrived there from Crete in a refugee ship to a *future* which would both haunt and inspire him.

Like Darley, he arrived during an air-raid, but whereas Darley was almost immediately recruited as a censor at the British Embassy, Durrell's progress was less smooth. A security sergeant challenged him by name and separated him off with all the other men, and while Nancy and Penelope went with the women and children to the Lunar Park Hotel in Cairo, Durrell was to be taken to Agame Camp just outside Alexandria for interrogation. But the Sergeant was a big fan of Miller's, had read *The Black Book* and knew Durrell's poetry, and was determined to have Durrell to himself for a while. They crouched for the rest of that night in a slit-trench against a sky full of anti-aircraft tracer-bullets and talked about poetry. After a few days at the camp, Durrell joined his family at the Lunar Park Hotel, which he christened 'Lunatic Park', claiming that it had once been a brothel.

Cairo (a hot copper pan between two deserts, according to Durrell)[1] was in the middle of the khamseen – a hot dry southerly wind off the Sahara which smothers everything with a thin choking layer of sand. And it must have been uncomfortable crowded into a cheap tourist hotel. It was packed with refugees from the Nazi-occupied Balkans. Nor did he find the Egypt outside the hotel elevating. The dirt, the squalor, the sand-clogged air, the heat, the lice, the dead bodies in the streets covered with flies, the diseased beggars deformed in every conceivable way, and the cheap brothels – all this both fascinated and repelled him. The general air of corruption in Farouk's feudal kingdom, symbolized somehow by the fetid waters of the Nile, weighed down on him, he said, like being slowly crushed under the weight of great elephants.[2] And he found the pervasiveness of Islam oppressive. He was to find no holy connection with the spirit of *this* place as he had with Greece.

By contrast to the grim Cairo of poverty-stricken Egyptians

was the affluent lifestyle of others. The Egyptian government was supposedly neutral, and the cities had been declared 'open'. Although the harbour at Alexandria was bombed, Cairo remained untouched, and after dark was a blaze of lights. Shops were full, restaurants offered every delicacy and the nightclubs flourished. Visitors from an England suffering from air-raids and shortages were shocked, while the contrast was even greater for the battle-stained soldiers on leave from the desert.

Larry and Nancy were broke, and funds could not be easily sent out from London, so Durrell looked for work. His old British Council friends Abercrombie, Southam and Spencer were there, but because he had been recruited locally in Greece he was no longer on the Council's payroll. He managed to find a job writing occasional editorials and funny pieces featuring his Aunt Norah for the English-Language *Egyptian Times* – the paper for which E. M. Forster wrote when stranded in Egypt in 1915. When Theodore Stephanides, now a lieutenant in the Royal Army Medical Corps, arrived in Egypt from Crete aboard the HMAS *Perth* on 1 June 1941, he found Larry and Nancy still holed up at the Lunar Park Hotel, to which David Abercrombie had directed him.

In August Durrell's fortunes changed. Robin Fedden, having worked with a Quaker ambulance unit in Syria, was now teaching at King Fuad I University, and sharing a flat with Bernard Burrows from the British Embassy. He must have mentioned Durrell and his many virtues, including his fluent Greek and propaganda work in Athens, and, as a result, Walter Smart, oriental counsellor at the Embassy, recruited Durrell as a junior in the Foreign Press Department there. Smart, a tall figure with a Wellingtonian profile and a wicked sense of humour, had been first oriental secretary and then counsellor to the Cairo Residency since 1926. He was a connoisseur of art and artists, and Durrell warmed to him instantly. The cultivated Smart impressed the cynical Durrell with his obvious probity. A diplomat from the old world of Empire, he had seen Egypt move from British control towards independence in 1936, the experience Durrell later gave to his British diplomat David Mountolive in *The Alexandria Quartet*. What may have most commended Smart to Durrell, however, was that he had known Cavafy, the Greek poet he most admired.

To Bernard Burrows, Durrell was an entirely non-establishment figure, an unpredictable *enfant terrible*, but he thought it was to the Embassy's credit that they still employed him; and he was, in any case, extremely good at his job.[3] Durrell's duties involved liaising with the Greek press and keeping abreast of affairs in occupied Greece. The job brought him back in touch with his old friend Seferis, now working in Cairo with the Greek government in exile. The other advantage of his new post was a salary, and being able officially to get funds from England. In this new state of relative affluence, the family moved to an apartment at a guest house in the prosperous Cairo suburb of Gezira, where Durrell could entertain friends from the Embassy, the British Council and the Greek community working in Cairo.

If Durrell had felt like an exile all his life, as he said, then his forced exile from Greece was probably more painful even than his exile from India. They were, he told Seferis, inhabitants of what Zarian called 'the Enormous Eye' (Greece), but were on the wrong side of the Mediterranean. His deep sense of yearning for Greece gave a new dimension to his poetry and brought him closer than ever to the great Greek poet of exile, Constantin Cavafy of Alexandria. It would also give considerable poignancy to the book on Corfu, *Prospero's Cell*, which he had half finished before leaving Greece.

The place for writers to meet in Cairo was the Anglo-Egyptian Union, once the residence of the Sirdar, the British Commander in Egypt, when it was under British control. During the war the Union was given the role of bringing together English people and Egyptians with a taste for the arts. In fact, few Egyptians went, but English artists in Cairo, or soldier–artists on leave from the desert fighting, found it a pleasant cultural oasis in which to relax over a drink or a game of billiards. The garden of the Union was an especially exquisite retreat, and it was there in the late summer of 1941 that Durrell, Fedden and Spencer hit on the idea of creating a poetry magazine to provide an outlet for their work. Fedden described its aim as being 'to emphasize the importance of personal life and values when the current of all thought and feeling around us [was] set strongly in the channels of war, and when it was proving evermore difficult to exist outside the "war effort" '.[4] Fedden and Spencer, as pacifists, were out of sympathy with the prevailing martial culture, and Durrell 'was clearly irked by the canalization of thought and response which the atmosphere of wartime Cairo imposed'.[5] (If he felt at all guilty about not being in uniform, contact with the military in Egypt probably altered that.) They got support from Terence Tiller, also teaching at the university in Cairo, and from Walter Smart. Durrell persuaded the Greek President in exile to fund the magazine, and Fedden got the French Archaeological Institute to print it. The idea was to produce some 200 copies, and sell it at five piastres through the best Cairo bookshops.

In September, Durrell began exploring Egypt, making an expedition to the Pyramids with Theodore Stephanides and the American Professor Reisner, senior archaeologist at Cairo University. In October he told Seferis that, for men of the subtropics like them, Africa was not their element. He did not warm to Egyptians as he did to Greeks, and if he already hated 'cannibalistic' Christianity, he found Islam suffocating and beastly. In December, an echo from another lost world came in a letter from Miller, sending love from Anaïs in New York and telling him that Alf Perlès was now in Scotland serving in the Pioneer Corps. Pearl Harbor and Hitler's declaration of war on the USA had occurred three weeks before, but Miller seemed still detached from the war. He had just returned from a 25,000-mile trip around the country with over 500 pages of a new book, *The Air-Conditioned Nightmare*, and was deeply in debt. Even so, he still spoke of making a trip in search of his Shangri-la – Mexico, India, China or Tibet. Wars were other people's affairs.

The first issue of *Personal Landscape*, a 'magazine of exile', appeared in January 1942. In it were poems Durrell had written in Greece, including 'Argos' and 'To Ping-Kû Asleep', and one which is an important psychological statement, 'Je est un autre' (a title taken from Rimbaud), reflecting his continuing meditation upon the nature of the self. He also contributed a short essay, 'Ideas about Poetry'. Spencer's recent Greek poems were there too, as was Fedden's poem 'Personal Landscape', from which the magazine took its title. Reception was so good that circulation increased to 800 over the next eight months.[6] John Lehmann judged it 'one of the rare "little" magazines that have made literary history in our time'.[7] Durrell sent a copy to Eliot (assuring him that it was to be kept 'select'), inviting him to contribute a poem, but without success.[8]

There was a considerable social life for Durrell to enjoy. Walter Smart and his wife, the Syrian painter Amy Nimr, held open house at their home at Zamalek, and here he could relax in civilized and literate company from London, Paris, New York and around the Middle East, including Elizabeth Gwynne (the cookery writer Elizabeth David-to-be), Ines Walter, later to marry Bernard Burrows, and writer and traveller Freya Stark. Smart's library particularly impressed Durrell, as a great melting pot of ideas from east and west. Here he found many books which were to influence his thinking about Egypt, including E. M. Forster's *Alexandria: A History and a Guide*. At the Smarts' he also met Patrick Leigh Fermor, the intrepid commando, and the two men struck up an instant rapport. Leigh Fermor found Durrell an ebullient presence, 'a man who pumped the oxygen back into the air', a man of 'wit, intelligence, charm, comic sense, a vast array of interests and a staunch-less fluency ... unrelenting toil all day ... punishing nights, hangovers that slink off next day like beaten dogs ... a faultless eye and ear, skill in drawing and painting, a deft touch on stringed instruments ... a delightful pitch of voice for talks and songs, and the speed of a dolphin in the sea ...'.[9]

Larry's marriage, however, was in a poor state. His relationship with Nancy had become increasingly strained, something to do with his finding Egypt difficult to adjust to and the unreality of wartime Cairo. Theodore Stephanides visited him at the end of February, a few days after Durrell's thirtieth birthday. He found Durrell busy with his job, busy with *Personal Landscape*, busy compiling notes about Egypt, which would inform and add to his *Book of the Dead*. When writing an account of his visit Dr Stephanides made no mention of Nancy.

Not only was Durrell reading Cavafy and reflecting on the

A Family of Empire: Lawrence Samuel and Louisa Durrell with their three eldest children, Larry, Leslie and Margo, in India. Lawrence Samuel was committed to the colonial ideal, and his poetic mouthpiece was Rudyard Kipling, one of the authors who first inspired young Larry.

St Saviour's and St Olave's Grammar School, 1925. Durrell (top, far right) is standing near 'Jammy' Firth, who reported Durrell as 'mentally indolent'. An earlier teacher wrote that he was 'too frivolous' and would become 'a mine of misinformation'.

St Edmund's School, Canterbury. Durrell (bottom, far left) is said to have been more interested in looking at models in glossy magazines than the sports cars that fascinated his contemporaries. The master in the centre is Walter Stephen-Jones who Durrell claimed taught him to box.

G. P. 'Holly' Hollingworth was the teacher at St Edmund's who encouraged Durrell's interest in French and France by passing on to him the literary pages of *Le Monde*.

Richard Aldington was a great influence on Durrell as a young writer. They first exchanged letters in 1933, but did not meet until 1957, when Aldington advised Durrell on places to live in the South of France.

The Queen's Hotel. The Queen's Hotel in London's West Norwood was the model for the decaying Regina Hotel in *The Black Book*. The Durrells moved here in 1930 but Louisa's rumbustuous young family were too much for the other residents, and she moved them to a large house near Bournemouth the following year.

The conservative poet John Gawsworth (here in Egypt in 1944) was someone Durrell thought highly of as a youth, although Dylan Thomas called him 'a boil on the armpit of the nineties . . .'

My Family and Others: the Durrells in Corfu, circa 1937. Larry (standing on the wall) is flanked (from left to right) by Leslie Durrell, Spyros Chalikiopoulos ('Spiro Americanus' in Gerry's *My Family and Other Animals*), Alan Thomas, Louisa Durrell, Nancy Durrell and a friend, possibly Veronica Tester.

The White House, Corfu. This is the house that Durrell and his first wife Nancy rented from a local fisherman in 1935. Durrell later had the upper storey built. Here he entertained his friends, notably Henry Miller, who tells of his visit in *The Collossus of Maroussi*.

Villa Seurat, Paris. Durrell and Nancy first met Henry Miller here in August 1937, when they were staying on the ground floor of this building and Miller was living on the first.

Dylan Thomas. Thomas and Durrell met
in December 1937 when Thomas was on a
visit to the poet Anna Wickham, and
refused to be tempted to visit Durrell in
Greece. In 1939, when he heard that
Durrell had overstayed his planned visit to
London, he wrote asking, 'Has somebody
moved Corfu?'

Tambimuttu, who Durrell referred to as 'a
crazy Tamil', edited *Poetry London*.
Durrell claimed to have discovered him in
a flat off the Tottenham Court Road where
he stored poems for his magazine in an
outsize chamber pot.

David Gascoyne was considered the
handsomest poet of his generation, and
enchanted Anaïs Nin when they first met.
In Paris in 1938, he declared Durrell's *The
Black Book* to have done for England
what Céline had done for France and
Henry Miller for America.

Henry Miller, 1933. Henry Miller was about to publish *Tropic of Cancer*, the book which turned Durrell from the writer of 'romantic' novels into a more self-tortured and morally abandoned author, committed to shocking his reader and overturning existing sexual mores.

Anaïs Nin, 1933. The passionate and adulterous love affair between Anaïs Nin and Henry Miller had somewhat abated when they met Durrell in 1937. Durrell was struck by the sensual dream-like quality of her fiction and declared her 'the first woman writer'.

Durrell edited the magazine *Private Landscape* with Robin Fedden in Egypt during the war. It was Fedden who reported someone saying that when Durrell entered the room, 'it was though someone had uncorked a bottle of vintage champagne'.

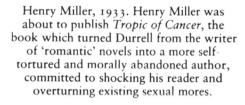

No. 2.1144

MILITARY PASS TO ENTER THE DOCKS ALEXANDRIA

Signature of Holder حامل الوثيقة

Lawrence Durrell

Durrell's official pass for the Alexandria docks, circa 1943. One of his friends in the British Secret Service in wartime Egypt was puzzled as to why Durrell, as Press Attaché, would need such a pass, but it enabled him to meet and interview Noël Coward on a ship anchored in the harbour.

Bernard Spencer was Durrell's close friend and collaborator, with Robin Fedden, on *Personal Landscape*. He was a slow worker, who Durrell found frustrating, while Spencer thought that phrase-makers like Durrell were ambitious to the point of insanity.

(*opposite page*) Eve Cohen Durrell in Turkish peasant costume, 1947. When this was taken, Eve and Larry were living in the Villa Cleobolus, an idylllic cottage inside the grounds of a Turkish cemetary on Rhodes. Durrell once implied that Eve was the model for his enigmatic heroine Justine in *The Alexandria Quartet*.

Return to Pudding Island, 1947. Recently married to Eve and
returned from Rhodes, Durrell relaxes at a picnic organized by his
friend Bernard Burrows. He had just failed to get the post of British
Council Director for the Dodecanese Islands, and was about to
embark on a disastrous year in Argentina.

Reunion in Sommières, 1958. Anaïs Nin visited the Durrells at the
Villa Louis. With her here are Claude Forde (later Durrell),
Claude's two children Diana and Barry, and, on the left, the young
Sappho. Anaïs and Durrell had not met for twenty years. Impressed
by the success of *Justine* she told him they should have eloped when
they first met in Paris in 1937.

Heraldic Universe, but he was also discovering books about Egypt's past, such as E. W. Lane's *Manners and Customs of Modern Egyptians* (1836) and Joseph McPherson's *The Moulids of Egypt* (1941), both of which described religious festivals and practices in the early nineteenth century. In Cairo, too, he found Gerard de Nerval's *Women of Cairo*, from which he learned about child prostitution, Dervishes and Copts, and other matters strange to him. All this reading went to swell the notebook and the mind as *The Book of the Dead* underwent a powerful metamorphosis. Eliot had said it would be far better after his resurrection from the war's ashes.[10]

Personal Landscape largely carried the poetry of civilians like Durrell. Other magazines, like *Orientations*, set up by G. S. Fraser (then working in Cairo for the Forces magazine, *Parade*), catered more for soldier–poets and emphasized more the shared experience of war. In *Orientations* No. 1, Durrell had a short essay, 'A Landmark Gone', extracted from his Corfu book. It was a snapshot of his idyllic life at Kalami, which summed up the impact Greece had had on him, and the cruel loss he felt being exiled from it. Oddly enough, it appears under the name Charles Norden, billed as 'author of the promising first novel, *Panic Spring*' – as if he still wanted to cling on to his romantic *alter ego*. The *Personal Landscape* people considered themselves more polished and cosmopolitan than the amateurs encouraged by the other magazines, and there was little contact between the two groups, except through Fraser and John Waller, a lieutenant in the Royal Army Service Corps.

The *Personal Landscape* editors were all quite different in temperament. Fedden was the languid charmer, with an engaging stammer – an occasional poet rather than a professional like the others. Spencer had a feline character, sleek as a black cat (it was said), and was generally considered the most talented poet among them. He was modest but had a great sense of fun and was widely liked. Durrell, by contrast, was a catalyst, a force, a galvanizing presence.

Some of his new poems, intended for his Faber collection, had fallen into the hands of Tambimuttu, who put them into an anthology he was editing for Faber, *Poetry in Wartime*. Eliot felt he could not now include them in the Faber collection, and Durrell was doubly annoyed to find that Tambi, without permission, had published in *Poetry London* every poem he had left with him in 1939. However, he liked Tambi, and when the 'batty' Ceylonese wrote to say he was broke and practically starving, Durrell forgave him. Perhaps he was soothed by Faber assuring him that they would definitely be bringing out a collection of his poems once he had replaced those which had been lifted. Having got permission to use the diplomatic bag (a sign of status in the Diplomatic Corps) Durrell promptly sent Eliot parcels of his early poems, including his Hamlet soliloquy and 'Uncebunke' cycle, and some from Spencer, whom he believed to be a rare, undiscovered talent.

While Durrell was sometimes frustrated by Spencer's lethargy, Spencer regarded Durrell with friendly scepticism, once saying to him, very shrewdly, that the trouble with phrase-makers like him was that they were ambitious to the point of insanity.[11] Despite his drive and ambition, however, Durrell was finding it difficult to write in Egypt: the climate was exhausting and the war seemed to offer no future.[12]

One of the poems included in Tambi's *Poetry in Wartime* was 'Letter to Seferis the Greek', written in Kalamata. It is a quiet anthem to friendship and to Greece, with a haunting note of impending loss.[13] Durrell's friendship with Seferis was an important one. In May, just before the Greek was transferred to Cape Town, he and Nancy went to dinner with him and his wife Marika. Seferis, suffering from an anti-typhus injection, was slightly delirious, and rambled on about a bizarre character called Ramon Gomez de Serna. This eccentric had once delivered a lecture from the back of an elephant at a Paris circus, and had set up a society for the protection of inanimate objects, once offering a home to a lonely looking lamp-post. These stories seemed to mesmerize Durrell, and the following day he came back and asked to hear more about Ramon. A year later, he produced a poem, 'Mythologies II', which was an ode to what he called 'men of the Marmion class', a celebration of magnificent oddballs, grand failures perhaps, among whom he included the eccentric Ramon and also Katsimbalis, perhaps because by then he had read Miller's *Colossus of Maroussi*, which turned the not very great Greek poet into a legendary giant.

The desert war was hotting up. Theodore Stephanides left for a field hospital near Alexandria. A new German offensive began in May, when Rommel's Afrika Corps attacked Allied forces on a wide front from Gazala to the Mediterranean. Tobruk and Mersa Matruh were taken, and by the 25th the Allies had retreated across the Egyptian border to make a stand at Sidi Barani. The great 'open' cities of Egypt were now directly under threat. By the end of June, Rommel's tanks were at El Alamein, a mere eighty miles from Alexandria, threatening to engulf it. The British fleet withdrew, so precipitating the famous 'Flap', when the Cairo Embassy and British Military HQ burned all their documents, filling the air with smoke and bits of charred paper, and the evacuation of British wives and children was hurriedly organized. The jokers had it that Rommel had already booked the best room at Cairo's Shepheard's Hotel.[14] But not everyone panicked. Durrell claimed that on the day of the Flap the British Ambassador held a huge banquet for foreign ambassadors, as if nothing at all was amiss – a triumph of the stiff upper lip.[15] As to himself, he told Artemis Cooper that on that day, 1 July, he was sent to Alexandria to check on the Press Office (and oversee the burning of papers, presumably). He arrived to find the office shelled and the streets all but deserted. Walking around the city he saw that some traders had put out signs of welcome for the Germans. He coolly noted down their names and later had their shops declared out of bounds to British troops.[16]

Nancy did not join in the first evacuation, and it was some time in July that an Embassy man got her and Penelope a lift to Palestine with a Free French unit.[17] This was the parting of the ways for Durrell and Nancy. One account of their break-up says Nancy found him too possessive,[18] the other is that she confessed to having had an affair, and was furious when he took it so calmly.[19] Whatever the precise circumstances, she must have grown tired of the regular sparring matches they were now said to be giving one another, and it is doubtful if at the time of their departure Durrell knew that he would not be seeing her again, nor seeing his little daughter for a very long time.

The reason for the failure of his first marriage is hinted at by Durrell in letters to his friends – he felt that marriage was constricting to a creative artist. His great inspirer, Miller, had rid himself of his wives and lived as a free spirit. When they met, and for the first two years of their marriage, Nancy was a shy young woman, who was no doubt dominated by her small, dynamic husband. And when the burning ambition to produce an important and serious work, with *The Black Book*, pushed him towards madness, she was the nearest object of his pent-up creative fury. Meeting Nin and Miller in Paris probably gave Nancy the strong feeling that she was an artist and a person in her own right – she came out of her shell, as Miller noted. But that did not quite fit into Durrell's idea of what a wife should be – a bedmate and a support for him in his creative life, tolerating his egocentric behaviour and putting up with his emotional tantrums. There is no doubt that he had the predisposition to be violent to his women, just as he had the talent to sparkle for his friends; the happy joker could quickly turn into the brooding ogre, especially under the influence of drink. Much as he loved his little daughter, she must have represented even more the bourgeois trap into which Lawrence Lucifer dreads being drawn in *The Black Book*. Nancy no doubt found his attitude, and perhaps his increasingly sadistic sexual demands, unbearable, and if he did show indifference to her confessed infidelity that could have been the final straw. With Nancy's departure, that prospect was avoided, but he had to live again with his own terrifying sense of solitude.

Left alone, he moved in with Bernard Spencer, who had a first-floor flat at 27 Sharia Malika Farida, opposite the Mohammed Ali Club, where editorial meetings for *Personal Landscape* now took place, and where the magazine had its mailing address. In the June issue of the magazine, Durrell's contribution was a prose poem, 'Conon in Exile'. Conon, an imaginary Greek philosopher, was also himself, or at least one of his masks. In exile on a Greek island the philosopher meditates on the women he has known, and, as age encroaches, realizes that the dance of love is but a rehearsal for the dance of death – a bitter reflection by Durrell on his own crumbled marriage perhaps.

By 9 July the situation on the western front had stabilized and the panic in Cairo subsided. In the aftermath of this extraordinary crisis, Walter Smart got his 'K' (to use the diplomatic jargon which so amused Durrell), and became Sir Walter Smart, KCMG. When General Montgomery arrived in August and turned the tide of the desert war in October with his great attack at El Alamein, some evacuated wives and children returned. Durrell, however, heard nothing from Nancy, who now saw their marriage as over. He never quite recovered from the loss, if not of Nancy then of his young daughter Penelope. The theme of the lost child was to recur in his later fiction, a mark of how long-lasting the scar was to be.

Durrell, like Spencer, seems to have turned to other women for comfort. The flat became known as the Orgy Flat – the scene of many a wild party. He did not allow the war or his own personal circumstances to get him down and outwardly was as brimming as ever with bonhomie.[20] Fraser captures well the jaunty Durrell (perhaps drinking at Groppi's or the Anglo-Egyptian Union) in his poetic snapshot, 'Monologue for a Cairo Evening':

> Cairo was full of characters. I shall
> Remember Larry stocky against a bar,
> The round face and the tartan scarf, looking
> like a jovial commercial traveller.
>
> Talking like the occasional angel who descends
> By the ladder of alcohol to the banal rocks
> Of the wars we do not start and cannot justify
> But how the psyche cushions all its shocks . . .
>
> Leaving a plot for a story: leaving a shocker
> To sell for sixpence at the chemist's stores,
> Describing six neuroses at six a penny
> Seeing in one labyrinth six minotaurs . . .

Another 'character' who cropped up in Cairo was Gawsworth, who caused Durrell problems by insulting the monarchy (he was a staunch Jacobite) and needing to be vouched for as harmless rather than subversive.

In August, Dr Stephanides found Durrell still in Cairo lodged with Spencer, still working at the Embassy, and still producing *Personal Landscape*. The autumn issue carried an essay on the Heraldic Universe, perhaps his most succinct explanation of an idea which seemed to defy succinctness. It was contrary to logic and causality, he said, which had limits in trying to describe the world. Rather, poetry belonged to the realm of unreason, where ideas were not related causally but by way of a mysterious sympathy. It is a symbolic world, a plane of reality to which man's spirit aspired. Poetry could only explore and treat the unknown obliquely, like holding a smoked glass up to enable us to stare at the sun.[21] This essay revealed the thinking that would shape his future novels as he became more and more intent on giving his fiction the sense of poetry. And, like a poet, he was to create in his fiction an irrational symbolic world where the normal laws of causality do not apply.

Fedden got married in October to a beautiful, enigmatic, Italian–Greek Alexandrian, Renée Catzeflis. There was a great party at the Orgy Flat on 11 November, ostensibly to celebrate a new issue of *Personal Landscape*, but also to toast the marriage in suitably poetic style, and to celebrate Durrell's departure for Alexandria, where he had been appointed press attaché. By now, with the Germans in retreat, the government had moved to winter quarters in Alexandria, and a man on the spot was important for the Foreign Office. To begin with, Durrell took up quarters at the Cecil Hotel, the grand imperial pile where anyone of substance stayed in Alexandria. But soon he moved into a flat with Gwyn Williams, who lectured at the King Farouk University with Robert Liddell and Harold Evans, and settled down to a carefree bachelor lifestyle again.

Durrell had always wanted his own command, and the Alexandria posting was a turning-point in his life. It placed him in close touch with a city and culture which he was to make famous. But this move did not cut him off entirely from his Cairo friends; he would often commute at weekends, travelling by train or by car between the two cities.

However, Alexandria was another epiphanic experience for Durrell, and yet a strange one, because while he hated what he thought of as a broken-down version of Naples he was also in love with it. On the one hand, it was a small, parochial place – the remains of Alexander's city could be walked round in ten minutes – while at the end of the street stood the desert, a great dead hinterland, with the city clinging to the coast by its fingertips. On the other hand, there was the city of his imagination woven from the most exotic strands, especially the highly erotic, sensual atmosphere which Europeans found so seductive about Egypt, with its air of mysticism and intrigue. Alexandria in those days was hardly an Egyptian city, its population mostly Greek, Jewish and British. During the war there was a great influx of other nationalities, mostly refugees from around the Mediterranean, many in the uniforms of the various allies. The rich mixture of cultures and races, and the large numbers of beautiful women in the city, with its air of decadence, produced a heightened sense of sexual freedom even in wartime, when moral standards were in any case some-what relaxed.

But Alexandria struck another chord in Durrell. Its predomin-antly Greek culture not only aroused in him the sensuous poet, but also excited his thirst for ideas, his enduring metaphysical curiosity. If Cavafy was his poetic guide to the sensuous pleasures of Alexandria, F. M. Forster guided him back towards the history of ideas. Forster had been exiled there in the First World War, and his *Guide to Alexandria* was Durrell's introduction to the place. With the aid of these important predecessors and his own accumulated reading, he turned the city into his own Heraldic Universe, which was after all, in his view, the true function of the poet.

What intrigued him was the fact that he found diametrically opposite ideas sitting comfortably side by side, and every version of every religion and metaphysical belief together in one place – the best of Jewish thought, of the early Christians, and of Greek ideas, especially about mathematics. Wine was invented there, as was land measurement, and there were strange African influences – Plotinus, for example, most likely a Nubian. He was fascinated by the idea that European history

– 2,000 years of blood-letting under the banner of religion –
might have been different if the Alexandrian example of tolerance had been followed.[22]

While he could reflect that Cavafy and Rimbaud had walked
the city's streets, the spirit of the place did not draw him into
a holy embrace as Greece had done, but produced a strong
alchemical reaction. What he saw as dross would, through the
ferment of ideas it provoked in him, ultimately be turned into
gold. He would transform this city into one through whose
streets also walked characters such as Justine, Balthazar,
Mountolive and Clea, threading in and out of one another's
lives, characters 'damaged in their sex': comedians, murderers,
grotesques, deceivers, seductresses, wily debauchees and writers
– who make up the cast-list of his *Alexandria Quartet*.

His thinking was now beginning to diverge from Miller's.
He still held to his old beliefs about the role of the artist, about
the Heraldic Universe, and still agreed with Lawrence that the
idea of the unitary personality was unsustainable. Now added
to this was the notion, developed over the past few years, of
the determining influence of landscape on culture, as well as
new ideas about the kind of novel he should write to embody
these thoughts in fictional form. The focus of his writing had
gradually shifted from Athens to Alexandria – love's 'great
wine-press' according to Nessim in *Justine*, and, according to
Durrell, the great hinge where oriental and occidental cultures
met – the ancient source of so much western culture.

He never tried to become a classical scholar, preferring the
demotic form of Greek, and helping, with Robert Liddell,
Bernard Spencer and Terence Tiller, to translate modern Greek
verse into English. It was thanks mostly to their work that
poets such as Cavafy, Seferis, Palamas and Sikelianos are as
well known to English readers as they are. *Personal Landscape*
carried translations of Greek poets, including Seferis' 'King of
Asine' and some by the socialist poet Elie Papadimitriou, whose
republican sentiments he shared at that time.

Durrell's job as what amounted to censor, put him in charge
of some 250 press people, many of whom became his friends
after finding themselves being shaved side by side in barbers'
shops, meeting at cocktail parties, at country houses or on

shooting excursions on Lake Mareotis. He learned a great deal
from them, and this enabled him to create characters such as
Nessim and Narouz in his *Quartet*. And it was a young man
at his office who first introduced him to the Copts, and
intrigued him by announcing that he was leaving to live in a
Coptic monastery out in the desert. His job also gave him
a special vantage-point for viewing the city of Alexander and
Cavafy, a city of clubs and cafés and taverns where prospective
poets sat smoking the long narghiles and drinking Turkish
black coffee.[23]

He was also enjoying himself with the available women in
both Cairo and Alexandria. At parties, Durrell gave the distinct
air of being 'fancy free', and, according to George Lassalle, an
MI5 man and friend of Robin Fedden, 'When an attractive
woman entered the room, he would often leap up like a puppy-
dog and clutch at her breasts ... a frolic everyone involved
found entertaining.'[24] No doubt this direct approach sometimes
paid off; certainly his letters to Miller suggest that in Alexandria he clocked up a considerable number of conquests, many
of them girls from his office – beautiful mixtures of Egyptian,
Coptic, Syrian, Moroccan and Spanish, with eastern looks,
olive complexions and explosive natures.[25] And no doubt he
found, if he had not known before, that his poetic gifts also
conferred a sexual power, the power to spin a seductive web
of words into which to draw some unsuspecting female. It was
a power already there in his poems, but one which achieved its
fullest flowering in his *Alexandria Quartet*. The highly neurotic
atmosphere was partly due, he said, to the fact that Egyptians,
who normally went to Europe for six months of the year,
were bottled up at home. Even old women and scholars were
transformed into votaries of Bacchus.[26]

The ebb and flow of Allied troops through an already culturally mixed society made frequent and fleeting sexual liaisons
commonplace in wartime Alexandria. The bright young English
poets and scholars were not slow to indulge those vices which
the English Death had so successfully stifled in Pudding Island.
Dorian Cooke claimed to have slept with five women in one
day, and Durrell regaled Miller with tales of such wild sexuality
that the American said he could hardly wait to get to Egypt to

taste its delights. However, Durrell warned him, the sole talk of the town was money; even *l'amour* was reduced to a question of lucre.[27]

Despite the physical isolation of Egypt, Durrell was still in contact with the outside literary world. In the New Year he received strange literary missives from Porteus, stationed with the RAF on the Suez Canal, and an airgraph from Tambimuttu asking for an essay on poetry in Cairo for *Poetry London*, and for more poems for another *Poetry in Wartime*. Word also came from Eliot in April 1943 that, having tried in vain to contact him, he and Anne Ridler had assembled his book of poems for spring publication, and had given it the title he wanted, *A Private Country*.

By June he seems to have realized that Nancy would not return, but he still managed, on Ping-Kû's second birthday out of Greece, to write a bitter-sweet poem of yearning for them called 'Echo'.[28] He told Theodore Stephanides and Anne Ridler that he had had no news of them at all. The June *Personal Landscape* carried two of his poems, 'Mythology', which Seferis' stories had inspired, and 'On First Looking into Loeb's Horace', a poem which reflected on the Roman attitude to self. It also had for the first time a poem by Keith Douglas, the dashing soldier–poet, who went to war in a tank with his cavalry regiment much as he might have gone riding to hounds with his local hunt. In August, Durrell met and interviewed Noël Coward in Alexandria on a Middle East tour.

In the autumn Durrell left Williams's place and moved in with Paul and Billie Gotch, who had a large flat in a house in Moharrem Bey, with a tower on top of it. It had a marvelous view over the rooftops of Alexandria to Pompey's Pillar and beyond to Lake Mareotis. The tower was where he worked and entertained – the perfect place, away from his office, to play the poet to friends, or to any girl he could entice up there. It was here that he finished the poems which were to make up his second collection for Faber.

The poetry scene was enlivened at the year's end by a spat provoked by G. S. Fraser, who in the September *Orientations* dared to describe 'Lawrence Durrell's *Personal Landscape*' as isolationist. Durrell then accused Fraser of self-publicity, and after several lively, rather personal exchanges, the editor put an end to this correspondence. A quarrel between two high-flown over-sensitive poets seemed out of place in a magazine mainly devoted to the ordinary soldier and his future. Despite this paper war, Durrell quite admired Fraser as a poet, though he told Fedden he considered him a journalistic desperado.[29]

One of Fraser's implied criticisms of *Personal Landscape* was that Durrell and the others preferred to withdraw from ghastly western civilization into small, mystical utopias dominated by habit and familiarity – Greece, ancient and modern, being for Durrell the epitome of virtuous living. Reviews of *A Private Country* echoed this view. The *TLS* congratulated Durrell on his honest title. His *was* a private country, but, while Greece was a recognizable setting, that of 'Uncebunke' and 'Hamlet' were so private as to be impenetrable.[30] The *Poetry Review* said that 'the seeker after enlightenment can only feel a thicker darkness gather round him as he reads'.[31] But both recognized the power of his imagination and the vigour and inventiveness of his language. His most enthusiastic review came from John Bayliss in *Poetry Quarterly*, who hailed him as 'one of the best poets writing in English today'.[32] Alex Comfort, who reviewed the poems in *Tribune*, wrote to Durrell separately, saying, 'I'd like to add my personal admiration of it as a single work of art.'[33]

Strangely enough, after some eight years as a Faber author, *A Private Country* was the first book which Faber & Faber published under the name Lawrence Durrell. Eliot, who knew as much about Durrell's work and his potential as anyone, was to be his key ally and sponsor in achieving a reputation after the war, though Miller also helped enormously. When Durrell wrote to Eliot in the autumn of 1943 saying that he would be very willing now for Faber to bring out *The Black Book* with those few offending words removed, Eliot was against it. The time was wrong, he said, and people did not want to be reminded of the 1930s. After the success of his poems, readers would be on the lookout for something new from him. *The Black Book* could come out after his reputation had been established.[34] Anne Ridler wrote to him in much the same terms. 'I want to see another big work published first,' she told him, '– that book that has been bottled up inside you all this time.'[35]

That bottled-up book, *The Book of the Dead*, although not being written down, except in note form, was being constantly revised. He now thought that Alexandria, that huge cauldron of intrigue and deceit, that great axis between eastern and western culture, was a far more suitable setting than Athens. And soon he was to discover the final ingredient to add to this rich brew which would eventually give us *The Alexandria Quartet*.

At a party, he met Eve Cohen, a sumptuously beautiful Alexandrian Jewess, both passionate and temperamental, who was to become the model for the character of Justine. She was born in Alexandria, the first child of Tunisian parents, her father a Jew whose family were from Carthage and her mother a Greek from Smyrna of Spanish–Sephardic origins. Her father was an unsuccessful moneylender and she grew up in great poverty. Mr Cohen was tyrannical and possessive and was furious when, on leaving school, she found a job as a typist with a film company. The ructions this created in the family caused her to leave home and find lodgings with her employer. Bored with teenage life in Alexandria, she had withdrawn into herself, yearning for intelligent company. She found it in Durrell, who was immediately attracted by her dark beauty, and gave her his telephone number. At first she was not interested, but in a low moment phoned him. He took her to Pastroudi's, where she found she was with someone who treated her with seriousness and was ready to discuss her ideas with her. Soon they were meeting regularly, and Durrell's curiosity led him to quiz her closely and challenge her most fundamental beliefs.[36] He, in his turn, thought of her as a refugee like him, and one of the few people he had found he could talk to.[37] She met some of his friends, the Gotches and Gwyn Williams, who remembered her as 'a ... stateless journalist'.[38] No doubt Durrell found her some writing work to do.

In the warm afterglow from the good reception of his poems, he wrote to Eliot proposing a book for Faber about Greece. Eliot considered it a good idea, with Greece more in the public eye, but wanted something popular – more Durrellian than Byronic, in which he allowed his own particular viewpoint and style to come through.[39] Exactly what Durrell had in mind is difficult to tell, but he was closely in touch with Greek affairs through the government in exile and through his many contacts with Greeks in Alexandria and Cairo. He corresponded with Compton Mackenzie, the novelist and graecophile, and they agreed that the internal vendetta between left and right among Greeks at that time was a disaster that had to be addressed.

But there was still time for diversions. In November, there began a friendly exchange of rhymed insults between the poets of Cairo and those in Alexandria.[40] There had been no better 'bash-up' since Troy, thought Durrell.

The dawn of 1944 found him in a frustrated and depressed state. He told Alex Comfort that he had written nothing for six months, and informed Gawsworth that he was leaving Curtis Brown. The war seemed unending. It had destroyed his career and left him and so many others feeling eaten up. After the war he said he felt that six years had been torn out of the calendar, and at a critical age for him.[41] He had ended up in the insignificant role of propagandist and censor. As a mere information officer, he thought himself a man of little importance who had merely prostituted himself to the war, and, like Lao Tse, who had withdrawn to his library, he had shelved his ambitions. Then, for eighteen months he had had no news of Nancy or his daughter, who were in Jerusalem; he felt a failure as both a husband and a father.[42]

Shortly into the New Year, he took a holiday in Beirut, where he sat down to reassess his life. This painful process of self-examination resulted in one of his most important poems, 'Cities, Plains and People'. When he said later that his biography was to be found in his poetry, this is the poem he must have had most in mind. And to remind him once again of his roots came news of the death of Big Granny. Dora Durrell had died aged eighty-one. She had not lived quite long enough to see the sun set on the British Raj.

Perhaps to shake himself back into a working mood, he suggested to Tambimuttu, now commissioning and editing books for Nicholson and Watson in London, that he bring out an anthology drawn from *Personal Landscape* – 'an anthology of exile', guaranteed to be better than any other anthology of Middle East writing from any publisher.[43] Tambi liked the idea, and Durrell promptly got the thing organized, dividing responsibility for different sections of the book between himself and the other two editors. He was particularly keen to include translations of the Greek poets they had published – Cavafy, Seferis and Sikelianos.

In a continuing mood of introspection, in the March issue of *Personal Landscape* he had a self-mocking review of his own book, *A Private Country*, and also contributed the first of a string of biographical poems, 'La Rochefoucauld'.[44] In the following issue he had 'Byron',[45] and the minor comic master-piece 'A Ballad of the Good Lord Nelson' – Rabelais raising a satirical eyebrow in salutation to Freud.[46] Humour was, of course, one of Durrell's main defences against depression, but he also learned at about this time what he called 'The Three Minute Egg', a Chinese system of meditation which he now employed whenever events began to get on top of him.[47]

On 6 February, at the Cairo house of Bernard and Ines Burrows, Robin Fedden met the dancer Diana Gould, just arrived with a touring company playing *The Merry Widow*. She fell for the handsome Fedden, who told her about *Personal Landscape* and said that when she was in Alexandria she *must* meet Durrell; he gave her a letter of introduction to him. When the show went there she took up the suggestion and they met at her hotel. Setting off for a tour of the city in a horse-drawn gharry, the horse refused to budge, and Gould got it going by pelting it with chocolates given to her by an eager stage-door johnny.[48] Up in Durrell's tower, he performed his poetry for her; they shared ideas, and found themselves remarkably *en rapport*. He was enchanted by her intelligence and beauty, she by his vivacious personality and bewitching power with words. He had, she thought, a beautiful, even noble, head. Durrell chaperoned her around the city, once with Gwyn Williams driving her around Lake Mareotis, which inspired a poem in him.

They saw quite a lot of one another, even though she realized they looked strange together – she so tall and dark, he so tiny and fair. Eve, however, became furiously jealous of them, and the next time he met Gould he turned up with deep scratches down his cheek. But it was Fedden she had fallen in love with, and Durrell reunited the pair by inviting Robin to Alexandria to deliver a lecture. Almost as soon as the dancer left Egypt with her company for Sicily, Durrell sent her two poems dedicated to her.

By this time he had accumulated enough poetry, he thought, for another collection to send to Eliot. The centre-piece of it was to be 'Cities, Plains and People', also to be the title of the book. Eliot preferred him to publish a prose work first, but was told that the Greek book was simply not progressing. However, he liked the idea of a book just on Corfu, which Durrell proposed instead, and hoped that it would be ready to follow the poems, which were now scheduled for 1945.[49] In fact, Durrell was already at work on *Prospero's Cell*, though he had not yet chosen a title. It was a way for him to return to Corfu to celebrate its landscape and people. He had been reading books on the history of the island and re-reading Miller's *Colossus of Maroussi*.[50] It would serve, like his long autobiographical poem, to take care of 'time past' so that he could anticipate 'time future'.[51]

Reminders of 'time past' kept occurring. In Beirut he met Barclay Hudson, who had first given him *Tropic of Cancer* to read in Corfu, and was now engaged, like him, in propaganda. And Miller, now at Big Sur in California, working on a great new opus, *The Rosy Crucifixion*, wrote to say that Alf Perlès was to marry a certain Anne from Dumfries, and that he and Anaïs had split up.[52] Durrell met Xan Fielding for what Fielding called an 'unforgettable evening' in Cairo, singing through their repertoire of Greek songs together. Fielding had just returned from fighting with guerillas in Crete, where he had been kidnapped by the Gestapo before making a daring escape.[53] In Cairo, too, he met Lord Patrick Kinross, an RAF hero and now director of the Publicity Section at the Embassy, and Paddy Leigh Fermor, also back from guerrilla fighting in Crete. Fermor – both mad and Irish according to Durrell[54] – had actually captured a German general and smuggled him out of Crete to

Egypt. Later, Durrell was to embody something of these heroic friends in the characters of the guilt-ridden Captain John Baird in his Cretan mystery *Cefalû*, and of his James Bondish spy hero Methuen in his Cold War thriller *White Eagles over Serbia*, set in Tito's Yugoslavia. Another soldier he knew, Keith Douglas, is probably glimpsed in his soldier–writer John Keats in the *Quartet*. Spies and soldiers, as well as diplomats, were to people the pages of his fiction from this time on, and crop up again and again in the intricate tales of espionage, intrigue and deceit of which he became a master.

On one level he found the atmosphere of promiscuity and decadence profoundly boring, on another it supplied him with the material which he was to weave into his Egyptian novel. He saw love and death as the opposite sides of the same coin, and death in Alexandria as something Proustian and unhurried; dissolution by way of drugs or pederasty. But the superb and uncared-for women of the city were available in profusion; there was nothing more beautiful nor more vacant, and their vacuity was like the touch of love, like having sex with a void, though the act of love with them was like a savage razor-fight. He urged Miller to visit Alexandria when the war was over, there to rid himself of earthly concerns and prepare himself suitably for his Tibetan pilgrimage.[55] And yet there *were* Alexandrian woman who could inspire him. Eve was one, another was Clea Baduro, a blonde Greek painter, whose studio he would visit, and who became the initial model for the Clea in *The Alexandria Quartet*.

Durrell was still smitten with the beautiful Diana Gould, now with the *Merry Widow* company entertaining the troops in Naples. One of the two poems he dedicated to her, 'Mareotis', was Egyptian, an exquisite poem of place shot through with nostalgia. The other poem, 'Delos', is about Greece and the islands. He included both of these in the *Personal Landscape* anthology for Tambimuttu, and added three of Gould's clerihews. Theirs was to be an extraordinarily honest friendship conducted through a lifelong exchange of passionately frank letters. Durrell probably never had a more straightforward and perceptive critic of his work. From Egypt, after hearing that Fedden had not written to her, he wrote to her proposing marriage, but it was not in the stars, and she wrote back sweetly to him saying how touched she was.[56]

Durrell's mood of pessimism was not helped by a letter from Miller announcing that he had seventeen books due out in America – mostly reprints of early work for which Laughlin had US rights. But Miller was broke, as usual, and sent around a letter inviting someone to sponsor him at $50 a week. Durrell replied from the depth of a self-proclaimed limbo, in which everyone, he felt, had expired or was expiring.[57] Anaïs had published *Under a Glass Bell* and 400 had sold in a week after a good review by Edmund Wilson in the *New Yorker*. Miller was donating half of his income to her to help her bring out the diary. His tail was up and he talked brightly about reunions of all the Villa Seurat regulars after the war.[58] The past five years had not diminished their friendship nor Durrell's admiration for him.

Eve Cohen had come to play more and more of a part in Larry's life. She was different from the other women he chased – not only beautiful, but passionately uninhibited and able to talk to him in detail about the dark underside of Alexandrian life. He drank in greedily her tales of drugs, female circumcision, sex among the Arabs, sadism and murder. For her it was probably therapy, for him it was rich material for his *Book of the Dead*. With no word from Nancy (touched by old-fashioned English guilt, he thought) the passionate Eve was a tonic. To retire to a Greek island with 'Gypsy' Cohen now became a dream of the future – a sexual relation which was also a non-possessive friendship seemed to him the idyllic prospect. The means to write, a shady tree, a girl to fuck and some bosom pals was all he asked.[59] One day in May he took Eve through the battlefields of the western desert, through Bourg El Arab, to a beach on the coast where they bathed naked in the warm Mediterranean, against a background of sand dunes and the scattered debris of war. It was the experience he later gave to Darley and Clea in the last volume of *The Alexandria Quartet*.

By August he had managed to secure a tentative posting to a Greek island after the war.[60] The dream of the shady tree, the typewriter and the woman seemed just a little closer to fulfilment. He badly needed to escape from the deathly atmosphere of Alexandria, but to take with him everything he had learned. He was bursting to write and was anticipating his new creative life with delight. The *Personal Landscape* anthology was in preparation, *Cities, Plains and People* was due out in the spring, and *Prospero's Cell* was finished. The latter he saw as an attempt to recapture the flavour of words. He was also heavily pregnant with the idea for his Alexandrian novel, but felt he could not get down to it until he was free. In the meantime he thought he might write an anatomy of Anglo-Saxon taboos – perhaps pondering something humorous about English diplomats and *their* comical taboos. Miller, meantime, reported having met a twenty-one-year-old Polish girl (Lepska) in New York whom he was taking back to Big Sur as his wife.

One person Durrell did not get on very well with in Egypt was Reggie Smith, the large affable British Council man and the model for Guy Pringle in his wife Olivia Manning's *Balkan Trilogy*. Reggie and Olivia dubbed Durrell 'the magician'.[61] Reggie was not very keen on Durrell's poetry, which may have irritated him, and Olivia, whom Durrell depicted cruelly as a beaky bird of prey, wrote a piece for *Horizon* about exiled poets in Egypt which aroused Durrell's wrath. She was just determined to be in the swim, he sneered. He was no doubt also incensed by her saying of Bernard Spencer's poems, 'Unlike Lawrence Durrell's work, they never pretend to be more than they are . . .'[62] He had his own account of exiled poets, 'Airgraph on Refugee Poets in Africa', in the December special number of *Poetry London*, in which he focused generously on George Seferis and Eli Papadimitriou.[63] Fraser's *Orientations* article on Cairo poetry which had so annoyed Durrell was also included. Tambi added a postscript to it defending *Personal Landscape* as standing for 'the circular ciné-view which is inclusive'.[64] Perhaps out of gratitude, Durrell offered him the English rights of *The Black Book*. More cheering was a letter in October from Anne Ridler, who had read Durrell's new collection of poetry in manuscript and had been much struck by it. It was as impressive as ever, and more of a piece. Eliot had asked her to arrange them for publication.[65]

British troops had landed in Greece on 14 October, but civil war was brewing there and the country was in ruins following the German withdrawal. Seferis returned to Athens. News came from Europe that Keith Douglas had been killed three days after the Normandy landings. Another epoch seemed to be drawing to a close.

With *Prospero's Cell* finished, Durrell began a novel which had been incubating over the past years, about a group of people who get lost in a Cretan labyrinth (or 'lost in the womb', he told Miller), eventually published as *Cefalû* (later *The Dark Labyrinth*). It was, he confessed, something of a potboiler, a novel of action meant as a correction to the overwriting to which he was prone, to rid him of writer's cramp and loosen him up for the major work ahead. On top of that he had written something more challenging, part of a book about twins, turning on the Oedipus question – no doubt that part of his *Alexandria Quartet* dealing with Narouz and Nessim. The twin-self he found in Freud he replaced in his later fiction by something even more fluid and unstable. And another psychologist was soon to engage his mind. In September he told Miller he was deep into Georg Groddeck's *Book of the It*. A few weeks later he sent a copy to Miller. It was far superior to Howe or Rank, he thought, and the very man he and Miller had been seeking at the Villa Seurat. He made no distinction, as Freud did, between the conscious and unconscious. It was Freud used organically rather than mechanically, and the first western scientific statement of the Taoist belief in the identity of opposites. The 'It' is what man is lived by; illness is a disposition of the It, illnesses are chosen by the It. Durrell believed that it chimed exactly with his own experience. He had discovered psychosomatic medicine.

The prospect for peace was now real. In February 1945, Durrell was put down to work for the Overseas Information Service as director of public relations on the Aegean island of Rhodes, in the Dodecanese. Until liberated, it had been under Italian occupation, and once peace treaties were signed it was to be taken over by Greece. Spirits rose when he heard from Miller that Obelisk Press books were on sale in Paris shops, and soldiers were madly buying them up. Kahane's son Maurice was now in charge of the firm, and there might be royalties. Miller's own books were selling well in America (over 10,000 copies of *Tropic of Cancer* alone), and he had sold 300 paintings in 1944. At Big Sur, he was living in a cabin costing ten dollars a month, married to his twenty-one-year-old Pole with a baby expected. He could see the sun rise over the mountains from his door; the surrounding nature was enchanting.[66]

Durrell told Miller that he had taken a month's leave to write *Cefalû*, and that Gypsy Cohen had gone along too to help preserve him. Although apparently a thriller, it was a morality at heart, and his characters (everyday English tourists lost in the Cretan labyrinth just as the Minotaur threatens to return) would stand for Virtues and Vices, like Sinfulness, Self-deception, the Righteous Life and so on. Some perish underground; others emerge into the sunlight.

Two of the characters find Shangri-la, the land of visions where the imagination rules. It is a familiar Durrell message, the same message discovered by Lawrence Lucifer after finding his way through the more convoluted psychological labyrinth of *The Black Book*, to the idyllic Greek island with its healing spirit of place.

The new *Book of the Dead*, Durrell declared in late February, was about incest in Alexandria and he had already written twenty pages. He thought it would take a year to write, and it was unlikely to be publishable in England. He had stumbled across a strange group of cabbalists living around the Mediterranean, pre-Christian masters, who were trying to achieve consciousness of the essential symbol, not according to any rational scheme, but through a Pythagorean system which, among other things, made clear the significance of the Tarot. A Mr Baltazian, a banker on a small scale, was the local man who had access to this coterie, and all of this was going into his *Book of the Dead*.[67] It was probably through Baltazian that he learned of the Syrian Gnostics, of which a few adepts also remained. He became so fascinated by this form of early Christianity that he came to consider himself part of a select group who were privy to its secrets, and read its widely dispersed texts – the Hermetica, Poemandres and the pre-Socratics.[68] The idea of heresy and turning the conventional ethical system on its head gave a philosophical gloss to his own subversive notions. Gnostic ideas were to inform his Alexandrian novels, the non-deterministic, fleeting method being partly suggested by the scattered fragmentary nature of the Gnostic texts, and to become the wider historical background to his *Avignon Quintet*.

Miller and Durrell continued exchanging manuscripts and books. Durrell sent the complete file of *Personal Landscape* and a novel by a young Syrian writer, Albert Cossery, which Miller sent on to Maurice Kahane (now Girodias) in Paris. The news from France was that his pre-war literary heroes, Céline and Giono, were in deep trouble for collaborating. The news from England was mixed. Margo had had a son, and Diana Gould was depressed, having been given twenty-eight days to find a job or be sent to work in a factory. And Eliot had just discovered that eleven of Durrell's twenty-two poems intended for his new collection were to be published in the *Personal Landscape* anthology, ruling them out of *Cities, Plains and People*, already in galley-proofs, which would have to be postponed and he would have to come up with eleven new poems. Eliot also wrote separately to turn down *Cefalû*. It was more Durrell than Norden, but as Durrell it was not good enough, he said. He recommended that he either do a serious work or one which was low-brow but intelligent. Undeterred by this rejection Durrell sent the novel to Tambimuttu.

Eliot had ended by asking him whether he wanted to be primarily a poet or a prose writer.[69] The answer to Eliot's question seems to have been that his poetry phase in Egypt was over and that he was now planning something truly ambitious. He sent Eliot ten poems to replace the ones in the anthology, plus a three-fold outline of his grand design. Apart from some shifting of titles, it was much like one he had sketched out to Miller before the war. The first part was an agon, about dislocation – *The Black Book*. The second part was a pathos, about union – his *Book of the Dead*. The third part was to be an anagnorisis, about the acceptance of death, to be called *The Book of Time*. At the end of his life, Durrell was to claim to have worked through this scheme exactly according to plan.

Eve had become very much a part of his life, and the prospect of Rhodes without Gypsy Cohen suddenly seemed less than exciting. He had arranged to take her along as his secretary, but she was a stateless person and her father had an arranged marriage in mind for her. Gwyn Williams was recruited to help:

> Larry's divorce from Nancy had not then come through but he decided to loosen Eve from her family ties . . . Eve was to pretend to visit Cairo on journalistic work but was to get off the train at the suburban station Sidi Gabr, only a few miles from the city centre. I was to be waiting outside the station in my car. The plan worked. Eve crossed to my car and I drove at once to my villa on the Rue Sirdar. There she hid for three days until the hue and cry for her died down and Larry brought a taxi to take her to his flat in Moharrem Bey.[70]

The last number of *Personal Landscape* appeared in May to coincide with the end of the European war. It contained Durrell's 'Conon in Alexandria', some Cavafy translations by Amy Nimr, and a sad obituary to Keith Douglas, its only soldier-contributor, and perhaps the best English Second World War poet. It was a fitting tribute to three years' hectic creativity, and marked the impending breakup of that little group who had made it possible. The dispersal of friends was another recurrent theme in Durrell's fiction and poetry. 'Alexandria', a poem written a year later, is a nostalgic celebration of sleepless ghosts of friendships forged in the heat of war and of Egypt.[71]

Not long after the anthology appeared, Durrell set off for ten days to Rhodes. His journey across the Mediterranean to the island in an HDML (Heavy Duty Motor Launch) forms the opening chapter of the book he later wrote about Rhodes, *Reflections on a Marine Venus*. The island still bore the weight of the aftermath of war – demolished tanks, barbed wire, abandoned arms and general shortages, especially of food. He quickly reconnoitred the place, found himself an office in the headquarters of the erstwhile Italian Governor of the island, and surveyed his kingdom – his staff and the printing press from which he was to oversee the printing of newspapers in Greek, Turkish and Italian, as well as English. Once he had sized up the situation, he could return to Alexandria for Eve.

CHAPTER 8

Return to Greece:
Reflections on a Marine
Venus (1945–1947)

'Ah, yes,' roared Katsimbalis, 'that would
be Larry. Always wanting to be king of the
islands!'

John Waller, 'Athens in Spring', 1947

When Durrell returned from his ten days in Rhodes he was
still not sure that he would be posted there. But if he had the
slightest of qualms about going, it was not because of the mess
made by the war, but because of the mess made by the Italian
'restoration' of the island – architecture on the grand, ornate
scale and the countryside disfigured by craftily contrived hide-
aways and walled gardens swamped with bougainvillaea. He
comforted himself with the thought that, once the Greeks took
it over, all this picturesque orderliness would be reduced to
something far more basic and chaotic. As for himself, he felt
dissatisfied because he had his Egyptian book inside him
wanting to be written and yet he felt still locked into a military
system of uniforms and procedures. If one epoch was over, the
new one seemed somewhat unwilling to dawn.[1]

By the end of July 1945 his Rhodes job was confirmed; he
would be attached to the army, who were the ruling authority
on the island. Taking Eve along proved to be more of a problem
than he had anticipated, because she had no papers, but in his
usual clever way he wove a path between the army, the Embassy
and the Egyptians, and smuggled her on to a Norwegian tanker
in Alexandria harbour. After an eleventh-hour fright when a

policeman tried to obstruct them, they set sail, leaving Egypt and, for Durrell, three years of exile behind. When they arrived on Rhodes they set themselves up in a luxury hotel, Albergo della Rosa, on the beach there. They went swimming at six every morning, but, because the food was poor, lived mainly on fruit. It was an idyllic life; the only thing to mar the scene for Durrell was the military, whose ways he considered both crude and phoney.[2]

After Egypt, which he had found so stifling, Rhodes was a fresh-air paradise. His change of mood on being back among the mostly Greek population only went to confirm his theory about the spirit of place – how climate and country affect personality. He was always in his element in Greece, almost always out of it elsewhere. But although he was glad to be free of Egypt, he felt a strong sense of nostalgia when the *Personal Landscape* anthology was published in June. It was given a sympathetic reception, though ironically, considering its elitist stance, the *TLS* said of it: 'There is an appeal to the common reader, though the collection emphasizes the rarity of lyrical poetry in these overcast years.'[3] The anthology seemed to sum up his war, he said. On the other hand his peace would not begin very peacefully. Nancy wished to divorce him and marry someone she had met in Palestine. He told Eliot that his first priority now was to raise enough money to pay for this. He had received a £200 advance on *Prospero's Cell*, but half had gone in tax; now he had sold his labyrinth book to Tambimuttu. George Leite was trying to publish *The Black Book* in America, with a foreword by Miller, but could not raise the money. As for *The Book of the Dead*, the boredom of his present job prevented him getting down to it. However, he had discovered a library with a huge amount of material for a possible book on Rhodes, along the lines of *Prospero's Cell*, if Eliot was interested.[4]

In his new position as director of information, Durrell set out to inspect the island in more detail. He commandeered a large German staff car, and took Eve to visit the ancient cities of Lindos, Cameirus and Ialysos, meantime keeping an eye open for a suitable house in which to settle. The sight of Cameirus Castello struck him in particular, standing high on a bluff

overlooking the sea with a vast emptiness below, like the scene
in *Cefalû* – a high cliff and a dizzying drop into nothingness.
Perhaps that is how he saw his future. He needed to plunge
off into freedom and risk landing safely below, but still clung
to the cliff-top unable to make the leap.

   In letters to friends describing his new island, he wrote passages of such lyrical rapture that they give the impression of
being sketches for his projected book. Eliot liked the idea, but
thought he needed to live there longer, as he had on Corfu, to
be sure he was not just reacting to the island with the values
of a Baedecker – like the tripper who hides inside us all. Perhaps
aware that in *Prospero's Cell* he seemed unsure whether he
was a poet or a prose writer Eliot again asked Durrell which
of the two he was. He thought he should choose, adding that
he believed that twenty years hence he would be one but not
the other.[5]

   In the eyes of some of his most ardent admirers, Durrell's
island books are his best achievement. They are, of course,
more accessible than much of his poetry and his more complex
fictions, though he weaves poetry and ideas into them with the
same smooth dexterity. While *Prospero's Cell* was based on
real experiences it was fundamentally a work of the imagination, and the method used was that which he had recommended
to Theodore Stephanides – the French anecdotal method
interlaced with history, folklore and flora and fauna, using
imaginary characters as need be.

   The influence of D. H. Lawrence and Norman Douglas is
probably more evident than he would like to have admitted,
especially in its feeling for landscape, awareness of colour, of
light and shade, of historical resonance and the spirit of place.
Add to this the camera eye for detail, the novelist's grasp of
character, and the poet's subtle alchemy with words, and you
get Durrell's own sublime literary cocktail. By this method he
transformed the island into something all his own, each of the
seven main chapters another part of the whole tapestry woven
from numerous threads – experience, reading, folktales, poetry,
an acute sense of history, and a love for Greece and its people.
It was not just Corfu but Corcyria, and not just any Greek
island but Prospero's Isle in *The Tempest*. In that mood of

invention, few writers could capture so enchantingly the spirit of an island festival or the wicked black humour of the phallic puppet-figure Karaghiosis, or the carousing disquisitions at the Partridge with Zarian and company. The invented diary, suggesting that of an observant naturalist, was used to great effect, evoking the beauty of the island and the hedonistic life he and Nancy had lived there before the war. A fascination with form (and the use of the notebook, diary and letter) was, of course, one of the hallmarks of his work from the earliest days of his fiction writing. It is clear that Durrell was now writing with a new authority; as a stylist he had reached his maturity. The novelist in him was only awaiting the right opportunity to demonstrate his virtuosity at full stretch.

When the book appeared in England in October, it was prominently reviewed. G. W. Stonier in the *New Statesman* loved 'the charmed circle' which the island became in the book, a poet's timeless world broken into only when time and reality in the form of war impinge at the end. He had two reservations – Durrell presented Greece as a place in which to discover yourself, yet in this book we do not discover Durrell, and the 'sensitive description' is perhaps too consciously sensitive.[6] This apparent concealment of the self was to be noted by others.

However, one of the poems added to *Cities, Plains and People*, 'Eight Aspects of Melissa', was important from a biographical point of view. The image at the outset of the poem gives a clue to Durrell's developing view of personality as many-faceted. It is the image as a broken prism, so not just one broken image but a broken broken image. The subject of the poem, Melissa, who was Eve, he told George Leite,[7] is perhaps a preview of Melissa, the cabaret dancer and lover of Darley in *The Alexandria Quartet*, and also a view of Justine, the nymphomaniac intriguer, who can be seen as the dark side of the same coin. Darley's relationship with Melissa, a compliant Earth Mother and occasional prostitute, was one of pure but innocent sex, with Justine it was one of callous deception.

As he relaxed into his job on Rhodes, and felt more expansive, he told friends he felt all but governor of the twelve Dodecanese islands. He had a roomy office in a lovely medieval building covered with bougainvillaea, only occasionally disturbed by screams from a nearby hospital psychiatric ward. He had a local staff of 'characters' whom he was to immortalize in his book about Rhodes. He was responsible for censoring two daily newspapers, one Greek, one Italian, and a weekly Turkish one, and also had to deal with visiting pressmen. Enosis would occur after a peace conference when the British military would hand over the Dodecanese to the Greeks. But with civil war erupting in Greece and the British taking sides, the situation required delicate handling from the information officer.

His position carried a certain amount of kudos and authority and, anxious to avoid scandal, he and Eve lived separately in the hotel. Officially she was his secretary on a renewable three-monthly resident's permit. Durrell did some of the writing in both Greek and French, which he enjoyed, and she helped with proofreading and censoring. And when the presses were not busy he printed other material – translations of Seferis and Sikelianos, and Cavafy's love poems, and a small edition of 'Zero' and 'Asylum in the Snow' which he distributed to friends. The British community in Rhodes, mostly old Africa hands, were used to bossing servants around and displayed appalling attitudes towards the locals. Durrell scorned them as the poorest, dullest types to whom the Rhodean fisherman was distinctly superior. Even the Brigadier in charge was out of a comic opera.[8] This was the man who, according to Durrell, decided to test whether this 'writer fellow' (Durrell) was made of the right stuff by asking him what he thought of village cricket. When he said he loved it the Brig knew he had the right kind of fibre, and he was accepted.[9] The name of the army General in command in Greece was Scobie. Perhaps in giving his secret transvestite in *The Alexandria Quartet* the same name Durrell was striking an anarchic blow at the mindless military establishment he was forced to serve on Rhodes.

Now he could no longer exist in a private country, and found it torture having to contend with wider world events. It seemed, after all, that his job would last only a few months and he would have to move on. He also believed that within five years there would be an atomic war, so that time was running out.

For the moment, he could not write poems – something, he thought, to do with the change of scenery.[10]

When Romilly Summers, a friend from Cairo, turned up, Durrell and Eve took him on weekend tours of the island in their big German car, exploring every inch of the coast, and looking over the ancient sites. It was an archaeologist's paradise, the Germans having dug holes all over the place laying bare sites and relics from the ancient past. Later came Paddy Leigh Fermor, Xan Fielding and the painter John Craxton, drawn by Durrell's wholehearted conviviality and good humour. Despite these new pleasures, a Greek island and congenial friendships, he found that he missed the companionship of the procession of poets, desperadoes and undercover agents passing through wartime Egypt. And there were those ghastly vulgar Africa hands, who made him ashamed to be British, even if at arm's length. Nonetheless, for him Rhodes was greatly preferable to England, from where Gwyn Williams had written excitedly about the new Labour government and his hope for a better future, and Diana Gould had written gloomily about the prospect of living under a people's government.

They spent Christmas on one of the small surrounding islands. Patmos, which struck Durrell by its whiteness – white rocks and white buildings – was a haunted island. On it stood the Church of the Apocalypse built over the cleft rock into which St John is said to have placed his hand. They stayed at the nearby battlemented monastery as a guest of Father Porphirius and the other monks, and were to become regular visitors whenever Durrell could spare the time and find a caique to get them there.

Tambimuttu sent news from London of a reunion of old Egypt hands – Ruth Speirs, Bernard Spencer and Gwyn Williams. And he also heard from Gerald, still writing poetry, but now working as a student keeper at Whipsnade Zoo, well on his way to fulfilling his ambition to work with animals. Both Gerry and Leslie loathed post-war England, and Larry was not very keen to return there without an income of a thousand a year, he told Robin Fedden. The literary scene in England sounded dreadful – all apocalyptics and 'sweaty

Christians', or literary aristocrats, like the Sitwell brothers, who produced nothing but 'gentry-art'[11].

The situation in Greece was still dire. Durrell's old republican cronies were selling out on their principles, he thought, and, encouraged by the British, were supporting the return of the monarchy.[12] He was not impressed with the King, and felt glad that after all he had not lost a limb during the war for this man who now seemed to him a grotesque figure of fun.[13]

He got away in the New Year to Athens, where he met Patrick Reilly, the British Ambassador, and Stephen Runciman, who ran the British Council there, and some of those working with him, including Maurice Cardiff, Rex Warner and his old friend Wallace Southam. Paddy Leigh Fermor was also there (deputy to Runciman), as were two other old Cairo friends, John Waller and Osbert Lancaster (press attaché at the Embassy). With such well-placed friends, there was, he thought, a good chance of a job there once his Rhodes commission ended. He walked through familiar streets around the Plaka with Seferis and Katsimbalis, through a sad crowded Athens of homeless ill-fed people, and found Sikelianos starving. Katsimbalis, oddly enough, had been saved from starvation thanks to his new-found fame in Miller's Greek book. When Wallace Southam discovered that he was the 'Colossus of Maroussi', he employed him to give talks for the British Council and he become even more famous than before. Despite the grim situation there, Durrell found a gaiety and an intellectual hunger which astonished him, but also a sense of murder in the air under the shadow of civil war.

Just past his thirty-fourth birthday, Durrell decided after all to marry Eve. It would certainly solve the problem of her being stateless, a situation which he blamed on the Egyptians.

His duties included entertaining visiting journalists. One who came for a story was Stanley Maxted from the Forces' magazine *Parade*, and with him came a young photographer, Mary Mollo. She had read *The Black Book* in London at the suggestion of Julian Symons, and was expecting to find someone very superior when she met Durrell, but she had not anticipated the magnetic charm which immediately switched on when he met a pretty woman, and she was instantly enchanted. When she told him she had read his work it was his turn to be delighted. He admired very much her new camera, a Rolliflex, and she was later to make him a present of one.[14]

Durrell took Mollo, Maxted and Eve on a tour of the islands in a caique, interpreting for them as they went, and stopping off to bathe every so often, in spite of the cold water. It was evident to Mollo that Durrell was in his element speaking Greek and also in his element at sea in the caique. Back in Rhodes, Mollo was surprised and delighted when he casually threw a manuscript at her, saying, 'You can keep that; I'm through with it.' It was the manuscript of his *Cefalû*, soon to be published by Tambimuttu.[15] Durrell had a low opinion of this book – piddling his talent away, he considered it – but talked a lot about his *Book of the Dead* and urged Mollo to read Groddeck's *Book of the It*. He never read entirely out of intellectual curiosity, but was always searching for a key, some psychological or metaphysical system to replace the Christianity he had ditched as a youth.

Cities, Plains and People, published in April 1946, received a generally complimentary press. Hugh Gordon Porteus compared him to Joyce and Eliot in his powers of invention and the haunting intensity of his lines, and commended him for failing to attach himself to any movement or clique. His verse, he thought, was occasionally imperfect but always exhilarating.[16]

The settling-in process in Rhodes was completed when his books and manuscripts finally arrived via Athens, some retrieved from where he had left them in Kalamata in 1942. (Gerald found out later that the Germans had used some manuscript papers to light fires.) At the same time, in a graveyard at a Turkish mosque, he discovered a tiny house which could be rented cheaply; they would move in when the present tenant departed. But his writing got going in fits and starts. He had begun and immediately abandoned a play, but it was on his main opus that he was mostly reflecting. He told Eliot that he hated the new 'urbane' style which had crept into British writing, typified by the *Manchester Guardian* vilifying Miller, and he hated the God-obsessed poetry of the young. Sex, he thought, was the only subject worth writing about. He wanted to write a novel about sex in the Levant – its lustful and uninhibited nature – a world where Eros was everything. If he wrote it in French there would probably be no problem, but in writing it in English he would probably be crushed.[17] While bursting with ideas, he still could not get down to the big novel, feeling confused and in shock still from the war years, as if trying to write while tied up.

In June, his dream of a job in Greece came a little closer. Sir Patrick Reilly, the Ambassador, wrote to the Foreign Office, recommending a full-time salaried consul for the Dodecanese. He went on to recommend also that a British Council representative be appointed for the islands, and added: 'There is a good candidate available on the spot in Mr Lawrence Durrell, the present Director of Information. He is intelligent, full of ideas, speaks Greek admirably and French well and knows Greece and the Greeks well and wants to remain in the islands.'[18] Stephen Runciman also added his support.

Durrell was distressed by the state of famine in Greece and worried that he and Miller with their books about the country had produced a cult-following which would not be good for it in the long run.[19] The Cultural Affairs man at the FO, not having heard of Durrell, decided that he must return to London for an interview if he wanted the post. Durrell replied that he could not afford to make the trip, but with the approaching Enosis was eager to transfer from the Ministry of Information to the British Council. Reilly again wrote, strongly recommending him, so he was disappointed when the Foreign Office refused his request for bag facilities, something which would have enabled him to communicate more speedily with the rest of the world, and would have been a mark of status.

The proofs of *Cefalû* were sent off, and he plunged back into official duties. Celebrations of the island's independence from Italy and impending cession to Greece brought scores of foreign journalists to Rhodes, and he was forced to deal with their political questions, which to him were profoundly boring. In spite of his distaste for the colonials from Africa who had moved into Rhodes with the army, he had *some* British friends there, and these feature in *Reflections on a Marine Venus*.

There was the Scottish doctor, Ray Mills, senior medical officer at the Thermi Hospital in Rhodes, and the sedentary civil servant with a dicky heart, Hoyle (Edward Hoyland, later Consul General in Rhodes), and there was the (probably fictitious) soldier, the monocled Captain Gideon, who set his own private course through army life by inserting into Movement Orders the names of the places *he* wanted to visit. These three plus Durrell and a man called Sand set off, like five men on the bummel, to explore the island with Eve and Mills's wife in tow. And, if Durrell's book is to be believed, they had gentle English-style adventures along the way – a little wine, encounters with strange Greeks, amusing conversations, and sing-songs. Jerome K. Jerome could not have arranged things better. Durrell was especially *en rapport* with Mills, partly because of his fascination with medicine, but also because they shared an interest in peasant cures. They visited the lost cities on Rhodes, picking their way among the barbed wire and unexploded mines, went swimming, even in the coldest weather, and once had to rescue around 800 Jewish refugees, some of them injured, who had been shipwrecked, *en route* to Palestine, on a nearby island.[20]

In September, he returned briefly to Cairo, but soon came back to begin worrying again about his future, and feeling almost paralysed by the possibility of an atomic war.[21] Worries evaporated a little when finally they moved into the little house in the Turkish cemetery, the Villa Cleobolus – studio, bedroom, bathroom and kitchen. There were trees arching over it and a profusion of oleander around the graveyard gate. There was a shady sycamore tree to eat out under, and there the local Mufti came every morning, attracted by Eve's very good Turkish coffee. The peace and quiet of the little villa was in such contrast to hotel living, Durrell said, that his life had begun to recapture some of its old vivid glow.[22]

At the end of the summer, Xan Fielding, Paddy Leigh Fermor and Joan Eyres-Monsell, whom they christened the Corn Goddess, and whom Leigh Fermor later married, came for a week. Leigh Fermor and Fielding were both planning books, and conversation roamed not just over the adventurous past and the delights of Greek cuisine, but over literature and the sticky business of getting into print. They stayed up all night in the graveyard reading poetry and talking books, books, books, and Durrell had a small volume of Fielding's poems published on his presses. They visited the lost city of Camirus, exploring the bat-infested maze of underground water-conduits, and Durrell later dedicated a poem to his two friends. But they found him stuck in a job he disliked, uncertain about getting the one he wanted, and unfulfilled because he lacked the freedom to write at full throttle. At one point he said to Fielding, 'I'm dissatisfied with myself, and worried, but I don't want to commit suicide just yet.'[23]

The happy move to the Villa Cleobolus with its company of silent turbanned monoliths, and the coming of his friends in the late summer, seemed to have the effect of arousing his slumbering Muse, and by October he had a new collection of poems for Eliot.[24] These included some about islands, such as 'Patmos', and on Rhodean characters, including 'Manoli of Cos' and 'Dmitri of Carpathos'. But there were others which he had accumulated over the past months when inspiration struck through the melancholy, as in his delicately shaded and sensuous 'In the Garden: Villa Cleobolus', and the poem on 'The Lost Cities' dedicated to Leigh Fermor and Fielding. He wrote a five-stanza verse to commemorate the closing of the French brothels. This sad dirge to a paradise lost was dedicated, appropriately, to Henry Miller and George Katsimbalis. Durrell and Miller both blamed the puritanical socialist government in France, which also introduced stronger censorship, so that passages had been cut from the recent Obelisk edition of *Capricorn*.

When John Craxton visited, he found that Durrell was still painting his gouaches – something he had kept up in Egypt. With his sharp eye for detail and a strong awareness of tones and shades of colour, developed originally alongside Nancy, his poems were often verbal paintings, and his paintings were often visual poems. Painting would become more important to him later on, but was never more than a relaxation, and probably, along with poems and plays, an excuse to put off the plunge into the great fictional brew which was simmering inside

him. He wrote a lot about needing to clear the decks and
having the freedom to write the great opus, probably because
he remembered what writing *The Black Book* had taken out
of him, and how close to madness he had come. He would
need to break free from the orthodoxy and propriety of his job
if he was to dive into the maelstrom of creativity which lay
ahead.

The last of his books arrived, including signed first editions
of Miller's early trio, *Tropic of Cancer, Black Spring* and
Tropic of Capricorn. This prompted him to read them again
and to contemplate writing a full-length essay on Miller, an
extension of the short piece written for *The Happy Rock*, an
anthology of essays celebrating the American. Miller himself
had abandoned his gypsy life and was about to buy a
house at Big Sur, Girodias having finally paid him royalties of
$4,000. *Capricorn* alone had now sold 54,000 copies, but
there were hints of future trouble – Girodias and the French
publishers Gallimard and Denoël were to be tried for publishing French versions of his books. He was now, he told
Durrell proudly, a *cause célèbre* in France, like Dreyfus had
been. As for the US edition of *The Black Book*, it was at the
printers still but due to be published any day.[25]

At the end of October, a month after King George returned
to Athens, Durrell took Eve there to meet Katsimbalis and his
other Athenian friends. Sikelianos, broken down by the war
and famine, looked much older, he thought, though somehow
splendid, surrounded by a life in ruins; the others, nervous
because of the local tensions, were strangely optimistic. A
happy encounter with John Lehmann, editor of *New Writing
and Daylight*, who was visiting the city, led to Lehmann quickly
accepting Durrell's Rhodean portraits, 'Eternal Contemp-
ories'.[26] Durrell was delighted. Appearing in such magazines,
he told Lehmann, was particularly rewarding after having his
poetry rejected so often – a slight exaggeration, one might
think. He promised him some prose, though could not promise
when.[27] In fact his main prose effort was gradually focusing
upon his book about Rhodes.

On 15 November, he and Eve had something to celebrate.
He was granted a decree nisi. Meanwhile civil war flared up

in Macedonia. It was perhaps at this point that Durrell decided to take Eve to Corfu.[28] He was shocked by the condition of the people, and visiting Kalami again found that Athenaios' wife Eleni had died in 1940, starving herself to keep her children alive. Athenaios had married a local village girl, Kerkyra, and now had a young daughter of five. Durrell met again Nicholas the schoolteacher–fisherman and a boatman who asked for £100 for housing the *Van Norden* for six years during the war. The yacht, he discovered, had been confiscated by Germans in early 1943 but Durrell did not resent the impoverished Greeks trying to make money, even slightly dishonestly, because their situation was so desperate.

He had already made a small mark among readers of poetry in America. Now he received an important fan letter. This was from Lawrence Clark Powell, the librarian at the University of California at Los Angeles, and a friend of Miller and of Richard Aldington, who declared himself a devotee. He had all three of his Faber books and had read his work with ever-mounting delight and excitement. He wanted anything Durrell had ever published. With this newly kindled academic interest in him, Durrell's embryonic American reputation grew a fraction more, and he heard that someone was lecturing on him at the University of Wisconsin. He was delighted by this transatlantic interest, though wary, not wanting anyone to read the disastrous *Pied Piper of Lovers*. He hoped that his 'fans' would be patient, because he saw his career lying ahead of him rather than in the past. He did not mind recommending the US edition of *The Black Book*, which George Leite was still trying to publish, but was less enthusiastic about *Cefalû*, due out in the US from the New York publishers Reynal and Hitchcock.

Although he referred to it as 'amusing rubbish', it paid for his divorce.

Leite, who had published 'Eight Aspects of Melissa' in his magazine *Circle Nine* and was considering bringing out 'Zero', wrote in December to say that there might be a delay over *The Black Book*. Durrell, however, was not at all bothered by this hold-up; the last thing he needed now, with a job application to the British Council under consideration, was a highly publicized legal action against the book. If that happened he would certainly be dropped. The old pre-war Durrell who would publish and be damned was now a cautious man seeking office. It must have galled him, but if he wanted to stay in Greece, get remarried and support a decent lifestyle, he needed that Council appointment.

The lack of direction in his writing is evident in the disparate kinds of work he was undertaking. He began a translation from the Greek of Emmanuel Royidis' mildly scurrilous anti-clerical novel *Pope Joan*, about a supposed woman pope. He had first come across the book while walking around Athens in 1939 with Katsimbalis, who had pointed it out in a bookshop window.[29] An anti-Catholic jibe was unlikely to upset the Orthodox Greeks, nor even, for that matter, the gentlemen of the British Council. In any case, translation was at a scholarly arm's length from authorship.

By the end of the year he had finished his first poetic drama, *Sappho*. The story was not that of the legendary Sappho of Lesbos, who wrote amorous poems to young girls and finally leapt to her death from the cliffs of Lefkas when her love for a beautiful boatman, Phaon, was spurned. Durrell's story of Sappho, apart from the setting, seems to be a product of his own, rich imagination. In Durrell's play, no lesbian feelings are hinted at, and there is no suicidal leap from the cliffs. Instead, the poet, discovered as a lost child after an earthquake, is married to Kreon, ruler of Lesbos (perhaps her own father, it is suggested), and is terrified of growing old and at the prospect of death. Lesbos is at war with Athens, and Sappho is bored. Phaon is here depicted as a gentle artist, returned to Lesbos after a long exile. He and Sappho become lovers. When Pittakos, Phaon's twin and a previous lover of Sappho, returns after triumphing over Athens, the debate is joined – Pittakos, man of action, and Phaon, peace-loving artist, arguing the nature of truth and of free-will. No one, we are told by Sappho, masquerading as an oracle, can escape his fate. Sappho's fate is that of an embittered exile. There is a great deal of talk and very little action. This renders the play more interesting as poetry than as drama, and gives Durrell the opportunity to air his pet ideas about art and

solitude and death, and to present two images of himself –
action-man and poetic exile.

On 16 December, he received the bad news that the job he
had hoped for had been axed from the British Council budget.
He was asked if he would consider taking a post outside Greece
and if he was likely soon to be in England where he could be
formally interviewed for such a position. What he may not
have known about was an exchange of letters between the
Foreign Office and the Council. The Council's director of
appointments said they felt morally obliged to find Durrell a
job in the Middle East if possible. 'Durrell did good work for
us before the war and if he really wants to come back to us, I
think we should probably be glad to re-employ him.'[30] The FO
told Patrick Reilly in Athens that if the Council could not find
him a post they would do their utmost to fit him in somewhere,
'because of the good work he had done in the past'.[31]

With the British occupation of Rhodes coming to an end at
the beginning of 1947, his work with the Overseas Information
Service was wound up and he faced the future without a job
in prospect. He announced that he planned to marry Eve in
February, and meanwhile to finish *Reflections on a Marine
Venus*. Robert Liddell reported from Egypt that he had asked
Eddie Gathorne-Hardy if they should send him a wedding
present, and Gathorne-Hardy had replied, '*Quite* unnecessary.'

Perhaps it was a sign of Durrell's and Miller's insecurity that
they exchanged mammoth letters in February. Miller, now the
father of a daughter *and* a son, finally sent a copy of *The
Happy Rock*, to which Durrell had contributed two years
before. However, Durrell found the book coarse, trite and in
no way worthy of its subject, Miller. So few of the contributors
seemed at all conscious of the literary revolution for which he
was responsible. Even so, he confessed to a sudden loss of
confidence in himself and a feeling of hysteria, due, he believed,
to never having got over losing his little daughter. *That*, he
thought, was the heart of the matter. Now he was possessed
by an acute yearning for the Villa Seurat days, a time, of course,
when his confidence had been brimming over.[32]

Somehow Durrell had managed to persuade the Overseas

Information Office to send him back to England on paid leave. His divorce from Nancy had been made absolute on 13 January, but there is some confusion about the date in February on which Lawrence Durrell married Yvette Cohen. He wrote to Miller in a letter dated the 27th, saying that he had got married the day before, but his divorce papers indicate that he married on the 17th. In any event, Durrell packed his books and papers off to Alan Thomas in Bournemouth and prepared to leave Rhodes.

Eve was anxious to have her parents' blessing on the union, and so after the wedding at Military HQ in Rhodes they set out for Egypt, planning an Orthodox religious ceremony in Cairo, where her citizenship could also be established. Durrell said later of his second marriage that neither of them wanted to get married but Eve needed the papers in order not to be returned to Egypt. But once he had married her he did not regret it.[33] They travelled via Athens, where there was a last get-together with Seferis, Katsimbalis, Ghika and Rex Warner, listening to a disc sent to Durrell by Miller, a record of himself reading from *Tropic of Cancer*, reminiscent of similar readings in Paris and Corfu. The past, it seemed, was ever at his heels. Katsimbalis was moved to tears by the recording and Seferis sat as if bemused and declaring over and over that Miller was quite a fellow. Durrell in his turn was so moved by their reactions that he made a gift of the disc to them. They thanked him, he told Miller, as if he had presented them with a piece of his (Miller's) anatomy.[34]

The newlyweds flew from Athens to Cairo, where Durrell was told by the British Information Service that there was a post available for him with them in Istambul, but he quickly turned it down.[35] Perhaps the thought of going to Turkey was too much for his graeco-phile soul to take – or perhaps he was simply fed up with Information Service work, hobnobbing with hard-drinking, heavy-smoking journalists into the early hours and in a very real way 'lying for his country'. He was more intent, it seems, on throwing in his lot once more with the British Council, whose Athens people had tipped him off that there might be a job for him there.[36]

The attempt by Eve to settle matters with her parents almost came to grief. According to the account she gave to Artemis Cooper, the first problem was that though she had a birth certificate she was stateless. Her ancestors had arrived in Alexandria as refugees several generations before, but they had never become citizens of any country. Her parents were opposed to her marrying Durrell and, with the aid of the Chief Rabbi of Alexandria, sought to have her committed to an asylum. She managed to communicate all this to Durrell, who told her to get out and head for Tanta, halfway between Alexandria and Cairo, where his friend Gwyn Williams would give her sanctuary. He then cabled Williams telling him to lock her in his loft and not let her out of his sight. With the Chief Rabbi's help, Eve's parents were calmed down, the relevant papers were signed, and Larry and Eve went through an Orthodox marriage ceremony in Cairo. In order to convince Eve's parents, Durrell had a friend at the Cairo Embassy transform the ordinary-looking marriage certificate into something impressive with the aid of a grand red Embassy seal.[37] Whether this mollified them is not known. It is possible that Durrell exacted a subtle revenge on Eve's father by naming the elderly sugar-daddy of Melissa in *The Alexandria Quartet* Cohen.

So without a job, but with a new wife, he returned to England for the first time in eight years, and settled down temporarily with his family at 52 St Alban's Avenue in Bournemouth. There, too, apart from Louisa, were Margaret with her husband John and their two-year-old son Nicholas, thirty-two-year-old Leslie, who had spent the war working in a munitions factory; and young Gerald, now a poet as well as a zoologist, highly critical of his eldest brother's work, and just about to set off on his first zoo quest, to West Africa, to gather wild animals for English zoos.

Larry told Curtis Brown that he had already written two-thirds of his Rhodes book (an exaggeration). They in turn told him that George Leite's *Black Book* contract had expired some months before, and asked him to authorize its sale in America to Laughlin at *New Directions*. He agreed, writing himself to Leite to inform him of this.[38] Nevertheless, Leite still went ahead and published Durrell's 'bughouse' stories, 'Zero' and 'Asylum in the Snow', in a single small volume.

In London he met again Eliot and Tambimuttu, who gave him the news that David Gascoyne had had a mental breakdown. Durrell could, he thought, cure him if he could work on him for a couple of months – doubtless feeling that he had now found the answer to such maladies in the medical psychotherapy of Georg Groddeck. Even so, after the Mediterranean he found England freezing and soon succumbed to a dose of influenza. Despite feeling wretched he was struck by the contrast between post-war Britain and post-war Greece. He thought highly of the Labour government's success in all-but abolishing unemployment and maintaining fair rationing. He thought they had prevented the country from sinking and even the poor were well looked after. However, what was not so good was that when he contacted the British Council he was told that all Athens vacancies had been filled, and he would have to wait until something else acceptable to him came up.[39]

Two publications marked his return to England in 1947. One was a piece in *Windmill*, 'From a Writer's Journal', a mixture of literary reflections and jottings on Rhodes, and 'From a Winter Journal', mostly about the lost Rhodean city of Lindos, in John Lehmann's *Penguin New Writing*. The first contained a slighting reference to 'gentry-art', which led to a sour exchange of letters with Osbert Sitwell.

In June, Durrell was finally invited for interview by the British Council with a posting to South America in view. Whether he was keen on the idea is difficult to tell. He would have preferred the Levant, but he had long been curious about the New World, and had thought of moving to America more than once. He was offered and accepted a two-year appointment as lecturer with the Council in Argentina.

Suddenly he became fond of the previously hated Pudding Island. He now thought that England was a much more pleasant and civilized place to live than any other European country, thanks to the Labour government's rationing and employment policies. He was both impressed and delighted, especially because there had been no loss of freedoms as there had been in totalitarian countries.[40] Sorting through the papers which Thomas had in store, Durrell came across a large bundle of the letters he had received from Miller over the years, and spent a whole morning reading through them.

Now that his appointment to the British Council had been settled he had time to relax, sort out his papers and earn a little money from journalism. He continued translating *Pope Joan* and had an article on Rhodes accepted by the *Geographical Magazine* and a talk on Miller rejected by the BBC. He then offered two more radio talks which were accepted. When he went to London to record them for the BBC, one of his producers, he discovered, was another hero of his youth, the pugnaciously right-wing poet Roy Campbell. They became firm friends until Campbell's death some ten years later. Durrell's talks began a long-time relationship with the broadcast media. He was a natural broadcaster, even better, it transpired, without a script. 'Greek Peasant Superstitions' took him back to the folktales he had used so successfully in *Prospero's Cell*, and which he was also including in *Reflections on a Marine Venus*. In 'Dreams and Divinations' he explored that area of the irrational which so appealed to him and which formed the basis of his engagement with metaphysical systems of all sorts. Its appearance in the *Listener* brought a letter from Jung in Zurich, a contact which, strangely, Durrell seems not to have pursued very far.[41]

Another foretaste of his Rhodes book appeared when his article 'The Island of the Rose' was published in the *Geographical Magazine*, with photographs taken with the Rolliflex given him by Mary Mollo. Apart from pictures of the lost ancient cities of Lindos and Cameirus, he cheekily inserted photographs of his Turkish graveyard and Mollo's photograph of Eve posing as a modern Rhodean beauty in a fourteenth-century Turkish costume.

Before leaving, he sent Eliot manuscripts of *Sappho*, and a new collection of poems, *On Seeming to Presume*. *Pope Joan* went to Rodney Phillips and Green, and some translations for a collection of Seferis' poetry, *King of Asine*, were left with John Lehmann. He also gave Tambi a poem for a Festschrift to Eliot he proposed to publish, and discussed with him the idea of bringing out a selection of Miller's work which Durrell would edit.

He had not misused his free-time in England, but he had still not felt free enough to start on his *Book of the Dead*, which, with his notes on Rhodes, again went along in his baggage.

CHAPTER 9

In the Wilderness:
Argentina and Yugoslavia

(1947–1953)

La vraie vie n'est pas absente, mais
ailleurs. The right life is not absent, but
elsewhere.

Rimbaud

Sir, money is a whore, a bawd, a drudge;
Fit to run out on errands; let her go.

Ben Jonson, *The Devil Is an Ass*

The Durrells sailed for Argentina on the SS *Brazil Star* on 28 October 1947. *En route*, the ship called at Lisbon, where there was a reunion with the newly widowed Bernard Spencer, now with the British Council there. The Atlantic crossing was pleasant enough, and Durrell thrilled at first seeing Rio de Janeiro – a quite fantastic sight, he thought, a white city, a fine harbour surrounded by towering skyscrapers dominated by a stone figure of Christ and intertwined with jungle.[1]

Behind him he left a growing reputation. He needed praise because he was about to descend into a shadowland of creative depression which would engulf him for some time ahead.

Argentina, when he arrived there, was the world's fifth-richest country, with a thriving beef export trade. From the outset, it left him with a strange impression. There was, he thought, a lack of spiritual gravity about the place, which left one floating. The angst-ridden European was oddly displaced there; all that was possible was melancholia. The individual was overwhelmed by a society, symbolized by skyscrapers and exaggerations which extended even to dances like the jitterbug. There was nothing of worth there, besides European panic and bad conscience in a spiritual void.[2] Durrell hated Buenos Aires – too hot, too materialistic, too little culture – but he did meet some interesting people there, such as T. E. Lawrence's brother, and the Argentinian writer Jorge Luis Borges.

Soon after arriving, he was appointed, as from the end of February 1948, British Council director in Cordoba – a pleasant place, he thought – an old university town ('the Oxford of Argentina'). His appointment had, however, ruffled some feathers, it being felt that the post should have been subject to special interview in London rather than filled locally.[3] But Durrell complained to friends that he was being exploited for his literary reputation, and paid a mere junior lecturer's salary. In fact, the salaries were quite handsome and were paid in US dollars, and Durrell was not unimpressed by his sudden affluence. In Buenos Aires once, a colleague recalled him insisting on paying for drinks with the remark, 'Look, I'm stiff with dollars!'

But the dream of US dollars from writing faded when Reynal and Hitchcock, due to bring out both *Cefalû*, as *The Dark Labyrinth*, and *Prospero's Cell*, were taken over by Harcourt Brace, and his titles were dropped. In England *Cefalû* appeared almost unnoticed at the end of the year. On 25 January, Miller's dreams of riches also crashed when the French franc was devalued and some 30,000 dollars being held from him in Paris suddenly became 5,000.[4] Amid the general gloom, Durrell was heartened to hear from Eliot, who wrote to say how highly he thought of his new poetry collection, *On Seeming to Presume*.[5]

By February, still in Buenos Aires, he was complaining of boredom. He told Mary Mollo (now Mary Hadkinson) that, handsome though the country was, it was also a melancholy, characterless vista. The air was fetid and the place was swarming with businessmen ceaselessly consuming beef and Coca-Cola. Even England was preferable. He thought the people were pleasant but shallow and infantile; however, he hoped for better things in Cordoba. Meanwhile, he surveyed his literary situation. *Pope Joan* was now in proof form, *Cefalû* just published, *On Seeming to Presume* about to go to press, his verse play *Sappho* under consideration for production, and he was toying with an idea for another poetic drama.[6]

In March he took up his new post in Cordoba, and was soon hard-pressed to find time for his Rhodes book, of which he had some 150 pages, mostly notes. By the time summer came he felt trapped in a nightmare. The heat and dust of Cordoba did not help, and a pampero wind to match the khamseen only deepened the gloom. His nightmare was not only local, but global. The communist eclipse of eastern Europe had begun with the take-over of Czechoslovakia and rising tension over Berlin, and this he found profoundly depressing, feeling that Europe would be the centre of a nuclear war. Nevertheless, he still felt drawn towards that darkening continent.

He made good, cultured and stimulating friends in Cordoba, such as the Llambi Campbell de Ferreyras, a rich local family who gave frequent parties to which the Durrells were always invited. Larry introduced them to Groddeck, and Jorge Ferreyra swore that he helped cure him of tuberculosis. Through the Ferreyras, Durrell met William Walton, to whom he later sent a copy of *Sappho*, hoping he would turn it into an opera.[7] He was to dedicate his play gratefully to Fany de Llambi Campbell de Ferreyra of Cordoba.

Whatever his social life, 'the Oxford of Argentina', founded by Jesuits, failed to impress him, just as, it seems, *he* failed to impress some of his Council colleagues. Although he was regarded as a good, animated lecturer, he was also thought to have a hard edge. One colleague recalled how he made little effort to disguise his prejudices or his low opinion of the rather gauche Argentinians who were so eager to learn from him – once complaining after a reception that the party 'creaked'. He made no concessions to students, content to lecture above their heads, and making it clear that he thought Greece to be the centre of the civilized western world, something his young students found difficult to understand. He told Lawrence Clark Powell that the Argentinians were little more than likeable automata,[8] and having to travel to remote towns over the pampas to speak on Shakespeare or Modern Poetry to such people seemed to him quite a ludicrous thing to have to do.

His position made him more than usually conscious of not having been to university. He said later that among his university-educated British Council colleagues he felt he had to appear more widely read and to speak in more cultivated tones to conceal his own lack of formal education. With this in mind, he turned back to his planned thesis on Elizabethan writers, admitting that this was intended to compensate him for having failed to get into Cambridge. For a time he became intensely interested in the transcendental metaphysics of Giordano Bruno, the sixteenth-century Italian philosopher and mystic, whose ideas on time, he thought, made him as modern as Einstein. He also pursued his interest in Groddeck, whom he admired not only philosophically but as a healer.

In May Durrell wrote to Patrick Reilly to say that coming to South America had been a grave error of judgment, and he may have now regretted turning down the Istanbul job. He thought that even being conscripted into an English coalmine would be preferable to Argentina. He told friends that he and Eve would probably become alcoholic before he could escape back to Europe.[9]

Stimulated by boredom, he tried his hand again at comic writing, and wrote to P. G. Wodehouse enquiring about the origin of Jeeves. Wodehouse kindly replied, explaining how he had turned Jeeves from a butler who merely opened doors into the ingenious manservant forever retrieving his silly-ass master from catastrophes of his own making.[10] Durrell was obviously feeling his way towards his own comic invention, the diplomat–raconteur Antrobus. In the same vein, he introduced a course on the limerick, illustrated with his own compositions, determined to shock his parochial students (stifled by Jesuitical censorship) or make them laugh.

In more serious mood, he decided to compose a textbook from lectures he had given at the university at Tucuman,[11] a book later to appear in Britain as *Key to Modern Poetry*. In this he expounded some of his ideas about poetry and art and how it connected to the major ideas of the twentieth century, especially those of Freud and Einstein. He began by apologizing for his lack of real scholarship and asserting his disdain for scientific rationalism as a basis for analysing poetry. He favoured the random approach matching his own reading, applying a psychoanalytic theory here and scientific hypothesis there. If he was trying to explore 'the natural history of poetry', his major influences were Wyndham Lewis's *Time and Western Man* and Edmund Wilson's *Axel's Castle*, and his main perspective was taken from anthropologists such as Tylor, Frazer and Rivers, psychologists such as Freud, Rank, Jung and Groddeck, and scientists such as Eddington, Whitehead and Einstein. He saw links and cross-pollination between these disciplines. He made no claim to originality; rather, he outlined a Method. He stressed the provisional nature of truth, and wanted to avoid thinking along straight lines when science informs us that time is curved. He rejected the Victorian notion of science with its proof for everything, and its implied clear-cut relation between subject and object. Einstein's theory had relativized not only our view of the material world but also the human personality. Dickens and Dostoevsky, whose narratives progress along a straight line, represent the old thinking; Joyce, Proust and Eliot, whose work proceeds through spiralling and counter-spiralling motions, represent the new. Eliot captures the elusive and deceptive nature of past and present in the famous opening lines of *Burnt Norton*: 'Time present and time past / Are both perhaps present in time future / And time future contained in time past. / If all time is eternally present / All time is unredeemable'.[12]

Freud opens the path into the human interior, no longer clear, whole and fixed, but obscure, divided and unstable. His ideas on sex lead away from its being seen as a unifying and joining process towards the view that it is one of division and disjunction. Analysis was moving away from causal explanation towards the idea of creative balance; similarly the artist is moving from the self-contemplative form towards the resolution of contradictions for the sake of the overall pattern.[13] All this anticipates and underpins his *Alexandria Quartet*. When he wrote that time and the ego were the two central concerns of modern poets, he could have added novelists – at least novelists, who, like himself, have a considerable poetic genius at their disposal.

After a comparison between Tennyson and Eliot, and an excursion through Einstein, Huxley, Freud, Groddeck and Rank, Durrell surveyed the poetry of the 1890s, the Georgians and imagists, Eliot, Hopkins and poets of his own generation, in the context of the ideas discussed at the outset. What this book tells us is that, frustrating though he may have felt his time in Argentina was to his artistic development, here he was preparing the intellectual ground for the great *Book of the Dead* which was still gestating.

Eliot wrote saying that he liked *Sappho*, and that it was good to come upon a poet who knew that prose underpinned all poetry and that poetry was no more than prose in flight.[14] However, he warned that poetry was not selling and it would be better to see how *On Seeming to Presume* went before tackling the verse-play. Furthermore, he said, *Sappho* was overlength and would therefore be too pricey for the poorer poetry lovers. Nevertheless, he would still recommend Faber to publish it. He pointed out certain anachronisms, inappropriate usages (which Durrell insisted on keeping), and argued that the revelation (in the first version) that there were two Sapphos and two Kreons was highly confusing and even laughable. Durrell had to remove this device from his play, but he was to use it to great effect in his final set of novels, *The Avignon Quintet*. Eliot was probably right in suggesting that prose fiction was his natural element and in pointing out a dramatic weakness in *Sappho* – too much talk for the amount of action.[15]

Since landing in Buenos Aires, Durrell had suffered from poet's block, and receiving proofs of his poems from Faber in July must have made him wish for a climate friendlier to poetry. Having exposed, as he saw it, the wellsprings of twentieth-century English poetry in his lectures at Tucuman, he was unable to draw on those waters in Argentina. He did manage to paint, but not enough to lighten his gloomy sense of displacement. Furthermore, the climate left him with frequent colds and 'flu, and the inability to write had stretched his nerves so that he turned to drink and drugs (Tincture of Valerian) to relieve the stress, even coming close, he said, to a nervous breakdown. The Rhodes book and *The Book of the Dead* remained unwritten; his letters briefly turned viperish. He accused Eliot of 'acidity' in his comments on *Sappho*,[16] and in letters to friends he made catty remarks about a whole string of contemporary poets, including G. S. Fraser, David Gascoyne and even his champion Porteus.

By September he had given notice to the British Council, that he intended to leave well before his contract expired. One student reported that he sometimes did not turn up to lectures, preferring to stay home and take a siesta. It was rumoured that he had taken to his bed and refused to teach until the British Council sent him his ticket back to England.[17]

His *Pope Joan* translation and *On Seeming to Presume* appeared in October, as if heralding his return to a more congenial writing climate. The *TLS* praised the poems for their intellectual power and sensual imagery, and compared his treatment of landscape to that of Shelley, though in his 'intellectual bite and appetite for pleasure' he showed a poetic temperament that was closer to the Byron of *Don Juan*.[18] The comparison with Byron and Shelley was shrewd, for he mostly identified now with the traditions of romanticism and exile.

A round of farewells brought the Durrells one evening to the house of Miguel Alfredo Olivera, who was to do the Spanish translation of *Sappho*. Olivera was struck by the beautiful Eve, 'as still as a statue and as white as wax', and speaking an ancient Spanish mixed with Arabic which she had inherited from her Sephardic ancestors. Ironically, Durrell said that in Cordoba he had been 'learning to suffer and not condemn', and expressed his usual strong views about what writing should consist of. 'Books should be made with our own material or they shouldn't exist at all. The fight does not consist in registering what is experienced, but in registering oneself to oneself.'[19]

With a broken contract behind him but with a great sense of relief, Durrell left Buenos Aires with Eve on board the SS *Andes* on 4 December. He could not wait to leave the muddy waters of the River Plate behind him, and a letter written to Miller from Santos in Brazil already reveals a lightening of his mood.

Back in Britain it was confirmed that the British Council had decided to dispense with his services.

Margo had now separated from her husband and was living with her son on the opposite side St Alban's Avenue, at number 51, where she had set herself up as a landlady, filling her house with lodgers – which she was to describe with great comic effect later in a book, *Whatever Happened to Margo?*, not published until 1994. Leslie was still around, busily misbehaving and dicing with the law, offering to sell people yachts which did not belong to him. He was seeing a woman who ran a local off-licence, and they would soon be married.[20]

At something of a loose end, Durrell began to re-establish himself with old friends. He sent Diana Gould, now married to Yehudi Menuhin, a copy of *Black Honey* (a play he had written about Baudelaire's black mistress), asking her professional opinion of it, and went up to London to congratulate Eliot on the Nobel Prize he had won the previous December. And he was given a rousing welcome-home party at the Old Crown pub in Museum Street by the new King of Redonda, Gawsworth (M.P. Shiel now having died), and two old acquaintances from Egypt, G.S. Fraser (about whom he had recently been very catty to friends) and Ian Fletcher, now designated the King's Chamberlain. He found Tambimuttu nearly broke, and any chance of his bringing out a 'Best of Miller' seemed remote. In general he thought the English literary scene as idiotic and boring as ever, with the 'sweaty Christians' still much in evidence and publishers urging authors to be ever more pious.[21] He missed Anne Ridler, now in Oxford, where Vivian worked for the University Press, but she was actively trying to get producers interested in *Sappho*, which she said Eliot was steering towards publication.

When Gawsworth, now editor of the *Poetry Review*, wrote asking for poems, he had to admit that he had nothing new to offer. And now he was faced with no job, no income and the prospect of being unable to meet his obligation to contribute towards Penelope's upbringing. But, for the first time since 1942, he was reunited with his young daughter, and was able for a while to see her quite often. The deep wound he had suffered at losing her in Egypt was to some extent healed. But it must have made him even more conscious of the need to find a job, and the idea of starving in Athens was abandoned.

Bernard Burrows, still at the Foreign Office, may have encouraged him to apply to them for a job. He also had Patrick Reilly's backing. By April 1949 he had been appointed press attaché to the British Embassy in Belgrade on a three-year contract at the very handsome salary for that time of £5,000 a year, plus perks and accommodation. Miller was delighted. Durrell would be well placed to do the work he wanted to do; there was nothing more soul-destroying than having to write for money, he said.

Although Durrell had worked on an occasional basis for the Foreign Office, in Athens, Cairo and Alexandria, he had never appeared on the Foreign Office List. Now he sat there proudly with the rank of first secretary, and with full bag facilities – a definite move up the diplomatic pecking order. However, he would go to Yugoslavia as a 'contract officer' on a slightly different basis from that of a career diplomat. In *The Alexandria Quartet*, the novelist Pursewarden, a 'contract officer', was considered much less dependable than 'officers of the career', and was subject to the discomfort of being posted anywhere, often to places he found uncongenial.[22]. But this move into Foreign Office circles would provide a new, informed dimension to *The Book of the Dead*, especially that dealing with characters like Mountolive and Pursewarden, who first meet at a pub near Westminster Bridge – the very stamping ground of bowler-hatted 'dips'.

In preparation for the move, Durrell attended a four-day FO briefing about the Yugoslavian situation. Relations between the Soviet Union and the Tito government in Belgrade were rapidly deteriorating. The Durrells travelled to Belgrade via Paris and for a few hours he was able to savour that city's old charm, little changed since the 1930s.

He had not been in Belgrade long before he was hit by the appalling conditions of living under a communist dictatorship – a depressed and fearful citizenry, heavy censorship, no food, a ubiquitous secret police, and shuffling lines of political prisoners watched by machine gunners. The whole deathly system was one of relentless corruption, both moral and spiritual. No matter that Tito was at loggerheads with Stalin, life under the Yugoslav Marshal's brand of communism was insufferable for a creative individualist; Durrell quickly informed friends that politically he had shifted decisively and dramatically to the right. Perhaps the shifting-point came when he tried to befriend a Yugoslav writer, who was almost immediately arrested for having contact with an imperialist spy. Capitalism, he decided, was after all worth defending, as was his own sanity. He asked for a supply of vitamin pills to help lighten his sagging spirits.[23]

Before Yugoslavia, Durrell was probably slightly on the left politically, a republican where Greece was concerned, and rather admiring of the way the socialists in Britain had handled the post-war crisis. Within days of landing in Belgrade he had become a fierce anti-communist – both monarchist and fascist, he told friends.[24]

Not surprisingly, when Orwell's *1984* came out in June, Durrell was riveted, and wrote to the *Booster*'s old adversary expressing his unreserved admiration for so courageous a book. To read it in a communist country, he said, was extraordinary because what Orwell had written about he was experiencing at first hand.[25] The bad climate and stifling political atmosphere in Belgrade made him dream of getting down to Greece, and he ordered a small car from England with a view to driving south to Salonika, just to enjoy the pleasure of speaking Greek again.

The debt owed to Miller was in part repaid when his essay 'Studies in Genius – Henry Miller' appeared in *Horizon* on 20 July. In it he argued that Miller's genius lay in his commitment to writing as a means of self-fulfilment rather than as conscious art. This distinguished him from a Joyce or a Proust (who in their own ways, he believed were mummifiers of the culture), and his wild streak of anarchic comedy set him apart even from D.H. Lawrence, with whom otherwise he had much in common. He did not offer, as Lawrence did, a moral justification for obscenity, but while regarding sex as a sacred act also saw it as convulsively hilarious. He was not a 'literary man' nor an 'artist' but a fructifying 'force'. His talent was uneven, and sometimes he wrote badly, but behind his work lay much painful experience and suffering which had enabled him to grasp the labyrinthine nature of life and the fragmentation of the self, perceived as it is through the fractured prisms of memory. His work signalled the demise of urban man, and he pointed to the sources of Truth and Beauty lying beyond the shabby facade with which science obscured the real world. He lamented that most Anglo-Saxon readers could read Miller only in bowdlerized forms.[26] Miller saw the article in manuscript and was delighted. Only Durrell could intoxicate the English in this way, he wrote, though he felt that he had missed the chance to lambast the British for not having published his early books.[27]

Not long after arriving, the Durrells were struck down with laryngitis, and the shortage of drugs in Yugoslavia added to their suffering. The vitamin pills were most welcome, and Durrell asked Theodore Stephanides to make up a medical chest with a range of drugs including tannic acid, aspirin, sulphanilimide and penicillin. Groddeck at this point was not sufficient. However, in the summer of 1949 he obtained copyright permission to have the German's *Book of the It* republished, and this along with his *Horizon* article earned him the undying gratitude of Groddeck's widow.

By August Larry and Eve had moved into a house of their own. As the Yugoslav crisis gathered momentum, three Soviet armoured divisions were moved to the country's borders and Stalin denounced Tito as a 'renegade'. By the beginning of September an air and naval pact between the two countries was broken off. In the midst of all this, Durrell was sent a copy of Miller's *Sexus*, and after reading only the first part was, he told Miller, deeply disappointed. He considered it morally coarse and from an artistic point of view excruciating. It lacked humour and passion and at times was childishly obscene and inane. Worse, the little of mystical worth in it was swamped by lavatorial filth.[28] On 10 September, he cabled Miller urging him to withdraw the book before his reputation was ruined.[29] He wrote to Girodias explaining his embarrassment. He had agreed to review the book for several papers, convinced that he would like it, but was now in despair at what he thought was a squandering of talent – the author seemed puffed up with self-importance and the style was so bad he wondered if Miller had written it while drugged. He had a copy of the letter sent to Miller.[30] Perlès also saw the letter and wrote to Durrell, greatly distressed at what he saw as a breach between his two oldest friends. Was the letter necessary, he asked? Henry would be terribly hurt. He was a genius. And did not a genius have the right to write shit? If he was presently in hell he needed love and assistance, not to be hurt by his friends. Durrell was sufficiently touched by this letter to realize that he had overreacted. He cabled Miller abjectly apologizing for his unfair criticism and reaffirming his admiration.[31] The pressure he was under as the Yugoslav crisis worsened, and the embarrassment of having agreed to review the book and having eulogized it in advance in *Horizon*, had led him to panic. Also he was now keenly conscious of his position and anxious not to jeopardize it and his handsome salary by being associated with any scandalous publication. Miller seemed quite unconcerned by Durrell's attack. He had suffered worse assaults from those who were not his friends. Perhaps Durrell was correct, he said, and that he was done for, but that wasn't how he felt.[32] Durrell followed up his cable of apology with a letter to Girodias in much the same vein, giving permission for anything of his to be quoted in support of Miller. He said he must find a more constructive way to be critical in future.

Durrell managed to escape the pressures of office with a visit to Zagreb, an old Habsburg university town surrounded by hills with beautiful landscape to the north. He wrote to Anne Ridler about the trip, laid on for the diplomatic corps by the Yugoslavs, in which slightly drunken diplomats were sent off across the Croatian Plain on a train specially constructed by Yugoslav Light Industry. The toilets did not function and the lights fused; the carriages rocked so much that all were thrown into a confusion. This story later found its way, suitably embellished, into the comic annals of Antrobus. In fact, by the time he left Yugoslavia Durrell had enough material of this kind to fill several books. It seems as though he could make his job bearable only by seeing the funny side of things – something which came easily with his comic vision of the world of people who took themselves seriously. And there was much detail to salt away for his *Book of the Dead*. 'While I hated being a diplomat,' he said, 'I took my wisdom from Stendhal, who never hesitated to take notes.'[33]

Miller, never one to miss a chance to publicize himself, wrote suggesting that Durrell follow up his eulogistic essay in *Horizon* by persuading Cyril Connolly to let him review *Sexus*, and blasting it for all he was worth.[34] But Durrell had already written a long letter of apology and self-justification, eager not to offend the man to whom he owed so much. 'Joey' Perlès's letter had made him realize how ill-tempered and injurious he had been. Miller was one of the great geniuses of the century and nothing else counted.[35]

In October he took Eve on a trip to Sarejevo. He described it in a lyrical letter to Anne Ridler. The bold Tyrolean dress of the Bosnian peasants with hints of the orient he found pleasing, and he relished the dramatic plateau and ravines and cascading waterfalls which led up to the panorama of the town – the minarets and houses perched on the sheer mountainside, eagles soaring, the babble of Turkish women behind their black veils, the Turkish quarter and the trellises behind which girls lurked in purdah, cafés, houses, mosques and fezzes – something out of the last century from the mysterious east. They returned to the gloom of crisis-ridden Belgrade with great reluctance. He had to admit to Ridler, who was now editing *Modern Verse*, that he had no poems to offer her.[36]

There were other trips. At the end of October, just as Stalin made his final break with Tito, the Durrells left for a week in Salonika. The trip was 'duty', Durrell said, though also a delightful excuse to get away to the hills, away from drunken Serbs. He was so sick of communism that he even thought that the communist witch-hunting in the USA was probably the most intelligent way to deal with it. Muddle-headed liberals and guilt-ridden socialists were merely serving the interests of those who would destroy the very values on which writers depended.[37] When in the following June the United States took the initiative to help defend South Korea against invasion from the North, it confirmed his belief that America was the only country truly to recognize communism for what it was.

The nature of Durrell's 'duty' trip through Macedonia to the south is obscure, but he did submit a report of his trip to the Foreign Office, which suggests that part of the purpose of his trip was to spy out the land. He had had a penchant for spying ever since his intelligence-gathering job in Athens in 1939, and since identifying pro-Nazis in Alexandria in 1942. He was probably never a spy in the James Bond sense of the word, but merely kept his eyes open as all people involved in information work were expected to do. But it fed his passion, and gave him background for the spy thriller he later wrote set in Tito's Yugoslavia, *White Eagles over Serbia*. The detailed knowledge of topography and flora and fauna of the region which appears in that book suggests either that he kept a notebook or used his highly retentive memory for the purpose.

His hatred of communism changed his attitude also towards what had happened in Greece at the end of the war; he was now grateful that the communists had been kept out. The Yugoslav communists were worse than the Nazis, he thought, and he was irritated by the many well-meaning British and American left-wingers coming to Belgrade and complaining of the degeneracy of their own countries. He seems to have forgotten his 'Chronicle of the English Death' and Miller's *Air-Conditioned Nightmare* – but perhaps not entirely, for while he admitted that capitalism was ugly, ignoble and enslaving, it was, he thought, infinitely less so than countries which had became spell-bound by Marxism.[38] Meanwhile that western freedom he now admired was about to be put to the test in Paris after Miller's *Sexus* was seized by police and its publisher, Girodios, was soon to face trial.

Ever on the lookout for metaphysical revelation, Durrell now found another guru, to rival his pre-war psychological mentor Graham Howe. In April he told Miller that he had discovered an American, Francis J. Mott, whose width of vision left Rank, Jung and even Groddeck flattened on the canvas. Mott's book, *The Universal Design of Birth*, took the idea of the trauma of birth and went beyond it, supplying an incidental version of the womb experience. His work was linked to oriental and ancient religions, and he wrote movingly, said Durrell, about solitude and neglect[39] – experiences of his own which still haunted him. The message was apocalyptic – those who wished to save the world should join together in Mott's Life Society. Durrell was eager to share his new discovery with all his friends, and both Anne Ridler and the Burrowses remembered being urged to read Mott.

His hope that the anti-communist Churchill would win the election in April 1950 was dashed when Attlee's Labour government (whose members Durrell now considered a bunch of woolly apologists for dictatorship) was re-elected. He wrote grimly to Theodore Stephanides saying that physical conditions under communism were truly wretched, with a TB rate of around 80 per cent. He asked him for certain prescribed drugs, saying that as gifts they enabled him to make a few friends. This helped with his work of gathering information in a country where security was so rigid, and friendships with foreigners were frowned upon.[40] The spy in him was never entirely asleep.

In the middle of June, the Durrells went off for a month to Ischia, where Larry's old Corfu friend Constant Zarian was living. Xan Fielding was also there, and there were long debates about life, death, art and sex, sampling of the local vintage, and swimming in the Mediterranean. Durrell also wrote and had printed an important poem, certainly his best since before Argentina, 'Deus Loci'. It is a 100-line poem in ten stanzas, an affirmation and celebration of the spirit of place in preference to accursed and doomed religions. It was privately printed and he sent signed copies for sale to the Gotham Book Mart in New York, circulating others to friends. On trips to Capri he met Norman Douglas and Auden, which prompted him to compose a letter in verse to Anne Ridler.[41]

It was evident that he had found the change of scene productive. Returning refreshed from Ischia, he undertook another 'duty' trip, this time to Sarajevo and Dubrovnik and then north to Split and Zagreb – more background for his later thriller.

Sappho had been published in April, but had not been widely reviewed, though Peter Russell in *Time and Tide* thought well of it both as poetry and as a piece of theatre. Durrell's handling of characters, themes and denouements, he thought, showed remarkable skill for one who had not written for the theatre before. 'Let's hope', he concluded, 'that some theatrical producer will be discerning enough to risk a season for it.'[42] As if in response to this, at the end of August a letter came from the actress Margaret Rawlings asking for a year's option on the play.[43] Durrell was excited enough by this to think that perhaps after all he *was* a dramatist, and promptly began making notes for a new play. At the same time, a review of English poetry in the *TLS* judged his three volumes of poems 'something new in topographical verse'.

Nor was it all official gloom and long-distance literary recognition. Durrell, the tiny joker in the diplomatic pack, was a source of much hilarity – as he had been in Egypt during the war – seeing the funny side of even the most grimly sober events, as well as living out some of his spy fantasies. He was learning a great deal about public affairs and public behaviour. He thought that the way ahead for the novel lay with the Stendhalian epic rather than a jaded Proustian subjectivity.

Margaret Rawlings was eager to put *Sappho* on in London with herself in the lead. She suggested that Durrell enter it for an Arts Theatre Club competition for new plays, with a prize of £700 and production during the Festival of Britain. She would try to interest London producers, believing that the recent successes of Christopher Fry's verse plays would make it a little easier for them than hitherto.

He was still very dependent on his friends, including Theodore Stephanides and Gawsworth, who agreed to knock his *Key to Modern Poetry* manuscript into shape. Gawsworth wrote to tell him that he was putting 'Deus Loci' into the next *Poetry Review*, but then embarked on a catalogue of woe. His second marriage had collapsed and he was holed up in two rooms with just his books and three blankets. He had pleurisy, was stony-broke, and survived only by slowly selling off his precious library. In these circumstances, he said, working on Durrell's book would cost him ten rather than five pounds, and he could do with half on account; that would get him through one more week at least.[44] Hating proofreading and other minor chores associated with writing, Durrell readily agreed, asking Gawsworth for good measure to consider doing an index for the book. The man whom the young Durrell had all but worshipped was now his paid dogsbody.

When a fortune-teller read his coffee grounds he was told that a Dark Lady would bring him good fortune, and he wrote to tell Margaret Rawlings that the signs for *Sappho* seemed very good. She in turn was greatly encouraged by the huge success of Eliot's *The Cocktail Party*. She longed to do the play, she said, and had Jack Hawkins in mind for Pittakos and Michael Gough for Phaon.[45] When he heard from his agent that Knopf were to publish the play in the US, he felt sure this meant that he was after all a born dramatist, and pressed on with a new play. But the Dark Lady who would bring him good fortune was not called Sappho, but Justine.

He told Theodore that his Belgrade posting was three years' hard labour and that picking journalists' brains was like picking oakum.[46] Despite such complaints, however, meeting journalists and editors gave him valuable literary contacts. Malcolm Muggeridge, whom he met there, later interviewed him for television, and Kingsley Martin, editor of the *New Statesman*, began publishing his poems – in September 'Epitaph' and 'Water Colour of Venice' and in December 'Education of a Cloud'. All these, written in Yugoslavia, show the poet again in full spate. The Venice poem was sparked by Zarian saying that Florence was youth and Ravenna was age, while Venice was second childhood.[47] In January 1951 he had his first poem in the *TLS*, a lovely little piece on 'Sarajevo', including much of the imagery used earlier in his letter to Anne Ridler.[48] On 9 March, the BBC Third Programme broadcast a selection of his poems in a programme produced by his old Cairo friend Terence Tiller.

If he still missed his 'lost' daughter, there was now a new hopeful prospect in the fact that Eve was pregnant. She decided that the situation in Yugoslavia was so unsettled, with Stalin rattling his sabre and threatening to invade, that she would prefer to have her child in England.

Something absurdly Antrobus-like occurred to Durrell in February. On a visit to Trieste he discovered in a garage a vast, silver-grey, bullet-proof eight-cylinder, forty-horsepower German staff-car, a Horch which was once owned by Göring and then by the Nazi area commandant. Durrell bought it cheaply on impulse and drove it back to Belgrade. It was the sort of car in which Nazi leaders swept victoriously into capital cities, and the Diplomatic Corps were furious with him. He told Anne Ridler that it was the perfect car for a poet – no one but a madman would own a thing like that. He thought he might get a good price from Tito for it when he left.[49]

There was drama on the family front, too. The old family home of 52 St Alban's Avenue had been sold and everyone had moved across the road to Margo's house at number 51. On 26 February, brother Gerry, now twenty-six, and only just budding as a zoologist, got married at Bournemouth registry office to Jacqueline Rasen (born Wolfenden), a twenty-one-year-old music student, with Margo and her husband John as witnesses. A month later, Margo, now twenty-seven and divorced from John, also married a twenty-one-year-old – Malcolm Duncan, a corporal in the Life Guards. This time, Gerald and Jacqueline bore witness. Larry seems to have missed these two family occasions, but in May he took extended leave to bring Eve to England to have her baby. In Bournemouth they found Gerry out of work. Larry urged him to try the BBC, and to write a book about his animal expeditions and send it to Faber. The result would be *The Overloaded Ark* and a series of radio talks which would launch him on a career in writing and broadcasting which Larry always said far overshadowed his own success.

Eve chose Oxford as the place to have her baby, and they took a house at 84 Old Road in Headington, just a short drive from the Churchill Hospital where Eve was booked in for her confinement. The combination of Larry, Eve and the impending baby brought many of their friends to Oxford. Anne and Vivian Ridler were on the spot, and Louisa Durrell was driven up from Bournemouth by Alan Thomas. In at the birth also were Alf Perlès and his new wife Anna, and Mary Hadkinson, who remembers Eve being extremely nervous about the forthcoming delivery.

Their daughter was born on 30 May, under the sign of Taurus. Durrell was thrilled to have another daughter, this one charming and dark like Eve. While trying to think of a name

Mary jokingly suggested Sappho, and to her horror this was taken up with great enthusiasm by Durrell. She tried to retrieve the situation by proposing a simple English name to go with it, and so the Durrells' little daughter was called Sappho Jane. Larry's latest guru, John Mott, the 'trauma of birth' man, with whom he was conducting an earnest correspondence, became her godfather. According to Sappho, by her mother's account she was due two days earlier, but as delivery was likely to be in the middle of the night Eve was drugged to delay it, despite her objections. When she was eventually born she was so strange-looking that Durrell asked jokingly if the father could have been a Korean.[50] The implication was that the trauma of birth was rather more traumatic in her case than it might have been.

Eve stayed behind in England for a few months after the birth and returned to Belgrade at the end of August. The prospect of more years ahead in Yugoslavia weighed down on Durrell. A poem of his, 'The Sirens', which appeared in the *TLS* in late June, shows how strongly Greece was now calling to him. That, above all, was where he wanted to settle, and he urged Miller, for the sake of his own career, to come back to Europe. *The Rosy Crucifixion* seemed to him just rehashes of *Tropic of Cancer*, whereas Miller was capable of far greater things, which the more critical climate of Europe would inspire.[51]

Perhaps urged on by Anne Ridler and drawn by thoughts of Greece, Durrell now got down to completing his book on Rhodes, which had been lying untouched since before the Argentinian adventure. To this end he now conscripted the ever willing Theodore Stephanides to dig out material on the Turkish siege of Rhodes for him at the British Museum. But he found that trying to write was heavy-going because he was so busy with visiting journalists and fighting for air in a suffocating world of administration. A change of government in October, with Churchill's Conservatives coming to power, meant adjusting to different foreign policies and political personalities. Nevertheless, he managed to finish the book by January.

Reflections on a Marine Venus was as autobiographical as *Prospero's Cell* had been, and, like *Prospero's Cell*, equally unreliable as a biographical source, except as a record of Durrell's imaginative rendering of his experiences. As with his Corfu book, this one turned Rhodes into his private country with its own personal landscape. What was particularly successful was his handling of characters such as Mills, Sand, Hoyle, the mildly disreputable Captain Gideon and his colourful staff in Rhodes, who were utterly believable and thoroughly enjoyable company; and his set-piece description of a dance festival shows that he had lost none of his confidence as a writer of telling situations.

Margaret Rawlings was as good as her word and, although no stage production of *Sappho* was yet in sight, she arranged a successful reading of an abbreviated version of it at the French Institute Theatre in London on 21 January 1952. *The Times* next day gave it a favourable enough notice:

> Mr Durrell's verse had all the suppleness of prose while retaining the heightened imagery and atmosphere of poetry, and it says much for the quality of his play and also for the skill of the principle artists that they managed to create, on a bare stage set only with chairs, a good measure of dramatic illusion.[52]

Durrell was so buoyed up by this review that he agreed to tailor the text even more towards Sappho in the hope of getting the play properly produced with Margaret Rawlings in the lead. But he feared that the spirit of place in Yugoslavia was working against him. And, now forty, he was feeling that success had perhaps passed him by, and was looking for explanations. He spent time trying to expound Mott's psychology of consciousness to both Miller and Perlès. Miller simply replied that Mott was not for him; his idea of a Society of Life with its own constitution was not possible. And why worry about the possible destruction of life when it was, in any case, inextinguishable?[53] Perlès was far more brutal. He was not surprised that Durrell could raise little interest in Mott, whose writing was stultified and rambling, like Fraenkel's direst babblings. If the world was doomed, as Mott claimed, he wasn't much bothered, nor did he believe in such a thing as a 'collective brain' which would exert itself to prevent a coming holocaust. The world could be improved only through individual effort not by the organizational efforts of paranoid outfits like Mott's. He was, he said, surprised from the depth of his bowels that someone as creative as Durrell should swallow such garbage.[54]

In March there were more family nuptials, when thirty-five-year-old Leslie took the plunge and married his off-licensee love, Doris Hall, a divorcee some ten years older than himself. Miller, on the other hand, was now separated and on the loose, writing to Durrell that at last he, too, had found an 'Eve'. He would soon be sending Durrell his new book *Plexus* and one called *The World of Sex*, just published by Girodias in Paris.[55]

That spring, the siren call of Greece became so strong that Durrell decided to take Eve and the one-year-old Sappho on a six-week camping tour through Macedonia into Greece. They had already been camping beside the Danube and Sappho Jane had a little sky-blue tent of her own to sleep in.[56] Now she had to receive her Mediterranean baptism. He also planned to spend a few days in Athens, hoping to find a job in Greece. There was little chance that he would get a diplomatic job there because he had a serious drawback, he told friends – he spoke the language, which was considered not quite right for a diplomat.[57] The same applies to Mountolive in *The Alexandria Quartet* when he wonders why, with his Arabic, he is kept so long from a post in the Middle East. But that was how it was in the diplomatic pass-the-parcel game.

Meanwhile, *Key to Modern Poetry* was published in London and almost simultaneously in America. It got short shrift from the *TLS*.[58] The *New Statesman* objected to 'amateur philosophers' and judged Durrell 'not so much a critic by vocation as an imaginative writer doing his best off his main beat'.[59] The last point is well made because Durrell did not regard himself as a critic – an unproductive role, he thought. But he was a man of ideas, and in due course the realm of ideas would be seen exactly as Durrell's main beat.

There is no record of how or when Durrell disposed of Göring's Horch, and it is likely that when he drove south on their camping trip along rough, unsurfaced Balkan roads it was in the small car he had ordered from England. They ended up in Chalcidice, the area south-east of Salonika, one of whose three peninsulas leads to Mount Athos. A village woman was hired for cooking and cleaning and to keep an eye on the camp when they went exploring. He told Alan Thomas that he had been offered the Greek island of Olympiad, eight sea miles from Stavros – rugged, isolated, but with water and a harbour as well as groves of olive trees: applications in writing to the harbourmaster at Stavros. They stayed for over a month around Chalcidice.

Anne Ridler, having laboured long on his Rhodes book, had suggested that perhaps he need not deal with more than one siege of the island. He wrote to her from Bled energetically defending the second siege as a great turning-point, perhaps one of the greatest turning-points in modern history. He would rather lose some of the book's ghost stories, he told her. Bled, he thought, was beautiful and he loved the Slovenes. However, he and Eve were thinking of taking a house in Cyprus, which might be a good place to bring up Sappho – small and dark like a bird.[60]

The west was now openly backing Tito against the Russians and, on 18 September, Britain's new Foreign Secretary, Anthony Eden, arrived for a five-day visit, for which Durrell was in charge of publicity. There were meetings with Tito, a press conference in Belgrade, and two official dinner parties in Bled at which Durrell found himself in close proximity to the men who ran Yugoslavia. He did not record his feelings about them, but they can be easily imagined.

Before he departed on the 23rd, Eden publicly stated how impressed he was with Durrell's information team. But immediately the minister left, Durrell was fired. This probably meant that his three-year contract had expired and no renewal was offered, though he might have been granted an extension had he applied. No doubt someone at the Belgrade Embassy was happy to see the back of a 'non-establishment', unpredictable trickster like Durrell, with his cutting sense of humour and his impatience with stuffy proprieties. Bernard Burrows got the impression that there had been a serious clash of personalities between him and a senior official at the Embassy, and that the subsequent Antrobus stories, making out the diplomats there to be little more than a bunch of chinless buffoons, were his cunning revenge.

Seventeen years earlier, Durrell had asked George Wilkinson to find a villa for him in Corfu. In a strange repeat, he now asked him to find a villa in Cyprus. He chose Cyprus rather than Greece because of the chaotic condition of the Greek economy. In Cyprus he could spend his sterling savings without loss through currency exchange, and, important for a writer, the island's postal service was reliable. And he would be living among Greeks and able to speak Greek. He would take his tent and his car and sleep under the stars if need be. It seemed the ideal place to chance his arm as a man of letters.[61]

He asked Alan Thomas to post his notebooks, the drafted portions of his Egyptian novel and his signed copy of Forster's guide to Alexandria to him c/o George Wilkinson in Kyrenia, and his books to Limassol to await collection. The Durrells had saved enough money to buy a small house and to give Larry a year of blissful freedom in which to work on his Alexandrian opus.

Then, on the eve of departure, Eve had a nervous breakdown and plans were delayed while Durrell wondered what to do. Finally he sent her for treatment to a British Army hospital in Hanover (the nearest available psychiatric ward). Years later, Sappho gave an account of the circumstances in which Eve fell ill. Durrell was a drunkard, both fiendish and beligerent, always close to insanity, who could be extremely destructive – with a very cruel psychological precision. When Eve tried to explain that she felt like he must have felt in Argentina, he was scornful that anyone could suffer as he had. They had a great row, Eve removed her ring, and he attacked her. She did not fight back but after three nights of silent struggle he finally frightened the life out of her with what Sappho thought was an awful look – quite devilish. After that she was drugged and taken off to a military hospital.[62]

It was while stranded alone in Belgrade waiting for Eve to recover that Durrell got the idea of making money by writing thrillers. He said that he planned to do around a dozen, but only wrote one, which he was unable to sell. This story, *White*

Eagles over Serbia, was based on a true episode about which
he had some inside knowledge. It was in one sense James Bond
without the sex, and was written very quickly. He had learned
through writing press releases and editing journalists' copy
how to write clearly at speed, so the fluent style required for
an adventure book was at his fingertips. The story concerns
Methuen, a British agent sent into Serbia to discover the truth
about a group of right-wing guerrillas who had supposedly
discovered Royalist gold in the mountains. He makes his way
on foot into the area, contacts the guerrillas and is with them
when they are violently ambushed by Titoist troops. He escapes
to tell the tale to his Foreign Office handler. Durrell's grasp of
the form relating to agents and espionage, and his detailed
observations of the Serbian countryside, show us his observant
eye and retentive memory at work. Strip away the thriller
component and you have yet another Durrell travel book.

Eve returned but was still unwell, and, after a brief stay in
an observation ward in Trieste, went to England for further
treatment – a sad beginning to 1953. Durrell said later that
people thought she became ill because of his bad treatment of
her, but in fact it was a kind of 'Jewish hysteria' coupled with
religious mania to which she had fallen victim. However, his
record with women, on his own admission, was not a good
one, and he was prone to violence. Nancy had not been able
to stand the wildness which sometimes overcame him when
frustrated, and his time in Argentina and in Belgrade had been
perhaps the most frustrating in his life. He certainly complained
to friends – to Miller and to Anne Ridler – about the shackles
which family life imposed on a writer like him, who needed to
work up a kind of madness to write at full throttle. Living
with him in such a mood proved difficult for Nancy during the
writing of *The Black Book* in Corfu; that Eve should have
broken down under the same kind of pressure was not surprising. Genius makes an uneasy bedfellow, and Durrell's
genius was about to burst forth.

CHAPTER 10

The Bitter Lemons of Cyprus (1953–1956)

It is curious that the English, who can
rule so admirably, cannot like the
Romans also mix. They can impose their
laws but not their culture. That is why
English rule is the most efficient and the
least permanent in the world.

Robin Fedden, *The Land of Egypt*

Do you recognize the Temple with the
  vast peristyle,
And the bitter lemons in which your teeth
  left their mark,
And the grotto, fatal to heedless visitors,
Where the conquered seed of the
  conquered dragon sleeps?

Gerard de Nerval, 'Delifca'

When Durrell first went to Cyprus he retreated into meditation. After four years of Foreign Office musical chairs he was glad to have *his* chair taken away. He was no longer an unreliable 'contract officer' of the Diplomatic Corps, but a liberated spirit, free at last to commune with the inspiring muses of Mount Helicon rather than the hard-drinking hacks of Fleet Street. Even so, he had learned a lot from his years as a press officer. He had learned to write fast, clearly and concisely, had become aware of politics and of how great affairs of state are administered, had met powerful people and had further strengthened his own power to speak with authority, a skill already evident in his early letters to Miller.

In Trieste *en route* to Venice and Limassol, he visited Eve in the hospital observation ward just before she moved for further treatment to England. In Venice there was time for him to grasp at fragments of that city's history, to imagine Stendhal taking a glass of wine in Florian's and Baron Corvo darting about shadowy alleys, and to watch the *vaporetto* nudging down the Grand Canal. But now he was poised to embark for the Greek world he loved, the place which most inspired his own imaginative spirit.

In Cyprus he headed for Kyrenia, a lovely little Graeco-Turkish port on the north coast, where George Wilkinson had a small villa, and found two rooms to rent for himself and Sappho in the house of a Greek Cypriot schoolteacher called Panos. Here he began looking around the island for the dream house in which to write his great book, and here he first got to know local Greeks, who were highly impressed by an Englishman who spoke such good Greek. Through Panos, he met the harbourmaster, the grocer, the bookseller and the pharmacist, and in Clito's wine-shop he found congenial company. His book, *Bitter Lemons*, tells how he there disarmed a local braggart, Frangos (spoiling for a fight with this British interloper), by inventing a brother who had died in defence of Greece at Thermopylae.[1]

Cyprus is one of the most beautiful of Mediterranean islands, with a richly varied topography – the snow-capped Troodos Mountains, a hot central plateau, vine-clad slopes and pretty harbours. There are relics of the past civilizations which have dominated its history – Greece, Syria, Egypt, Rome, Turkey, as well as Crusaders and Templars. In the nineteenth century Rimbaud was there, helping to build the Governor's residence at Troodos, and the British had ruled since acquiring it from Turkey in 1878. The indigenous people were predominantly Greek, with Turks making up around a fifth of the population. At the time Durrell arrived, Sir Robert Armitage was the Governor and, although there was a minority movement among the Greeks for Enosis, the island was a haven of peace, a paradise for writers and artists.

It differed from other Greek islands mostly because of the British presence – red pillar-boxes, Morris Minors, and Union

Jacks fluttering above police stations, though significantly hardly anywhere else. The British community was, in Durrell's eyes, boorish and almost entirely insensitive to local feelings and local culture. In Kyrenia, houses had sprung up which were straight out of English suburbia, with names like Mon Repos and The Gables. There were more milk-bars than wine-bars, and, of course, practically no one among the British spoke Greek.

By the end of March 1953, Durrell had found a Turkish house in the small Greek village of Bellapaix under a medieval castle called Buffavento, a few miles east of Kyrenia and four miles from the sea. It stood on a hillside close to a twelfth-century Gothic Lusignan abbey built by the medieval Order of St Norbert. In the village square stood the Tree of Idleness, whose shadow, said the legend, robbed one of the power to work. In a celebrated chapter in *Bitter Lemons*, Durrell tells the story of how he bought his delightful house in this picturesque village. A roguish Turkish estate agent from Kyrenia, Sabri Tahir, cunningly persuaded a peasant family to sell it for a mere £300. The same house, after Durrell's and others' renovations, sold for £160,000 in 1995.

Durrell found himself in a landscape of orange and lemon trees in a village permeated with Turkish and Venetian influences, where roses and almond and peach blossoms grew in profusion. His house, which stood on the hillside above the village, had immense chiselled doors with an ancient pistol-lock, carved window screens and balcony from which one could see from Bellapaix to Kyrenia and the Taurus Mountains in Turkey beyond. His garden was a garden of trees – lemon, tangerine, pomegranate, mulberry and walnut. The people of Bellapaix, said Panos, who had taught there, were the laziest and the best-natured of people. Durrell's first impression was that there was something eerie and malign about Cyprus, which was unlike any Greek island he knew, with more of an eastern flavour. He found the local Greeks more formal and more reserved than metropolitan Greeks, and the climate far from sexy, which made it a mystery to him how Aphrodite came to be born there – a view he later changed.

The house needed work before he could move in, and buying

it and supporting Eve in England had made a big hole in his savings. While building work began he continued living with Panos in Kyrenia. Getting by was difficult, but the trick, he knew, was to live not on the British level but on the cheaper Greek one, something he was used to and quite enjoyed. Finding him fluent in Greek and knowledgeable about Greece, the villagers, after some initial suspicion, welcomed him in great style. He met the affable Andreas Menas, the large, moustachioed Michaelis, Dmitri the café owner, Anthemos the grocer and the welcoming village *muktar*. Those who were hostile he won over by embracing in the name of Greek hospitality. And there too was the roaring Frangos, his pugilistic friend from Clito's wine-shop.

Overseeing work on the house and looking after little Sappho was a full-time job. However, his notebooks had arrived and he was able to start on his Alexandrian novel by working at night after she had gone to sleep. The notebooks – he called them 'quarry books' – were a repository of memories from which he hoped to cut and carve his great opus. But, finding it difficult to settle to work, he blamed his marriages and the commitments which they had brought: still having to pay for Penelope's upbringing, and now for Eve's stay in England.[2]

Meanwhile, he had made contact with Seferis, now Greek Minister in Beirut, and wrote to Miller, congratulating him on his success with reprints of his early novels and publication of *Sexus*. Miller, who had survived police prosecution in France, replied from Paris. He was there touring Europe with his Eve, and expecting war at any moment. Once things looked dangerous, he said, he was beating it straight back to the States.[3] He and his Eve had a grand reunion with Perlès and his wife in Barcelona, a hilarious occasion at which they could not stop laughing recalling the old Paris days. Durrell may have felt left out, stuck as he was on his small sweltering island, but his mother had arrived to help with Sappho, and there was cause for celebration – the appearance of Gerry's book, *The Overloaded Ark*, and his own *Reflections on a Marine Venus*. Gerry's book was a big success, becoming a Book Society Choice and a *Daily Mail* Book of the Month, and selling 27,000 copies in a very short time. At twenty-eight,

Gerry became an instant celebrity. *Reflections on a Marine Venus* was also to receive excellent notices and confirm Durrell as an 'islomane' of subtle power and artistry. A review by Sir Harold Nicolson in the *Observer* crowned the book's success: 'This is a gay and lovely book. I hope that those who are unable to journey to the Sporades will read it and catch something of the sun-god's happiness and the tang of resinated wine.' The pleasure of the book was the rare conjunction of 'an ideal subject with a writer of quite unusual distinction'.[4] Anne Ridler wrote to say that Nicholson's review would help enormously with sales, and quoted an advertisement that declared, 'A glorious press for the brothers Durrell'.[5]

Without Eve, his eye began to wander. As when Nancy had left him in Egypt, he had the opportunity again to exercise his poetic powers of seduction. One young woman he fell for in quite a big way was Marie, the daughter of a famous British diplomat, Sir Eugen Millington-Drake. Marie, like Durrell a restless traveller, was thinking of putting down roots in Cyprus and was looking for a spot to build her perfect house. When she died in the 1970s, he was deeply upset and in his final island book, *Sicilian Carousel*, describes his deep attachment to her.

By the autumn of 1953, he was halfway through his novel, now called *Justine in Alexandria* – a bizarre concoction of sex and espionage, which would be widely denounced, he joked,[6] but he thought it the best thing he had done since *The Black Book*. With his house still unfinished and still living in cramped quarters, working on it was difficult. However, it had been building up in him for so many years it was now bursting to get out, and any spare moment served. Louisa was there to care for Sappho, but his remaining funds were being eaten up by the house, and he could not afford even to buy books.

When the money had almost run out, he took a job teaching English at the Pancyprian Gymnasium in Nicosia. It meant getting up at 4.30 a.m., writing for an hour (in pencil not on the typewriter in order not to wake the sleeping child), then driving into the capital, watching the sun rise as he went. He taught from 7 a.m. till 2 p.m., then drove thirty miles back to Kyrenia. He was by no means a dedicated teacher, but the sixth-form girls were apt to leave red roses on his desk, and the boys also warmed to this lively, laughing little Englishman who spoke Greek and so obviously loved the Greece of which so many of them longed to be a part.

He moved into the house at Bellapaix towards the end of October. The work was barely finished and he had not even a table to write on. But he now began to hint at the kind of novel he was writing – it was set in Alexandria and was 'four-dimensional'. The problem was to keep it tight and concise, but he was in great shape for writing, and at ease with himself. Eve had said she might be arriving in Cyprus soon, but in any case the book occupied most of his thinking. Even so, he was occasionally diverted by some strange beauty or other whose attentions he found soothing. He seems to have changed his mind about Cyprus being a sexless place, and now, in late October, told Miller that it was an island for the sybarite.[7] His interest in deviant sexuality had no doubt been somewhat repressed during his time with the Diplomatic Corps. Now, more of an artistic free agent, he could again indulge his fasci-nation with Freud and de Sade, explore the multiple nature of sexuality, and the condition of hermaphroditism, which had fascinated him among Gerald's insect specimens in Corfu. He told Miller that Cyprus had the highest number of genuine hermaphrodites in the world.[8]

With the house finished he was able to entertain his friends. Paddy Leigh Fermor came in late October and they had riotous times together, and John Lehmann visited in November. Zarian said he planned to settle there to start up a newspaper, and Freya Stark paid a visit while staying with an architect friend of Marie's, Austen Harrison. Harrison, an architect based in Cyprus (a noble-looking Norman Douglas or a figure from a youthful novel of Huxley, thought Durrell), lived at Lapithos in an old converted wine-magazine, which for Durrell embodied a whole philosophy of the good life. Two Yugoslav ballet dancers also came – one for whom he had a specially soft spot, a delec-table girl called Fosca, whom he borrowed for his *Alexandria Quartet*. Cyprus, like Egypt, was becoming a movable feast for exiled and travelling writers and artists.

His discussions with Harrison and a Greek architect called

Christophides led Durrell to sketch out a novel called *The Village of the Turtle-Doves*, intended to follow his Alexandria story. It concerned Peristerona (Turtle-Dove), a perfect Greek village, conceived by a Falstaffian architect Caradoc – a place which attracts idealists like the young architect Dmitri and his filmstar girlfriend Beba. The story, as far as it went, involved the clash between idealism and corrupt politicians. The ideal village is meant to replace an old village underneath which lie valuable antiquities. Caradoc survived into *Tunc/Nunquam*, as did the filmstar figure, there called Iolanthe. Durrell probably abandoned this novel when he realized it was going nowhere and that he was writing a far better one in *Justine*.[9]

He found the Gymnasium an ideal laboratory for the study of Cypriot sentiment. There he witnessed the gradual shift of feeling from love of both England and Greece to an anarchistic opposition towards British rule on the island. When Seferis came visiting from Beirut in mid-November, looking, he thought, much older and wiser at fifty-four, Durrell took him to meet his class. He gave an address which received a great ovation, and boosted Durrell's kudos, as friend of the great Greek poet. Many of his students were increasingly torn between an almost religious passion for Enosis and an affection for the British who had helped Greece gain independence from Turkey.

By now, Larry had ceased to care much whether Eve returned or not, except that they were connected by Sappho. He told Miller that women were a wearisome interference with work – although they thought they were persons, they were merely illustrative of some general law or biological urge. The best way to enjoy them was to bother about them as little as possible.[10] He planned to spend most of the coming winter with his Elizabethans now that his books had arrived from England.[11] But he continued to comfort himself with liaisons; whatever they lacked in stability, they made up for in spice and variety. Meanwhile the novel grew at roughly 1,500 words a week.

Eve was staying with the Burrowses in London when Durrell finally sent her a cable asking her to return to him in Cyprus.

Perhaps Louisa, at sixty-eight, was finding baby-minding a bit
taxing, and Sappho was missing her mother. Also Durrell could
perhaps avoid the 'woman trouble' which Miller had run into.[12]
Having Eve back would at least help to protect him from any
emotional backlash from casually discarded lovers. By the end
of March 1954 she was there, looking, he thought, delightful
and in good spirits.[13] She loved the house and Sappho was
thrilled to have her mother back. Louisa returned to Bournemouth, Margo and St Alban's Avenue. Sappho later made out
that being cared for by Mrs Durrell in Cyprus was a rough and
frightening experience, that Louisa hated caring for children,
especially when they soiled themselves, and put her into corduroy trousers lined with napples. When Eve saw her she was
horrified and wanted to remove her. There then began a
struggle for her soul between her father and mother.[14]

But Durrell was trying to engender that difficult mental state
he thought it took in order to write something important. He
told Eliot that progress on the novel was hindered by his having
to teach; he therefore lacked time for the nervous breakdown
essential for giving his book its edge. He was feeling ancient
and was now quite unable to compose poetry. His only
pleasures were love-making and sunbathing, a new awareness
of the significance of pleasure being his main achievement.[15]
Epicurus, his mentor in such things, would have nodded
approvingly. He did have other pleasures, such as entertaining,
and that spring he had visits from Osbert Lancaster, Sir Harry
Luke, Katsimbalis, and, later on, Ines Burrows and Daphne
and Xan Fielding (whose war memoir, *Hide and Seek*, was just
out).

The British had foolishly closed the door to Enosis, and, as
trouble began to brew on the island, the Colonial Secretary, a
friend of Austen Harrison, suggested that Durrell might like to
take on the job of director of information services for the
island. Durrell accepted. The job, he thought, would be more
congenial than teaching, and would put him back on a decent
salary. He met the Governor, who thought that the situation
could be kept a colonial one; Durrell thought that once Athens
and Ankara became involved it would become a European,
even a world issue, and events would slip from the Governor's

grasp. But at that time, despite strikes and demonstrations, the island was relatively quiet and the press remained ungagged.

Having rejoined the establishment, Durrell found himself with a large shabby office in Nicosia, a Greek assistant called Achilles, and a car of his choice – an Opel. According to Penelope Tremayne, 'He loved fast cars, and drove the Opel with spectacular effect.'[16] However, he was so exhausted from hard work that the book ground to a halt, and he began to detest it for tormenting him so.[17] He was lifted a little out of his slough of despond when, on 10 June, he was invited to become a Fellow of the Royal Society of Literature, an offer he was pleased to accept. And if his book had bogged down he did manage to get poems into print. Two written in Belgrade during Eve's breakdown, 'On Mirrors' and 'Letters in Darkness', appeared – the first in the *TLS* in August and the second in the September *London Magazine*, which in October also included translations of four Cypriot poets by Durrell and Maurice Cardiff, a British Council teacher in Nicosia.

Part of his inheritance as information service director was a monthly magazine, *Cyprus Review*, a glossy public-relations effort promoting a benevolent image of the colonial administration, not unlike the *Booster* when it belonged to the American Country Club of Paris. Durrell was determined to make it into a worthwhile literary magazine, and at the same time promote Cyprus and British culture.[18] He brought in George Wilkinson as editor, but retained editorial control himself. He wrote to his many writer friends soliciting contributions.

As press interest in the Cyprus situation increased, and journalists queued up for copy, Durrell must have wondered what on earth he was doing back in much the same situation he had escaped from in Belgrade – back from Helicon to the hacks of Fleet Street. Cyprus was not communist Yugoslavia, but now, rather than helping to expose what he thought of as a false line in propaganda, he was in danger of becoming a propagandist himself. However, he believed that only one side of the story had so far been put, and there needed to be a respectable outlet to express the British viewpoint.[19]

If Larry's career was temporarily bogged down, Gerry's was

shooting skywards. After the success of *The Overloaded Ark*, from which he had so for earned £3,000, his second book, *Three Singles to Adventure*, had already sold 10,000, and his third, *The Bafut Beagles*, had just come out, selling 10,000 prior to publication. He was busy giving radio talks and trying to get into television, and he had a grand project to found a trust devoted to breeding endangered animals, for which he was eagerly seeking rich backers.[20] Meanwhile, Margo, now separated from her husband, still lived at 51 St Alban's Avenue with her two sons, and Leslie had gone to work for the Kenyan government, in some civil engineering capacity, and had taken up painting.[21] Larry's painting had been on hold since Argentina, but he had not abandoned the art by any means. As for poetry, his new book, *The Tree of Idleness*, was due out in March with a harder, more ironic style which was, he thought, more Taoist.

Initially, the approaching tragedy on the island seemed to Durrell a bit like a comic-opera. While storm clouds gathered, he still had his place in the sun, and was enjoying his house in Bellapaix and his friendships with the villagers and other Greek friends such as Panos. He had pushed his book, which he jokingly called 'Sex and the Secret Service', to 200 pages by mid-December, and intimated to friends that he himself was involved in Stendhalian intrigues which were leading him into the darker regions of human motivation. His relationship with Eve was also coursing through unchartable regions of the soul. Although she had recovered from her break-down, he saw himself in the same situation of which F. Scott Fitzgerald had written in *Tender Is the Night*. He told Anne Ridler that his family was a weight around his neck and he would have done better to marry a rich sterile widow. But if he had done that, replied Ridler, where would such poems as 'Clouds of Glory' and 'Aspects of Melissa' have been?[22] Sappho, meanwhile, was growing up to be beautiful – dark with big black eyes, and a mixture of whimsicality and devilishness.

On 18 December, the UN decided to shelve the demand of the Greek government for Cypriot self-determination. Demonstrations became riots, Union Jacks were burned, British-owned bars stoned and cars set alight. Students were shot and arrested.

The director of information services found himself under mounting pressure from journalists. Charles Foley, editor of the *Cyprus Times*, remembered Durrell, 'short and square, with rock-crystal eyes set in a craggy face and the grin of a good-natured satyr',[23] feeding them the official line. Britain supported self-determination, but it was 'not on' for Cyprus. British withdrawals from the Middle East had to end for the sake of the western alliance and for the benefit of the Cypriots, too. Since the war there had been great progress on the island – piped water, reafforestation and eradication of malaria. For the Greek government to take over could be disastrous for the Cypriots. The island was essential to NATO's defences, which had brought business and prosperity to the locals. The Turkish minority was against change and Turkey was a vital member of NATO. Foley saw, however, that Durrell was as free from humbug as a Cyprus official could be, and probably did not believe in the policy.

But he did believe in the *Cyprus Review*, which flourished on a subsidy, and its January edition gave a list of authors lined up for 1955, which reads a bit like Larry's own visitors' list: Gerald Durrell, Freya Stark, Lord Kinross, Osbert Lancaster, Sir Harry Luke, Patrick Leigh Fermor, Vernon Bartlett, John Lehmann and John Pudney. In February, as if there were not a cloud in the political sky, the March edition ran articles on a tree-planting festival and on winter sailing at Kyrenia. It also mentioned a new director for Cyprus Radio, which was also under Durrell's control – a radio which would put the British line over on the air.

Gerald arrived at the end of March to make a film and to finish a book. He was amused to find Larry about to move into a splendid new palatial office with a desk the size of a billiard table. While he was there, a letter arrived from Faber with a cheque for *The Tree of Idleness* for the grand sum of £5 11s 6d. Larry sighed. He would have to be careful, he said, or he'd soon be up to six pounds![24] With the Bellapaix house now smartened up, he took everyone back to the village for a weekend. But it was a little too unsettled for him to return there permanently, as sentiment was turning ever more against the British, and, friendly though he was with the villagers, he was also a member of the increasingly hated island government.

Gerry and Jacquie left at the end of May but there was a flying visit from Paddy Leigh Fermor, who came to lecture at the British Institute in Nicosia, a visit which coincided with the publication of *The Tree of Idleness*. Leigh Fermor read it straight off and pronounced it the best Larry had done so far. He had read it through twice and felt 'aswoon'.[25]

When the immensely tall British Colonial Secretary, Lennox-Boyd, visited Nicosia in July for talks with the Greek Cypriot leader, Archbishop Makarios, Charles Foley caught him and the information director together in an amusing snapshot at a press conference:

> The Minister was accompanied by the Governor, a man of moderate height whose head was level with the visitor's collar-band, and Larry Durrell, who came a little lower again. The sight of the Secretary of State stooping to talk to the Director of Information was reminiscent of a Max Beerbohm cartoon: 'Watts-Dutton reprimanding Swinburne for drinking absinthe'.[26]

His relationship with Eve had now broken down irretrievably, and in mid-August she left for England, taking Sappho with her. Durrell, it seems, had grown bored with his marriage, seeing it far too often as a curb on his creativity, much as he had his marriage to Nancy. Eve was a beautiful woman and had stuck by him through bad times in Argentina and Yugoslavia. Unhappily, he found it difficult to stick by her when things turned badly for her. He needed strong women who could put up with his sometimes outrageous and violent behaviour and continue to love him. Eve, it turned out, was too sensitive and, when she saw his growing impatience with her, had the courage to leave him. The ogre from whom Nancy had fled had also finally driven Eve away.

The deteriorating political situation may also have had something to do with it. But Sappho gave her version of events some thirty years later. She said that Larry had treated Eve with violence at times bordering on madness,[27] and that she had decided to go with her mother rather than stay with her father. Being deprived a second time of a daughter left Larry with a deep emotional wound. The theme of the lost child would now take on a sharper edge than ever.

Left alone in his official residence in Nicosia he felt completely worn out. He told Freya Stark that he hoped that the following year would bring some enchantment into his life. Even so, whatever he was going through, he was gathering valuable experience from it all.[28] Like Miller, who turned a wretched early life to good use in his *Tropic* books, Durrell had never given up the great urge to turn whatever misery he suffered into literature. For the moment, his official position meant that he was forbidden from writing about events, though he did a few anonymous pieces for the *Economist*. As always, the writer inside him was noting and retaining, with future books in mind.

He did not live alone for long. One evening, in the bar of Nicosia's Cosmopolitan Club, he got into conversation with a young ex-Guards officer, Richard Lumley, who was travelling around the Middle East, and, finding he had nowhere to stay, invited him to his place for the night. In the event, Lumley stayed for about six months, and Durrell was able to help him find a job, first at the new Cyprus Radio station and then on the *Times of Cyprus*, through Charles Foley. Lumley was heir to Lord Scarborough, a member of the royal household. There were leisurely and hilarious conversations, much conviviality and some farce. On one occasion, after a good night's drinking together at the Cosmopolitan, lurking figures were spotted in nearby bushes and Cyril the barman decided that Durrell was a terrorist target. Larry and Lumley had to escape in an infantry-style zigzagging dash from the club's back door. Under pressure, friends noticed, Durrell had become a chain-smoker. He also armed himself, as Lumley soon found out. Arriving back late one evening he found that he had lost his key. He hammered on the door, but no response. Finally, the door was opened and there stood Durrell, stark naked with a revolver clutched in his hand.[29]

EOKA, the terrorist organization committed to Enosis, was now the force with which the British had to contend. Talks in London between Britain, Greece and Turkey broke up without agreement in September. The situation promptly became an international one, as Durrell had predicted, and the Greek radio began vitriolic attacks on Britain and its lackeys, such as Durrell, who were described as enemies of the Cypriot people. On 15 September, EOKA was outlawed, and on the 18th the British Institute in Nicosia was attacked. At the end of the month, Sir Robert Armitage was replaced as Governor by a soldier, Field Marshal Sir John Harding.

It was evident that, at least for now, Durrell could no longer live in Bellapaix, and so the house he had lovingly converted was locked up, and he took to spending time alone at a deserted mosque on the coast where he had made friends with the Turkish *Hodja*, a shy old man and a recluse, said to have been banished there for rape and murder. There was a Turkish burial ground where he found himself close to happiness – it was like Rhodes all over again. The deserted beach near by was a place to take a woman or to meet Greek friends such as Panos who might have been compromised now had they met more openly. Those he took there he enjoined to absolute secrecy. This was his private country to which he could escape from the stress of daily life. And the isolated mosque suited his new contemplative mood; he was now reading Suzuki's dissertations on Zen Buddhism.[30]

His novel was all but finished, and actually fitted into the scheme he had outlined to Miller before the war, following the form of youth, maturity and age. Although he said later that his characters were not based on anyone in particular, but built up from many sources, he told Miller that his book, now called *Justine* and set in pre-war Alexandria, was about Eve. The choice of title also betrayed his attachment to de Sade, as did one of the epigraphs he used for the book from de Sade's *Justine*:

> There are two positions available to us – either crime which renders us happy, or the noose, which prevents us from being unhappy. I ask whether there can be any hesitation, lovely Thérèse, and where will your little mind find an argument able to combat that one?

And there was one from Freud's letters which underlines his fascination with the many faces of sexuality:

I am accustoming myself to the idea of regarding every sexual act as a process in which four persons are involved. We shall have a lot to discuss about that.

The Nicosia house was a place not just for bachelor carousing, but also for dispensing information and booze to the world's press. Durrell was careful to meet at the airport and house himself journalists who he thought might be hostile to the British line so that he could contaminate their minds more effectively. He estimated seeing 600 journalists in six months, and a river of gin flowed through the house, and not only gin, as Kingsley Martin, editor of the *New Statesman*, remembered:

> Lawrence Durrell is the only public relations officer I can recall giving me red wine and talking about poetry over a wood fire. That is how I recall an evening with him in Cyprus at the beginning of 1956. That was before things had passed the point of no return . . . It was before Durrell was sure he could no longer remain working with Sir John Harding, in spite of his admiration for him as a personality and soldier; before he knew he could not return to live in the house he had built with such passionate joy in Bellapaix; before his demi-paradise of love and friendship had been transformed into the saddest and most reluctant inferno of superstition and murder.[31]

The Cyprus situation was moving towards its violent denouement. Durrell found the harsher military policy under Harding difficult to stomach. But the social Durrell continued to function. The day after Martin's visit, and with a heavy hangover, Durrell dashed to meet Diana and Yehudi Menuhin, whose tour ship had put in at Larnaca. There he had a brief reunion with Diana, who had so entranced him twelve years earlier. He and Yehudi hit it off immediately, each having a voracious and open mind, each fascinated by eastern religions. Diana found him not quite as certain of himself as he had been when they had met in Alexandria. She told him later that she had never met anyone who was able to combine such cleverness, kindness and precious generosity; he and Yehudi were fraternal spirits.[32]

Miller counselled Durrell not to find another mate in too much of a hurry. But Durrell did not need any advice from Miller on the subject of women, and had already found someone. Dick Lumley remembers him coming back from a party one night with the woman in charge of the French section of Radio Cyprus. Before long she had moved in. Her name was Claude Forde, a married woman with two children, whose English husband was in the navy but who seemed to live a life of her own. Pretty, blonde, intelligent and loquacious, she was fluent in seven languages. She had been born Claude Vincendon in, of all places, Alexandria, the daughter of a French banker and a Jewish mother. She had lived in Ireland and in Israel, where she had trained as an electrician. She was also a writer, working on a book about having kept a pub in Cork. She might have walked straight out of the pages of Durrell's novel. When she moved in with him, they worked together on their books with the noise of bombs and shootings outside (and Durrell in constant touch with Government House on the phone), helping one another as they went. Claude did his typing, and Durrell joked later that some of the odd punctuation in *Justine* was caused by her jumping at the sound of bombs exploding. He said he finished *Justine* with a map of old Alexandria spread out on the table, and Claude helping him to recall streets and parks and bordellos which he had forgotten. Out in the country, revolution raged, but inside they were lost in a fantasy of being somewhere else – the Alexandria of memory he was now exploring.[33] When he finished the book he calculated that, excluding the time absorbed by the crisis, it had taken him around four months to write.[34]

Like *The Black Book*, the whole Alexandria sequence is set inside different frames. In *Justine*, pre-war Alexandria is recalled by the exiled Darley (schoolmaster and would-be novelist), from an island in the Cyclades – perhaps Mykonos. But, in the way the memory works, he recaptures the past not in strictly chronological form, but in sometimes fleeting images or set-piece events, so that the narrative reveals itself only gradually through these epiphanic recollections. The instability of memory expresses what Durrell had come to think of as the instability of the self and the uncertainty of history. Justine, the beautiful, dark, seductive nymphomaniac Jewess, traumatized by childhood rape and desolated by having had a child kidnapped, stands as the mystery at the core of the novel. Her inscrutable husband Nessim, the Coptic banker and business tycoon, only compounds and confuses the enigma. Together with Darley and his mistress Melissa, the Greek dancer and prostitute, these two make up the four faces of love alluded to in the Freudian epigraph. Justine is the dark focus of the book, and all other characters seem to be defined in relation to her. She is projected not only as a real presence, but also as a prismatic psyche and as a godlike force, giving the book both a psychological and a metaphysical resonance.

The cast of other characters – Balthazar (homosexual, doctor and cabbalist), Clea (artist and lesbian), Pombal (French diplomat and womanizer), Toto de Brunel (French diplomat and homosexual), Scobie (ex-naval commander, Vice Squad officer and pederast), Mnemjian (barber, pimp and spy), Capodistria (ageing one-eyed moneylender, sensualist and rapist of the young Justine), Cohen (furrier and 'protector' of Melissa) and Pursewarden (diplomat and novelist) – are also unknowable except through fleeting memories and provisionally constructed stereotypes liable to be undermined by different versions of them seen from others' viewpoints. All these characters are sexually damaged, and Alexandria, the capital of memory, is a place of intrigue and deception – of false lovers, spies and dark plots. Darley, who loves Melissa, the mistress of Cohen, is seduced by Justine, Nessim's wife and the lover of Pursewarden and also of Clea, who may have made love to Justine. This kind of oriental *La Ronde* is explored with the ironic detachment and luxurious langour of a Cavafy, against the backdrop of an Alexandria seen through a soft-focus lens and imprinted through a language vibrant with allusion and colour. The city, with all its squalor, cruelty, vice and voluptuousness, is transformed into Durrell's own Heraldic Universe, his own private country. At the same time, it stands, as some of its critics have observed, for something wider: a universe of ideas which Durrell had evolved through his own metaphysical quest for meaning and his exploration of unorthodox ideas – oriental religions, the Cabbala, de Sade, and his own spin on Einstein and Freud (Freud reworked by Rank, Howe, Groddeck and Mott).

Darley's reconstruction of the past, centring around these connected figures, is interleaved by a book about Justine by her previous husband, Arnauti, called *Moeurs*, in which there is a diary, purported to be Justine's own account of her life, and reinterpreted through a letter written by Clea. From these stories within stories within stories (the Chinese box) is drawn the unsteady and imperfect narrative which by the end of the book we have extricated through the pen of Darley. Justine is deceiving Nessim and Pursewarden, Darley is betraying Melissa, who deceives Darley with Nessim. So that, even though Darley gives us his fragmented account retrieved from his haunted memory, it is an unstable account, for in this atmosphere of deception no one's words can be trusted. By the end of the novel Justine is no longer the power she was; she has left to work on a kibbutz in Palestine (Claude's influence on Durrell perhaps); Melissa is dead (leaving behind Nessim's child), Pursewarden dead by suicide, Scobie murdered, Capodistria murdered, Cohen dying, Nessim deserted, Darley gone to teach in Upper Egypt. An old Durrell theme – the scattering of a company of acquaintances – brings the novel to a conclusion. In 'Workpoints' at the end of the novel, Durrell quotes Pursewarden's idea of the three-part 'n-dimensional' novel – a forward-running narrative with contrapuntal retrospective references giving it a strangely slow-spinning, extra-temporal impression revealing the overall pattern simultaneously. Causality therefore is not the dominant mode, but events can move between past, present and future, not necessarily in that order.[35]

Behind this intricate and seductive book, so Durrell later claimed, he was attempting to embody Einstein's theory of relativity in literature. It must have been an extension and elaboration of the idea which had been put to him in 1938 by E. Graham Howe. Einsteinian theory showed that events appear only relative to the observer, whose presence also undermines the truthfulness of the vision. On this view, truth is no longer something objectively demonstrable, but unstable and provisional – and the truth not just of history and external events, but also of biography and of the self. Others had reached the same conclusion, including Ford Madox Ford in *The Good Soldier* (which Durrell had not then read) and André

Gide in *The Counterfeiters*. But the way in which Durrell got to this point is the intriguing story of a curious, self-tutored mind untrammelled by institutional learning. And the haunting quality of his poetic prose, here brought to perfection, made this an extraordinarily distinctive literary achievement.

Dick Lumley did not care for Claude's presence; he found her bossy and opinionated, and much too talkative. He advised Durrell to get rid of her, and Durrell promised to do so. However, she remained, and on one occasion, when she said that her husband was due to visit Cyprus, Durrell became very nervous, pacing up and down and saying to Lumley, 'Do you think he'll hit me?'[36] What happened in the event is not recorded, but somehow it became understood that Larry and Claude were a pair. And perhaps he began to see her as a model for Clea in *Justine* – that is what is widely thought, although there was also Clea Baduro, the beautiful Alexandrian painter, whom Durrell had known, and who some think has a greater claim to being the original. Probably the character grew more like Claude as Durrell wrote.

Just how non-establishment Durrell was Dick Lumley discovered one evening when he received a phone call from some senior civil servant at Government House.

> A lot of the colonial administrators didn't know what the hell to make of Larry. And I can . . . see him now, sitting in the hall, fairly pissed one evening, and the telephone goes and a long, increasingly angry conversation [ensued]. And this is one of the top in the administration. And Larry's punchline I'll never forget. 'Anyway, you're an inept cunt!' Howls of laughter and he puts the receiver down. And you see, this didn't figure in the manual when you went to wherever you went to learn about colonial administration. So he was a wild card, obviously. But then . . . John Harding [brought] a lot of new people in . . . they were a much higher calibre and *they* appreciated Larry, you know . . .[37]

On 9 March 1956, Archbishop Makarios was deported to the Seychelles. Strikes and riots followed what was widely thought of as a gross political blunder forced on the Conservative government by its Empire Loyalist right wing. Later, on the day of the deportation, the appointment of Durrell as government press censor was announced. Taking on the role of censor again must have been anathema to a literary anarchist like Durrell, and he was now speaking openly about returning to England and of going on to live in France with Claude.

Perhaps prophetically, on 10 March, the *New Statesman* printed his poem, 'Bitter Lemons'. After completing *Justine*, he had probably already begun to sketch out his third, and some would say his best, island book. He had turned also in relief to writing comic sketches about life at the Belgrade Embassy, which according to Claude he wrote very quickly at odd moments in his office. So was born Antrobus, the old diplomatic hand with a Wodehousean line in humour, a character whom Durrell, the mimic, must have aired at congenial moments among his friends. In his casual inventing of Antrobus he had struck a goldmine.

The deportation of Makarios was compounded by the execution on 10 May of Michalakis Karaolides for murder. On the morning of the execution, Durrell made his last visit to Bellapaix to retrieve some books and papers. Instead of the usual cheery greetings he was met by a wall of silence. After the hanging, EOKA had its first martyr, and the British case was doomed. The revolt grew in savagery and if Durrell had ever hesitated about leaving the island his mind must have been made up as the situation became irretrievable. Diana Menuhin wrote hoping that some unhappy terrorist would not turn him into a Rupert Brooke and some corner of a Cyprus field into a piece of Pudding Island forever.[38]

He found a new friend in Penelope Tremayne, the English poet, working in Cyprus with the Red Cross, whom he met through Maurice Cardiff. They instantly became friends and she found Claude as impressive as him. 'She was tiny, exquisitely pretty, and bubbling both with vitality and good nature. She was absolutely sweet, and very intelligent.'[39] Larry, she discovered, was planning to escape from Cyprus and the official life which had so fractured his relationships with the Greeks he loved.

He said, 'When I leave here I'm going to live in the south of France, where the cigarettes are a shilling a packet and wine is sixpence a bottle, and I've got enough in the kitty to live for a year like that, by the end of which I shall have written a book that will really sell.' So I said, 'Splendid, and what is it going to be?' 'Well,' he said, 'there's only one thing that really sells in the present day and that's pornography. But it's got to be thriller pornography – James Bond, if you can do it,' he said. '[But] I'm never going to be able to write that sort of stuff, so I'm going to write high-brow pornography and they'll all swallow it.'[40]

Dick Lumley, perhaps unable to put up with the bossy Claude, moved out and soon thereafter became ADC to the Governor, Field Marshal Harding.

Some youths threw a bomb at a house opposite Durrell's in Nicosia – a bomb probably intended for him.[41] He moved house. His schoolmaster friend from Kyrenia, Panos, was shot dead by EOKA (possibly for associating with him). This may have been the final straw. In *Bitter Lemons*, he says that Harding asked him to stay on.[42] However, a successor was appointed.

He wrote to Alan Thomas, sending him the manuscript of *Justine* and a clutch of letters from famous writers which he thought would be worth keeping. One definitely worth keeping, though containing disappointing news, came from Laurence Olivier in July, rejecting Larry's play *Sappho* for theatrical production. Sir William Walton had passed on the script to him, but Olivier said that while there were some lovely things in it – 'fine verse and lovely sounds' – the whole thing did not add up to a play for him. The characters were unbelievable and did not engage him emotionally. It was a play for the ear rather than for the eye. And while it made good reading it would not, he thought, make for an exciting evening in the theatre.[43] Meanwhile, in America, the faithful Miller was trying to get the film actress Geraldine Fitzgerald interested in the play – also to no avail.[44]

On the night Lawrence Durrell left Cyprus he invited Penelope Tremayne to dinner at the Ledra Palace Hotel. Afterwards, he and Claude climbed on to the airport bus, and Durrell, leaning out of the window, threw Tremayne the keys of his house and told her she could have it rent-free. Then, just as the bus was about to leave, he leaned out of the window again.

'You'd better have this, too, if you're going to live up there,' he said, and dropped his revolver at her feet.

Tremayne was horrified. She had no licence, and if a Red Cross nurse went armed it would compromise her entirely. She turned it in to the Special Branch. It was probably an indication of how hastily he had to leave the island that he left behind his treasured library, which it would take him some time to retrieve.

Back in England, he was broke and utterly without prospects. Claude hoped to find a place for them to live in France, but meanwhile he sent *Justine* and *White Eagles over Serbia* to Faber, and obtained a contract from them to write the book he had already begun about his Cyprus experience (*Bitter Lemons*). He was given a three-month deadline of December. Miller told him not to worry; he had a charmed life – full of fascination and beautiful books.[45] Fortunately, *Justine* was soon accepted and Faber also decided that *White Eagles* might be suitable for the juvenile market.

Eve asked him to look after Sappho while she found a job and got settled in London, and his need for funds became even more pressing. He had a small nest-egg of about £400, intended to see him through his first few months in France. His settled income was gone or about to go, he had to support his daughter and he needed somewhere quiet in which to finish *Bitter Lemons*. Hoping to make a few guineas, he offered the BBC a talk on 'Politics and Terrorism in Cyprus'. But a Foreign Office man (used in those days to vet politically delicate material at the Corporation) investigated him and decided that he was unsound on Cyprus, so the idea was squashed.[46] No doubt someone at the FO had wreaked revenge on him for some past insult. The BBC was, in the event, the loser. They would probably have got a preview of *Bitter Lemons*, undoubtedly the finest piece of literature to come out of the Cyprus affair. Instead they got from him some recordings of his most recent poems, and a review of Kazantzakis' book, *Freedom and Death*.

Shortly after recording his broadcasts, for which he earned eleven guineas, plans to live in Paris fell through. In desperation, he got back in touch with Cecily Mackworth, his friend from Villa Seurat days, who had just married a French marquis and was living in a château in Normandy. She was amazed to get a letter suggesting that he come to work for her as her gardener while he finished *Bitter Lemons*. As a newlywed she thought the last person she wanted around was Larry Durrell.[47] A friend, Diana Ladas, however, lent him a small cottage at Donhead St Andrew, near Shaftesbury in Dorset. It was a charming cottage set over a rushing stream and buried deep in the countryside, well away from prying eyes or vengeful EOKA men. Although the move was only temporary, he and Claude took Sappho and arranged for her to attend the local village school, while he raced on with *Bitter Lemons*, and Claude, who had finished off her novel about Ireland, *Mrs O'*, submitted it to Faber.

This move almost exactly coincided with Eve petitioning Durrell for divorce in early October. Even so, *Justine*, now at the press, was dedicated to her, and there was no apparent feeling of acrimony between them, though Durrell resented the idea of having to pay out more alimony and more child support. Poverty was what he feared most, and his greatest nightmare was having to return to the Foreign Office.[48]

The divorce petition also coincided with the publication of his *Selected Poems*, dedicated to his two daughters. It was divided into lyrical poems, short biographical poems, and landscapes and ballads, and was sympathetically reviewed in the *New Statesman* by his friend Fraser, who applauded the formal completeness of his verse, and celebrated his 'sense of landscape, fantastic humour, occasional direct sad tenderness . . . as original and enjoyable as the poetic handling.'[49] *The Times* also felt he had a new confidence[50] and the *TLS* said that 'He can bring a landscape to life more beautifully and economically than any living English (or American) poet.'[51] Meanwhile, another Durrell was making his mark. Gerry had published *My Family and Other Animals*, to an enthusiastic press, and the Durrell family became famous overnight. It was something out of *Pickwick Papers*, thought Larry.

Larry found Sappho a bit of a handful, and was eager to complete *Bitter Lemons* and get her settled back with Eve so

that he could get on to the second novel of his sequence, a
book he called simply 'Justine II'. He reverted to rising before
dawn and working for fourteen hours a day. The ability to
write clearly and fast, which he had learned as a journalist and
press officer, now paid off. While he ploughed away at *Bitter
Lemons*, the Suez affair was rumbling in the background. The
same men at the Foreign Office who had blundered so badly
over Cyprus were now blundering badly over Egypt. By 21
November, it was all over, and the British had to hand the Canal
Zone over to the UN. Larry's Cyprus book was completed on
time. It had taken some six weeks to write, and now he could
clear the decks ready for France. He was exhilarated. He had
escaped the trap of paid employment, and was with the woman
he loved. But he had no intention of getting back on to the
marriage merry-go-round again.

In *Bitter Lemons*, despite Durrell saying that it was not a
book about politics, the increasingly vocal and then violent
movement for Enosis constitutes the whole brooding background. And yet it is the story of the Cyprus affair from a very
odd angle. We meet the villagers of Bellapaix, the Turkish estate
agent Sabri Tahir, Clito the wine-shop owner, the reclusive
Hodja, the students of the Pancyrian Gymnasium in Nicosia
gradually turning from protestors to bombers. We meet Panos,
the doomed schoolteacher. And we learn of the strangely
ambivalent attitude of the Greek Cypriots towards the British.
They had, they said, to continue to kill the British, though they
did so sadly and even with love.[52] We see the stiff, uncomprehending British administrators, not knowing Greek, completely
oblivious to Greek sensibilities, and under pressure from
equally uncomprehending politicians in London. Durrell
watches all this, powerless to avert the oncoming tragedy. His
loyalties are torn. But he renders the whole sad story with such
ease and style and sureness of touch that it can be seen just
how fluent and assured his writing had become. There is also,
as always in a Durrell island book, a strong sense of history,
and of his romantic attachment to the whole Graeco-Roman
world. The tragic tale, of a paradise island in the process of
being lost, had brought out the best in one of our very best
Epicurean writers.

He was worried that he had no US publisher, even though he had several books due out in England – *Bitter Lemons, Justine, White Eagles over Serbia* and *Esprit de Corps,* the first of his Antrobus books – not to mention the recent *Selected Poems.* Miller suggested he ask Larry Powell, his librarian friend at UCLA. He was a great fan of Durrell's work and would do anything to find him a publisher if he wished, though he warned that he was regarded in America as difficult, a writer for the elected few. Meanwhile Miller continued dreaming of finding his Shangri-la – Japan, Burma. Siam, Java, India.[53] But Durrell was not looking so far afield; his mind was now set firmly on France.

CHAPTER II

Variations on a Theme of Love (1957–1958)

This man understood the secrets of the
flesh; he understood its past as well as
its future, by studying the present.

Balzac, 'The Atheist's Mass'

Justine was due out on 1 February 1957 and Durrell was
interviewed by *Books and Bookman.* Asked for his life-story
he said, 'My poems constitute the only honest sketch of myself
I have ever made. I suggest you reprint them all and let your
readers judge.' The magazine declined. He deplored much of
his past work, he said, and only wrote on in the hope of getting
better. He thought he had not yet produced the mature work
of his middle years, but continued to pursue the elusive ghost
of perfection.

> I regard writing as a fascinating bore, and wish it were better paid.
> *Justine* is only the opening flourish of a projected three- or five-
> volume novel. Apparent obscurities will all be cleared up later. I am
> hoping to settle in France. I have no other ambitions. I would accept
> £1,000 a year or someone's discarded rich mistress to shut up
> altogether.

The magazine commended *Justine's* power and magic and the
innovative nature of its form, and hailed the birth of a new
literary star.[1] But *Justine* got off to a slightly rocky start: some
250 errors were later found in the first edition, no doubt in
part reflecting Durrell's hatred of proof-reading.

He soon found an American publisher. Elliot Macrae of
Dutton, in London in January, was given a copy of *Justine* by

Faber. Within three-quarters of an hour of starting to read it he had phoned Curtis Brown to ask for an option.[2] Realizing that Durrell's novel sequence could make its author a celebrity, he bought the US rights to the whole cycle and to *Bitter Lemons*. Durrell was stunned, and began to think that his luck had changed. As if to confirm this, Terence Tiller agreed a contract to produce *Sappho* for BBC radio – a pleasant enough farewell present from Pudding Island – and he asked the BBC to ensure the cheque was paid after the end of the financial year to save on his tax bill.[3] There was a send-off present for Claude, too; Faber accepted her novel, *Mrs O'*.

An article on Richard Aldington next to a review of his own *Selected Poems* in *The Times* may have prompted Durrell to write for the second time since 1933 to this hero of his youth. He asked Aldington, then living in Montpellier, to suggest places to live on the Mediterranean coast. Aldington replied in detail saying this was a good time to go down there because there were nasty outbreaks of tourism at Eastertime.[4] He would be happy to meet him any time he was in Montpellier, he said.[5] Durrell was delighted. But first he and Claude spent some days in Paris, exploring his old haunts – Alèsia, Rue de la Tombe-Issoire, the Villa Seurat, the Cloiserie des Lilas. They found Paris very expensive and, as their £400 was being quickly eaten up, decided not to linger. Durrell may have hoped to get royalties for *The Black Book* from Girodias, but all the publisher's titles had been suppressed in France, and he was having to fight the decision in the courts.[6]

They headed for the Côte d'Azur, then travelled by local buses in search of a quiet place to settle, but found it disappointingly like the English south coast. Finally they went inland to Montpellier, where they met Aldington and his sixteen-year-old daughter Catherine for lunch in a café. It was a meeting of minds. They found themselves in accord on their right-wing politics, and their antipathy to England and to Jews, though Aldington was far more virulent in his views than Durrell. He had had a gripe against England ever since suffering on its behalf in the First World War, and hated the establishment that had led Britain into war. Now he hated it even more for turning on him over his biography suggesting that T. E.

Lawrence was homosexual, which was why, he thought, his recent biography of Frédérique Mistral (the Provencal poet and Nobel Prize winner) had not been reviewed in England. Durrell said he would try to review it for the *New Statesman*.

Larry and Claude set off to explore the area between Montpellier and Nîmes, hoping to find a small town on a swimmable river. They found it in the picturesque medieval town of Sommières on the Vidourle with its ancient Roman bridge, not far from St Rémy, the birthplace of Nostradamus. There they rented a small villa, the Villa Louis, on a hill below a medieval castle just above the railway station. They took it for six months, hoping to find something large, strange and more permanent in the meantime. Thanks to Claude's hard business head they got it for a mere £2 a week, but it was fairly primitive, with just well-water and no toilet, so to perform certain necessary functions meant squatting among the vines in the garden with a small shovel in hand. The house was cold and decrepit: they washed in a bucket, slept in sleeping bags. The only stick of furniture was an ancient sofa which they found in the attic and which they christened 'Elizabeth Browning'. They lived cheaply, their only luxuries being Gauloise cigarettes and a weekly bottle of *vieux marc*, the local firewater. There was a splendid farmer's market selling excellent local bread and Camembert, a wide variety of vegetables, and fine inexpensive wine. And in summer the river would be excellent for swimming.[7] Durrell thought it an ideal spot to bring their children during the holidays.

Reactions to *Justine* began to filter through, at first from friends. Freya Stark wrote to say what a splendid book it was. She liked his 'visual grip' in depicting the tough, luminous quality of the Levant, heartless but benign. She felt that writing it had taken its toll. And, detecting how important his freedom was to him, she urged him to love but avoid matrimony, since freedom was life to him and marriage only offered freedom when merged with religion.[8] Miller wrote telling him that his handling of the English language was beyond compare. Justine was just what he imagined Eve to be, only magnified.[9] Diana Menuhin thought *Justine* 'tremendous' but also found it suffocating, and complained about Justine's humourlessness and tasteless promiscuity, which made her so boring.[10]

The English reviewers seemed somewhat bewildered by the book – especially faced with his publisher's claim that it pointed the way to the novel of the future. There were expressions of awe at the verbal power and brilliance of Durrell's writing, and at the strange enchantment of his mythical Alexandria and its enigmatic characters. (John Davenport in the *Observer* had 'no hesitation in calling this a great novel'.) But there was also scepticism about what seemed to be too much cleverness, complexity, even arrogance and pretentiousness. Cyril Connolly, who had, he claimed, read and enjoyed everything Durrell had done, wrote, 'I think that in *Justine* . . . he has found a form, a blend of imagination and memory, or analysis and dream, poetry and prose, which enables him, in the sun of Alexandria and in the shade of Cavafy, to come into his own.'[11] But Stephen Spender wrote to him personally saying that he had 'grave reservations' about the book.[12]

Most exciting for Durrell was a talk by Christopher Middleton on the BBC Third Programme, giving *Justine* the intellectual imprimatur he was most anxious to receive. Middleton, in a subtle and perceptive analysis, argued that the book could not be understood in isolation from *The Black Book* and *Key to Modern Poetry*:

> I believe that Durrell has aimed here to create, within the framework of a psychological novel, a vision of reality that is based on myth . . . [and] has considerably enlarged the range of the psychological novel as a literary form.

The only question was, he concluded, whether Durrell could sustain this exploration of the no-man's land between psychology and myth; could the poet as novelist turn himself into a visionary?[13] It was probably the very question that Durrell was asking himself.

On his forty-fifth birthday, 27 February, Durrell had good reason to look with satisfaction at what he had achieved since leaving Cyprus just six months earlier. Two books out and three in the pipeline, and *Sappho* soon due for a radio airing.

And even if some critics had strong reservations about *Justine*, others were saying that it was unusually brilliant. He had flung off the yoke of a salaried 'position', and was now a full-time writer for the first time since 1939. He quickly got to work on 'Justine II'.

He was beginning to 'take in' the part of France in which he now found himself. It was the Midi – more precisely Languedoc. At Sommières the Vidourle flooded each year, sometimes sweeping away people and houses, but the locals seemed not to care; they enjoyed the bullfight, but in its local form where the bullfighter had to remove a cockade from the bull, not kill it. Larry and Claude soon found a favourite place to relax, the Café du Glacier, where they could sit with drinks and books under huge shady plane-trees beside the Vidourle. He still owned a house in Cyprus, but returning there then was out of the question.[14] Penelope Tremayne, who was living in it, wrote to say that a deputation of villagers had come to her door and told her that they had had a meeting the night before, and had voted *not* to kill her.[15] Money worries were pressing, yet even under stress Durrell seemed never to get ill. When illness threatened, he said, he just read Groddeck and immediately revived.[16] However, this was his make-or-break year. Claude, a fine executive secretary, had offered to take a job, so determined was she that he be free to write, which is why they planned to stay close to a big town, Nîmes, Toulouse or Avignon.

Since Durrell could not afford to visit Aldington, and since Aldington was a bad traveller and petrol was rationed, they settled for letter-writing. This became a great correspondence in Durrell's life, second only to that with Miller. Aldington advised him to get a French resident's visa, otherwise his UK publishers would automatically deduct 42 per cent of his earnings. The best thing was to pay French tax. He should sort this out as a matter of priority.[17]

Meanwhile, Claude, whose first novel had gone well, had finished a second, *A Rum Go*, a humorous story based on her days as a young secretary for the navy in Alexandria, which probably owed something to the author of Antrobus, if only by way of sympathetic association. Now she was busy on a third, drawing on her time in Israel. Durrell thought all this work was very good for her; it stopped her chattering.[18] He himself now settled back into his routine of rising early and working right through the day, hoping to deliver Justine II to Faber by the end of June.

Terence Tiller's radio version of *Sappho* in late March brought a brief notice in *The Times* calling it 'a play of intended surprises' which failed to surprise because of 'too leisurely a style and by disregard of tempo'.[19] The *Listener* was also less than complimentary. 'Lawrence Durrell's *Sappho* . . . had an Oedipus plot and several others, and failed to make a coherent drama of them, though there was some fine poetry.'[20] But money was more on his mind than was his play. At the end of March he estimated they had enough to last for two more months, so he speeded up work on Justine II. He was fearful of having to return to the Foreign Office, though he must have known that once his Antrobus stories appeared he might no longer be welcome there.

When Aldington wrote saying he was feeling wretched because of low blood pressure, Durrell diagnosed oxygen deficiency, and prescribed aspirins and hard liquor, such as *grappa* or geneva. He suggested valerian too, which he had found helpful in Argentina – a dated but effective remedy.[21] But he also thought Aldington's illness was depression over criticisms of his T.E. Lawrence book,[22] and vowed to do everything he could to help him win back his readership. Durrell was always ready to act out his old dream of being a doctor; even in his work one finds a belief in the healing power of literature.

When Roy Campbell was killed in a car crash in Portugal on 24 April, Aldington was devastated, Campbell being one of the very few English-language poets he had time for. Durrell and Claude met Aldington and his daughter in Nîmes, close to the bullring where Campbell sometimes fought, to commiserate and try to raise his dashed spirits. It helped that a few days later, on 4 May, Durrell's review of Aldington's Mistral book appeared in the *New Statesman*.[23] And for Durrell the cheering news was that *Bitter Lemons* had been made a *Daily Mail* Book Society choice for July. He also heard from Miller that,

at his prompting, Hans Ledig of Rowohlt would probably soon
be making a very attractive offer for *Justine*. At least, he felt,
he could avoid having to take another job until 1958.[24] And
even *White Eagles over Serbia* had its limited success, being
named a Young Elizabethans Book Choice for July, and some
reviewers compared him to Buchan. Others, however, considered it unsuitable for young readers – too stylistically clotted
and too violent – and more a travel book than an adventure.
Durrell concluded that he had no talent for thriller writing.

By the end of April he had all but finished Justine II and Claude
was typing it as he went. The whole novel cycle had now taken
shape. There would be four in all: the second one (with a
spatial form like the first) told the same story as the first
but from a different viewpoint (the idea, he hinted, was from
Giordano Bruno); the third one would be a naturalistic novel
and so quite different from the second; number four would
add a new dimension to the sequence, the dimension of time.
Justine II had taken him just six weeks to complete, and he
decided to have a month off to recharge his batteries. While
relaxing, he heard that *Justine* was to be published in Germany,
France and Sweden. Miller's efforts with various European
publishers had led to a scramble. And Rowohlt took not only
Justine but *Sappho*, too, with the prospect of a theatrical production. Durrell had been in Miller's debt since *The Black
Book*; now the American was helping to put him on the world
map.
    When Durrell moved to Languedoc, he had, in some respects,
retired from the world. He calculated that over the previous
ten years he had met 10,000 people, and now wanted to catch
up on lost time just writing his books. The world would now
have to come to him – strictly by invitation, of course. Paying
tax in France meant declaring himself an emigrant. He did not
mind that. The tax inspector in Nîmes, on discovering that he
was a writer, had shaken his hand.
    American readers got a preview of *Justine* when Kenneth
Rexroth reviewed the British edition together with the US
edition of *Selected Poems*, in the *Nation* of 18 May. Durrell
could hardly have wished for a better trailer. Rexroth called

him 'one of the most civilized writers in England today ...
gifted with a gentle, unselfconscious eroticism very rare in our
nasty and Puritan world'. He applauded the influence on his
poetry of Cavafy. The novel was 'almost a novelification ... of
Cavafy's poetry', and, following Cavafy, 'Not only is the city
[Alexandria] so real that it envelops you like a cloud in its own
miasmas, but the people are more real than real.' Soon after
this, Durrell heard from Gerald Sykes, the novelist husband of
his old friend Buffie Johnson, saying that he was reviewing
Justine for the *New York Times*. He was so enthusiastic about
it that Durrell could be assured that Rexroth's cheers would
be fully echoed by Sykes.[25]

The immediate fear of poverty and having to return to diplo-
macy was lifted when in June he received an advance from
Dutton for *Bitter Lemons*. This, added to the money for the
Book Society choice, would keep them afloat till Christmas at
least. He was doubly cheered when an Egyptian woman friend
of Miller's sent him a book about Shaw accompanied by two
nude photographs of herself. More relaxed and expansive now,
he had time to ponder on what he was doing. The story he
was telling, from *Justine* to Justine II to Justine III was now
spreading from the subjective centre out towards the realm of
the objective. Justine IV would return to the subjective.[26] The
novelist in him was edging out the poet, but he still valued his
poetic reputation. American reviews of *Selected Poems* were
mixed. After Kenneth Rexroth, who had compared him to
Cavafy and Horace, came W. T. Scott in the *Saturday Review*
who thought that the traditional lyric line he used was only
rescued from banality by the freshness of his language. Robert
Stock, in *Poetry*, thought it a very uneven selection, and some
poems best left unmentioned.[27] When Aldington read *Selected
Poems*, he said it delighted him to read a poet who said pleas-
ingly what he intended to say. Why, he wondered, had
MacSpaunday not eliminated him?[28]

Bitter Lemons was published in England in July.[29] Reviews
were generally enthusiastic. Kingsley Martin in the *New
Statesman* observed quite rightly that Durrell's position as a
Greek speaker with friends among the Greek Cypriots put him
in a perfect position to see how the situation arose. 'Eschewing

politics, it says more about them than all our leading articles and in describing a political tragedy, it often has great poetic beauty.'[30] The book was given a prominent notice in the *TLS*, which applauded him for seeing what the politicians had failed to see, that the Cyprus problem was a European and not a colonial one.[31] His friend Spencer, reviewing it in the *London Magazine*, judged *Bitter Lemons* the best of Durrell's island books, which was, he said, saying a great deal.[32] There were also complimentary reviews from Harold Nicolson and Peter Quennell, and his friend Porteus wrote to say, 'You are doing the best writing since the heyday of poor old Wyndham, and nothing should be allowed to stop the rich heady flow.'[33]

In early July, Claude went to London for ten days to see Faber about her second novel, and to buy a chemical toilet for the Villa. Durrell found he missed her a great deal more than he thought he would, and realized just how many chores she dealt with, leaving him free to work. He consoled himself by going to see a French film version of *Lady Chatterley's Lover*, and by reflecting on French attitudes towards sex and defecation – far healthier than Anglo-Saxon ones which reduced these basic functions to mere rituals. And the worshipful attitude of the French towards the artist was greatly to be cherished.[34] In France, he felt, he had found his true home.

Because of Rowohlt's contract, Faber were constrained to offer him a more generous contract in return for two books a year (£500 advance for each novel delivered), so freeing him to do nothing but write – a major turning-point in his life, he told Miller. And there was a further $1,400 due from Dutton when *Justine* was published in America. It meant financial security for him and Sappho's school fees paid for a whole year ahead. (She was now at Bedales, a co-educational school at Petersfield in Hampshire, where, it seems, she was very happy. Eve was matron in charge of the juniors and they lived next to the school.) It also meant that he could commit himself to a future in France, something he had always wanted to do. There was further cause for celebration when Claude returned from London with a contract for her second novel,[35] and *two* chemical toilets to stand out in the vineyard.

*

Faber were excited about Justine II and sent it to the press under a new title, *Balthazar*. This novel (dedicated to his mother and Alexandria), the second in what became known as *The Alexandria Quartet*, was to put Durrell on the literary map, not only because critics and readers now realized that something extraordinary was being attempted, but also because in it he laid out his theory of the novel and his plan for the whole cycle in a brief prefatory note. He regarded the book as more a sibling than a sequel to *Justine*, and, while the characters were invented, the city was real. He had sought for Unities not in contemporary literature, but in science and the theory of relativity. The four novels consisted of three of space and one of time – the whole thing forming a 'continuum' of words. The first three 'spatial' novels were not continuously linked, but interlaced and overlaid while chronology was suspended. Part four, a postscript to the others, was the only one which moved through time. The subjective first two would move to an objective third, called *Mountolive*, which would transform the earlier narrator into an objective participant. This idea he had first come across in Lewis's *Time and Western Man*, and was a better means of representing 'Space-Time' than Bergsonian 'Duration', the preferred method of Joyce and Proust. The quartet was concerned, at its centre, with exploring modern love. If all this seemed pretentious, the research was worthwhile if a 'classical' structure for today might be revealed – even if what emerged was literally 'science-fiction'. He gave the dateline on this short manifesto as 'Asconia, 1957', a fictional place, to imply spacelessness and to put people off the scent of where he was really living.

This book carried *two* epigraphs from de Sade's *Justine*. One concerned the failure of men of learning to reveal to us 'the gigantic idiosyncrasies' of the human heart; the other read, 'The mirror sees the man as beautiful, the mirror loves the man; another mirror sees the man as frightful and hates him; and it is always the same being who produces the impressions.' Thus he prefigures the pattern of the book, revealing to us the deceptive nature of memory, as recorded by Darley in *Justine*. Balthazar, who has read Darley's account questions his sources – Arnauti's book, Justine's diaries, Nessim's words. From him

Darley retrieves his manuscript covered with notes, insertions, question marks. This is Balthazar's 'interlinear' which revises the story told in *Justine*. In it he learns some cruel truths. He had believed that Justine loved him, but discovers that she merely used him as a decoy to deflect Nessim's suspicion from her love affair with Pursewarden. Scobie, the old Vice Squad man with 'Tendencies', appointed to the secret service, asks Darley to spy on Balthazar's cabbalists, who are suspected of plotting against the state. He reveals to Darley that at full moon he feels compelled to dress as a woman, and asks him to dispose of his female clothing. The suspected love affair between Justine and Clea is confirmed, and we hear the circumstances of Justine marrying Nessim – she does not love him but hopes his money will help her find her stolen child. Darley learns that much of Arnauti's book, *Moeurs*, was invented. The story of Mountolive's youthful love for Leila unfolds, as does the relationship between her two sons, Nessim the banker and Narouz the farmer. The story also emerges of Pursewarden as philosophical novelist, and perhaps spy, and as the object of Justine's desire. The mysterious, violent and unpredictable Narouz, obsessively in love with Clea, learns from mystics that Justine's child is dead. Scobie dies on a transvestite evening out, kicked to death by a sailor. At a masked ball during the annual Alexandrian carnival, Toto de Brunel is fatally stabbed. Because he is wearing Justine's ring it is thought that a jealous Nessim has killed her. But Narouz confesses the murder to Clea, thinking that he has stabbed Justine.

Balthazar gives another and sharper focus to the events narrated, and raises fascinating questions about the nature of truth and reality. New characters in the book include Leila (Coptic beauty, mother of Nessim and Narouz), Mountolive (diplomat lover of Leila) and Keats (hard-bitten journalist). Many characters are disfigured (Narouz, Leila) or blind (Liza) or one-eyed (Capodistria, Scobie and Hamid) – probably haunting images of disfeatured beggars from Durrell's days in India, Cairo and Alexandria as well as an embodiment of Groddeck's belief that the physical is somehow a reflection of the mental. Scobie is also Tiresias, and so, said Durrell, was he.

It was now evident that Durrell had pre-planned the *Quartet* only in the general terms outlined in his preface to *Balthazar*. He was in fact feeling his way forward, like a blind man, and at this stage probably not always confident that he would be able to bring the thing off. Had Faber asked him to finish the whole cycle first it would have been different; he could have gone back and forth, checking and correcting and amending. Fortunately, the complex, unstable nature of the narrative enabled him to complete the cycle more successfully than if he had chosen a more conventional form.

Some of the philosophical ideas, discussed by Pursewarden, may throw light on Durrell himself – the idea that a woman may sleep with a poet who may immortalize her; the idea that corruption and confusion may be creative; the idea that the physical act of love alone is the way to self-knowledge. If the *Quartet* is high-class pornography, as Durrell joked, it is also a textbook of seduction.

Miller, having read the manuscript, was duly amazed. The carnival scenes were breathtaking and rivetting. He was enchanted, and Durrell's contemplations about art and religion reminded him of Paul Valéry. Nothing in English literature matched it.[36] Shortly afterwards he urged Durrell to contribute to *Playboy*, they paid so well, and to send them *Justine* to review.[37] Durrell was touched, as ever, by his mentor's praise, and in return said admiring things about *A Devil in Paradise*. The company which his correspondence with Miller provided would become more important to him as Aldington moved from Montpellier to Sury-en-Vaux in Cher, where he had been lent a house. There was a farewell party at which Durrell first met Jacques Temple, then working for the magazine *Entretiens*.

Claude's two children, Diana (eleven) and Barry (eight), Sappho (six), plus Margo and her son Nicholas (twelve), had flown in by seaplane to Marseilles in early August, and were keeping them busy at the Villa Louis – swimming and fishing in the Vidourle, sleeping in tents in the garden, visiting the bullfights. At the same time Durrell was encouraging Theodore Stephanides to come out from England, which he thought was done for – so many downcast, would-be-communists everywhere. Nor was Cyprus a place to return to; the British, having stirred up the Turks, had left it with an uncertain future. He knew this need not have happened if the right decisions had been taken earlier. In *Bitter Lemons* he had settled for the dispassionate approach of the classic Greek tragedy, but he could have said far more than he did. The conflict in Cyprus had cured him of his infatuation with Greece; now he had reverted to an earlier passion – France. An indication that his Cyprus book had achieved an impersonal detachment came when he received a letter from Sir John Harding thanking him for writing about him fairly.[38]

When *Justine* appeared in America, the critics there were as interested in the author as they were in his work. Gerald Sykes in the *New York Times Book Review* hailed it as 'the best new work of fiction I have read in some years'. He mentioned *The Black Book* and *Cefalû*, and then compared *Justine* to Proust's *Remembrance of Things Past*. Durrell was now 'a truly important writer' and 'a genuine poet' who had 'survived morally and literarily the disasters that have typically shattered his post-Joycean, post-Proustian generation'. He was a 'waste-land man' who had come through and who had surpassed his master, Miller.[39] *Time* gave it a prominent review, finding it 'a sensuous and beautifully written hymn to the "post-coital sadness" of mankind . . . [and] . . . a hymn to Alexandria . . . where sects as well as sex proliferate'.[40] The *Atlantic* complimented him on his poetic writing, but found the setting more convincing than the characters, who embraced 'with the cool click of algebraic formulas', and so permitted him to be 'remarkably outspoken without becoming offensive'.[41] The 'high-class pornographer', it seems, had got under the guard of the puritanical Americans.

Even while the children were filling the Villa Louis with their noise and confusions, Durrell had plunged into writing *Justine III* (*Mountolive*) – his Stendhalian one of the three, he sometimes called it. Miller had sent him a copy of Denis de Rougement's *Love in the Western World*, in which there were passages about the beliefs and heresies of the Cathars, and how their love poetry concealed a shared mystical revelation between lovers. It seemed to mesh with his own thinking about ancient sects such as the Copts and the cabbalists, with which

he was dealing in the *Quartet*. Thus was born a fascination
with the Cathars, whose home had been in Languedoc, a fascination which was to last the rest of his life.

After the children had flown home at the end of the holidays
he set out to finish *Mountolive* by Christmas. Faber reported
20,000 copies of *Bitter Lemons* sold in less than three months,
thanks to its having been a Book Society choice, and undertook
to publish *The Black Book* uncensored once the *Quartet* was
fully out. As much as Durrell loathed England, he still needed
her. His cultural heritage was English as was his whole manner,
however sometimes ebulliently 'Irish'. He spoke French with a
pronounced English accent and spoke English with a degree of
refinement unusual even among the English. But he proclaimed
himself a European, at deadly odds with English provincialism.

When Eve was granted a decree nisi, Durrell again became
a free man. No co-respondent was named, so the grounds were
either desertion or cruelty. Claude, however, was still married.
When Eve left him, Durrell had been quite contemptuous of
women and determined never to marry again. Even so, he knew
he found it impossible to exist without a woman to take care
of his needs, to leave him free to write and to enjoy her admiration. Anaïs, having read *Justine*, wrote from Los Angeles,
applauding his new-found literary power. She should have run
away with him in 1937, she told him.

Diana Menuhin, not easily carried away by encomiastic
reviews, wrote saying how delighted she was that he was
enjoying financial success but warned him not to pour away
his beautiful talent too recklessly. The gemlike qualities of his
writing were so easily roughened and scratched. She urged him
to make sure he read his own proofs thoroughly, so that, unlike
Justine, Balthazar would not be riddled with errors.[42]

Hearing also from Perlès, Durrell replied in an excess of
pleasure about his new home in France: the French fucked
better, ate better, had the best wine, and enjoyed a tax rate a
third that of England.[43] But Perlès would have none of this
anglophobia. England had saved his life. He had seen an
advance copy of *Esprit de Corps* he said and had been weep-
ing with laughter over it.[44]

Mountolive was now finished; it had taken Durrell a little

under two months. He immediately began to wonder about
the final novel of the quartet, concerned about how he could
tie up all the loose ends. As with the previous two, *Mountolive*
left many questions unanswered. Unlike the other two, it is a
straightforward third-person narrative telling the story of
British diplomat Mountolive and his affair with Leila Hosnani.
It introduces Pursewarden and his blind sister Liza, to whom
Mountolive is also attracted. Memories of Mountolive's childhood echo Durrell's – India, Tibetan lamas, a cruel expulsion
back to England, a father he never sees again. Sent as
ambassador to Egypt, he takes on Pursewarden as political
adviser on the strength of his dismissal of the report about
a Coptic conspiracy against Egyptian nationalism involving
Nessim. There is a re-run of the carnival and the masked ball
(this novel covers the same time-span as the previous two) and
the murder of Toto de Brunel. Pursewarden confesses to
Melissa that he has been his sister Liza's lover, implying that
only Anglo-Saxons were unimaginative enough not to
appreciate the deliciousness of the many varieties of sexual
love. Melissa in turn tells him that her old protector, Cohen,
was involved in a plot with Nessim to smuggle arms to Israel,
and she thinks Cohen was poisoned for knowing too much.

When Pursewarden commits suicide he leaves this information for Mountolive. Nessim proposes to Justine, whom,
after their marriage, he launches into Alexandrian society. She
discovers Darley's fascination with her diaries, and, not
knowing that she had copied out Arnauti's fictional diaries
in her own hand at one time, he accepts them as authentic.
Capodistria's murder at the duck-shoot is revealed as faked
because he is a compromised party to the arms-smuggling plot.
Meanwhile Narouz has fallen under the influence of a Coptic
mystic and is making inflammatory speeches which could bring
the sect under suspicion. Mountolive meets Leila again after
many years – she is now disfigured by smallpox. In disgust he
gets drunk, stumbles into a house of child prostitutes and is
doubly disgusted. Finally, Narouz is strangely murdered.

As Durrell told Richard Aldington, the *Quartet* was deliberately Rider-Haggardish in parts. But *Mountolive* was the hinge
of the whole sequence, and provided its rationale.[45]

November brought him even closer to France. He was invited by some friendly locals – the butcher, the baker and some of the regulars at the local café – to the annual reunion of the Class of 1930–2 (soldiers and resistance fighters), and simultaneously heard that his Paris publishers (Buchet-Chastel of Corrêa), delighted with Roger Giroux's translation of *Justine*, would bring it out in December. It was some indication that, now that he had accepted France, France was accepting him. The proofs of *Balthazar* had arrived and he was determined to read them carefully. Claude meanwhile had got an American publisher for *Mrs O'*.

But the surprise of the year came when Durrell was declared winner of the Duff Cooper Memorial Award for *Bitter Lemons*. He was invited to London to receive it from the hands of the Queen Mother, something he swore he would never do, and it took all Claude's persuasive powers to change his mind.[46]

Louisa could not attend the ceremony, she said, because she had nothing to wear, and Gerry had left her in charge of a chimp he had not yet found a home for. A mistress was not acceptable in the royal presence, so Durrell's daughter, Pinky (tall, blonde, cool and seventeen), was chosen to accompany him. Once there, he was horrified to find that a gaggle of Bournemouth aunts (Prudence and company) had wangled their way in, but he finally saw the funny side of it – after all, they looked a bit like Giles cartoon figures, he thought. The *Sunday Times* described the occasion:

> The Queen Mother entered the drawing-room and sat at a table with a glass of champagne in front of her. Lord David Cecil, on her left, took a last peep at his notes. The Author, on her right, looked out over the audience with a massive calm as we disposed ourselves, standing round the table. The profile of the seated Lady Diana Cooper had the serene gravity of a head on a Greek white-figure vase.
>
> [*Bitter Lemons*] . . . said Lord David Cecil justly, [was] the kind of book which is extremely well done today: a narrative of fact recorded with poetic feeling.
>
> The Queen Mother spoke fetchingly before presenting Mr Durrell with a specially bound copy of Duff Cooper's 'Old Men Forget'. With it went a cheque for £150 [actually £200]. Many of the

subscribers to the fund were present. They must have been delighted, moved even, by the whole affair.[47]

Durrell was very nervous at having to make a short speech, and, being long-sighted and rather vain about wearing glasses, had written it out in very large letters. Afterwards the Queen Mother came over and said, 'Mr Durrell, I just wanted to tell you once more how very much I enjoyed your book, and how truly excellent it is.'[48] Despite his declared distaste for England, this must have been one of the high points in the life of the self-declared fascist–monarchist. He declared the Queen Mother a 'merry widow'.[49]

On the same day there appeared his book of Antrobus stories, *Esprit de Corps* (dedicated to members of the Belgrade Embassy of 1951). Larry, like Gerry, had collected a zooful of his own characters – species of old diplomats, preserved and pinned into his collection (one thinks of the butterflies of his lepidopterist friend in India). Some of his FO friends, Bernard Burrows among them, thought these comic stories well below his level of ability, tending, as they did, to bring the Diplomatic Corps into contempt.[50] Durrell, however, was lampooning the English he had so long despised, and the Empire which he saw collapsing around the bumbling figures vainly trying to run it.

He quickly acquired one great fan – the equally anglophobe Aldington – who declared him a new Wodehouse, only greater.[51] *Esprit de Corps* exploited a familiar vein of British self-mockery, and was well received in Britain, John Betjeman writing that 'Whatever wars there may be and whatever crises, there will still, please heaven, be the diplomatic corps, with its protocol and formalities as a field for humour which I have never seen better used than in these stories.' Later American reactions revealed some confusion about a man working in two different genres. R. W. Flint in *Commentary* found the book 'passably funny but also embarrassing, as an obvious potboiler by a first-rate novelist is embarrassing'.[52] Miller hated them, telling him flatly that they were 'terrible' – his readers did not know whether he was a serious writer or a comedian. But Faber sold 6,000 copies within a month, and *Argosy, Vogue* and *Lilliput* all bought stories. Antrobus showed how the amusing Durrell could compensate for the wicked Durrell who haunted the *Quartet*.[53]

A new civilian Governor, Sir Hugh Foot, was appointed in Cyprus, and Durrell received a letter from him congratulating him on *Bitter Lemons*, just as he had from Sir John Harding. By some Durrellian magic he had satisfied both the soft- and hard-liners on the Cyprus problem.

But he felt that he had compromised himself too much ever to return to the island or to Greece again.

The New Year saw him at last on French tax, but, since Eve received her degree absolute in November, he was back on English alimony again. He got down to completing a final draft of *Mountolive*, and, while Claude typed it, he dashed off another book of Antrobus stories, which after the big novel he found relaxing. They had brought a small record-player back from London, and spent their evenings listening to Mozart by candlelight. Then, during the day, he took time out to pick up his painting, which he had abandoned since Cyprus. The French *Justine* had arrived, and they were delighted by the fluency and integrity of the translation.

Fame was creeping up on him, and in January 1958 the *Observer* asked him to go to Algeria to cover the uprising there, an offer he was happy to decline. But he had begun to worry about being sought out by importunate fans and bores and people who were just curious – Miller had told him some horrendous stories of people breaking into his house and abusing him for things he had written. Faced with this awful prospect, he thought of padlocking the gate and putting up signs about savage dogs or a plaque to the 'late' Lawrence Durrell who *used* to live there.

In January, Faber sold Antrobus stories to *Harpers* and the *Atlantic* in America, and his agents, Curtis Brown, had swung a deal with the *Sunday Times* for six stories a year in return for a retainer, which pleased him immensely; he had never been comfortable, as Miller had been, to dispense with a basic salary. In this more secure and relaxed atmosphere, he initiated a correspondence with Perlès about Miller and his place in literature, a correspondence in which Miller was later to join and which would be published as *Art and Outrage*.

Miller had had Claude's and Larry's star charts read by a Danish astrologer. Claude, she declared, was 'very lovable' and they were well suited. Durrell should write more about unfortunates in prisons, brothels or mental homes. He was due for a long journey or would move the following October. Venus and Aquarius together meant that he was unconventional in love. Claude confirmed that Durrell was not only 'unconventional' when it came to love, but she would say 'unique'.

The French reviews of *Justine* confirmed to him that he was in tune with the spirit of place there. Jacques Howlett, in *Les Lettres Nouvelles*, saw the novel as a mirage displaying mysteries to be solved, leaving 'an air of deep profundity'.[54] Dominique Aury in *La Nouvelle Revue Française* wrote of the book's enchantment. 'The romantic part of *Justine* is in fact constantly overflowing at the same time that it is supported – by a silent and secret violence which does not reveal its true nature, but gives to each episode a second significance.[55] Françoise Erval in *L'Express* admired the prismatic effect and the 'game of mirrors' which the characters play with themselves, but, as to Durrell's theory about time, she warned that aesthetic theories are best applied to art when the artist has forgotten them. After a decade asleep, she wrote, English literature had woken up with William Golding, Angus Wilson and John Osborne and the 'angry young men', but Durrell was not a part of any school; he was sufficient unto himself.[56]

Durrell was thrilled by this blessing from French critics, whom he regarded far more highly than English ones. He was also immensely pleased with a review sent to him by Jean Fanchette, the young Mauritian editor of a French student magazine, which he thought more acute and complimentary about *Justine* than any so far. By the end of February he was told that the book was having a big success. Fanchette pointed out to him that women critics seemed to have been romping delightedly through what they saw as his slow-burning eroticism.[57] He was eager to meet Durrell and, when he said that he was medical student, Durrell was equally eager to meet *him*.

He would surrender everything to be a medical man, he told him.

Their peace was shattered when their landlord said he needed the Villa Louis for his own family (perhaps those chemical toilets, the only ones in Sommières, were the attraction), but Miller's friend Temple got a local lawyer on to the problem to ensure they had the place at least until after the summer when the children were again due out from England. This endeared Temple to Durrell, and they became close friends.

Eliot had persuaded Faber to do *The Black Book*, and Durrell asked Miller to write a preface for it, mischievously suggesting that while he was at it he should do an illustrated children's book on a passage in *Sexus*, which, he thought, would cause great interest and amusement. He was himself amused to hear that Gerry had become a television star, thanks to a highly versatile chimp brought back from the Congo, the one that had kept his mother away from the award ceremony in London. And he was extremely proud of his two beautiful daughters. Pinky had become a ballet dancer, and Sappho was showing signs of being strongly unconventional.[58]

When *Bitter Lemons* appeared in the US, his friend Freya Stark, in the *New York Times Book Review*[59] and George Steiner in the *Yale Review* placed Durrell among the exceptional giants of literature, like Milton and Dryden, Thucydides, Shakespeare and Tolstoy. The book, said Steiner, was a chronicle of 'the twilight of European colonialism . . . a twilight full of tragic absurdity'.[60] A rather personal attack on him appeared in the *New Republic*, entitled 'Will Lawrence Durrell Spoil America?' The author, Gordon Merrick, argued that Durrell's exotic prose obscured 'just another psychologically displaced person' creating a picturesque cult 'to screen from view the howling emptiness of peasant life, self-pitying, totally irresponsible'. And the same went for Durrell himself, whose attitude towards women in *Justine* was 'adolescent and . . . self-pitying'. 'He is obscure, to a point where one may legitimately wonder if obscurity isn't simply a device to disguise his own emptiness.'[61]

He was in the literary headlines in England, too, when *Balthazar* came out there on 15 April. Anaïs, now in Brussels, wrote saying that *Balthazar* was 'a feast for the intelligence' and for the heart.[62]

In late April, Anaïs and Hugh came to Sommières. Anaïs was impressed with the Villa Louis – primitive like a monastery – with many of Larry's paintings, photographs and reviews on display and found Claude her vivacious self; but Durrell was, she thought, strangely cold and impersonal. Anaïs felt that he had an obsession with succeeding, probably because of his earlier poverty, and she was touched by Claude's devotion to him, her gaiety, sauciness and humour.[63]

When Larry and Claude set off for Paris on 19 May in an old Peugeot 203 he had bought, serious trouble was brewing. A few days earlier French settlers had taken over in Algiers and an invasion of paratroopers was expected any day. Undaunted, they went carousing with Fanchette (described by Anaïs as 'a young and beautiful Negro'),[64] attended the party thrown by Buchet and met Penelope and Sappho, who spent a couple of days with them in Paris before they all drove back to Sommières. The crisis which brought General de Gaulle back to power on 29 May seems to have left them unaffected. They all got back with fatigue colds. Claude had an attack of bronchitis, and Sappho went down with chickenpox. Faber sent news that *Balthazar* had sold 7,000 copies in a month, which may have made him feel better about having spent unearned money on a painting by an Israeli friend of Fanchette's, Zvi Milstein. It was called *The Clowns*, and he hung it on his bedroom wall where he could see it while lying in bed, something to inspire him with his own painting. Feeling sorry for the impoverished Fanchette, he sent him the printer's copy of *Mountolive*, saying that after he was famous it would be worth money.

When, at Larry's suggestion, Anaïs met Jean Fanchette at the café Les Deux Magots in St Germain des Près, she was immediately taken by the 'delicious' Mauritian. Fanchette explained his plan to launch an Anglo-French literary magazine called *Two Cities*, to be edited in both Paris and London, and she liked the idea so much that she agreed to back it and help edit it. She spent a 'divided life' – with 'Hugo the father' in New York and 'Rupert the son' in California.[65] Now, when

Hugo left for Britanny, she left for London to meet her paramour Rupert Pole, guitar player and dreamer, performing what she called her 'trapeze act' between the two men.

With the children back in England, Durrell began to search for a new house. He found the ruined Mazet Michel offered for rent for five years, with an option to buy, just off the road near Uzès on the Nîmes–Avignon road in an area called Engances, reminiscent of a remote part of Crete or Cyprus. With it went three square kilometres of garrigue (scrubland), which included a couple of hundred olive trees stricken by frost. He hoped Theodore Stephanides might advise him how to make his desert bloom. It was a bit of a blasted heath, across which the mistral howled. There was some wildlife, but the land was rocky, with pine shoots, wild flowers, holm oak. He did not mention that the French Air Force used the area as a shooting range, which was probably why the rent was so reasonable. There were drawbacks to living in France so far from publishers and agents, but a mazet a (small farmhouse) on the garrigue would be better than living in poverty in South Kensington. In passing his future address to selected friends, he swore them to secrecy,[66] and again urged Stephanides to abandon ship and join them to help cultivate their brown patch.[67]

To make more money, he began churning out what he regarded as rubbish. He had already dashed off a few stories for British newspapers; now he did a piece on Cyprus for the *Nation*, and offered his services to *Holiday* magazine, which was said to pay very well. But when they asked him to do a travel article on Egypt, he declined. That was one country he never wanted to see again.[68] Miller helped, insisting that he receive half the royalties for the Miller anthology. There was also a growing interest in Durrell's paintings; since his success, they had been fetching as much as £45 a time in America.

Gerald Sykes sent an advance copy of his encomiastic review of *Balthazar* for the *New York Times*, but cautioned him against writing too fast if he was to sustain the level of perfection he had achieved in the *Quartet* so far.[69] Durrell was grateful for Sykes's magnificent boost, but was in no mood to slow up. *Balthazar* had now sold 10,000 copies in England, while *Justine* had gone into seven languages. He knew he was working too fast, but where the writing was limp he hoped that it would be submerged by the whole cycle.[70]

Balthazar came out in America, attracting from the critics a strange range of comparisons. Sykes in his *New York Times* review praised Durrell's descriptive powers,[71] and *Time* magazine lauded the Einsteinian shifting of perspectives[72] while Paul Bowles, writing in the *Saturday Review*, suspected an attraction to the prurient side of de Sade as much as to the rational.[73] Interestingly, one of the most dismissive reviews came in *Atlantic Monthly* from Charles Rollo, who had grown up in Alexandria. He found Durrell's city utterly unreal.[74]

When Aldington asked him to support Potocki in a publishing project, Durrell demurred. Potocki's connections with Oswald Mosley, the British fascist, and his admiration for Hitler did not commend him, and anyway he found his conscious English eccentricity tedious. And although Durrell was anti-Jewish, he was left speechless by Potocki's approval of Belsen.[75] Durrell told Aldington he had lived under a fascist government in pre-war Greece (in Cyprus, too, when the British showed their fascist tendencies) and was a Royalist, the only way for a poet who put values before politics.[76] This was not good enough for Aldington, who said that he also had experience of fascist governments, in Italy and Spain, and they were infinitely better than the workers' anarchy they had replaced.[77]

Durrell went to Grenoble to research a travel article for *Holiday*. What fascinated him (apart from the large fee) was that it was the native city of Stendhal. At the university he talked with medical students about poetry, science and cadavers. He found a vine planted by Stendhal's uncle, wandered through the author's house, saw his manuscripts, and handled one of his notebooks.[78]

On his return, they packed ready to move to Engances. It was the end of an epoch. Durrell had arrived in France with £400, soon down to £200. Now he was on the brink of fame and fortune.

Living With Fame (1958–1960)

A celebrity is a person who works hard
all his life to become known, then wears
dark glasses to avoid being recognized.

Fred Allen, *Treadmill to Oblivion*

The Mazet Michel was a return to the primitive life. They were without heating, running water or lavatory, and the ground was rather too hard for the vineyard-and-shovel routine. They had a water-pump and a lavatory installed, courtesy of $1,000 from *Holiday* magazine for the Grenoble article. Claude put up shelves and Durrell wrote asking Alan Thomas for his books (retrieved by Penelope Tremayne from Bellapaix), especially ones on Egypt which he needed for Justine IV (*Clea*). He noticed a lot of dry freestone lying around and thought he could do some building of his own. There was plenty of game on the garrigue, and he decided to save for a twelve-bore shotgun; that way, together with a little kitchen garden they would plant, they might be able to keep the pot full over the winter. The mazet's owner said that they could, if they wished, buy the place after three years, so there was the prospect of owning a house again. As an even better omen for the future, he was told by Buchet, his Paris publisher at Corrêa, that *Justine* was short-listed with Robert Musil's *Man without Qualities* for the Best Foreign Book of the Year Prize. It did not win, but he thought it a tremendous compliment from the French, who seemed to have taken him to their bosoms.

Success brought him invitations to do lecture tours in America, Holland and Sweden, all of which he refused, and an invitation from Walter Wanger in Hollywood to script a film about Cleopatra, which he thought hilarious. Fanchette wrote to say that he was amazed to find how enthusiastic females of a certain age were about *Justine*.[1] And more and more people wanted to visit him. But Durrell was now very jealous of his privacy, and his friends had strict instructions not to pass on his address, even though the mazet was remote and hard to find. There was no phone, radio or television; they just had the gramophone and Durrell's guitar.[2] This remoteness suited him, and slowly he collected his thoughts enough to get down to *Clea*. In preparation, he was reading Stendhal, Strindberg and Hamsun, and pondering on the very process of constructing fiction itself.

Mountolive (dedicated to Claude) came out in England in October. The straightforward narrative recommended itself to the English critics, who had been rather puzzled by the *roman fleuve* style of the first two books, and it received quite prominent reviews. John Davenport, who had liked the first two novels, wrote, 'One's admiration grows ... Mr Durrell is an artist,' and Richard Mayne said, 'His prose beguiles us with marvels of virtuosity ... it touches brilliantly on an urgent and compelling political theme.' Even a sceptical Frank Kermode admitted that he had probably misjudged the sequence at an earlier stage, and now thought there could no longer be any doubt about Durrell's achievement.[3] But there were always those who thought his novels were deathly, corrupt or empty of meaning. Pamela Hansford Johnson, for example, thought that his vision was so private that, like Peer Gynt, he had difficulty finding his own moral and intellectual core, which might not be there at all. 'Mr Durrell's sequence is an entrancing, odorous maze without a centre.'[4] Durrell himself had no illusions about his Justine III – he knew he had hit the dartboard, but not by any means the bull's-eye.

Fanchette sent him his review of *Mountolive*, lauding it as a *tour de force* reversion to the traditional narrative form. They met briefly when Durrell made a flying visit to Paris in November, and Fanchette talked eagerly about *Two Cities*, the first issue of which he planned to make a homage to Durrell. Anaïs Nin had fallen for the handsome Mauritian, and told

Durrell that, after the damage that living in America had done to her, he seemed to be a healing force in her life.[5] Advances from America and Germany had secured Durrell's future for some time. *Mountolive* had sold 10,000 copies in November, and then came news that it had been accepted by the American Book of the Month Club, bringing him a guaranteed $20,000. Two days later, his second book of Antrobus stories, *Stiff Upper Lip*, was published, and Claude's divorce came through. By February they would both be free. But, weighed down, as he saw it, by alimony, Durrell had no desire to marry again.

With all this new-found wealth in prospect, he secured Sappho's immediate future by paying her school fees at Bedales for five years ahead, something which horrified the impoverished Aldington. But Durrell felt committed to the school and its co-educational tradition, and Eve was living almost next door to it. And fortune threatened even greater fame. Aldington said he had written to *The Times* supporting him for the Nobel Prize, and Miller told him that he, too, was nominating him.[6] As if in answer to this he was sent a review of *Justine* from the German paper *Die Zeit* headlined, 'A Sure Contestant for the Nobel!'

Anaïs asked him to write a preface to her novel *Children of the Albatross*, to be published by Peter Owen in London. She felt that America had misrepresented her, and consequently she was unknown in Europe. Would he, she asked, say something out of the depth of his wisdom and perceptiveness?[7] Owen needed it in a hurry and she wanted a preface that would also go into an American edition. Despite the pressure of work, he agreed. Such distractions made it difficult for him to get started on *Clea*, and he busied himself laying down a courtyard in front of the mazet with variously coloured flat stones gathered from the garrigue. Then, with the help of a local mason, he built a long wall around it, and after that began whitewashing the house, inside and out.[8]

Clea was further delayed by a sudden cold snap and a blasting mistral which laid Durrell low with the flu. Not only was he confined to bed but he had nothing to read, his books not yet having arrived from England. Claude offered some sound Groddeckian advice, saying that suffering was a form of self-aggrandizement, and that he was only wanting to be coddled, but he refused to be either cured or comforted. Echoing his poor health, notices for *Stiff Upper Lip* were also below par. For some reviewers the joke had soon worn off, for others it was too close to Wodehouse. But if Durrell was upset, he was upset all the way to the bank.

The preface he had dashed off for Anaïs's *Children of the Albatross*, however, pitched him into an unexpected storm. When she read it she wrote complaining angrily at having been misled into thinking that he was a friend who understood her, but his preface was full of uncaring distortion. The claim that she had grown up in a grand hotel and had been married to a wealthy man, living a chauffeur-driven lifestyle and able to support Henry Miller at the Villa Seurat, was all a fantasy. Then, in describing her work he had used expressions like 'soap bubbles', 'embalming' and 'feminine subjective work'. It was humiliating. She would not use what he had written.[9] Durrell quickly wrote an emollient letter explaining that he was overworked and had written the preface at speed; if she wanted it cut or rewritten he was quite happy. This did the trick and she replied immediately regretting her 'emotionalism'. She put great store in being one of the Three Musketeers. They had best forget the whole thing, she said.[10] But she did not forget the whole thing.

Another female friend who took him to task was Diana Menuhin, who wrote saying how much she had enjoyed *Mountolive* and that she had found his various characters maddening, brilliant and absorbing. But why, she asked, was the sex so cold – lacking generosity, sweetness and humour? The characters were cold and rapacious; they could not caress but only grab. One longed for joy and passion or real sensuality. The relationship between Nessim and Justine seemed entirely cerebral; Mountolive was gutless in not going after Leila for himself. And she quoted Donne's lover: 'Filled with her love would I be rather grown *Mad* with much heart than idiot with none . . .'. But perhaps in Alexandria that's how it was, with the desert sand invading and stilting even the human heart.[11] He had no more telling critic.

*

Perhaps because of the pressure of having to come up with something special to round off his *Quartet* there were several false starts to *Clea*. The first effort got the point of view wrong, the second had to be rewritten. However, on Christmas Day he sat down determined to write 1,000 words to get the thing started. Soon he was able to settle back into his early-morning routine, rising at 6.30 and writing until he had managed 2,000 words, sometimes working up to fourteen hours in a day. Occasionally he took time off to do some stone-walling or to shoot for the pot with his newly acquired shot gun – a means, perhaps, of venting that build-up of madness he thought necessary to give his work its final spark. If so, Claude was spared the extremes to which Nancy and Eve had been subjected.

Aldington came for a day shortly after New Year with Jacques Temple, despite the bitterly cold weather. They talked about the coming launch of *Two Cities*, the 'Durrell edition' to which Aldington and Temple had been invited to contribute. Writing to Aldington, Fanchette had addressed him by mistake as 'Adlington', which produced an angry letter to Durrell about the impertinence of this 'frawg'. Aldington had quite forgotten that in 1933 he had addressed Durrell as 'Dummell'.

Fanchette sent Durrell a list of questions, compiled with his London editor of *Two Cities*, Edwin Mullins. These together with Larry's answers were to appear in the first issue. Asked whether the role of 'foreigner' had been essential to him, he replied that in Anglo-Saxon society the real 'foreigner' is the artist, which is why France was so appealing. Exiles were inclined to be 'more British than the British', and he did not want to be that; despite his 'love–hate' for England he did not wish to become a 'professional foreigner'.[12] The French recognized that love was 'a form of metaphysical enquiry', the English thought it had 'something to do with the plumbing'.[13] *Justine*, he claimed, was invented, but a common type to be found around the Mediterranean. His characters were his pets, his toys, his inventions, his recreation. And about the complete *Quartet*, he now thought that if he had written all four first and then matched them before publication it would have been different, but lack of money led him to compose it as he did, piecemeal. Later he would be able to eliminate the minor discrepancies which had got into the works.[14]

He was still struggling through the early pages of *Clea*, and still worrying that he might let his fans down if he did not get it quite right. One of his fans, Aldington, said he was fuming about the way men had treated Melissa, and that he was most upset at him killing off old Scobie; the sailors should have let him off. This prompted Durrell to consider how he might conveniently resurrect so obviously successful a character. He admitted that in creating some of his grotesques he had been influenced by the Elizabethans and even by Victorian melodrama. Then D. H. Lawrence and Freud had provided him with a modern mysticism where divinity and perversity, goodness and badness were to be seen in all people. Scobie was no sodomist but an emblem of mystical union.[15] And on the overall structure of his scheme, it was not necessary to go back to Homer for a form, as Joyce had done; his form was detached from literature, and he was curious to see where his scientific model led him.[16]

By page 60 of *Clea* he was happy to inform Aldington that Scobie was back. It had taken all his ingenuity to resurrect the old reprobate.[17]

Working so doggedly at his book, and not being able to exercise as he liked to, hiking and swimming, he became concerned about his increasingly pear-like shape. His intake of local wine could not have helped. Once he had lauded the French attitude to defecation; now he sang of the pleasures of modern indoor plumbing.

News came that *Sappho* was to be staged in Germany, according to contract, and that American film companies were showing interest in the *Quartet*. Then Claude's divorce was made absolute at the very moment that an American impresario paid her $1,000 for the stage rights of *Mrs O'*. It seemed impossible for anything to go wrong for them.

Jokingly, he told Aldington that he was running out of metaphors and at the same time asked Thomas for his copies of de Sade's *Justine* and *Brewer's Dictionary of Phrase and Fable*. By mid-March 1959, *Clea* had grown to 130 pages. He worked very quickly straight on to the typewriter, and when he had a difficult passage he stopped and worked it out by hand. He never read what he had written, leaving that to Claude. Rather than work in sentences, he preferred working in great blocks of 10,000 words at a time. He told an interviewer, 'When I'm on top form and it really comes I don't stop for twenty-four hours! Then I just knock off and go for a swim in the sea, or cut wood for a couple of hours, or sometimes Claude . . . and I will go on a drink for a couple of days until we come back to ourselves!'[18]

The American reception of *Mountolive* lifted his spirits on the final sprint to finish *Clea*. The coverage was generally enthusiastic. The Book of the Month Club called it the most subtle novel of its generation, and the *New York Times* spoke of 'Durrell's vertiginous erudition, his felicity of phrase and his astonishing powers of description'.[19] There were those who thought him misleading and even unwholesome, even while they appreciated his creative brilliance,[20] and those who saw the three completed novels as examples of a contemporary tendency to treat the most repellent themes with the most ingenious literary skill – turning sensuality, disfigurement, perversion and sadism into what amounted to a literary *tour de force*.[21] The public mood in America was changing. Not only was the sensuality, perversion and sadism in the *Quartet* tolerated and even applauded, but Miller's *Tropic* books were finally on sale in the bookstores. Durrell told Miller that it would be *he* who would get the Nobel, and looked forward to seeing him in Sommières, where they had found him a flat with the only flush toilet in town, and a cheap Spanish maid whom they could vouch for.

By the beginning of April a draft of *Clea* was finished, and Claude was typing it for him to revise. He got a fan letter from David Niven, saying he would love to play Mountolive. Aldington wrote in good ascerbic form to say that Niven was typecast for Scobie, but that Hollywood would come knocking at his door soon enough. He was peeved that Durrell had refused to contribute towards a printing press for Potocki, and said he would get him to christen it the Melissa Press.[22] Aldington also disliked Fanchette's *Two Cities*, which he thought amateur.

In April Durrell was awarded the French prize for the Best Foreign Book of the Year (the Prix de Meilleur Livre Etranger) for *Balthazar*, which further put back revision of *Clea*, bringing as it did a flood of requests for interviews from newspapers and radio. And on 23 April he received the ultimate accolade short of the Nobel – an interview with the *Paris Review*. At the beginning of May, the Carnival scene from *Balthazar* was serialized in *Les Lettres Nouvelles*, as a curtain-raiser for the publication, and Buchet arranged a launch party for Monday the 4th. Durrell took Claude to Paris, and met Miller for the first time in twenty years.

Miller and Eve (to whom he was now married) had taken an apartment near his old stamping ground of Montparnasse. Durrell was amazed that Miller, now sixty-eight, was so spry and active. Claude was pleased to find him less of the monster she had imagined from his books. They both thought Eve delightful. In the splendid apartment on Boulevard St Michel, which Fanchette had set up for their reunion, Miller stood around dressed in a loud tartan shirt, being admired and talking in a slow drawl, while Durrell was holding forth in his emphatic refined voice to a circle of journalists and young artistic hopefuls. Buchet was there, rather miffed because *he* had planned to host the Durrell–Miller reunion and had been scooped by Fanchette.[23]

There was trouble on the Paris streets that night, as the Algerian crisis rumbled on. Nevertheless, Larry and Claude, the Millers and Miller's daughter Val, Gerald and Buffie Sykes, Raja Rao, André and Odette Bay, Edward Mullins, Fanchette and his wife Martine went on to chez Papille. Over dinner, Miller, back in his old element, entranced his audience with his eccentric trains of thought and recollections of times past with Durrell in Paris and Greece. Fanchette got very drunk and at some stage threw his meal out of the window; afterwards he could not remember a thing.[24]

Next day Miller dragged Durrell off on one of the prodigious walks they used to take around Paris, stalking ahead and leaving the diminutive and overweight Durrell breathlessly trying to keep abreast. Later, at Buchet's office, they found a ping-pong table and Miller played seven games in a row and beat everyone who took him on. He put his fitness down entirely to Buddhism. Miller and Durrell were interviewed together for the radio and the newspapers, and discovered that they were a natural double act – they had so much in common, had corresponded for so long, each seemed to be party to the other's thought processes. The Paris visit was topped off with the long-planned celebration for them at the Corrêa offices laid on by Edmond Buchet and Jean Chastel, to which Girodias turned up, and said he wanted to reissue *The Black Book*.

The French critics were enormously impressed by *Balthazar*. *Les Lettres Françaises* called Durrell a 'great writer and remarkable stylist', and *Combat* greeted the novel as a true advance in modern literature.

Interviewing Durrell, wrote Jean Cau in *L'Express*, was like trying to pin down a shadow. Questioning 'this little man with a large sensual nose and a laugh as fresh as the vin blanc which we drank' was impossible. He seemed to believe, like Plato, that although we think ourselves responsible for our actions they are only expressions of Ideas within us; all creation was to him, therefore, poetic. He spoke always of the 'poet', never of the 'writer'. Access to his interior world was, concluded Cau, difficult and secret:

> Either there is the Poem or there is Life [Durrell told him], and evidently the Poem and the Life are the same thing. The existence of the poet confirms the life of society, the existence of the society is imaginary and the world is created by poets. Understand, of course, that the poetic experience is not exceptional. On the contrary.

After an hour of this, said Cau, one got used to the language, and the reversal of reality, like turning a glove inside out, was fascinating. Durrell went on to say that, in constructing his 'continuum', Einstein used algebraic characters; *he* used beings, like de Sade, whose 'sadistic' explorations were really explorations of himself. He referred himself to Plotinus, Plato, the cabbalists and the Gnostics and what he called 'the whole Alexandria way of thinking'. He was an idealist who rejected Marxist economic explanations of art. 'All works of art are

Promethean: Rimbaudian Man, Proustian Man steals the fire.'
Art was Rimbaudian illumination. Cau decided that there was
no connecting Durrell to the ordinary man's earth and life. On
'love' he said:

> Love is culpability. Love consists in discovering the impossibility to
> 'give' to the other. Love which is the essential rapport is at the same
> time the impossible rapport. Love is no more than to discover the
> opportunity to live your solitude in front of a mirror. A man and a
> woman who love are two absolute solitudes who grow, contemplate
> and reflect . . . [Sex] is the door to hell or paradise in which one
> begins to know oneself. Sexual rapport confirms the solitude; at the
> same time, as you understand it . . . it gives you illumination.

France, said Durrell, was an idea to be found in everything the
French say, the air they breathe, their ways and their spiritual
art of living. 'An artist in an Anglo-Saxon country is always
more or less sought by Scotland Yard . . . In France an artist is
at least a good Camembert.'[25]

That same evening, he met Mary Hadkinson, his photographer friend from Rhodes, at the café Les Deux Magots in St
Germain des Près. She found she was unable to hold a sustained
conversation with him because he was surrounded by a throng
of bobby-soxers hanging on to every word 'le maître' spoke.[26]
His experience in public relations, although he had loathed it,
had taught him to speak with authority, and now he did so as
an author. And the presence of beautiful young women always
gave wings to his seductive eloquence. His tone of conviction
and gift of the tongue fitted him well for the role of guru
when the 1960s arrived, enchanting impressionable youth and
dazzling interviewers with his pontificating not only on novel
writing, but on the art of living and loving too. He could
indulge his sense of fun by toying with his listeners and mysti-
fying them with his verbal power, a power which could also
be used for purposes of seduction, as he had demonstrated in
the *Quartet*. Gerald told of a woman friend of his wanting to
meet Larry, and sitting enraptured by him for a long time and
never once speaking to him. She told Gerry afterwards that it
was pleasure enough just to listen to him talk. But not all fell
for the Durrell charm. At one party a woman told him that he
was nothing but 'a sex-obsessed dwarf'.[27]

*

Back in his den at the mazet, Durrell slept for twenty-four hours. He heard that Twentieth Century-Fox had taken an option on the *Quartet* and Walter Wanger was asking again about the scripting of *Cleopatra*. And news came that *Sappho* was set to open in Hamburg in October. Alan Pringle at Faber, who had seen an advance carbon of *Clea*, thought it a considerable achievement. Some passages were magnificent, and, despite a few queries, he thought it would be an inspiration to young writers.[28] From Paris, Fanchette reported a life-size photograph of Durrell in the window of Gagliani's, and Girodias sent a contract for the reissue of *The Black Book*, which Dutton also scheduled for American publication in 1960. Both Dutton and Faber now wanted to do his *Collected Poems*, and Fanchette asked to publish an extract from *Clea* in *Two Cities*, but Durrell suggested instead something from *The Black Book*. To relax, he got back to his freestone-walling, and entertained a few friends. Cathy Aldington and Jacques Temple came one evening, staying until almost midnight, and friends of Gerry, Mai Zetterling and David Hughes, also came and were treated to a marvellous leisurely and elaborate lunch.[29]

Around mid-June his revision of *Clea* went off to Faber. The novel extends the time continuum occupied by the first three in the sequence, the action taking place after the events previously covered. Now it is wartime. Darley is summoned by Nessim back to Alexandria from his island in the Cyclades, bringing Melissa's child with him. He arrives, much as Durrell had done, during an air-raid. He finds that Menmjian has become the richest barber in Alexandria, Pombal is in love with a beautiful married woman, Fosca, Justine is back from Palestine but no longer the delectable woman who had so enchanted him. Her beauty has faded, her perfume is nauseating to him and her company less than appealing. At heart, she tells him, her love has always been for Nessim. Darley's obsession with her is broken. Nessim, who has lost an eye and is guilt-ridden about the death of Narouz, takes the child. From Balthazar, who has been badly treated by a homosexual love and has tried to cut off his hands, Darley learns that the Cabal is no more and that Capodistria's 'death' had been faked by Nessim to enable him to avoid being compromised over the arms-to-Palestine plot, and to claim the insurance and so escape bankruptcy. From Clea he learns that Scobie is now venerated by the locals and a *mulid* (festival) is held every St George's Day. Clea, it seems, can mimic Scobie with uncanny accuracy, and so he is reincarnated once more through her voice. One of their acquaintances, Amaril, fell in love with a girl at a masked ball, who turned out to have lost a nose through Lupus, but, loving her, he replaces it with plastic surgery and she now makes an appearance. Clea also tells Darley that, unsure about her own sexuality she had thrown herself at Pursewarden and been rebuffed. She became pregnant by Amaril and had an abortion. As an artist, she now knows that sex is knowledge, and understands both the male and female aspects of it. Clea and Darley become lovers.

Liza Pursewarden, about to marry Mountolive, hears that the journalist Keats is to write a scurrilous biography of her brother, and invites Darley to read letters which reveal that it was Pursewarden's incest with Liza that drove him to suicide. On Darley's advice they burn the letters. Keats, who has discovered himself as a writer, goes off to the desert war, Fosca is accidentally shot by French sailors, and Clea and Darley find a lovely little island off which to swim. After accidentally being harpooned through her right hand, her painting hand, Clea leaves to live and work in France. She writes to Darley saying that she has met Nessim and Justine in Paris; Nessim's fortunes have been somehow restored; they plan to live in Switzerland. And she, who has learned to paint with her artificial hand, has discovered herself at last. She suspects that Darley too has come into his own as an artist, and she awaits his letter or his coming to Paris.

For those wishing to find autobiographical traces in the *Quartet*, there are obvious parallels with Durrell's time in Egypt. He admitted to Fanchette that he himself was both Pursewarden and Darley in his different moods. And perhaps he was Mountolive when aspiring to diplomatic eminence, Scobie when feeling outrageously camp, Keats when wanting to emulate his brave soldier friends, Nessim when suavely conspiratorial, and Narouz when brutal and sadistic. But in certain moods he was also Scobie or Balthazar as Tiresias – the seer whose voice might be heard in his poetry as much as in the *Quartet*. The shifting of identities was a theme he was to take up later in his *Avignon Quintet*.

The novels after *Justine* had been produced at high speed, in great sustained bursts of creativity. *Balthazar*, said Durrell, took six weeks, *Mountolive* twelve and *Clea* eight. Even if there was an element of exaggeration there, the rapidity of their production is unquestionable and astonishing. After each great effort, he said, 'I just collapsed into bed for two or three weeks.' But picking up the thread again afterwards produced errors of continuity. 'Brown eyes on one page had become blue a week later, and characters who had come into a room wearing one dress went out of it in a totally different one. But I think we caught most of those in the proof-sheets.'[30] When the *Quartet* was published under one cover in 1962, there were minor changes and additions.

When *Clea* was published, the *Quartet* was completely available for the first time. Durrell received a very serious and careful critical assessment, not just from reviewers in the daily and weekly press, but also more and more in academic journals and theses. Scholars have found many a message in Durrell's highly complex masterpiece. But perhaps the message at the end of *Clea* is the one which he meant to have most effect. Keats and Clea are transformed into artists. Then, there are the letters of Pursewarden to Darley (entitled 'My Conversations with Brother Ass'), which seem to embody Durrell's own outlook on art – anti the Anglo-Saxons and pro the Europe of Rabelais and de Sade. Art is seen as therapeutic against perverse beliefs such as Original Sin, and against the damage we cause to each other through sexual love. There is something Groddeckian in this: in getting the mind straightened out, physical wellbeing can only follow. By the same token, getting the mind straight about sex, by booting out Original Sin, can only result in sexual wellbeing. These notions link to his seductive idea that self-fulfilment through sex can occur only when it is raised to the level of art. And art, too, has brought order out of chaos; Darley's fragmentary understanding of his Alexandrian past has, through the relative perspectives of time and space, achieved wholeness.

Miller, who had read a carbon of the book, wrote from Le Chambon. He found it stunning, exquisite and luxuriant. Pursewarden, however, he found not believable as a great writer, and Darley too self-depreciating. Keats and some of the lesser characters were handled brilliantly. Technique in the whole *Quartet* reminded him of a bullfight – exciting and hazardous cape-work. He had immortalized Alexandria. There was horror and beauty in *Clea*. Like Homer's gods he had stood aside and skewered morality in the process. Through the characters, Alexandria was living herself. He shouted his hosannas.[31]

The various children arrived for the summer at the end of June – Eve, on a rare visit to her ex-husband, bringing Sappho from London: a timely visit from the real Justine at the completion of the books she had helped to inspire. Soon afterwards, the Millers arrived for a big reunion. Temple and Aldington joined them one evening at the mazet, dining in a tent which Durrell had erected outside, and being serenaded by him on the guitar with scurrilous songs from the repertoire of Joshua Scobie. Larry took Miller to the bullfight and introduced him to fiery *vieux marc*. The two men caught up on the past twenty years, went to Nîmes and Avignon and the Pont du Gard, down to Saintes Maries de la Mer for the children to go swimming, and took a trip up the Rhône together. Anaïs wrote from Paris saying how much she wished he was there; however, instead she spent her time in the city enjoying Fanchette and his healing powers. There was also a visit from Girodias. Durrell was finding himself in ever greater demand.

Clea was supposed to appear before the end of the year, but a printers' strike in England delayed the proofs for a couple of months. The fans, eager to know the end of the Alexandrian saga, would have to be patient. Meanwhile Durrell planned to take Sappho back to England at the beginning of September. Then in October he and Claude would head for Germany for the opening of *Sappho* at the Deutsches Schauspielhaus in Hamburg. As Durrell intended bringing back as many of his books as possible from Alan Thomas's attic, they took the car, driving to Calais and crossing the Channel by ferry. Behind

them they left a local mason building an extension to the mazet
– three extra rooms for the children when they came. Sappho
was duly delivered to Eve, and Larry and Claude then headed
for London, where Leigh Fermor had lent them his house in
Chester Row. Durrell found England transformed. There had
been three months of uninterrupted sunshine, and everyone was
in great good humour – tanned, cheerful, kind, well-mannered,
lively and devil-may-care. The food was better than before,
though he did wonder whether his fame meant he was just
being fed a better class of meal.

He embarked on a publicity round for Faber. He met again
some of his old Fleet Street acquaintances from his press attaché
days, and was annoyed to hear some of them suggest that it
was unpatriotic to live abroad. But all this attention from the
press gave him a chance further to develop his own legend.
One interview, published in the *News Chronicle* under the title
'Why Mr Durrell Can't Afford to Write Poetry', quoted him
as saying, 'The English novel is too anaemic. I am trying to
make it more full-blooded.' It named him the most interesting
author to emerge in the 1950s. He had shaken up the novel
by providing it with a new form, primarily because of his poetic
skill and his powerful use of language. But he had ceased to
write poetry, he said, because a poem took at least two weeks
to gestate and one could empty one's mind of a third of a novel
in one good poem. He still felt insecure, despite paying the
lower French tax, but would not like to be a millionaire. He
was a fan of Evelyn Waugh and Graham Greene and thought
Amis's *Lucky Jim* was 'a little masterpiece', but 'There are too
many people writing about policies and not enough about
values.' The main task of the writer was to arouse the artistic
spirit which lies in everyone; only in that way could a person
ever live. 'I have no ethical position,' he concluded, 'I believe
that humour is the solution to the problems of the World, the
Flesh and the Devil.' His next novel, he said, would be a big
humorous novel. Miller would have been proud of him; after
all, he had once believed that if only he could get to Berlin to
make Hitler laugh there would be no war.[32]

He appeared on the BBC Television *Tonight* programme, and
found that he was a 'natural' television performer, rather like

Gerry, who was by now a celebrity through his TV appearances with animals. Larry fell in love with the medium: his fluent charm lent itself to live performance.

The London visit suddenly took a downturn. Claude fell ill and had to go into hospital for investigations. It was feared she would have to have her ovaries removed, but fortunately it was only a cyst which required nothing more than a routine operation. They stayed in Bournemouth while she recuperated, and there Durrell began to retrieve his books and papers from Thomas's attic. He found there all his letters from Miller dating back to 1935, and letters from Dylan Thomas and George Bernard Shaw. He even found the little Jupiter diary which Miller had handwritten for him in 1939, a gem of a thing full of exquisite drawings and quotations from Zen. He packed his books on the Elizabethans, determined to spend time on them when he could escape back to the solitude of Engances. Claude and Larry spent a couple of congenial evenings with the Thomases, knocking a hole in their cellar, before heading back over the Channel to France.

On their return they found the mazet in chaos. The mason they had left working there had got drunk on their wine and damaged their water-pump, leaving the well dried out and the house flooded. It took them almost two weeks to clean and tidy up the place. Fortunately, word came from Hamburg that *Sappho* had been postponed until November. Larry felt exhausted after his trip, and was content to rest at home for a while. There was a letter from Miller, hard at work on *Plexus*, asking him to get his letters microfilmed with a view to Larry Powell, the librarian, editing the Miller–Durrell correspondence. Powell had just completed a fifty-page Durrell bibliography with Thomas, so he seemed a suitable person for the job.[33]

The spread of Durrell's fame (he had now been translated into thirteen languages) made him more reclusive than ever. The mazet had now become home in more ways than one, a place to which he and Claude had become attached, a foxhole in which to hide from the increasing demands of celebrity, and to feel at one with rugged nature. They decided to buy it outright and became joint owners (helped by a huge advance for *Clea* from Buchet); it was only the second house that Durrell had owned; the first still languished unoccupied in Cyprus. Their children were delighted; it seemed to be the end of the nomadic life, and they would now each have rooms of their own. To preserve the solitude it represented, Durrell put up a notice on the track approaching the house, indicating that uninvited and unexpected visitors were unwelcome. 'This is a workshop – please write.'[34]

Encouraged by the forthcoming production of *Sappho*, he had begun a new verse play, *Acte*, about a Christian girl in the court of Nero, which was meant to express the return to the melodrama which had marked the final pages of *Clea*. His identification with the Elizabethans was now intense, and he felt ever more keenly that he had been born 350 years too late. He implied that there were two influences on him in writing *Acte* – the desire to introduce an element of Grand Guignol into the theatre and the desire to return to the bloody passions of the writers like Thomas Kyd. The story certainly held those possibilities for him. Acte is a Scythian princess who has been blinded by a cruel satrap. (Blindness and blind women held a strange fascination for Durrell.) Sent to Rome as a hostage for Nero's pleasure, she hopes to work her charms on the malign Emperor, but fails. She is loved by and in love with a Roman general, Fabius. Both are banished to Egypt but die in a failed rebellion. The cynical writer, Petronius Arbiter, comments chorus-like on all this and, as in *Sappho*, tragic events are more often reported than seen onstage.

In November, Miller was suffering a crisis, having apparently fallen in love with an artist's model of twenty-five. He and Eve partly separated, though she did not think the infatuation would last. Still in a state of nostalgia, prompted by his writing of *Plexus*, Miller urged Durrell to go to St Rémy, the birthplace of Nostradamus, and to the ruined château of de Sade at Lacoste, both of which he had visited on a cycle tour of France before the war. He continued to hanker after the mysterious east, something incomprehensible to Durrell, who remembered India as a place of squalor and disease to which he never wished to return. *His* east was an imaginary Tibet – mountainous, solitary and exclusive.

With Claude, Durrell flew to Hamburg for the opening of *Sappho* on 2 November. They were given a great reception by Rowohlt, who lodged them at a luxury hotel. Rowohlt planned to wring every ounce of publicity from his author's visit, as he was publishing the German edition of *Mountolive* on the 25th, and had all the press and media lined up to interview him. The play was performed at the Deutsches Schauspielhaus, starring Elisabeth Flickenschildt as Sappho and the young Maximilian Schell as Phaon. Gustaf Gründgens (a one-time friend of Thomas Mann's children, and during the Nazi era a friend of Göring) directed. On that first night there were thirty-six curtain calls, six for the author. Durrell was overwhelmed. A play he had written ten years before had turned into a theatrical triumph. He wondered if this was where his talent truly lay, in the company of his Elizabethans – Tourneur, Decker, Ford and the rest. Rawlings, who had flown out from England for the play, was distinctly underwhelmed, finding the production static and the declamatory style of the actors positively boring. It would have fallen flat on its face in England, she thought, and returned immediately to London, preferring to deliver her verdict to Durrell in a letter. She blamed the poor production on 'Municipal Money' used for 'Noble Experiments' rather than the good hit-and-miss methods of the English theatre. But she still believed in the play and was determined to see it done properly in England.

Durrell, however anti-socialist he might have been, loved the German subsidized theatre. To him, the production was a great success; he thought Elisabeth Flickenschildt was a wonder to behold in the role of Sappho. Interviews, photographs, phone-calls, lavish dinners and television appearances followed. Durrell got on famously with Gründgens, who was eager to see his next play, *Acte*. He felt he had learned a great deal and the new play would be better constructed. He was proud to know that *Sappho* would go into repertoire, alternating with plays by Schiller and Goethe. Television again conferred celebrity on him and again he was chased by bobby-soxers anxious to get their copies of his books autographed.

Durrell told Aldington that a writer only *existed* when he wrote. But he also admitted that once *Acte* was finished he had no idea what to write next. The great comic novel (still not more than a set of notes) seemed to have disappeared from the menu. Perhaps he was put off by Rowohlt, who asked him please to do no more Antrobus books, but to concentrate on serious work. And French reviews of *Mountolive* brought him back to his more sober work. *Le Figaro Littéraire* applauded Durrell's 'intelligent and powerful presence' in France.[35]

Art and Outrage appeared at the end of November. Miller called it a taste of caviar. Durrell thought that Miller's letters in the collection completely eclipsed his and Perlès's paltry efforts. He had been reluctant to have his larger body of letters to Miller published, but now Miller again urged him to agree to both sides of the correspondence coming out, cutting whatever he thought unsuitable.

On 17 December, with Eve in hospital, Durrell flew to England to bring back Sappho, taking Miller's letters to Bournemouth for Thomas to microfilm for Lawrence Powell. On his way back, in Paris, where Fanchette threw a surprise party, he met Curtis Cate, the Paris representative of *Atlantic Monthly*, Gaït Frogé, owner of the English Bookshop in Paris, and George Whitman, who ran the Mistral Bookshop on the Rue de la Bûcherie beside the Seine (now called Shakespeare and Company after Sylvia Beach's more famous pre-war shop).

Sappho joined Claude's children for Christmas at the mazet, which Claude and Larry now owned. *The Best of Henry Miller* anthology, which Durrell had edited, arrived from Heinemann, together with news that it was also a Book Society choice. Meanwhile he carried on working on *Acte*, which was about half done. In the New Year he expected an invasion of interviewers wanting to talk about *Clea*, due for publication by Faber in February. Brassaï was also coming to take his photograph, something of an honour he thought.

The New Year was to confirm his arrival as a major literary figure. The publication of *Clea* would be followed by his

Collected Poems, reissues of *The Black Book*, *Prospero's Cell*, *Reflections on a Marine Venus* and *Pope Joan*. *Art and Outrage* was published by Rowohlt, and *The Best of Henry Miller* appeared as well as a new edition of E.M. Forster's *Alexandria: A History and a Guide* with a preface by Durrell. The journalistic commissions also kept coming. In January he had a long piece in *Holiday* about the River Rhône and one in the *Sunday Times* about a Cypriot troubadour called Janis. The Rhône article was quintessential Durrell travel-writing – urbane, poetic and subtle. It brought the reader from the river's Alpine source, through Lyons, Vienne, Condriu, Tournon, Valance, Montelimar, Avignon and Arles, to the wide Delta, Saintes Maries de la Mer and the wild Camargue.[36] Aldington was against such enticements to American tourists to visit this relatively unspoiled part of the world, and he also complained to Durrell about his agreeing to be televised at Saintes Maries.

But there was more television to come. In early January a BBC team arrived for three days' filming at the mazet. Durrell was interviewed by Huw Wheldon, the high priest of British arts television. The director insisted he be interviewed high up in the Roman arena at Nîmes, where he suffered an attack of vertigo. But he got his own back once the tape started rolling, he claimed, by saying, 'What I'd like to say, with my friend Henry Miller, is that I like pornography and hate obscenity, but I won't say it because you have nine million muffin-faced viewers who won't buy my books.' The tape was restarted.[37] They ranged over his life and writing, and as usual he gave a characteristically fluent performance as the dazzlingly gifted English exile. No doubt it won for him a whole new raft of British readers when it was transmitted in February to coincide with the publication of *Clea*.

The French literary scene was overshadowed by the death of Albert Camus on 4 January 1960. Durrell's scene was overshadowed by the appearance of Jean-Paul Weber's portrait–interview of him in *Le Figaro Littéraire* on the 9th. Headed 'Dinner on the Garrigue with Lawrence Durrell', the tone throughout was one of barely veiled mockery. He began with a caricature of the *Quartet*. The yellow covers were like dried blood – the yellow blood of Huns (a friend's joke). Durrell's

Alexandria was a city of vice peopled by disfigured women and mad Copts. There followed a caricature of Durrell – 'shabbily dressed, powerful torso, arms of a fairground Hercules', and of his Heath Robinson-type car performing beyond what the factory had intended it to by 'walking' across the garrigue like a horse, which forced a postman to throw himself and his bicycle into the gorse in a panic. When Durrell spoke, Weber religiously included his grammatical errors. 'The postman . . . she is old. When the mistral blows she can no longer ride her bicycle . . . She is a communist . . . I do not like Nationalist Communists . . . Churchill she was a big man . . . You know ideas rule the world.' His views on Britain and the Common Market (it should include the USSR, with the British monarch in charge), obviously meant for comic effect, were reported as if they were the serious political opinions of a simpleton. The noise of shooting from the nearby firing range was a cue to be ironic about Durrell's search for peace and quiet out on the garrigue. Claude was presented as a beautiful, glamorous wife. Durrell, by contrast, came across as an opinionated buffoon, boasting and semi-articulate, while the interviewer was presented as a cold, knowing intellectual who had expected to find a profoundly philosophical writer, an intellectual equal, but had found a man who could not stop talking about 'bloody Christianity' and the importance to poets of having been boxers. The 'illustrious' writer then took the interviewer inside the mazet to look at his 'naive' watercolours and drink coffee. If they talked about his work at all, there was nothing of it reported in *Le Figaro*.

Durrell was upset, feeling he had been 'had' by Weber, who had, according to him, promised not to mention Claude, and had presented himself as someone at *Le Figaro*, which he was not. He had also afforded him a whole day of hospitality, food and wine. In future he would avoid such people. Fanchette was furious, saying that Weber would never appear in *Two Cities* again, and Aldington offered the assistance of two Paris boxers to go and 'duff up' the offending critic. Declining this offer, Durrell (showing more English phlegm than Irish spleen) dismissed Weber's derision.

Books and Bookmen ran an interview with him in February

called 'Lawrence Durrell: Is He the Greatest Novelist of the Fifties?' It was an agreeable way in which to bid farewell to the first decade of his success.

CHAPTER 13

Après le Déluge:
After the *Quartet* (1960–1961)

Every true work of art must create the
very taste with which it is to be judged.

Wordsworth

With the publication of *Clea* the great tetralogy was complete.
The Alexandria Quartet, which had emerged from the breathless dash towards completion, was more than it claimed to be
– 'an investigation of modern love'.

Clothing the whole project in theories of space and time,
and infusing it with mysticism, was probably an expression
of something deeply personal. Years of feeling deprived of a
university education could perhaps be assuaged by this claim
to profundity. Some critical reaction he received afforded him
the distinction he felt he deserved.

As the final volume in the *Quartet, Clea* was given wide
coverage on the review pages in Britain, though critical opinion
ranged from the encomiastic through the sceptical to the down-
right contemptuous. Some critics compared him unflatteringly
to Charles Morgan, another English writer popular in France.
Hints at imperfection in the *Quartet* produced an angry reaction from Durrell's committed disciple Fanchette: 'These little
creeps' were jealous of his success, and would never forgive his
criticizing their insularity.[1] And Aldington was equally scathing.
Durrell was a genius, his critics were incestuous 'farts'.[2] Durrell
himself took the long view as usual. Now that his books were
selling so well in Britain and in the US, what was in his account
at Grindlay's Bank mattered more than what was in the

columns of the *Observer*. And far more cheering was a fan letter from a South African woman who said that he must have done a lot of things with women to write so well about them.[3]

The recipient of all this critical attention was suffering from a writer's block and directing his energies to more wall-building. He undertook some journalistic commissions, including a piece for *Holiday* on Geneva. Staying at the Touring-Balance Hotel where Casanova once stayed, he visited the Palais de Nations, headquarters of the UN where his old diplomatic friend from Rhodes, Hoyland, now worked. One of the translators there, Alexander Blokh, an expatriate Russian who wrote novels under the pseudonym Jean Blot, recognized him and followed him into the men's toilets. There, relieving himself in the next stall, he introduced himself. Blokh invited Durrell home to meet his beautiful wife Nadia, a painter and also a translator, and they all became great friends. Durrell was conscious of Geneva's literary and artistic ghosts. Here had come Stendhal, Dickens, Balzac, Ruskin and Wagner. Geneva was to become an important setting for Durrell's later fiction, especially *The Avignon Quintet*.

Not long after his return from Switzerland, he heard that Miller, having been chosen as a judge for the Cannes Film Festival, was coming to France in May, without Eve but planning to meet up with his inamorata, Caryl Thomas, a model from Big Sur. And Fanchette, just back from London, sent news that *Clea* was a best-seller in England,[4] while Perlès wrote from Rome in April to say that his books were in every shop there, the Italian edition of *Justine* bearing the label 'Lady erotica'.

In America, where *Clea* was published in April, Durrell's brilliance was recognized, and the completed *Quartet* was often greeted as something revolutionary in fiction. *Time*, for example, which also carried an interview, said that what he had brought off 'has not been duplicated by any postwar writer',[5] and the *Saturday Review* called the *Quartet* 'a disquieting work', and 'a brilliant technical experiment . . . more fascinating than a mystery story'.[6] The *New Republic* greeted the whole opus as 'a new kind of novel – and one of the few really important works to come out of England since the war'.[7]

The spring saw Durrell and Claude back in Paris for ten days for the launching of the French edition of *Clea*, which coincided with the publication of his *Collected Poems* in London. He also spent time having a scenario discussion with Twentieth Century-Fox about the scripting of *Cleopatra*, then being directed by Rouben Mamoulian and produced by Walter Wanger, who had also bought film rights of the *Quartet*. Mamoulian, who already had a script, wanted to produce a poem for the camera – a romance somewhat after Shakespeare, and asked Durrell to write some of the scenes.[8] They stayed in great style for once at the Georges V Hotel close to the Arc de Triomphe, and again he was trotted out before television cameras, received masses of fan letters, and held court for the worshipful bobby-soxers at the St Germain cafés.

And again the French critics took Durrell to their hearts. *Figaro Littéraire* said that, given the cycle's originality, beauty and strength, and its technical conception, its completion incontestably placed Durrell among the big contemporary novelists. 'It is in the artistic and liberating act of creativity that the book ends, and also on a homage to France which the French reader will be greatly touched by' – a reference to a sentence claiming that the healing grass of art grew best in France.[9] Jacques Vallette in *Cahiers du Sud* wrote that in each generation the French sky needed an English meteor, and that meteor had arrived in the person of Durrell. The key to Durrell lay, as he himself claimed, in his just-published poems. Vallette thought *Clea* enclosed the whole tetralogy, giving us, most significantly, 'a new figure in the adult novel'. We might think we could embody in one phrase the quintessence of the work – like Justine's speaking of 'the secret of growth' – but it would be inept to reduce to one maxim an aesthetic work which quivers with words, with life and with perfumes.[10] Paulette Michot in *Revue des Langues Vivantes* stressed the 'stereoscopic effect' of the book and its mesmerizing powers. So enthusiastic was the French press for him that Durrell later said that as an author he was invented by the French, and attributed their enthusiasm to a dissatisfaction with the aridity of the *nouveau roman* – so precise, so analytic, so devoid of feeling.

Miller arrived in Cannes on 2 May and in Nîmes at the end of the month. Simultaneously, Mai Zetterling and David Hughes arrived in the Camargue to film the Gypsy Festival at Saintes Maries de la Mer. Miller had his Californian lover in tow. There were drunken evenings knocking back *vieux marc* at the mazet, where Zetterling felt quite cut out of the conversation and decided that Miller and Durrell were 'a fine pair of misogynists'. However, she recalled with some relish an amusing end to one of these evenings, driving back to their hotel with Miller in the front of their Land Rover and his girlfriend being seduced in the back by their cameraman, much to Miller's annoyance – 'he, supposedly the sex maniac of all time . . . being cuckolded in his own presence'.[11] However, according to Miller's biographer, he had already fallen for a beautiful German woman working for Rowholt in Hamburg, Renate Gerhardt, and was actually pushing Caryl at other men – a *Quartet*-like contradiction of perceptions.[12]

In Nîmes they dined next to the Arènes with the Sykeses, who were touring Europe, and were also joined there one day by a wild American writer, Charles Haldeman, who impressed Miller greatly. He later came out to the mazet, got drunk and caused an explosive scene. However, Durrell forgave him and even asked him to visit Frau Groddeck for him in Baden-Baden. Limes Verlag, the German publishers, were interested in reprinting Groddeck's work, and Durrell proposed that they also bring out in pamphlet form his essay on Groddeck from *Horizon*. He wanted Haldeman to give the news to Frau Groddeck and to greet her for him. Back in the USA, Miller was complaining about Big Sur being overrun by 'homos' and about young teenage girls sleeping around.[13] The sexual scene was shifting and, strangely, Miller did not seem to see himself as part of it or show any awareness of how far he might have contributed to it.

One of the fruits of Durrell's success was that publishers were now prepared to publish his *Collected Poems*. Although in the years since Cyprus the pressing need for money and the writing of the *Quartet* had reduced the amount of poetry he wrote, the volume included over 150 poems, covering most of his poetic life. And, perhaps still under the influence of his recent experiment in Space–Time, he placed them not in chronological order, but according to some order of significance private to himself.

The strong division of taste which Durrell met with in Britain is seen in the range of the opinions his poetry evoked in the wake of his *Quartet*. The most frequent complaint was of intellectualism and obscurantism. In America, where Dutton published the collection, the obscurity of his verse was often seen as due to sloppiness or to a wilful attempt to hide what was not there. *Time* noted the puzzling play of Durrell's poems, which was seen as partly a reluctance to allow his reader into the hidden recesses of his own feelings.

June saw him back in London for a fortnight's work on *Cleopatra*, this time living and feasting on smoked salmon at the luxurious Westbury Hotel in Conduit Street. The work was hard but the money was unbelievable. The BBC snapped him up for radio interviews and another television appearance on *Tonight*, where he held forth about British diplomats abroad. At the end of his visit, the filmscript went back with him to France for a tenth rewrite, but he did not consider screenwriting difficult, and it only meant more dollars. When he got back home to the mazet, he found his well had been dried up yet again by the mason, and both he and Claude came down with the flu once more.

The *Quartet* became the subject of more weighty academic appraisal. In June, essays appeared in the *Yale Review* from George Steiner and Martin Green which raised the issue 'Durrell: charlatan or genius?' And these two critiques represent the two poles from which Durrell was approached both then and later. For Steiner, his 'command of the light and music of language' was a sheer delight in an unimaginative, illiterate world of impoverished sensibility. Durrell also saw clearly the way in which the truth was constituted and he had drawn powerful metaphors from Dante, the Metaphysicals, the Gnostics and especially Lawrence, who, like Durrell, believed that the act of love was a significant affirmation of human identity – 'the only true bridge for the soul'. His Alexandria was a major imaginative monument like Proust's Paris or Joyce's

Dublin. The technique of superimposing text upon text was like that of the painter returning to the same scene under different lights, like the angled vision of the Japanese *Rashomon* fable and Pirandello's plays. There were perils in this risky method, said Steiner, but he applauded the magnitude of the *Quartet*, declaring that all concerned with the future of the language had to 'get to grips with this singular work'. And, however posterity judged the *Quartet*, Durrell would find an enduring place in the history of English literature.[14]

Martin Green deplored the proliferation of works coming from Durrell and the esteem accorded them, which left him feeling uneasy. He criticized his use of language as contrived and pretentious, and his underlying philosophy as 'paganism'. His attack on middle-class Protestant morality reached back to the nineteenth century, the hedonistic escape route to the Mediterranean had been trodden before – Lawrence, Forster, Norman Douglas. The greatest influence on him was Douglas, but in the Alexandrian novels the depravity was greater and less attractive than anything in *South Wind* – the voice of the narrator was emotionally, morally and philosophically exhausted; style and structure were more important than classical culture. These elements probably were traceable to the Paris of Miller and his hangers-on. Green then attacked Durrell's British Romantic expatriate attitude, especially in *Bitter Lemons*, where his attachment to a romantic view of the Greek peasantry and his irrational respect for British administration blinded him for a long time to political reality and to a recognition of the rights of the Greek Cypriots. He questioned the attachment of Britons to this type of sensibility as a pathway to truth and beauty.[15]

Since rocketing to prominence, Durrell found his opinion being solicited on every kind of weird and burning topic. Asked to contribute to a series on the 'Limits of Control' in the *TLS*, he offered a philosophy of quietism, of salvation through self-knowledge – much the view of Miller in the 1930s – and said that writers' opinions were not especially worthy of interest, and artists could contribute nothing towards solving world crises.[16] Ironically, in another piece in the *New York Times Book Review*, he did offer a solution in outlining his idea of the spirit of place and explaining how character is mostly derived from landscape. Here he argued that many world problems arise from people not being in tune with the spirit of place, and in literature one of the qualities of truly 'big' books is their expression of that spirit.[17] He was not claiming originality for this idea, acknowledging that it was incorporated in certain major works. Indeed, one of his critics had pointed out that Conrad, Maugham and Graham Greene all present characters as the embodiment of their location – a characteristic of what he called 'tropical literature'.[18]

Despite cautionary and even hard words from certain American academics, the transatlantic love affair with Durrell continued apace. Carl Bode, ex-American Cultural Attaché in London, now a critic, wrote asking about the genesis of the *Quartet* for a paper to be delivered to the Modern Language Association. And Fanchette, on a visit to the US, wrote to report that everyone was climbing on the Durrell bandwagon, and he was even a hero in Greenwich Village.[19] In London the price of fame came in a different form It was discovered that notebooks and paintings purporting to be Durrell's, but probably fakes, were on sale at a London second-hand bookshop.[20]

The thirst for articles about him continued, and, in spite of the Weber episode, he found it hard to resist being interviewed. In July, the novelist and playwright Nigel Dennis (author of *Cards of Identity*) wrote stating that he was doing a long piece on him for *Life* magazine, and asking if he might visit.[21] Durrell, who had still not finished *Acte*, and had been informed that Margaret Rawlings and the Bristol Old Vic would be taking *Sappho* to the Edinburgh Festival in 1961, welcomed the chance to meet a fellow playwright. Dennis and his young wife Beatrice stayed at a Nîmes hotel and Durrell collected them daily in the old Peugeot. The couples found themselves instantly *en rapport*. The two men were different – Dennis the tall, reserved, sardonic leptosome (in Kretschmer's scheme of physical types); Durrell the squat, extrovert, Rabelaisian pyknic – but found that they complemented one another perfectly. Dennis had spent many years in America enjoying the expatriate life, though, like Durrell, in manner and speech he was typically English.

Beatrice was very impressed by Claude, finding her sophisticated, charming, intelligent and fun, and a tremendous
organizer of Larry's life for him. Her snapshot of the mazet
was very sharply focused:

> It was a little, basic, peasant house, on a hillside, stone-building,
> whitewashed walls, very, very simple inside with just a few rugs on
> the floor and rather simple cotton covers to the beds, you know,
> and a sofa with a rug thrown over the back and quite a practical
> kitchen. And then there was a garden which they were very keen
> on, with lots of stone walls and paths, and they were planting trees,
> and planning to buy the hillside behind the house where they were
> going to plant an olive grove.[22]

There was also a room where the walls were hung with what
she called Durrell's 'bold extraordinary paintings', and the
extension for the children which they called 'Troy'. The
Dennises spent the week being taken around the local sights
and being entertained, enjoying Claude's *terrine*, and being
plied with Pernod, *vieux marc* and another explosive local
drink called *arquebuse*. Compared to the Durrells, however,
they were not heavy drinkers, and occasionally they would
take a stroll in the garden outside the mazet and deposit their
Pernod or *vieux marc* behind a convenient shrub.[23]

The invasion of children from England occurred in July, and
this time Durrell rented a room in a house at Saintes Marie de
la Mer in which they could sleep in camp beds just a stone's
throw from the beach. He was still working on that tenth
rewrite of *Cleopatra*, the money from which he hoped would
fund a trip to Italy. He had enough to live on for the coming
two years, but felt he was being gnawed at by people forcing
themselves on him. His concentration was not helped by the
children having brought jazz records to inflict on him and
generally spreading disorder through his life. It made him feel
grateful that he had enough money to keep them at school in
England rather than have them impinging more on his life at
the mazet. Nevertheless he managed to complete and send
off the script and then turned to enjoying the bathing, getting
some weight off and trying to cut down on his heavy smoking.

The announcement earlier that year that Allen Lane's Penguin

Books was to publish an unexpurgated *Lady Chatterley's Lover* began to exercise Durrell and Aldington. *The Black Book* had been published in France to what Durrell thought was a 'charitable' reception, but he was slightly anxious that it might run into trouble with the courts in the US. However, he was prepared to testify at the Old Bailey to the quality of D. H. Lawrence's book, and wrote to Lane accordingly.

Reflecting on what various critics had said about his work, Durrell accepted the view that using Einstein was mathematical nonsense, but considered that it was philosophically and teleologically valuable in his investigation of the human personality. There were faults in the *Quartet*, but that was the creative risk all artists ran. He was not interested in instigating disputes but in illumination. No one could predict its status a decade hence.

However, American universities were prepared to gamble on future greatness, and Aldington warned him to hang on to all his scripts and letters which might bring him a goodly price when the time came. The changing moral climate in America boded well for publication of *The Black Book* there, but after the encomiums heaped on the *Quartet* it had a very mixed reception. It was seen as either 'dull', rhetorical, pompous, fatuous, and flatulent' or as the *Quartet* in embryo. Within six weeks, it was nevertheless an American best-seller.

Durrell was genuinely surprised that *The Black Book* was not prosecuted in the US, but the successful defence in England of the unexpurgated *Lady Chatterley* (cleared of being 'obscene' on 2 November), set the seal on the changed situation. From now on, obstacles to previously banned books would begin to fall away. In these circumstances it is puzzling that Faber did not follow America's lead or Eliot's advice and publish *The Black Book* themselves. Perhaps they were less stout-hearted and adventurous than Allen Lane, or perhaps they felt it had by then, a quarter of a century after being written, lost its impact. Durrell said later that he had declined to have it published in England for fear of embarrassing his children by ending up in court.

At the risk of making readers feel sated by Durrell, Faber published *The Dark Labyrinth (Cefalû)* in October, and Dutton brought out *Prospero's Cell* and *Reflections on a Marine Venus* in November. *Cefalû* was known in Britain, and received only passing notice. In America Durrell was fortunate to have his travel books reviewed by friends. Freya Stark was generous in her praise. *Prospero's Cell* was, she wrote, 'in its gem-like quality, among the best books ever written'. The Rhodes book did not quite hold the same magic for her, but the style was 'equally remarkable and constantly arresting'. She placed Durrell beside Paddy Leigh Fermor, praising them for re-interpreting the classics and for capturing something of the lives of poor Greek peasants.[24] Kimon Friar compared him to Kazantzakis for pouring out 'so unstintingly of his creative powers into his travel books. Ultimately, the books of both men are an exploration of self; this is why Durrell has discovered that for centuries Greece has been the land of self-exploration and not of self-exploitation.'[25] Strangely (or perhaps not so strangely), his friends, unlike some of his critics, saw his work as somehow expressive of his self rather than obscuring it.

Acte was now completed – gaslit melodrama, he joked, or a new *Spanish Tragedy*.[26] Pondering on verse drama, with half an eye always on the Elizabethans, he decided that he agreed with something Eliot had once put to him, that writers in Shakespeare's day did not make a distinction between prose and verse, but wrote as the spirit moved them. Language alone ruled![27] He might also have admitted that language was the powerful key to understanding not just Elizabethan writers but also Lawrence Durrell.

Gerry, now running a zoo in Jersey, had invited Larry, Claude and Sappho to spend Christmas with him and Jacquie. Louisa, Margo and her two boys would also be there. As they were about to leave for Jersey, Durrell had a hint of things to come. Fanchette wrote to say that Southern Illinois University was interested in buying the carbon copy of *Mountolive* which Durrell had given to him, and asking whether he minded if he sold it. *Two Cities* had fallen into the red after an edition devoted to Rabindranath Tagore failed to sell, and would sink without this money.[28] The Durrell Family Reunion on Jersey was caught for the cameras by *Life* magazine – Louisa, Margo, Larry, Gerry, Jacquie and Lulu the chimp. The only absentee was Leslie, still abroad, though Claude did not appear in the photographs either, presumably not being legally yet 'one of the family'.

After leaving Jersey Durrell spent a couple of days in London, discussing *Acte* with his agent, Juliet O'Hea of Curtis Brown, who confirmed that it had been taken for Hamburg again by Gründgens, who hoped to put it on in the autumn, about the time *Sappho* would be opening in Edinburgh. Gründgens thought the play better structured than *Sappho*. Durrell also spent time in London discussing his screenplay of *Cleopatra* and trying to buy an elephant (or so he joked) for Gerry – one animal he did *not* have in his zoo. They returned to France early when Claude went down with influenza.

With New Year's resolutions in mind, no doubt, he finally decided that the time was right to sell his house in Cyprus. He also made arrangements in London to marry Claude there on their next visit. Only a few weeks earlier he had been urging Miller not to embark on matrimony ever again. Now, in his new family mood, he warned Aldington, about to accept an invitation to go the Russia for his seventieth birthday, to be sure to pay his respects to the much persecuted Pasternak family.[29]

At Gründgens' suggestion, and inspired by the thought that his plays were both to be put on in 1961, he got down to writing a third – this one, at the German director's suggestion, based on the Faust story, but set in Ireland. It was Gründgens' performance as Goethe's *Faust* in the 1930s which had brought him to the attention of Göring's wife, which in turn led to his directorship of the State Theatre under Hitler. Klaus Mann had depicted him as Mephistopheles in a post-war novel, and for him to ask for a Faust play had strange resonances which Durrell only partly grasped. Nigel Dennis wrote to say that *his* play, *August for the People*, was also to play at Edinburgh, scheduled to follow *Sappho* at the Lyceum Theatre.

Anne Ridler had declined to edit the Durrell–Miller letters and the mantle had fallen on George Wickes, though at this stage Durrell's preference was for Lawrence Clark Powell. He felt a bit sickened that his letters, written in private, would be available for students to read. He was irritated that a London typist who had undertaken to type *The Black Book*, and to whom he had written some thirty letters, had just sold them through a London dealer for $20,000. The vultures, he felt, were standing around him having a feast. He was able to sublimate his feelings by working on his new play – a return to bloody Jacobean drama, he thought, but even the play did not deter him from making money, when he was invited back to London to work again on *Cleopatra*.

Wanger had replaced Mamoulian with Joseph L. Mankiewicz, whose approach to the film was completely different. Mankiewicz wanted the political tensions between the major characters emphasized and to give the film more epic proportions. An entirely new script was required, though some non-location scenes were already being shot with Elizabeth Taylor in the title role. Curtis Brown had negotiated a fee of $2,500 a week for a six-week stint, plus travel expenses to and from London. Durrell left almost immediately, on 17 February 1961. In London he and Claude were lodged at the smart Basil Street Hotel, which reminded Larry of the Planters' Club in Darjeeling. And he wondered what his father would have thought of him hobnobbing with Hollywood film stars and moguls. However, he had never been to more than one Elizabeth Taylor film and did not get to see her in London because almost as soon as he arrived she was rushed into hospital with double pneumonia.

He was not the only writer working on the script. Sidney Buchman, with a long list of film credits, was to be his co-writer. They spent four days in conference with Mankiewicz, working out the whole film, shot by shot, scene by scene. By the middle of March they had a third of the script composed between them. Durrell considered the whole experience a study in form. He did not see film-writing as a new career, and prior to coming to London had turned down an offer to do a screenplay of Proust's *Remembrance of Things Past*, which he thought would take forever, and which in any case he did not feel up to. But in general he found film-writing terribly easy, though unsatisfying, believing that the image was enemy to the word, and that his own love affair was with words – often superfluous in the cinema. Nonetheless, he got on well with the thoughtful Mankiewicz, who had already produced a scenario of the *Quartet* for Wanger.[30]

In an interview with the *Guardian*, Durrell talked about his next novel being a comic, bawdy one. 'If you don't keep the bawdiness, you lose the tenderness,' he said. Returning to England had enabled him to reflect back upon his own exile. He now felt a dedicated European, and thought the current English redbrick-university writers were limited by provincialism. However, he was far more impressed with the England of the 1960s than with that of the 1930s, and even thought of doing a travel book based on a walking tour of the country. Even so, he still thought that the culture in England was morally oppressive and that was what turned the artist into a sort of refugee. It was different in France, where the artist was savoured like a good cheese or wine.[31]

On 27 March, Lawrence George Durrell (forty-nine, writer, of the Basil Street Hotel) married Claude Marie Forde (thirty-five, writer, also of the Basil Street Hotel), at the Chelsea registry office – not, as he then thought, where Joyce and Lawrence got married (that was Kensington). But Dickens had been married in a nearby Chelsea church, so he could at least claim some vague affinity with his old friend Pickwick. Afterwards, they caught the train to Broxborough and announced to the Dennises, 'We've got hitched!'[32] A letter came from Aldington to say that he had read in the local paper that they had 'committed matrimony', and Fanchette wrote to tell them that he had laid on a big party for them in Paris – not many invited, he added, only about twenty-five. He said that thanks to the sale of the *Mountolive* manuscript he had been able to buy his wife a washing-machine.[33]

Miller was in Montpellier, and after Paris there was another joyful reunion and a wedding celebration at the Auberge du Pont Roman beside the Vidourle in Sommières. Miller, now divorced from Eve, seemed determined to marry Renate and settle somewhere in Europe. He had something else to celebrate. In June, *Tropic of Cancer* was finally to be published in America (the Olympia edition was already on sale there). Perhaps the non-prosecution of *The Black Book* had encouraged his publishers to take the risk – Durrell in some way repaying the debt he owed to his mentor. When it appeared on 24 June, it sold 68,000 copies in a week, and the libertarian 1960s were given yet another kick on their way.

There was a growing interest in Durrell's letters, and Harry T. Moore told him that his university was negotiating for those he had written to Gerald Sykes. Moore's book of essays on Durrell, now ready for press, also included his letters to Fanchette, though whether these were being offered for sale is not clear. In fact, Fanchette's financial problems were about to end; that summer he graduated as a doctor. Durrell must have been delighted but somewhat envious. The old dream had never quite left him, and he still read the *British Medical Journal* whenever he had the chance.

Stories had begun to reach Durrell that women at smart parties were modelling themselves on the women in his books, some claiming to be the original Justine. Such fame led to ever more exotic journalistic commissions. In June, *Réalités* published an article by him on 'Women of the Mediterranean'. These, he maintained, were a distinctive species, the descendants of Aphrodite. Not only was Durrell a consummate ladies' men, he was also a poet of the sex – the source of his seductive power.[34]

His thinking on the subject of sex took on a new philosophical lease when he made friends with Denis de Rougemont, whose work he had long admired, especially *Passion and Society*. Its survey of religious, mystical and mythological treatments of love and passion took in Petrarch, Freud, de Sade, the Cathars and Gnostics as well as classical and Romantic ideas of love and death, thus embracing a wide spread of Durrell's own passions in one book.[35] A few days after de Rougemont's visit he wrote his first poem for six years – possibly 'Aphrodite' – with Mediterranean women much on his mind.

There was a quick trip to Paris and a party given there by Curtis Cate of *Atlantic Monthly* before the arrival of the children in July meant more time at Saintes Maries de la Mer, more time on the beach. News came that Renate had split up with Miller and that Miller was feeling suicidal. Perlès thought that the seventy-year-old Miller was just too old to run after younger women. Eve had been the best wife he had had, but they were now divorced and that was that.[36] However, Miller soon bounced back, and decided to go to England and then travel on to Ireland. Durrell meantime was looking towards Scotland and his trip to the Edinburgh Festival, where friends in Britain were beginning to anticipate another reunion. Alan Thomas and his wife were sent tickets for the first night of *Sappho*, and Dr Ray Mills, his friend in Rhodes, who now lived in Edinburgh, would be there too. There was also a mysterious French woman to whom he sent a copy of the play and an invitation to meet him in Edinburgh.

The first night of *Sappho* was scheduled for 21 August at the Lyceum. The cast included Margaret Rawlings as Sappho, Nigel Davenport as Pittakos, Richard Gale as Phaon and Henry Woolf as Pythocritos. John Hale directed. In the afternoon the Scottish PEN Club held a reception in Durrell's honour, and that day a cartoon of him appeared prominently in the *Scotsman*. He met the director and cast, and Henry Woolf remembered thinking that he was 'not unaware of his talents', – though in the light of the huge success of the *Quartet*, he thought, 'Fair enough!'[37]

Although the house was full (and one reviewer mentioned a 'rapturous reception'), the notices were rather poor. Most reviewers had good words to say for the verse and for the staging and for Margaret Rawlings' 'tragic intensity'.[38] But the heavyweight critics were the ones who had the power to hurt most. Harold Hobson, of the *Sunday Times*, noted that despite the beautiful writing and acting the play was dead.[39] The smartest critic in England, Kenneth Tynan, devoted half his column to it in the *Observer*. 'To write a verse play about the life of a poet is clearly a hazardous undertaking.' he wrote, 'for what in the world is the point of a poet in a world where everyone speaks verse anyway?' Sappho's lesbianism, he noted, was only geographical. Her whole character spoke of boredom. And 'like so many poets who attempt the theatre, Mr Durrell has mistaken plot for action; as if a series of unexpected events were an adequate substitute for the vital interplay of fully realized human beings'. Once again Durrell was haunted by an unwelcome comparison: 'I wish I could love Mr Durrell's style, for it is lonely not to; but as I survey his swelling European reputation I think of Charles Morgan and am suddenly reconciled to my solitude.'[40]

Durrell was unlucky, not only in some of his critics, but also in his timing. The age of the verse drama, of Eliot and Christopher Fry, of Anouilh and Giraudoux, was past. (Tynan put it rather brutally: 'Few sights in the arts are sadder than that of a man who climbs belatedly onto a bandwagon that has broken down.') Now it was eclipsed by the more earthy 'kitchen sink' drama of Joan Littlewood's Theatre Royal at Stratford East, and the English Stage Company at the Royal Court Theatre. Symbolically, the first night of *Sappho* coincided with the Edinburgh first night of John Osborne's *Luther*, with Albert Finney as the turbulent (and flatulent) priest. Durrell thought that the English critics were out to 'get him' because of his success with the *Quartet*.

The young French woman who was supposed to rendezvous with him in Edinburgh did not turn up, her excuse being that she got so engrossed reading his play at the airport that she missed her flight.[41] Then, on 31 August, he realized that he had used up his two tax-free months allowed in Britain, and had to leave the country in a hurry. This meant missing his Edinburgh reunion with Nigel Dennis. But at least he had the satisfaction of knowing that, whatever the press may have said, the play ran to full houses every night and had completely covered its costs. There was even talk of a West End run, which Durrell did not take seriously, made aware by the London critics that his style of play was not in accordance with metropolitan tastes. However, he could still look forward to the German production of *Acte* in Hamburg, where theatre-going was more of a religion.

On his return to the mazet, with the children back in England, he had other things on his mind. With the Cold War hotting up following the building of the Berlin Wall in August, he worried about their future, reflecting on what he had felt like in similarly tense times in the late 1930s. A voice from pre-war Athens, Robin Fedden, wrote to say that he had found a folder of letters from *Personal Landscape* days and wondered

if Durrell would object to him selling them; he promised a
splendid dinner for him and Bernard Spencer the next time
they were in London. And among the mountain of letters
awaiting him was one from Theodore Stephanides, holidaying
in Corfu, where he had resumed his studies of the flora and
fauna, interrupted in 1939. He was the latest of Durrell's
friends to ask permission to sell his letters, and was advised to
ask Alan Thomas's advice.

In November, the Durrells spent a few days with the Blokhs
in Geneva before heading for the opening night of *Acte* in
Hamburg. There was another loud success for Gründgens's
production, though it was later reported that the producer had
taken liberties with the script to give the play an edge of
Teutonic gloom more suited to the German mood. In Hamburg,
Ledig, Durrell's publisher at Rowohlt, told him that he had
come within two votes of winning the Nobel Prize that year,
but Durrell considered this so much eyewash – the Prize was
just a game of chance. In fact it went to the Serb, Ivo Andric
– Durrell was tempted, no doubt, to let Antrobus have his say
on the matter. The Hamburg trip coincided with the publication
by Limes Verlag of Groddeck's *The Book of the It* with Durrell's preface, together with the separate production (as a
pamphlet) of his *Horizon* essay on the psychiatrist. Durrell was
sent greetings by Groddeck's widow, who was thrilled by what
he was doing to resurrect her late husband's reputation.
When he and Claude arrived at the mazet for Christmas, both
were feeling very bronchial. They were met by freezing weather
and the biting blast of the mistral.

As a Christmas present, it seemed, he featured on the front
cover of the December *Atlantic Monthly* with Curtis Cate's
long essay on him inside. It began in complimentary fashion,
saying that the originality of Durrell's novels lay in their dem-
onstration of the elusive nature of 'truth', although he owed
much to Proust and Joyce and Groddeck. It then went on to
argue that the 'autodidact' Durrell's ideas were all borrowed
and that the novels failed to live up to the principles which
the characters themselves enunciate and even Durrell's own
declared aim, to move back from de Sade to Rabelais.
The *Quartet*, said Cate, lacked 'both the Marquis de Sade's

philosophical interest and Rabelais's lusty bawdiness'. However, he thought Durrell extraordinarily gifted and his *Quartet* an important achievement.[42] Despite Cate's critical tone, Durrell liked him personally and recognized the benefits of being afforded so much space in a major magazine.

After such a burst of effort and a rush of publication, Durrell was back to the incubation stage, mulling particularly over a book with a background of city building in Greece.

CHAPTER 14

Incubating (1962–1967)

Either I start a novel or I commit suicide.

Lawrence Durrell

The success of *Acte* in Germany was confirmed when a television production of it was initiated there, and encouraged by this Durrell again began to think of embarking on that book about Elizabethan writers. However, as he was having difficulty concentrating, and as Claude was busy translating a novel by Marc Peyre, *The Captive of Zour*, he went off on his own for a few days, first to Aix for a night with Aldington, before tramping off alone with a rucksack around the local French countryside. In Aix, he and Aldington were brought down to size by a sailor who said he had never heard of either of them, and in any case the boys on his ship only ever read 'Westerns'. It was a salutary experience which they both quite enjoyed.[1]

By mid-February 1962 the end of *An Irish Faustus* was in sight and Durrell looked forward to a break of several days for wall-building before turning to his next novel, tentatively entitled *La Machin au plaisir*, which picked up a few threads from the *Turtle-Dove* novel begun in Cyprus, and was to end up as *Tunc/Nunquam*. But the end of the play was proving difficult, and he became gloomy. He was also not feeling very well – thanks, he thought, to too much smoking and wine-drinking.

George Wickes was at odds with his editor at Dutton, who wanted him to put back into the Durrell–Miller letters certain 'personal' things he had excluded. Durrell thought that Miller, who was coming to France, should bring the manuscript over with him so that they could sort the matter out together. And still others were discovering that his letters had value. Wallace Southam, his old British Council friend from pre-war Athens, was the latest to write asking if he could sell those he had kept. He suggested that some of the money might be put towards funding a Lawrence Durrell prize or be given to his daughter Penny, but Durrell told him that any money should go towards Southam's recording business, Jupiter Records, which he ran from London's Kensington Church Street. In any case Durrell was in his debt for past kindnesses.

Durrell also agreed to record some of his poetry for Jupiter – the best of his Greek poems, he thought, plus some recent ones. Under pressure again from the UK tax authorities, who, he thought, watched the papers sedulously for any reports of him visiting Britain, he went to sound studios in Montpellier. The selection included 'Nemea', 'Argos', 'In Arcadia', 'Asphodels: Chalcidice', 'Lesbos' and 'Matapan', as well as the more recent 'Aphrodite'. His rather feminine, highly refined voice was well suited to reading what were among the best of his lyrical poems. When the record was finished ready for release in June, Seferis agreed to write a note for the cover; it declared 'He is not a landscape painter, he is mirrored in the *living eye*, he and his *Private Country*; in other words he uses Greek *objects* . . . in order to measure his own problems and his own longings as a man and as a poet of our times, tortured by our Western Culture.'[2] At the same time Durrell heard from the distinguished British composer Lennox Berkeley that he had set 'Lesbos' in a song cycle for tenor and piano for the Cheltenham Music Festival.

In early May D. G. Bridson visited him to make two programmes for the BBC and record him reading a brief selection of other poets of his choice. Since fame had come to him, his BBC fee had become inflated, from a few pounds in 1956 to around £50 in 1962 for each of three sessions (Conrad Aiken and Ezra Pound had received a mere £35). The interviews with Bridson lasted three days, and dealt in depth with the genesis of his works, from his very early poems and *Pied Piper of Lovers* to *The Alexandria Quartet*. At one point he talked about de Sade, saying jokingly (though revealingly) that newly married couples should read de Sade's works – they would find them funny at first and then instructive.

His Russian friends, the Blokhs, had moved from the UN in Geneva to UNESCO in Paris, and visited for a weekend in late April. No sooner had they left than he heard of the death of his old patron, Sir Walter Smart, who had died on 2 May. Smart had been crucial in giving Durrell the opportunity in Egypt to build up the experiences which led to the *Quartet*. Many of the books he had drawn on – Forster's *Alexandria*, Lane's *Manners and Customs of Modern Egypt*, MacPherson's *Moulids of Egypt* – he had found in the library of this charming, cultivated oriental counsellor, whose Cairo house stood at the crossroads of eastern and western cultures.[3] Claude's father died at the same time – in bed surrounded by his family, which Durrell thought was just as it should be. Even so, it meant a grim week in Paris arranging the funeral.

In the Queen's Birthday Honours that year, or so Durrell told Aldington, he had been offered an OBE, but had turned it down. Aldington cursed the bastard British for this insult, and said he should have been pretty firm about refusing it.[4] An Officer of the Order of the British Empire was low down on the scale of awards and, to Aldington, the thought that Richard Church and Stephen Spender had been given the superior CBE (Commander of the British Empire) was intolerable.

That summer, Aldington was in Moscow for the birthday celebrations laid on for him by the Russians. Feted as a great author, he was showered with gifts, and eulogies were read in his honour by the head of the State Publishing House. He even appeared on television there – ironic in view of his almost pathological hatred of communism and of appearing on television. Because of his health, he avoided the many vodka toasts and the heady Georgian wines on offer, but basked in the popularity his books enjoyed, especially his anti-war novels of the 1930s. Then, shortly after his return to France, on 26 July, he died of a heart-attack. An awkward man, deeply scarred by his war experiences and a sense of bitterness towards an England whose values he despised, he had lived the last years of his life under the cloud of British establishment disapproval of his book on T. E. Lawrence, and the consequent

reluctance of publishers to handle his books. Durrell's friendship and his championing of his old hero had doubtless made
those thin years far more agreeable than they would have been
otherwise. But Durrell was always conscious of his debts to
others and always generous in repaying them. He was also ever
more conscious of his own mortality.

He ventured to Britain that year for one of the distractions of
celebrity, the Writers' Festival at Edinburgh, which Miller had
also agreed to attend. Meeting Miller was his prime motive for
going, though he also relished the idea of locking horns with
some of the leading literary lights of the time. He had hoped
that Seferis would be there, but he had just relinquished his post
as ambassador to Britain and had left England for retirement in
Greece. Durrell hoped to see him in Athens later, because after
the Festival he and Claude planned to make their own long-
projected trip to Greece (a sentimental journey for him) after
first spending three weeks in Israel (a sentimental journey for
her).

Durrell and Miller appeared at the Writers' Festival in a
discussion on the novel in a packed hall on 21 August. Stephen
Spender recorded the occasion in his journals. Angus Wilson
and Mary McCarthy began in what Spender thought a 'promising' way, but then proceedings degenerated into 'back-
scratching, sly self-felicitation, over-modest disclaimers, [and]
special pleading of special groups' typical of such conferences.
'Lawrence Durrell was grand and simple and unhelpful. "The
only yardstick is to ask yourself three questions of a novel:
'Has it made me care? Has it brought me joy? Has it changed
your life at all?' " ' Muriel Spark later took fierce issue with
Durrell about this, saying that it was not the business of novelists to change people's lives. 'Don't let us forget the dignity of
our profession [Spender reports her saying], which is not to
change the public but to serve it.' In Spender's view:

> Lawrence Durrell's remark about the novel changing the reader's
> life is one of the hoariest clichés of modern criticism (I. A. Richards,
> Leavis, etc.). Durrell presumably had picked it up because he is a
> poet. Perhaps because she is a novelist, Muriel Spark seemed never
> to have heard of it.[5]

Durrell, however, was probably thinking of the novels which had changed his own life, and the author of one of them was sitting at his side. Miller, who had just been applauded by Colin MacInnes, rose to say that they were wasting their time discussing the novel as it had died over a hundred years before. He had come to Edinburgh in the hope that they might discuss 'something interesting, like painting'.[6]

The sentimental journeys to Israel and Greece were tempered by business. A film producer, Kurt Unger, had commissioned Durrell to write a short story about life on a kibbutz, which gave Claude the excuse to meet some of her kibbutzim friends again. In Greece, Durrell would be absorbing background for his projected novel, writing notes for a Greek travel magazine, and visiting Mykonos to meet the composer Peggy Glanville-Hicks, who might do an operatic version of *Sappho* for the San Francisco Opera.

Larry and Claude took a boat in September from Marseilles to Israel. Spending time on a kibbutz astonished Durrell because of the air of tolerance despite the presence of so many different creeds (from non-believers to religious extremists). In mid-October they travelled to Athens. It was Durrell's first trip to Greece for ten years and he feared that tourism might have ruined it. In Athens they met Seferis and Katsimbalis and plunged into an orgy of reminiscence – like a breath of oxygen to Larry, taking years off his life. The local paper, *Icones*, reported him as travelling 'incognito', visiting memorable scenes from the past and being delighted to find that the Plaka had not been changed beyond recognition with Coca-Cola signs or that whisky had replaced retsina in the cafés. He said that he found the Greek heart still beating to the Greek rhythm and that Greek cuisine was as it always had been. The wine had even improved. Referring to *Bitter Lemons*, the paper saluted him as a champion of the Greek Cypriot cause. The fear of being *persona non grata* in Greece because of his role in Cyprus was thereby dispelled; the incognito was unnecessary.[7]

Miller had returned to America to find a warrant for his arrest awaiting him in New York. He and the Grove Press were charged with publishing an obscene book, *Tropic of Cancer*. A year earlier it had been ruled 'obscene' by a Boston court, a decision later overturned by the Massachusetts Supreme Court. Now he was faced with the same charge in New York. He duly turned himself in, was given bail on the promise that he would not leave the US, and retreated back to California. Durrell immediately offered to send a letter in his support round for signature by prominent authors, but wondered whether support from 'decadent' Europe would carry any weight with an American court. In the event, the only circular letter he signed that December was one to *The Times*, supporting the return of the Elgin Marbles to Greece.[8]

Christmas 1962 was spent at the Jersey zoo with Gerry, Jacquie, Louisa and the chimps. That big comic novel was still incubating and, like all of his major works, would take time to hatch. Claude and Larry returned to the mazet to find the water pipes frozen and buckled, which he put down to atomic-bomb testing. Despite the cold, he managed to get down to writing *Judith*, the story set in Israel, which Kurt Unger had commissioned. He had a phone installed – but one restricted to outward calls only. Incoming ones could be taken by arrangement at a bar in Nîmes.

The letters which Durrell was so shy about publishing appeared as *Lawrence Durrell and Henry Miller: A Private Correspondence* in America in February, and was a major literary event. *Newsweek* thought they represented 'this century's most uninhibited mutual admiration society', mostly obsessed with money or 'the demands of the ego'.[9] The trusty Gerald Sykes in the *New York Times Book Review* saw the letters as 'the conscious effort of two ebulliently gifted writers of romantic temperament to blot out all in a hostile world that might mar the delightful private mythology they symbolically construct together, even when separated by wars and oceans'. They had the capacity to transcend the unpleasant by transforming fact into symbol or reducing tragedy to comedy.[10]

When the letters appeared in Britain a few months later, the critics were mostly dismissive, some positively hostile. *The Times* found the mutual admiration somewhat laughable: 'There has been nothing like this correspondence since, lading butter from alternate tubs, Stubbs buttered Freeman and Freeman buttered Stubbs.' Quoting the statement of Wickes, the book's editor, that the complete letters would not be ready to publish till the next century, the reviewer commented, 'We can wait.'[11] A scathing notice in *Encounter* by D. J. Enright said, 'It can only be supposed that ungrateful Messrs Faber have some enormous grudge against the two of them, since the making public of this "private correspondence" will hardly enhance the reputations which they have so painstakingly built up with the collaboration of an unnerved and gullible international public.' If Miller was 'the conscious anti-artist, the messiah', Durrell was 'the conscious artist, the aesthete'. There might be a small book in this, he concluded, but 'What is going to kill reading in our time is writing.'[12] Just before the correspondence was published, Robin Fedden reported selling Durrell's *Personal Landscape* letters for £110, which he thought a marvellous Christmas present. Why not, he asked, write a letter a week and they could split the profits?[13]

An Irish Faustus had been accepted for performance in Hamburg. By March 1963 Durrell had finished his *Judith* scenario, and he decided to take a few months off, first accompanying Claude to Geneva for a medical check-up. The plan was then to go on to Greece. He urged Miller to join them as it would pump fresh air into him. The bronchial chests Larry and Claude so often suffered out on the garrigue had revived his old obsession with breathing. Meanwhile Kurt Unger invited Durrell to Madrid to meet Sophia Loren, whom he had cast for the film version of *Judith*, and whom Durrell found very charming, dignified and stylish he said.[14]

After her check-up, it transpired that Claude had to have an operation for fibroids. Larry put off the trip to Greece, until she was well enough to go with him. Once there, however, discovering how cheap things were and that foreigners in Greece paid very little tax, Durrell thought it might be worth finding a place to live. Having just paid out a large amount of French tax, the idea of a tax haven was very appealing. He took Claude to Delphi to visit the Temple of Apollo and drank the sacred water of inspiration from the spring in the oracle's cave.[15] However, he realized that the problem was that in Greece you could find the perfect paradise in April which became overrun by Scandinavian tourists in August.[16] On their return to Engances the idea of moving to Greece seemed less attractive. Summer on the garrigue was not so bad after all now that they had, by slow effort, built up the house with rooms for all the children and made so many local contacts.

As usual Durrell found the presence of the children throughout the summer distracting – ferrying them to and from the sea and trying to sort out their commotions back at the mazet. However, they were growing beyond childhood. Claude's daughter Diana was seventeen, at school in Cheltenham, and hoping to study medicine. Barry was fourteen; and Sappho was twelve, soon to be entering the senior school at Bedales.

Another fond link to the past was severed when news came that Bernard Spencer had died in Vienna on 11 September, found dead on a railway track just outside the city. He had been ill and was thought to have a brain tumour, so whether it was suicide or an accident remained a mystery. The sad news came in a letter from Ruth Speirs in which she recalled their days all together in Cairo. Spencer died just six days after Louis MacNeice. When, a month later, Alan Ross, the new editor of the London Magazine, asked Durrell to write a memoir of Spencer, it took him back to pre-war Athens, Mykonos in 1940 and *Personal Landscape* days in Egypt during the war, as well as occasional meetings afterwards. He deplored the loss of such a talent, but the man had written too slowly and death had caught him before his true oeuvre was written.[17]

Poetry was slow in coming, and Durrell's novel had not yet got moving, but he could always turn to painting while his batteries were being recharged. The main means of recharging, however, were his 'quarry' notebooks, and by October the one he was using to prepare for his new novel (entitled *The Placebo*, part of a larger work called *An Attic Comedy*) was almost full and he was now feeling under the influence of St Augustine and Petronius if not yet of Spengler and Nietzsche. Greece, he still thought, was where all this would find utterance. Miller liked the idea of returning to Greece, and reported yet another great resurrection of the spirit, having plunged into a passionate love affair with a young Israeli actress.[18] The fact that he was in the middle of lawsuits, a bankruptcy action and a struggle with the US Revenue did not seem to affect him. At seventy-one, love conquered all. And if the Durrells could not get away to Greece immediately, Greece came to them in the form of George Katsimbalis, who visited in December, and the Fieldings, who were planning to convert a mazet close by them near Uzès. And they all had something to celebrate with the news that Seferis had won the Nobel Prize, thus putting Durrell and Miller out of their agony for yet another year.

The pilgrimage to Germany for the third coming of Durrell the playwright took place in mid-December, and they travelled via Paris to spend some time with the Blokhs, and there met up again with David Gascoyne. Nadia Blokh, who had seen some of Durrell's oil paintings, was keen to organize an exhibition of them in Paris, but he did not want to exhibit them under his own name for fear they would sell on that alone rather than on their quality. With Alex Blokh, he cooked up the pseudonym, 'Oscar Epfs'. The 'Oscar' he said, was because the painter deserved one, the 'Epfs', he sometimes said because it was unpronounceable, and sometimes because it sounded like a fart.

An Irish Faustus opened at the Schauspielhaus in Hamburg on 18 December, produced this time by Otto Schuh, Gründgens having died earlier that year. Will Quadflieg played Faustus (renamed Dr Morenius for the German production) and Judith Holzmeister was the crazed Queen Katherine of Ireland, intent on stealing the magic ring which is in Faustus' care. The Show Business Reporter from *Time* magazine was in the mood to be brutal. Hamburg, he said, had tolerated Durrell the playwright – *Sappho* for twelve performances and *Acte* for twenty-six – because they 'just could not believe that the author of vitally dramatic novels would write twice like a wooden Indian'. Incredibly, Hamburg had given Durrell a third chance with *An Irish Faustus*. 'Durrell describes it as a morality, but it is really a pretension. Durrell himself was hooted from the stage at the end.'[19] The London *Times* could not have been more enthusiastic. It saw the connection between medieval alchemy and modern nuclear science which Durrell was trying to draw, and found a parallel between the play and Durrenmatt's *The*

Physicists, adding: 'If the directors of the Dublin Theatre Festival are on the look-out for an outstanding play by an Irish author to put on this year, they need look no farther.' Durrell had written 'an Irish pantomime' which was 'a considerable advance on its two predecessors', and the play should endear itself to the Dublin public 'who have, after all, tasted something of the sort before in Yeats and Synge'.[20]

Durrell was often surprised and amused by the reactions to his plays. He admitted that *An Irish Faustus* was technically four centuries behind the times, but considered his message to be decades ahead. His concerns about the power which science gave over us were to gain momentum as he began to think more and more about his new novel.

A year earlier he had reluctantly agreed to edit the PEN poetry anthology for 1963, and, when it was published in November, it proved almost as controversial as his play – as if some reviewers wanted to jump on anything less than perfect from the writer who had become so rich and successful so rapidly. Durrell had managed to include some friends and acquaintances – Carl Bode, Hilary Corke, G. S. Fraser, Edith Sitwell, Bernard Spencer, Terence Tiller, Stephen Spender and even Oonagh Lahr, the daughter of Charlie Lahr, whose bookshop he had haunted in 1930s London. But he had taken in a large range of others – among them Philip Larkin, Kingsley Amis, Ted Hughes, Sylvia Plath, Stevie Smith and R. S. Thomas. The *TLS* thought his selection was 'interesting', though his bias showed with his nomination of Edith Sitwell as 'his star turn', and his apparently grudging acceptance of some poets whose style was not to his taste. This provoked a crushing response from Sitwell, who asked 'from under what dull, meaningless stone the writer of that review crawled'? Such persons were obviously malicious, empty-headed, illiterate and unable to write.[21]

Christmas was spent again in the unrestrained bosom of the family on Jersey, where his mother had now been living for a year or two with Gerry and Jacquie. Durrell had taken a few bottles of ouzo with him and was rather miffed to find that Gerry polished them off in a very short time. He might have been tempted to go to England to see Penny in the pantomime of *Mother Goose* at the Ashcroft Theatre, in which she appeared in a small ballet group, but there was always that fear of attracting the attentions of the tax man for overstaying his allowed time. Afterwards they spent New Year's Eve in Paris with Eleonore Hirt and Tonio Vargas, actors with Jean Louis Barrault's company, and arrived back at the garrigue to be greeted by snow and a shrieking mistral. But Durrell settled down for a time to add a few more oils to the dozen or so he thought worth offering for exhibition, and to do some background reading for his novel – a book on science applied to agriculture, and articles on computers. He was intrigued to learn that someone in Scotland had taught a computer to write blank verse, and one in France was being taught how to make love.[22]

On 24 January 1964, Louisa Durrell died, aged seventy-nine, in a Bournemouth nursing home. Larry flew to England for the funeral. Whatever feelings he had about her death he kept to himself. Later he recorded fleeting memories of the occasion in his notebook – the suburban cemetery, the lonely coffin, his mother's name being read out in full, 'Louisa Florence' (which conjured into his mind a young women of twenty-five), the presence of his Aunt Fan, aged eighty-nine (those never-ending aunts), and the stiff, meaningless Protestant service. There seemed something symbolic in this dreary ceremony and Louisa's passing – a year of so many deaths among his friends, and now his mother. He was probably far more moved by his mother's death than he would ever admit, though he did confess to a general feeling of gloom at these continuing reminders of death's haunting presence.

Plans were now afoot for his Oscar Epfs exhibition to be mounted in a Paris gallery in March (Durrell had told M. Tucher, the gallery owner, that Epfs was an impoverished friend who had asked him to sponsor him). But the idea of visiting Greece in June was threatened by clashes between Turks and Greeks in Cyprus. He also heard that in Crete it was said that he had helped Turks to get arms in Cyprus and that if he ever came there 'the boys' would 'get him'. He wrote a letter, which *The Times* published in May, condemning past British policy in Cyprus and putting the case for Enosis.[23]

The *vernissage* of Oscar Epfs's exhibition of oil paintings was held on 6 March at Galerie Connaitre at 36 Rue de Saints-Père, in Paris. Durrell and Nadia Blokh and Mary Hadkinson went round the bars and cafés of the *quartier* distributing cyclostyled notices advertising the show. Durrell claimed to be a 'friend' of Epfs, and Claude masqueraded as Epfs's sister. She was placed at the reception desk to spread misinformation. People were told that Epfs was a reclusive Dutchman working as *chef de gare* at Mount Athos and that he was too shy to put in an appearance. (Sometimes he was a Dane presently visiting Central Africa.) Durrell was delighted when a leading French art critic told him, 'Your friend's work is an anthology. He must find a style of his own.' During the proceedings, Durrell slipped out to a callbox, phoned M. Tuchet and, pretending to be Epfs calling from Greece, thanked him profusely for mounting the exhibition. Two weeks after the opening the truth leaked out in the magazine *Elle*. Durrell thought that Miriam Cendrars (the daughter of Blaise Cendrars), who worked for the magazine, was the one who had seen through the bluff.[24] The show ran for three weeks and brought in £60.

At the beginning of April, Perlès, now living with his wife in the house of Haldeman and John Craxton in Crete, set the minds of the Durrells at rest – there was no anti-British feeling there, and certainly no 'boys' who thought he had been on the wrong side in Cyprus.[25] Thus reassured, Larry and Claude left for Greece at the end of April, but got stuck in Corfu, at Paleocastrizza, after Claude fell and broke some ribs. So it was decided to abandon their planned tour and stay in Corfu, hire a villa and give her time to recover. Durrell's return to Kalami was a journey back into his past – the White House, the Anastasiou family, the little shrine of St Arsenius, catching up with the news, who had died, who had married whom.[26] Seferis came to visit from Athens, and Gerry and Jacquie joined them for a while. The children duly arrived for their first Greek holiday. Sappho, now thirteen, had started publishing poems in her school magazine, and on her return contributed a very Durrellian little essay about Corfu, showing that she had inherited something of her father's 'Pre-Raphaelite sensibility'.[27] In July, while they took in the sun and scenery of Corfu, *Judith* was being filmed in Israel, starring Loren, Jack Hawkins and Peter Finch. Durrell was invited, but had decided that films were no longer for him, and they could do what they wished with his story. Each time he had visited the company he had found they had changed the script and acquired a new writer. It all seemed too painfully familiar to him.

That autumn, *Two Cities* carried his 'Letters to Jean Fanchette', which irritated some of his friends, who thought that he had indulged Fanchette too much, especially Curtis Cate, who thought it was outrageous the way the Mauritian had exploited their friendship. But Durrell liked the young doctor and was more exercised by other things. In the autumn he received two PhD theses from America on the *Quartet*, together with three long critical articles. Such interpretations, he thought, did not unearth the 'meaning' of his work but rather gave an insight into the mind of the critic, simply using one work of art on which to construct another[28] – a perceptive deconstruction of the critical process as interpretation. He and Claude made two trips to Paris within two weeks, once to proofread the French translation of his *Selected Poems* for Gallimard, and once to give a lecture on Shakespeare at UNESCO, a visit arranged for him by the Blokhs ($750 for a twenty-minute talk).

Friendships with other writers, such as Fanchette and Alex Blokh, were important to him. He had discovered the work of another French writer, Claude Seignolle, who wrote tales of mystery and imagination in the Edgar Allen Poe vein. Always interested in the Gothic and grotesque, Durrell decided to boost him to a wider audience and had already written a preface to one of his books, *Un Corbeau de toutes couleurs*. When Ann Leslie of the *Daily Express* came to interview him in December, he chose to speak mostly about Seignolle, but in the process said many revealing things about himself. 'I'm just a stage Irishman, you know. A ham. But I've got the mental sluttishness of the Irish.' He told her: 'A woman wrote saying I must come and be her lover before the week was out or, as she was a sorceress, she would make sure I regretted not complying.' He also revealed the pressure he felt under to follow the *Quartet* with something as good. Hinting that he was being chased to finish something even then, he said he much preferred to tend to his vine trees.[29]

After a Christmas spent at the mazet with Cathy Aldington, Jacques Temple and Xan and Daphne Fielding, Claude succumbed to an attack of appendicitis (verging on peritonitis, Larry was told), and on New Year's Eve was rushed into a local clinic to have her appendix removed.

There was another death to sadden him. His mentor T.S. Eliot died on 4 January 1965. Through Alexander Blokh at UNESCO, Durrell was asked to write a memoir of him for the French magazine *Preuves*. He wrote it quickly, in his usual professional way. But he had written about him frequently over the years – to Miller and Aldington (who loathed him), to Anne Ridler and others of his friends. His essay was a personal one, remembering the many kindnesses he had received from the poet, and the very human side of a man whom many considered frosty and reserved.[30]

In April, Claude heard of a large house in Sommières being auctioned in Paris. She went to Paris on her own and, to Durrell's surprise, bought it. It was gloomy-looking place on the opposite side of the Vidourle from the ancient town, hidden behind a high stone wall and the vegetation of a large overgrown garden, with owls living in a disused water-tower – something, in fact, from the pages of Flaubert. It had large rooms with high ceilings, plenty of space for an extensive library and a grand piano, and high walls on which to hang paintings. There was a sunny conservatory at the rear – perfect for a studio – and plenty of hiding places to escape to if bores came visiting. Durrell was uncertain about it, but to Claude it was an investment, and it reminded her of Alexandria. Grudgingly he admitted that the mazet now smelt of mice and was overflowing with books – and separate rooms in which to work might prevent a divorce. The house was untypical of the South of France, being built at the turn of the century by a Madame Tartes, a local woman with social pretensions, and it came with one of the original maids, now very old, a Nancy Quiminal, whose name Durrell would borrow for his *Avignon Quintet*.

In the absence of a new novel, Faber decided that, to keep the Durrell pot boiling, a serious critical book about his work should be commissioned, and the choice to write it fell on his old Cairo rival and fellow Duke of Redonda, G. S. Fraser, now teaching English Literature at Leicester University. Alan Pringle at Faber also suggested that Alan Thomas might edit a volume of Durrell's travel letters.

In the summer the Durrells rented a villa at Paleocastrizza. Staying in a hotel were Cathy Aldington and a friend, a beautiful young ex-Schiaparelli model, Ghislaine de Boysson, now working as a journalist in Paris. Both girls were hoping to see something of Durrell, but he started drinking ouzo at eight in the morning, and always seemed to be drunk or asleep when they came around. They met Claude for dinner in the evening, and Ghislaine thought she looked very thin and was drinking too much.[31]

By September, Alan Thomas had moved from Bournemouth to London, to a house just off the King's Road in Chelsea, and was keen to get on with the collection of Durrell's travel writing for Faber, who hoped to have the book ready to hand by the autumn of 1967. His plan was to trawl through Durrell's friends, including Gawsworth, now rather pathetically living on National Assistance, suffering from diabetes, and asking Durrell's support for a grant from the Royal Literary Fund. Gawsworth urged his 'Duke' to write and to 'pour on the agony' for him.[32] Durrell obliged his 'King', who later wrote that he had 'saved the day' for him.[33]

Not having produced a novel for over five years, Durrell must have felt the need to keep himself in the public eye, and in October he travelled to London to be interviewed on television by an old journalist acquaintance, Malcolm Muggeridge. It was a lengthy session which ranged over Durrell's whole life, from India and the snowy peaks of Mount Everest, through his childhood and meeting Miller, to his philosophy of sex and life on the garrigue.[34] The programme's producer, Margaret

McCall, became a friend. On the flight back to Paris, he met a beautiful air hostess, an ex-trapeze artist, Diane Deriaz, whom he invited to dinner at the Cloiserie de Lilas, after which they walked around Paris all night, talking. They must have looked an odd couple, the tall willowy Deriaz and the diminutive Durrell, who was sporting a deerstalker and cape which he had got into the habit of wearing when he travelled – a Sherlock Holmes get-up well befitting a writer who posed so many mysteries and scattered so many clues throughout his fiction. He and Deriaz were to remain friends until his death twenty-five years later.

There was never any shortage of friends visiting the mazet. Marc Peyre came for an evening of feasting and philosophizing, and friends from England, James and Tania Stern, visited for a 'tipsy lunch' with talk about Groddeck 'under the plane trees'. The Fieldings and a neighbour, Paula Wislenef, were frequent callers, and George Katsimbalis and his wife Spatch appeared in November and were taken to visit Joseph Delteil and other writers around the Midi. Then, in December, Yehudi Menuhin arrived to give a concert at the Conservatoire in Montpellier with his sister Hepzibah, and he and Diana drove out to spend time with them at the mazet. They discussed eastern philosophy, and Menuhin strongly advised Durrell to give up smoking and take up yoga.

On 15 November, Alan Ross wrote to Claude offering to publish her translation of Marc Peyre's *Captive of Zour*; meanwhile, at Bedales, Sappho had been awarded a school prize for her short essay on Corfu. She was proving to have true talent as a writer, and her lyrical poems, now appearing regularly in the school magazine, bore many of the qualities of her father's – a feeling for landscape, a sharp eye for colour and detail, musical use of language.

By December Durrell was telling Miller that he now saw just where he had to go with his new novel, and had started it all over again – for the third time at least. Work on it gathered pace in the New Year, and Turkey was suddenly added to Greece as a background. He wrote to several friends – Lord Patrick Kinross, Alan Thomas, Freya Stark and Gwyn Williams – for books and information about Turkish history and about

Constantinople in particular. Thomas actually went on a cruise to Turkey and gathered first-hand material for him. However, in March 1966, Durrell was still feeling hestitant, wondering whether he had got the voice right, and by May he had abandoned yet another attempt. He felt uncertain about the impending move to Sommières, and thought that perhaps he could not launch himself into the novel fully until they had settled into the new house.

He thought that his fiction-writing had taken the sheen off his poetry and knew that his serious admirers often thought poorly of his Antrobus stories. However, the poetry had been ticking over and was being published at regular intervals in the *TLS*, *London Magazine* and *Encounter*, and he had also continued to turn out his comic tales of diplomatic life and publish them widely both in Britain and in America. Critical reaction to his new book of Antrobus stories was one of barely disguised weariness. The vein had been well and truly worked out. The two books which Faber published in 1966, *Sauve Qui Peut* and *Ikons* (published by Dutton the following year), collected his recently accumulated works of comedy and poetry. Durrell was realistic about these books, telling Audrey Beecham that he had lodged himself securely in the second rank with them, as well as with his travel articles for magazines such as *Holiday*. But in saying this he was only reminding himself of the vaunting ambition which was not quenched by mere celebrity. His problem, as he admitted to friends like Miller, was how to follow a great success like the *Quartet*. Everyone, including his publishers, expected him to write the same kind of thing again and again. But he was needing to do something closer to reality – a break from what had gone before.[35]

Alan Thomas's search for letters among Durrell's friends turned up one comic-tragedy from his youth. Thomas had written to Reginald Hutchings, who had edited *Janus*, in which Durrell's *Pied Piper of Lovers* had been so badly mauled in 1936, and mentioned Durrell's anger at the review and the limerick he had written in response to it. Hutchings was obviously upset by the pompous tone of Thomas's letter, and appalled that Durrell should have nursed a grudge against him all these years. He protested that John Mair and not he had written the offending review. Durrell left Thomas to sort out this misunderstanding, and Thomas maintained a rather high-handed tone with Hutchings, implying that he had been at least responsible as the editor of *Janus* for what Mair had written, which only made the situation worse. Thomas put Hutchings's irritated reaction down to a feeling of envy for Durrell's great success. But he did manage to trace enough letters which showed Durrell waxing lyrical about landscape – the theme of the collection. Anne Ridler, Diana Menuhin, Gwyn Williams, John Gawsorth and Freya Stark sent letters they had carefully preserved.

The work of renovating the house and installing central heating took up most of the summer. And furnishing it, too, was a great problem. Durrell managed to pick up a lovely Pleyel grand piano locally for practically nothing to go in the lounge-cum-library, but there were numerous large rooms which needed furniture. Meanwhile, Gerald and Jacquie were in Corfu. Gerald had had a mild heart-attack in June and had been told by his doctor to give up spirits and smoking. He managed to cut out the spirits but found smoking difficult to give up, and certainly could not resist the readily available Greek red wine. He wrote to Larry that he was horrified by what had happened to Corfu, overrun with tourists, like another Costa Brava. Nevertheless, he was thinking of finding some land there and building a house on it. But, as he was unable to get enough money out of Britain, he asked his brother if he could help. However, it was a bad time for Larry, and his money had all been eaten up by the new house, which his girls had told Gerry was a combination of Hampton Court and the Bastille.

They had decided to do up the mazet and keep it as an occasional hideaway or weekend cottage, or for when the children visited in the summer. At least, they thought, apart from Sappho, the children were now all grown up and more or less independent. Penny, who came to visit with a boyfriend – long-haired and blue-jeaned, Durrell noted – was making her way in the theatre. Claude's children – Barry, who had a job in London, and Diana, who was working in Geneva – visited briefly at the end of August to see the new house, but Sappho came for the whole summer. Durrell was very proud of his youngest daughter's progress both in writing poetry and in speaking French, in which she had suddenly leaped ahead.

By September, their new address was 15 Route de Sausines, Sommières. They acquired the services of a local girl, Marcelle, as a cleaner, and made the house ready to receive guests. Not long after moving in, Durrell took the children for ten days to Geneva to return Diana to her work, and to see the other two on their way to London. First, however, he kitted them out with a set of new clothes.

Amid the chaos of the new house, he received yet another letter from Anaïs about their relationship, complaining of what she saw as his negative comments on her diary, criticizing it for an absence of humour. She had also discovered, she claimed, that he had refused to write about it for the *New York Times.* Having re-read a letter he had written her from Greece in 1940, she was aware of a change in his attitude towards her, especially remembering his seemingly cool behaviour on her last visit to Sommières, and the preface of his which had so upset her. It would be recorded in her later diaries, she said, but she would like to understand it before it was written. She also thought he was far too friendly towards the man who had so humiliated her in a book he had written about Henry – Alfred Perlès, who now claimed to be the third musketeer along with him and Miller. How had she offended him? she wondered. She did not want to portray all this in the diary as a betrayal, but to restore their original friendship.[36]

Suddenly, in early December, Penny got married to her long-haired boyfriend, a fellow actor – so suddenly that Larry and Gerry knew about it only at the last moment, so were unable to attend the ceremony. Larry was anyway preoccupied with Claude, whose health had been fragile over the past few years (a succession of influenza and bronchial attacks, and two internal operations), and who was experiencing pain and trouble with her breathing. Doctors in Nîmes were unable to diagnose the problem. On the 9th, Durrell decided to take her to Geneva to get the very best medical attention available. He quickly cabled his friends to tell them that the Christmas celebration was off, and they left for Switzerland. At the Geneva clinic it was decided to keep Claude in for treatment, and Durrell returned to collect things she required. He despatched Christmas cards which had not been posted earlier, and sent the penurious Gawsworth ten pounds.

There was a silence after that. Friends who tried to get in touch found the house deserted. It was only in the New Year that the news leaked out. Claude had died of pulmonary cancer on 1 January 1967.

Durrell wrote a very moving account of the death of Claude in a book some fifteen years later – *A Smile in the Mind's Eye*.[37] She was cremated and he returned sadly with her ashes to the house she had made so much her own in Sommières.

Durrell's marriage to Claude is often seen as 'idyllic', and it was certainly the most consistently happy and fulfilled of his four marriages. However, even while Claude was alive, he hinted at numerous and often farcical 'adventures'.[38] And the 'idyllic' marriage was not absolutely free from eruptions, especially when he was drunk. According to Mary Hadkinson, Claude once came to her in tears, having been struck by him. There was a dark and violent side to Lawrence Durrell which Claude had somehow managed to contain.

Lord of the Dance. Durrell with Penelope at ballet school, 1960. Durrell never fully recovered from being separated from his first daughter after Nancy left Egypt with Penelope in 1942, and the theme of 'the lost child' recurs in his fiction. Here, the tall, cool Penelope humours her father's antics with amused detachment.

Durrell, Claude and Sappho, after Durrell and Claude's sudden marriage, 1962. Sappho was the second of Durrell's 'lost' daughters, and later seemed to accuse him of some kind of incestuous relationship. It was after Claude's death, five years later, that Sappho claims her father's attitude towards her changed dramatically for the worse.

The Family at the Zoo, Christmas 1960. Larry, Gerry, Margo and Louisa were reunited at Gerry's zoo in Jersey. The brothers had the warmest of relationships throughout their lives.

Hiding From Success, spring 1961. At their remote mazet on the garrigue, Durrell and Claude sit on one of the dry stone walls that Durrell was so proud to have built himself. When he felt 'creative madness' creeping over him, Durrell would divert his energies into building a series of these walls.

'The Vampire House', 15 Route de Saussines. This house was bought by Claude at a Paris auction. She died shortly after they moved in, and while Durrell continued to live there, he later complained that it was haunted by too many ghosts.

Henry Miller and Durrell, International Writers' Festival,
Edinburgh, 1962. Called upon to speak, Miller announced that the
novel was long dead and he had come to Edinburgh hoping to hear
someone say something interesting about painting.

G. S. Fraser. Fraser and Durrell became good friends after the war, and Fraser wrote the first full-length study of Durrell's work. But in wartime Egypt they were engaged in a lively critical, and sometimes personal, wrangle in the pages of the forces' magazine, *Orientations*. Durrell once referred to Fraser as 'a gangster-journalist'.

The Man Who Concealed his Nose with a Hat. Durrell told
Ghislaine that he wore funny hats to draw attention away from his
outsized nose.

Durrell with Ghislaine at 15 Route de Saussines. A couple of days
after he married Ghislaine, Durrell slept with another woman, but
reported to Ghislaine that the woman would not have sex with him
because, she said, he smelt. On the left of Ghislaine is Jacquie,
Gerry Durrell's first wife.

Author in Disguise, 1985. Durrell in an onion-seller's hat on his visit to England to publicize *Quinx*, the last of his *Avignon Quintet*. He was, he told a reporter, being pampered by pretty girls from his publishers, Faber & Faber.

St Julien de Salinelles, near Sommières. Durrell bought a plot for
his ashes in the cemetary of this little Romanesque church. It is
marked by a dog-rose and is the same spot on which the ashes of
Claude were scattered. Buddhist priests who instructed him,
however, claim that he has been reincarnated and is living as a
vineyard keeper in Burgundy.

CHAPTER 15

Back to Women and Fiction in a World of Sad Ghosts (1967–1971)

Wherever I turn
I see black ruins of my life.

C. P. Cavafy

Let copulation thrive!

Shakespeare, *King Lear*

Claude had shared, and been a part of, Durrell's enormous success with the *Quartet*. She had helped him to complete *Justine*, embodied his spirit of Alexandria, and probably survives partly in the character of Clea. She typed his work as fast as he composed it, and used her considerable secretarial skills to bring order to a life which tended towards disorder. And she managed their finances with the shrewdness one would expect from a banker's daughter. She had shared his privations when they first moved to France, camping in damp, unheated houses, shivering over wood stoves and bringing water from the well. Her health had undoubtedly suffered, and could not have been helped by the excessive drinking and smoking in which they both indulged.

Her loss was a crushing blow to him. The feeling of being deserted again was acute. For a time, to find his bearings, he decided to leave the house with its powerful associations with Claude.

After answering the many letters of condolence he received,

he went to England to stay with Alan Thomas at his new house in Chelsea. Early in February 1967, Thomas's wife Ella had gone missing, her clothes found at the edge of a lake, and suicide was presumed, so the two men had much to do consoling one another. After London, Durrell went on to Paris to stay with the Blokhs. There he talked about his new novel, now called *Tunc*, to which he planned a sequel called *Nunquam*, both to be dedicated to Claude. The titles were taken from Petronius – 'Aut Tunc, aut Nunquam' ('It was then or never').

Picking himself up after Claude's death, he wondered what to do with the house. Now that the children were grown up and, apart from Sappho, had not stayed long the previous summer, he considered selling it. He would keep the mazet, now fully renovated, to use as a winter base, buy a motorized caravan and spend his summers footloose around Greece. It was the sort of life he would like to have lived with Claude, but she disliked travel and preferred to stay at home. In the meantime he felt he must press on with the novel which had given him so much trouble. Marcelle, the cleaner, an earthy woman with a gusto for life which Durrell greatly appreciated, he kept to do the cooking and housekeeping. However, he was not encouraging visitors, though the Fieldings came over from Uzès from time to time, and in April Sappho and Barry came to stay while Diana visited at weekends. Their presence certainly cheered him up, though the atmosphere had been dampened by the news of the death of Miller's ex-wife Eve. Death, it seemed, was crowding in on him yet again, and he recorded his growing obsession, listing in his notebook the names of friends who had died over the past few years – Claude, her parents, his mother, Eve Miller, Bernard Spencer, Walter Smart, Roy Campbell, Aldington, Gustav Gründgens, Ella Thomas. This list was to grow over the coming years into what he later referred to as a 'death-map', and in *The Avignon Quintet* his character Piers also compiles one. His relative silence worried some of his friends, especially the Blokhs, who wrote asking if he was all right.

It was now that, according to Sappho, her relationship with

her father changed dramatically. With the loss of Claude, he turned to Sappho. The pattern he had consistently followed – that wives were idiot-prostitutes while Sappho was pure and sagacious – broke down. Sappho was turned into 'wife' and made to feel at the same time unthankful child. Durrell was the master of psychological cruelties and manipulative game-playing, and may have experimented with his daughter psychologically in researching character. How close this relationship developed into something akin to incest is unknown, though her notebooks and letters can be interpreted in that way. Certainly, he acted aggressively towards her, as he did towards his wives. And certainly, he confused her about her sexuality, by pointing out that her name, Sappho, would attract lesbians, and by drawing her into his own dark labyrinth of fantasies about sadistic sex.[1]

The deep anxieties expressed in her journals seem to centre around key fears: confusion about her own sexuality, fear of male sexual aggression, and a cruel psychological struggle between her and her father. A tense love–hatred for him appears to have suffused these later writings.

Durrell seemed to be searching for a Claude-substitute in other relationships, and the 'absurd escapades' in which he indulged included placing advertisements in lonely-hearts columns of papers and meeting strange women – in search of characters, it seems, as much as sex. His lifelong fascination with psychoanalysis did not extend to placing himself in the hands of a psychiatrist – he feared that analysis would destroy his creativity – but he happily analysed others, and the psychological games of which Sappho complained no doubt stemmed from this practice. When he was writing, he often found it difficult to distinguish between the world he was creating and the reality in which everyone else lived. People he knew became characters in his novels – something which more than one of his women recalled.[2] It seems, also, that women who experienced his 'unique' brand of love-making rarely came back for more.

Another way in which he coped with his anger at Claude's death was expressed in a notebook composed around the theme of blood – gory birth, vampire cults, sanguinary executions, and of course Christian blood-drinking, an old obsession. This he entitled the *Vampire Book*, and he referred to 15 Route de Saussines as the Vampire House.

The place was oppressive, and he needed to get away from old memories. In May he bought a Volkswagen camper, which he christened *L'Escargot*, and decided to drive it to Corfu, taking Margaret McCall with him. They were to discuss a film she planned to make in Athens starring Katsimbalis and Durrell, and, if he happened to come along, Henry Miller too. Miriam Cendrars also planned to be on the island, so he would be surrounded by beautiful women, some compensation for the heartache of losing Claude. A military *coup d'état* in April had brought a junta of Greek colonels to power, which Durrell thought would have put everyone in a bad mood, though it did not put him off going to Greece. Before leaving for Corfu, he finished *Tunc* and despatched it to Faber.

It was because he was attempting something quite different from the *Quartet*, he said, that *Tunc* had given him so many headaches. And the immediate impact of the novel is odd because it is not what had come to be thought of as familiar Durrell, although there are echoes of the Rabelaisian rhetoric of *The Black Book*, and certain recognizable Durrellian characters – the aspiring writer, the dying whore, the *femme fatale*. But there are also echoes of Wells and Huxley and Mary Shelley's *Frankenstein* and even of Ian Fleming, not to mention Poe, Petronius and Freud, and themes taken from Spengler, Neitzsche and de Sade. Durrell said that whereas the *Quartet* was essentially about the spirit of place, *Tunc/Nunquam* was about culture – based on ideas culled from Spengler's *Decline of the West*.

If in the *Quartet* Darley/Durrell achieves wholeness through artistic fulfilment, isolated on his Greek island, apart from modern civilization, in *Tunc/Nunquam* Felix Charlock/Durrell raises the question of whether such an escape is possible. The private country which Darley sought to create is threatened in the modern world by powerful economic and political forces from without. The integrity of the artist is deeply compromised by a world which turns his work into a product with a price on it. Felix is the inventor of the dactyl, a recording machine which automatically transcribes speech (and of Abel, the supreme computer). By means of the dactyl, Felix recalls, as Darley recalls through his writings, the events of his life and his efforts to reintegrate a seemingly disintegrated life. The cause of this sense of fragmentation is the multinational firm of Merlin's, which takes over Felix's invention, despite his reluctance to part with it. The novel and its sequel deal with the way Felix is seduced into the firm by the beautiful Benedicta Merlin, sister of the sinister brothers who run the firm, Jocas from Istanbul, Julian from London. By succumbing he loses his freedom, and the narrative deals with his struggles to free himself from the toils of the firm. Matters are complicated for Felix by his attachment to the warm-hearted Iolanthe, prostitute in Mrs Henniker's Athens brothel. As in the *Quartet*, here again are two brothers (like Nessim and Narouz – one cold and calculating, one more primitive and earthy), and two women whose lives are entangled with the narrator's (like Justine and Melissa – one devious and unpredictable, the other generous, open and trusting).

However, this is not the private country of Alexandria but the wide world of powerful capitalists with the power of life and death over the lone individual. The contract Merlin's offer Felix takes over not just his invention but him as well; his life of genteel poverty is transformed into one of conspicuous affluence; Bloomsbury and the British Museum are replaced by a Mayfair office and a jet-set lifestyle. In obediently marrying Benedicta, Felix strikes the Faustian bargain, and could pay the price others have paid. Key members of the Merlin family are blighted (the absent Merlin a leper, the shadowy Julian castrated, the unstable Benedicta sexually damaged) and all are capable of sadistic cruelties and murder. Iolanthe, by contrast, is the pure and honest love goddess of Greek mythology. Even when she murders her own brother, it is done from compassion rather than for perverted pleasure or gain. Having sold his soul to the firm, Felix has lost control of his creativity, of his inventions, and the firm can (and does) turn them at will into weapons of destruction.

The books are about the way in which culture and creative

artists are manipulated by commercial forces beyond their control. Even escaping to a remote island, like Gauguin (as Caradoc, the architect, attempts to do), does not succeed – the firm has a long arm. Great works of art in the past once reflected the deepest values of the society, embodying images of man and his place in the world. In the world of the firm, the world of modern capitalist society, works of art serve only commercial ends and reflect the values of profit and greed. The choice for the artist is between riches and poverty, success and castration, creative freedom and potency. For Felix this choice is dramatized in the competing attractions of Benedicta and Iolanthe. But Durrell sees the capitalist system in Freudian terms, as arising out of the gold = shit nexus – an idea which also obsessed Miller in the 1930s – an anal-fixated society. This, symbolized by Benedicta and Istanbul, also works against sexual fulfilment, symbolized by Iolanthe and Athens – and is the source of division within ourselves. The tensions tear Benedicta apart; the tensions inside Iolanthe lead her to compromise with wealth and success, and finally kill her through a breast-enlargement operation which goes wrong. Felix attempts to escape the firm by returning to Athens, where he was so happy with Iolanthe, and finally by fabricating his own death – but in such a way that the firm are bound to see through the deception.

The focus, because it is about culture, is therefore more anthropological than psychological, although Durrell thought that culture is based on association, which in turn is based on love. Asked later about his characters and why there were no heroes, he said:

> The whole notion of human personality is a sort of fiction. We think we are *personae*, but we are just a melting mass of electrons, a million personalities, and I always try to puppetize a bit, in the theatrical sense, precisely to bring that out. I don't want psychology in depth. Nevertheless, the fight between the group and the individual is also most basic to the nature of *Tunc*.[3]

The fluid, multi-faceted personality changing in different lights links the novel back to the *Quartet*; the wider context of power adds to the post-war writer something more basic perhaps than it was to Durrell/Darley. The links to the *Quartet* and *The Black Book* were not accidental. 'I like to see each of my books nod to each other on the way to the front,' he said.[4]

There is also a deliberately absurd element of play in *Tunc* which many reviewers missed, simply because they read it straightfaced and found it grotesquely exaggerated and incredible. His characters are puppets, as he admitted, and not psychological studies, and the shifting between reality and absurdity was done to make a point. It was therefore a book of ideas, not one of character and manners, so not much to the taste of English critics. It was the ideas, he admitted, that had given him most problems with this book and its sequel, but he had found it easier to write than the *Quartet*, where the luxuriant style he had chosen was very demanding.[5]

In Corfu he stayed at the Zefiros Beach Hotel, where he was joined by Gerry and Jacquie, making a television film about the island, called *The Garden of the Gods*, with Theodore Stephanides and sister Margo. Durrell toured in *L'Escargot* around old familiar places such as Kalami, and many tears were shed in memory of Claude. Corfu brought home to him the sense of so many friends lost, the feeling of being encircled by their graves. At Kalami, he also heard that his old fisherman friend at the White House, Athenaios, faced with creeping paralysis, had killed himself, and his wife Kerkyra had left the place.

He went to Athens with McCall to map out her film with Katsimbalis. When he had time to himself he painted what Denis de Rougemont called his 'rouge et noir et bleue' pictures of Corfu. On his return to Sommières, he found Oscar Epfs in enough demand to be offered another Paris exhibition, and there was news that Miller, just recovering from a hip operation, was due in Paris in September for an exhibition too. Meanwhile he was having to fight off journalists who had got wind of the new novel, and wanted to interview him at the Vampire House. All the same, he managed to prepare a second edition of his *Collected Poems* for Faber.

Just before leaving for Paris, Miller, now seventy-six, embarked on his fifth marriage, to twenty-eight-year-old Hiroko (Hoki)

Tokuda, a Japanese singer-pianist he had been pursuing over the previous year. There was a grand reunion at the preview of Miller's watercolour exhibition, to which Durrell also brought Margaret McCall and the Blokhs. In October, Durrell invited the Millers and Perlès down to Sommières for one of their reunions. They were joined by Miriam Cendrars and film director Jean Renoir, whom Miller had met in Hollywood in 1942. Marcelle, by now very much one of the household, did the cooking. The whole occasion was full of 'idiotic fun', according to Durrell, who found himself drawn to the young and sexually appealing Hoki, who in her turn, it seems, had taken a liking to his paunch.

A sense of uncertainty about his new book lingered. By October the proofs of *Tunc* had arrived and he learned from Juliet O'Hea at Curtis Brown that it was already sold in seven languages, and, realizing the high expectations which his readers placed on a new book from him, now feared that it might be a flop. In spite of such worries, he felt in the mood to work and threw himself into *Nunquam*.

Gawsworth wrote a pathetic letter saying that his landlord had sold the house over his head and that he was liable to be pushed out on the streets. He had even sold his book collection, including Sheil first editions, to make ends meet. He had also abdicated as King of Redonda, eight months before.[6] When he followed this up with yet another begging letter, Durrell wrote to tell him that he was strapped, had many commitments, and on this occasion could not help. In any case, someone had tipped him off that the ex-King was not as badly off as all that and he was just trying it on with his old friends.

Alone at the house in Sommières, attended by the patient Marcelle, Durrell worked on at *Nunquam*. Despite Miller's advice to him to find another wife, he was happy to enjoy the company of women when he needed it and do without it at other times. According to Diane Deriaz, scores of very beautiful women were desperate to sleep with him. His *Quartet* had struck exactly the right seductive note, and many a young woman saw herself as the embodiment of Justine or Melissa or Clea, and was ready to throw herself into the arms of the poetic 'master' of sexual love. And he no doubt could provide them with Darley or Nessim or Pursewarden, according to mood. Mistresses and typists were what he needed rather than any more wives, he thought, but often he settled for just friends. Miriam Cendrars, Paula Wislenef, the Fieldings and the Temples visited occasionally, so he did not want for company.[7] As a break from working on the novel, he sketched out a musical for Hoki to score.[8]

Durrell's place in English literature was by no means established, and he must have been nervous about the effect on his reputation his new novel would have. A reporter from the *Observer* came to talk to him and found him reading a textbook on Embalming Practice, being philosophical about some of the negative reviews of his books, and proclaiming himself a Blimp and a conformist. 'I like discipline,' he said, 'need it, always need something difficult to do.'[9]

But discipline did not always extend to decisiveness. Even while installing a swimmingpool, he was having second thoughts about keeping the house on – it seemed far too big, and he planned to spend much of his time abroad, mostly in Greece. Before the end of the year, he had three invitations to travel – one from G. S. Fraser to an Arts Festival in Leicester, where, he said, he would try to persuade the Phoenix Theatre to put on *An Irish Faustus*, one from Faber to go to London for the publication of *Tunc* in April, and one from Dutton to go to New York for the same purpose at the same time. He sent Fraser a manuscript of *Tunc* to read for his book, intimating that it was the same kind of puppet theatre as the *Quartet*, though with a different accent.[10]

Alan Thomas, who got a preview of *Tunc*, found some errors – Salisbury Plain had no chalk, as Durrell had suggested, and English country boys could not be referred to as peasants. However, he was stunned by the descriptions of Constantinople, which he thought brilliant considering Durrell had never been there.[11] Durrell visited him briefly in February 1968, and Thomas offered to drive him to Fraser's Arts Festival. At Leicester University, he made a great impression on the students, talking to them informally and reading from his work. Then on his first evening he appeared on a platform with Richard Hughes, author of *High Wind in Jamaica*, another writer who had spent his early years in exile and who had ambitions as a dramatist.

Back in London, he began the round of interviews preceding the publication of *Tunc*, while the smart new magazine *Nova* ran selections from the novel. He told a *Times* reporter that he was not at all put out by being accused of over-elaboration. 'The point is that when I move I move to the attack, I move smartly and with a pitchfork.' The book had taken him four years and he had discarded 200 pages trying to find the right tone of voice for it. To begin with it was too like Henry James, whom he admired – 'I doff my hat, but too precious, too leisurely.' Did having to jettison so much not discourage him? 'Sir, I am never discouraged. I am the spirit of hope, joy and plenitude. I believe in Heraclitus: "It rests by changing". I'm on the job 24 hours a day, even when I'm sleeping.' He suffered, if at all, from being 'a poor artist of an epoch relatively debased from the heroic mould' and from doing his best to make a good shadow play. 'The best way to read *Tunc* would be to undress and read it naked as a swallow.'[12]

It was in that playful mood that he now contemplated crossing the Atlantic to North America for the first time. He had told the *Paris Review* in 1959 that going to America was an experience he should save up for his late fifties.

On 12 March 1968, just two weeks after his fifty-sixth birthday, he took off for the US, first to visit Miller in California and then to promote his book in New York. By now, Miller was living in grand style with a ménage which included Hoki, her cousin and friends. Durrell was taken to see the sights, such as Forest Lawn and Disneyland. For him it was an eye-opener, because he had long thought of America as Miller's 'air-conditioned nightmare', a more urbanized version of Argentina. His visit coincided with widespread riots following the assassination of Martin Luther King on 9 April.

He had also told his 1959 *Paris Review* interviewers that if he went to America he would only fall in love with American girls. As it happened he fell in love (or in lust) with Hoki, and while the master of the house was otherwise engaged they debased themselves from the heroic mould. On his return to New York, she sent him a letter, spelling out her feelings. She wrote saying what a fabulous time she remembered them having together – brief and clandestine though it was. She was missing him, but had enjoyed the marvellous, unforgettable things he had said to her over the telephone the morning he left. She hoped he would not play around with too many other women and he would be continually in her mind. In fact she would be able to find little time for anyone else. Henry had been jealous, she told him, because she had more photographs of him than she had of Henry, but she could comfort herself in his absence with thinking about his warm stomach and how pleasant it was to sleep beside.[13]

And this was not the only amour during his transatlantic sojourn. On his outward flight from London he had charmed a young French Canadian woman, who wrote him a love letter on his return. In New York, he stayed at the Algonquin, from where he launched not only his book but himself on to the social scene with a great romantic flourish. At one talk he gave at the YMCA, John Unterecker, a teacher at Columbia University, was asked to do the introduction. Unterecker later recalled an epic night of carousing which would have done Durrell's friend Dylan Thomas proud. After countless champagne-cocktails, they had gone for a couple of scotch and waters at the Algonquin, where Durrell had chatted happily in Greek to the Greek staff. Then they had gone to dinner with a couple with whom they had consumed a bottle of wine apiece. After dinner Durrell and Unterecker had retired to the Algonquin for three more scotch and waters. The American, being drunk, had driven home extremely slowly at 3 a.m. Durrell had been up next day at 6.45 to give a television interview. It went well, he had later told Unterecker, but he had kept his eyes averted from the cameras to hide how bloodshot they were.

Someone later sent Durrell a large plastic head of Miller, which the Algonquin refused to place in its bar. Then came a quart of slivovitz from the Yugoslav Embassy, which Durrell is reported to have opened upside down for fear of it containing a bomb.[14] He was given all the razzmatazz appropriate to a

great visiting author. Miss Stelhoff gave him a party at the
Gotham Book Mart where he was a great success, according
to Marianne Moore who met him there, and he presented the
Mart with the plastic head of Miller. He was approached by a
movie-maker, who having heard about his trip to Disneyland
with Miller wanted them to return there to be filmed together;
he was sought after for interviews on every hand and was
reunited with Tambimuttu, now living in New York and editing
Poetry London–New York.

In America Dutton had printed 25,000 copies of *Tunc*. In
England, Faber had printed 20,000 and had to reprint even
before the book was launched. But the book's reception, on
both sides of the Atlantic, was mixed. *Time* saw in it overwriting, show-off phrases, mixed metaphors and leaden puns, but
all overridden by Durrell's gaiety, originality and sheer exuber-
ance.[15] Gerald Sykes played the honest friend in the *New York
Times Book Review*, acknowledging that people who could not
wait to see a successful author fall on his face would 'delight
maliciously in *Tunc*'. It was not on a level with the *Quartet*,
but what might seem like hollowness could well be this gifted
author moving in a new direction.[16] Another friend, Kenneth
Rexroth, in the *Nation* also saw self-mockery there, spotting
the deliberately absurd element, and argued that the world
of the firm was already to be found in places like Istanbul and
Athens – it was called the CIA. Miller and Durrell, he concluded, were prime candidates for the Nobel Prize.[17]

In Britain his most friendly review came in the *New
Statesman* from G. S. Fraser, who noted that it echoed the
'scabrous pantomimic humour' of *The Black Book*, shuffling
the characters of the *Quartet* into different roles, and turning
that work upside down to make them creatures of culture
rather than just of place. It was a new version of the Faust
story, even of the Arabian Nights, a modern 'Gothick' fairy
story with a 'disturbing sense ... of relevance'.[18] The most
negative notice (probably of his life) came from Robert Pitman
in the *Sunday Express*. He thought it all an outrageous confidence trick – daring sex gift-wrapped as culture. Despite claims
to the contrary, Durrell was not a good writer, and his descriptions of the English countryside were unrecognizable. And if

one were told that this was not a normal novel but an allegory, why had messages to be hidden in a free open society? It was 'good for a high-brow laugh' or as 'a cultural request number in a suburban library . . . But judged by the epic standards claimed by its admirers, the sad truth is that *Tunc* is bunk.'[19] When Durrell referred to hatchet-wielding English critics, no doubt it was Pitman that he had most in mind. He swore that they had it in for him because of things he had made Purse-warden say about them.[20]

But even the occasional bad review did not depress Durrell's now buoyant spirits, and his obvious popularity among his many women fans. Whatever 'adventures and idiocies' Durrell may have engaged in when Claude was alive, now that she was dead he was truly off the leash. He was certainly attracted to any nice-looking woman who came within range. He had shown this predilection at parties in Egypt after Nancy left him, and had indulged himself hugely in Alexandria, as well as enjoying women in Cyprus between Eve and Claude. Now he was ready to plunge again into affairs; and, perhaps from a sense of bitterness and with a thirst to revenge himself for the sudden loss of Claude, ready to drop the women cold straight afterwards. He had kept his hand in with the language of seduction in his poetry and fiction. In love, it seems, he preferred brutal rather than tender sex. Whatever dark sadistic forces lay hidden and repressed inside him (surfacing strongly in his fiction) now burst out in reaction to Claude's cruel death. On the other hand, he had been told by Conrad Moricand that he was destined to fertilize young goddesses, and had, he told a friend, always tried to fulfil that prediction.[21] One young goddess he met on a visit to Paris was a French girl he called 'Buttons'. It was a re-run of his first encounter with Gabrielle almost forty years before.[22] But the affair with Buttons, unlike that with Gabrielle, would continue for many years, on an occasional basis, whenever they could get together in the city.

Returning to France, he was in time for the student riots which hit Paris on 7 May. He heard from Perlès, who was writing a book on Cyprus, and Anaïs, sad that she had missed him in America. However, he saw something of Diane Deriaz in Paris and Miriam Cendrars, who came down to stay with him briefly. And Daphne Fielding finally got him started seriously on yoga, but unlike his father, he combined it with yogic meditation. He did about seven minutes every morning and evening, and found it helped his breathing considerably, although he had done nothing to cut back on his drinking and smoking. The strains of creativity had been replaced by the simple strains of coping with everyday life. Now the affairs which he had relied on Claude to handle – alimony, paying his bills, running two houses – became another pressure.

He also heard from Miller that Hoki was coming to Paris in May, hoping to do some journalistic interviews. In fact, her plan was to get together with Durrell and she went straight to Sommières to continue their liaison. While there, he tried to get her to score a musical with him, but she had lost interest in the piano and declined. After returning to the US, she continued writing to him, but her letters remained unanswered. Finally she wrote him the brief bitter letter of a discarded lover. She was fed up, she said, of writing letters in one direction only. Now he had lost her – a fantastic Japanese girl. She wished him all kinds of bad luck – that he would grow fatter and fatter, become an alcoholic, incapable of making love or of attracting women. Finally she hoped he would die alone and miserable. She signed off this message with a jovial, 'It's been nice knowing you!!'[23]

Alan Thomas, who was now living with a married woman (Shirley Celentano, an American, whom he had met somehow through Durrell), was trying to arrange for the Durrell manuscripts which he had been storing to be packed and sent off to him. Claude's son Barry had agreed to collect them in his Land Rover and ferry them back to Sommières. Thomas told Durrell that an American university would certainly pay a great amount for them if he wanted to sell them, and offered to come to Sommières with Shirley and help to catalogue them. He reported that Gawsworth was in hospital, threatened with eviction, and asking for money.

The strikes which had paralysed France were ended when De Gaulle won a landslide victory in the election on 30 June. But the postal service meanwhile was in chaos, and Durrell's isolation was complete. To relax after a morning slaving away at *Nunquam*, he worked on a musical, *Ulysses Come Homes* about the women that Ulysses had loved, Penelope, Nausicaa, Circe. The songs were pleasantly lyrical in a Noël Cowardish way, and he sang them in a suitably languid style accompanying himself at the piano – no doubt with cigarette-holder at the ready.

The filming of the *Quartet*, with script by Larry Marcus and directed by Joseph Strick, was soon to get under way in Tunisia, with Dirk Bogarde as Pursewarden, Michael York as Darley and Anouk Aimée as Justine. Durrell was invited to see the filming, but was keener to go to Corfu to spend the summer with Gerry and Jacquie. Meanwhile in June he was anxiously awaiting a visit from Diane Deriaz, his air hostess friend, the one-time circus acrobat (star of the Bal Tabarin), French women's wrestling champion, poet and friend of artists and poets, notably Picasso, Eluard and Audiberti, who had dedicated a play about Joan of Arc to her. Durrell found Diane intriguing as well as lovely, a cross between Anaïs and Claude. She was forty, beautiful and virginal, having had but one lover who had died at roughly the same time as Claude. He hoped she would agree to stay with him as his secretary. However, she resisted the Noël Coward songs and the swimmingpool, and declined to be anything other than a friend.

Another of Diana Menuhin's forthright letters came in July. She had loved the *Quartet* except for *Clea*, where she thought his technique showed too much. In *Tunc* she had found the same familiar ingredients – heartless, beautiful women, whores, clownish degenerates, weird intellectuals, fabulous cities, the sporting life, the concealed message – but no longer making the music his writing once had. And so many puns and aphorisms seemed to have gone straight from his notebook into the mouths of his characters, whether the words suited them or not. The vein had been worked out. Epic figures such as Justine, Scobie, Balthazar and Nessim could not be duplicated. She admired him enormously, which was why she wrote as she did, but the source needed to be refreshed, the soul reinvigorated.[24]

George Barker, down on his luck, wrote asking for help, but Durrell replied that Claude had put all their money into property and land, and he could hardly send him a field. On top of that he had to pay alimony and school fees, and then he had to face a 25 per cent tax hike in October. He was also unwilling to support his brother Leslie, who had long been a trial to the family. Leslie had returned under a cloud from Kenya, and had been living close to Margo in Bournemouth – begging and scrounging from them to get along. Finally he had found himself a job in London and moved there.[25]

The filming of *Justine* was delayed by a change of director. Strick was held up filming Miller's *Tropic of Cancer*, so George Cukor was put in charge of *Justine*. In any case, Durrell seems to have been past caring about it. He found himself stuck in Sommières, unable to get away even to Greece, partly because of *Nunquam*, partly because of a film being set up by Margaret McCall, and partly because of the weight of domestic matters which Claude had previously dealt with so efficiently. However, in September, Paddy and Joan Leigh Fermor (the 'Corn Goddess'), came by for some 'fun and feasting' which made up for having been pinned down for the summer.

The film for BBC Television, *Lawrence Durrell's Paris*, an examination of the 'myth' of the city, took him there twice in late September–early October. In it, he got the history wrong, saying that he was twenty-two when he arrived in Paris, that he had lived in Betty Ryan's flat for six months, that he had met Orwell there on his way to Spain. He expounded on the temperament of France – Protestant in the north, Catholic in the middle, and pagan in the south – and toured literary Paris in a fiacre. He talked to friends who for him epitomized the spirit of the place: Albert Cossery ('Egypt's Gogol', according to French critics), Diane Deriaz (about her life in the circus), George Whitman (about Shakespeare and Company) and Eleanore Hirt (about Paris theatre).

He spent Christmas in London, helping McCall edit the Paris film and planning another for the summer, about Katsimbalis and Athens. Staying with Thomas and Shirley in Chelsea, he was able to push *Nunquam* to within fifty pages of the end. Back in Sommières, he could look forward to *Spirit of Place* coming from Faber, and the French version of *Tunc* appearing in May 1969. First indications were that Roger Giroux's trans-

lation was being greeted with high excitement by those who
had read it.

Durrell was finding the seclusion of the big house very much
to his taste, reflecting that in the past a mother-fixation had
probably led him to become too dependent on women. He
preferred to see them when he felt like it – dinner and the
occasional night's stayover. Meanwhile he kept himself relaxed
with his regular yoga sessions and regulated breathing, and
completed his novel on time.

In *Nunquam*, Felix has been recaptured by the firm and
partly leucotomized. His past is a blank and he has lost the
will to rebel. Central to *Tunc* was the creation of Felix in
the firm's image and his escape from it; central to *Nunquam*
is the recreation of the dead Iolanthe in the firm's (Julian's)
image and her escape from that. *Tunc*, then, dilates on the
male's dilemma in the modern world, where his creativity is
overpowered by money; *Nunquam* expounds the female's situation – where she is transformed into an object for man's
gratification. And so, in *Nunquam*, 'Aphrodite revolts' and,
finally, Iolanthe and Julian pitch to their deaths from the Whis-
pering Gallery in St Paul's Cathedral. In death, Iolanthe has
found escape and a form of wholeness again. Felix is left in
charge of the firm and his final attempt to break its grip is to
burn all its microfilmed archives. The firm might disintegrate
with all its records and contacts gone; on the other hand it
might not. Wholeness for him could be as elusive as ever.

These two novels, *Tunc* and *Nunquam* (reissued together as
The Revolt of Aphrodite) embody, strangely one might think,
both neo-Marxist and Freudian analyses of capitalist society
as corrupting and destructive of the wholeness which comes
from artistic freedom and from sexual freedom. Art and sex,
however, cannot in themselves free one from the tentacles of
the firm; only the destruction of its legal basis can offer that
hope. But Durrell was no Marxist, and he hated communism.
His solution was psychological, something akin to that of
Wilhelm Reich – a form of socialism through free sexual
expression – though in a classical context, that of ancient
Greece. Sex and art were, as ever, closely connected in Durrell's
thinking. In any case, the alternatives are there – to conform

to commercial pressures and become a creature of the system, or to take the leap to freedom, even if it means risking one's life. On the other hand, the basis of that control could be destroyed. The choice must be made. It's now or never. 'Aut tunc, aut nunquam.'

There is not only continuity here with Durrell's earlier work – some rhetorical traces and character traces of *The Black Book*, structural similarities with that and the *Quartet* (the narrator recollecting in order to make sense of the past, the sliding-panel effect) – but also some characters who stray in from past works (a one-eyed Arab, references to Pursewarden and even to a poet called Durrell). There, too (this time in more gruesome detail), is Durrell's fascination with embalming. Other Durrellian ingredients include violent sex, homosexuality, narcissism, rape, incest, brothel scenes, adultery, dildos and (in Julian's love for the dead Io) necrophilia, not to mention the Oedipus and castration complexes, indispensable to a novelist, he thought. And to all that obsession with deviant sex can be added other biographical parallels. Two women, one dark, sexually alluring but fundamentally unstable and one blonde, warm and generous; brothers, one sinister, one earthy; a fascination with the shit=gold (cash) nexus which had obsessed Miller in the 1930s, with brothels, with hunting and with blindness; the perception of Muslim Turkey as 'a death culture' compared to the 'life culture' of Greece; and a distaste for English public schools.

Reading it through he did not feel it was an unworthy successor to the *Quartet*, but, now it was written, he felt at something of a loose end. However, relaxed after his creative effort, he was happier to welcome visitors. Mai Zetterling and David Hughes, who had been to America and visited California, returned with news of the Miller ménage; Simone Perier (a friend of Miller's) phoned regularly; and, in April, Thomas and Shirley came to stay. Thomas was keen to have Durrell's archive valued, and took everything back to England in his car. He also took the completed manuscript of *Nunquam* to give to Durrell's agent, Juliet O'Hea. On the journey the car caught fire and the precious manuscripts were saved only by a timely dousing with a fire-extinguisher from a roadside café.[26] The archive was later bought by the University of Southern Illinois for over £24,000.

Spirit of Place appeared in England in April and in America in June. It included letters, essays and poems illustrating Durrell's facility for writing about distant places, plus his 'bughouse' stories, all linked by a biographical narrative from Thomas. The core around which the collection centred was Durrell's idea that culture is a function of landscape. The English response to the book was muted, but his true fans were to be found reviewing in American magazines.

Intimations that all was not well with the film of *Justine* came in a letter from the writer Lawrence B. Marcus. The film, he wrote, was dreadful, and he should know, having written the screenplay. What the hell had happened, he did not know.[27] George Cukor, director of *My Fair Lady*, had taken a highly complex novel and reduced it to a simple story-line. Robbed of its intricate subtlety and mystery the characters and story became banal.[28] It was slammed by Penelope Gilliat in the *New Yorker*[29] and by Dan Wakefield in *Atlantic Monthly*.[30] Miller saw the film and wrote saying he had found it utterly confusing: the dialogue was difficult to catch, he was unsure who Dirk Bogarde and Michael York were playing, and the first scene, where sailors try to seduce a girl with Spanish fly, was dreadful. But it would be his turn next: he had found out that the actor who played him in *Quiet Days in Clichy* was homosexual.[31]

Durrell learned from other friends that it was about the worst film ever made. He had been wise to stay away from it. He had managed to get his musical half done and Wallace Southam was keen to see it produced. But what concerned him more immediately was a new BBC Television film directed by Margaret McCall. This was a variation on the theme of individual freedom which he had explored in *Tunc/Nunquam*. For the film, *The Lonely Road*, he roped in Diane Deriaz to join in the quest for a Provençal tramp, Blanco, who represented to him the kind of freedom denied to most of us. The story followed Diane and Larry's unsuccessful search for the elusive Blanco, a man utterly without attachments. Durrell was also still in search of a Claude-substitute, and was disappointed when both Deriaz and McCall showed a preference for friend-ship over something more involved.

The New Year offered the prospect of another trip to the USA in March for the publication of *Nunquam*. However, Miller sent word that he and Hoki had separated, though remained friends.[32]

Early March 1970 saw Durrell in London, again staying with Thomas. He talked on radio about his newly published novel, agreeing that he had once again been concerned with the role of memory in human identity, and the question of whether the personality is an illusion. That was why he had put doll-like characters into preposterous situations. Chal-lenged over what were seen as Charlock's surprisingly 'Blimpish' observations, he agreed, saying that he himself was a Blimp and the opinions were well grounded. He also said that his reputation as a poet had suffered since he started writing novels, but that he found writing poems far more pleasurable, especially when a poem came off, which it did less and less often. He also revealed that he was already toying with an idea for his next novel, though he was not certain what form it would take.[33] To coincide with the launch of *Nunquam*, McCall's film, *The Lonely Road*, went out on BBC Television. Whatever critics may have said about his work, he was definitely a celebrity.[34]

The British reviews were mixed, as ever. Some critics, like Francis Hope in the *New Statesman*, found the characterization in *Nunquam* 'lazy', and thought the aphorisms were obviously 'rejected items from a poet's notebook'. Durrell was not at home in the world of science and his 'schoolboy obscenities . . . [were] as unfunny as ever'. The *TLS* was also unenthusiastic, seeing neither *Tunc* nor *Nunquam* as investigating very fully or plausibly 'what a sustained attempt to be free would be like to experience'. It found Durrell's use of ideas 'more opportunist than rigorous'.[35] At the other critical pole, Richard Holmes in *The Times* gave it a highly respectful, reflective review, placing it in a wider literary context and recognizing the ideas which Durrell was trying to explore. 'This is no longer the world of Proust and Cavafy. This is Faustus, and Mary Shelley's *Frankenstein* and the hard satiric grappling with contemporary ideas of Aldous Huxley's middle period.'³⁶ And Malcolm Brad-bury in *New Society* applauded too. 'Durrell sets a cracking Gothic pace, shifting between an emotional involvement and a kind of comic distance, revelling in it all.'

He flew to New York, where he found the American reviews awaiting him. At the end of *Nunquam* he had said that his intention had been to move from the ridiculous to the sublime – the reviews tended to see it as one or the other. One, in the *New York Review of Books* by Christopher Ricks, strangely echoed that dismissively satirical review of his first novel in *Janus* which had so hurt him. He wrote about a female writer, 'Ellen Ward Curler' (an anagram of Lawrence Durrell which *Private Eye* had come up with), and said that 'taken straight, as a novel by Lawrence Durrell, *Nunquam* would be no more than labored pretentious infantility, the resonance and crackle of hi-sci-fi. But then, as Virginian Woolf said, no one "can possibly mistake a novel written by a man for a novel written by a woman".'³⁷ Richard Boston was hardly more complimen-tary about *Nunquam* in the *New York Times Book Review*, poking fun at the 'lavishly praised' Durrell and his 'lush writing', his same old game-playing, his obsession with blind-ness and mutilation.³⁸

In New York he gave an interview at his hotel, the Algon-quin, talking about his mental state when writing and confirming that as far as ideas were concerned he was a borrower:

> Well, I'm not an original philosopher, I'm just a burglar. I'm like a pedlar with a tin tray . . . it's the way I set up my merchandize that may have a trace of originality . . . When I get neurotic writing the bloody thing I select all the infantile anal-oral sludge that comes float-ing to the surface, and if I get panicky enough to infect the reader with my panic, then I am doing a useful job.³⁹

The rest of his time in New York was spent drinking with friends or eating seafood at one of his favourite hangouts, the Grand Central Station Oyster Bar.

He travelled around the northern states, visiting Pittsburgh and Chicago, reading his poetry and from his novels. While stranded in Chicago because of snow, he was entertained by a singer friend of Miller's, Fiddle Viracola, a lively New Yorker who, if not a Claude-substitute, became more than just a friend. He also spent time with her in New York before returning to London to help Wallace Southam produce his *Ulysses* record.

In May he was visited by Fiddle Viracola in Sommières, and took her walking across the garrigue and to the mazet, gathered flowers with her and built wood-fires, as they cut themselves off from the world for a while. After her departure he plunged back into work, and also got down to some serious painting, with the prospect of another Oscar Epfs exhibition in Paris later in the year. He did, however, take time out to fly to England and escort Sappho up to York, where she was applying for a place at the university's Derwent College to read English Literature. While there he was interviewed by the university's student magazine, *Nouse*, confirming that he saw himself not as an original thinker but more as a creative organizer of texts. 'The artist does not exactly think while he works. He uses the ratiocinative side of himself only when he comes to arrange and edit what he has written or painted.'[40]

Back in Sommières, he was searching for books about the Cathars, the Gnostic sect cruelly persecuted by the Inquisition in the mid-thirteenth century, and about the Templars (possibly also Gnostics), destroyed by the Inquisition in 1307. The Gnostics had long fascinated him (he reflected that Pursewarden's suicide was 'the sacrificial suicide of a true Cathar').[41]

John Gawsworth died on 23 September, aged fifty-eight. Over the past few years he had declined more and more into poverty and ill-health. The shining literary star whom Durrell had found so inspiring in the early 1930s had fallen so far that the previous December a few friends had published a letter in the *Listener*, pleading for help for this last vestige of neo-Georgianism. The young man who in 1939 had been awarded the A. C. Benson silver medal of the Royal Society of Literature for his services to poetry was to die forgotten, recalled only as a footnote in the lives of others.

Fiddle Viracola visited Durrell again and helped him gather together all his Epfs paintings, which they packed into his Volkswagen, *L'Escargot*, and transported to Paris, delivering them to Marthe Nochy's bookshop at 93 Rue de Seine, where they were to be exhibited in November. He said a sad farewell to Fiddle, who flew off on a singing tour of Japan, and returned to more visits from friends – the Fieldings, Jimmy Stern, Mai Zetterling, Simone Perrier and Claude's son Barry, now a naval radio officer. Between times, he began to sketch out his new novel, determined to get down to it seriously once his Paris show was over.

To publicize the exhibition he sent out invitations offering to sign copies of *Nunquam* at the same time. If anyone had had any doubt about the identity of Oscar Epfs, they would have been left with none now. *The Times* thought it a significant unmasking, and the paper's Diary column ran a piece about it. He was exhibiting around forty paintings, he told them. 'They're pleasant, but no great shakes. It's just a relaxation, nothing more serious. I don't paint as well as Victor Hugo.' He described himself as a post-impressionist. However, a Reuters report on the show took a more jaundiced view of his style. 'Ranging from abstract splashes of color to an impression of prehistoric cave drawings, they defy classification and seem in turn naive, impressionist, surrealist or existentialist.' Sometimes, it said, he used a style similar to that of early Picasso or Marc Chagall – a style forty years out of date. Some critics had decided not to take Durrell seriously as a painter, on the ground that 'If he does not take himself seriously, then we should not either.' The pictures were priced from $85 for unframed posters to $550 for the largest canvases. The best-sellers were the small ones, mostly splashes of colour, with no concern for shape or form, said the report. Asked why he had chosen the pseudonym Oscar Epfs, he said, 'Because it's unpronounceable.' Nothing about farts this time.[42]

For Christmas he had his two daughters, Penelope and Sappho, visit him in Sommières, and laid on everything for a full Christmas feast, plum puddings and all. He clearly took great pride in his creative offspring, especially Sappho, who combined intelligence with beauty and a talent for writing poetry, which he was happy to acclaim. When they left he felt rather empty.[43] Trying to sort out his ideas for the new novel sent him into a depression and he shut himself away, finally surfacing at the end of January 1971, apologizing to Miller for allowing their 'famous' correspondence to lapse. His ideas were focusing more and more upon Templars and the Gnostic heresies, but constructing the thing in his mind was a delicate matter and he was fearful that it might all suddenly collapse.[44] He was also balancing this with a precarious emotional life. To stave off his feelings of emptiness and misery he plunged into a series of love affairs – all of them unsatisfactory. He felt grimly frustrated and acted cruelly to the women he bedded. He put his sense of irritation down to the male menopause.[45] When he wrote to Miller about his string of affairs, his old mentor told him that he should not be afraid of making a few more mistakes. They were good for him and, if he could lose himself, then there were no taboos.[46]

He had developed a nasty case of eczema, which he put down to the seafood at the Grand Central Station Oyster Bar. It made him bad-tempered and affected his love-making, so he left for Geneva in late February to have it looked at. He then spent time with his philosopher friend de Rougemont, who knew a great deal about Gnosticism – Durrell regarded him as a member of the 'Hermetic circle' to which he, too, liked to feel he belonged. What fascinated him was that the order of Templars had once been a formidable fighting force with the power to conquer half of Europe, yet in a very short time they had been stripped of their authority, imprisoned, tortured and incinerated, without any apparent resistance. There was the mystery. What sin had rendered them impotent?

While in Geneva he also met Claude Kieffer, the beautiful French wife of a Swiss doctor, with whom he soon started a love affair, and whom he was to regard as his Muse.

Never averse to being cross-questioned about his life and work, he gave a series of interviews to Marc Alyn, the French poet and essayist, who lived in nearby Uzès. The book which emerged from this encounter in the following year, *The Big Supposer*, was probably the most complete account of himself he had given since D. G. Bridson's interviews in 1960. He made frequent reference to suicide, something which alarmed Miller when he read the book, but this was more of a romantic gesture, linked to his reading of the Cathars, than a serious intent. Few of his friends thought him capable of it.

He was conscious that the kind of novel which was fashionable in France, the *nouveau roman*, represented everything he was against, and that opinion among the rebellious young, Maoist in tendency, was antipathetic to his own philosophical outlook. His engagement with the irrational, and the writing of luscious prose, was a conscious rejection of anything smacking of determinism or social causation. With *The Alexandria Quartet* he had looked at Europe through an Alexandrian spyglass; now he would look at Alexandria from Europe.[47] The imaginative expansion of his novel took him on the research trail to Avignon, one-time seat of the Popes and centre of Inquisitional cruelty. He joined a local lunch club and, sporting a beret, spent time eating with locals under trees at city cafés, and playing boules. There he lapped up local history – local myths and legends, the history of the city during the German occupation.

In part his loneliness was mitigated by Gerry taking the mazet for a year, so the two brothers could get together more frequently. He also occasionally went to visit Cathy Aldington, who lived at Saintes Maries de la Mer, and through her met again the beautiful model Ghislaine de Boysson, who had been working in television and films. He was learning to relax through his yoga, extending it to an hour a day and adopting the lotus position while standing on his head. Now he found that, without planning to do it, he had simply given up smoking – it just went with the yoga. It also helped but did not entirely clear up his eczema. Despite the discomfort of this, in June he went to London for the publication of his book of poems, *Red Limbo Lingo*, which showed the outpouring of bitter violence which Claude's death had provoked. The press was not enamoured and the book probably did Durrell's poetic reputation little good. Fellow poet and novelist Robert Nye commented that in this 'poetry notebook' 'Durrell has set down his musings about blood . . . [which] seem in urgent need of a transfusion'.[48] While in London he visited the Menuhins at their home in Highgate, a happy reunion, and spent time comparing yoga notes with Yehudi.[49]

Margaret McCall visited him for a month in the summer, followed by a ten-day visit from Eleanor Hirt. Sappho also came, and told him that having seen her first W. C. Fields film she instantly recognized the shape of his nose. (Miller had likened him to Laurence Olivier, and the *New York Times* to Richard Burton – he was amused to note.)[50] With Sappho he produced an odd book in a limited edition, *The Suchness of the Old Boy*, which was published the following year by Turrett Books, the imprint of the London bookseller Bernard Stone, from his Turrett Bookshop in Kensington Church Street. Durrell wrote the seemingly encoded Lear-like text and Sappho did the eccentric drawings, which seem very much like a caustic commentary on the words, if not on the author.

In September, he used a magazine commission, for an article on the Swiss lakes, to hold a tryst with Claude Kieffer at Lake Orta, where Nietzsche had first talked to Lou Salomé about *Thus Spoke Zarathustra*. Here, sitting in a small tavern drinking coffee, he found in the *New York Times* an obituary for Seferis, who had died in Athens recently of pneumonia. He felt angry at the loss of one of his surrogate fathers. It was another name to add to his death-map.

CHAPTER 16

The Prince of Darkness or the Devil at Large

(1971–1975)

The further you go in the artistic world,
and the more successful you are in
communication, you often become more
and more disembodied in your personal
relations.

Lawrence Durrell, 1970

Durrell's interest in Gnosticism in all its forms, already acquired in Egypt, was becoming increasingly focused on the Templars and Cathars. He took out a subscription to the journal *Cahiers d'Etudes Cathars*, which gave a solid background of scholarship to his researches, to add to a book he had discovered earlier in 1971, Jacques Lacarrière's *The Gnostics*.[1]

For Christmas Durrell flew to Los Angeles in time to celebrate Miller's eightieth birthday on Boxing Day. It was thirty-seven years since Durrell had read *Tropic of Cancer* and thirty-five since they had first met in Paris. Miller, just recovered from his artery-replacement operation, was now crippled with a bad hip, but he continued to hanker after women and love affairs.

In January 1972, Durrell had the chance to indulge his 'stage Irishness' when Margaret McCall took him to Dublin, perhaps with a film in mind. There they toured the sights, including the Martello Tower which Joyce had put into *Ulysses*, and Durrell swilled back Guinness and whisky in the city's pubs, delighting in the seductive charm of the Dubliners, and perhaps seeing something of himself reflected back to him – the eyes, the smile, the unconstrained blarney. He visited Trinity College to hear a paper about his work, 'Sexual Curiosity and Metaphysical Speculation in the Work of', by the young Richard Pine, later to do a full treatise on Durrell's metaphysics.[2] Afterwards, he met and talked with what he called the 'younglings' of Trinity College. Later he did a no doubt lucrative article for *Vogue* called 'Duffy's Dublin',[3] a lot of which was about Guinness and the inside of bars.

Shortly after he arrived back at 15 Route de Saussine (his Vampire House), the Vidourle broke its banks and flooded his cellar, ruining part of his library which was stored there. Trying to cope without electricity, he caught a cold and was feeling low until Claude Kieffer arrived from Geneva to soothe him and take him off to the Hôtel de l'Europe in Avignon, after which he carried her off for a weekend of love-making and good talk in Vaucluse. When he returned home he withdrew into a sad, lonely self-isolation to await his sixtieth birthday on 27 February, praying without very much hope for some degree of reason and self-restraint.[4] For a man who had lived so active a life, enjoying the sun and the sea and the outdoor life in general, his advancing age was difficult to bear. He had stopped smoking, and wanted to cut down on drinking (because of the cost, apart from anything else), but this he found far more difficult. Then in March he met a herbalist from Arles, Ludovic Chardenon, who set up his stall in the market at Sommières once a month offering cures for all kinds of malady with his infusions. Durrell asked him to cure his eczema, and Chardenon sent him some dried herbs from which Marcelle brewed up a liquor. Within ten days his eczema had disappeared, and the miracle converted Durrell to Ludo's herbalist magic. He decided to talk to him and produce a pamphlet about him and his herbs. *The Plant-Magic Man* came out the following year, first in the *New York Herald Tribune*, then in *Midi Libre*, and finally as a booklet from the Capra Press in Santa Barbara.[5] Ludo would also feature in *The Avignon Quintet*.

Mary Hadkinson came to stay and help Durrell salvage the books from his cellar, and to catalogue his library.[6] And in the summer he again visited Saintes Maries de la Mer to see

Cathy Aldington and again met Ghislaine de Boysson. Since their first meeting, she had been married and divorced, had had a career in films and television, become a friend of Gary Cooper, and been proposed to by Bing Crosby. Durrell was somewhat smitten.

Old friends as well as women could deflect him from his course. Alf Perlès, now living in Cyprus, wrote to say that he and his wife would be in Paris in early September, for the reissue of his memoir of Miller, and suggested a reunion. Durrell was quite keen on the idea and alerted his friend Michèle Arnaud, who thought she would make a television film about the occasion. When they met, there was an orgy of reminiscing and champagne-drinking. Perlès thought that Durrell had changed very little since he first saw him at the Villa Seurat, and Durrell reciprocated the compliment. After meeting Perlès, he also enjoyed a few frolicsome days with Miriam Cendrars.[7] Where women were concerned he did not seem to know where to stop, and confessed his sense of confusion to Miller. His mentor, now embarked on a new love affair with a Chinese actress, Lisa Lu, advised him after all not to get married. They both had poor prospects in the House of Marriage, but a more favourable outlook in the House of Love.[8]

Once he got down to it, Durrell worked with discipline. By December he had completed 125 pages of his new book, was making progress with his yoga and had managed for two reasonable periods to refrain from drinking. When Yehudi Menuhin was in the area and visited him, they talked of little but their respective yoga regimes. The clean-living Menuhin was delighted to learn that Durrell had given up smoking and cut down on drinking. Durrell was proud to announce that he could stand on his head in the lotus position for five minutes at a time, which he did every morning. Menuhin trumped that by standing on *his* head and playing the violin.[9]

With the danger of prosecution long gone, and with his children grown up (Sappho now had a boyfriend at university), neither Faber nor Durrell had any fears about *The Black Book* finally appearing in England, and it was scheduled for the spring of 1973. Correcting the proofs in December, he became deeply nostalgic for his youth in Paris and in Greece. It was a mood which infused his new novel (to be called *Monsieur, or the Prince of Darkness*). Here he was establishing the pre-war lives of characters who would eventually bring the complex baggage of their youth into the post-war world, though at this stage he may have been thinking of it as a one-off novel. But elements from *The Black Book* and even the *Quartet* would seep through into it, as if he wanted to spread himself on to a wider canvas.

After another idyllic visit from Claude Kieffer, he spent Christmas in Paris. When he returned he found that the house had been burgled. Some of his prized books on the Elizabethans had gone, as had his most valued paintings, including *The Clowns* by Zvi Milstein, which he had once hung in sight of his bed at the mazet. Paintings by himself and Oscar Epfs had been left behind – a cruel critical comment, he thought. Also missing were three typewriters, which reduced him to writing by hand. He took to sleeping with a loaded revolver at his bedside.

In February 1973 he flew to Los Angeles to work with Michèle Arnaud on a television film about Miller. There he talked of his anxieties about the new book, saying that he would have preferred to do something big to compare with the *Quartet*. Returning to France his plane was diverted to Geneva, an unexpected opportunity to spend time with his lover, Claude Kieffer. He then took the train back to Nîmes – from the freezing Swiss winter to the howling mistral of the Gard – where his gloom was only deepened by the news that Katsimbalis' wife Spatch had died – and he duly inscribed her name on his death-map.

In March his selection of Wordsworth was published. In his introduction he dwelt on the love between Wordsworth and his sister, harping still on the incest theme. His obsession with sex was one he happily shared with Miller in his letters, detailing his liaisons and bemoaning his inability to dispense with alcohol. Miller reassured him: the itch would pass as well as the urge to drink.[10] But Durrell lamented recent periods of hysteria and booze, which he put down to the self-disgust inspired by his eczema.

In May, he had to go to London for the publication, after

thirty-six years, of *The Black Book*. He took Ghislaine de Boysson along, and they stayed at his usual London lodging, the Thomases' house in Chelsea. The publication of *The Black Book* in England was certainly a media event, if not a critical one. He did his usual stint on television and radio, and attended book-signings at bookshops. *The Times* reported that in one day Durrell signed 220 copies of the book at Hatchard's bookshop in Piccadilly.[11]

He was on good form when he met the British press, saying of the book to a young woman from the *Sunday Times* that 'It's so tame now that it might have been written by an elderly spinster in Chelsea.' And when she asked why he had written it knowing it to be unpublishable in Britain, he replied in round Johnsonian fashion, 'I was striving for laurels, madam, not for royalties, and I was amply rewarded when I was accorded a small laurel by T. S. Eliot.'[12] He was equally expansive to Philip Howard of *The Times*, telling him, 'It's alarming, but I think I'm becoming respectable. I'm glad that my mother's not here to see it. But don't call me a guru yet.' He accepted that the same themes recurred in his novels, and quoted Eliot once saying to him, 'The maddening thing is that we only have one thing to say, but must keep on finding new forms of saying it.' He also said that he agreed with D. H. Lawrence in believing that sex was the way to escape the impoverishment caused to life by industrial society.[13] Paul Theroux's review in *The Times* treated *The Black Book* with a degree of amused contempt 'It's not good and it's fairly dirty,' he wrote. 'On the other hand, it is original . . .' It was in the tradition of Kyd and Tourneur, and 'the corpse-poems of Baudelaire and the sad haunted imagery of early Eliot'. And while it had been inspired by Miller's *Tropic of Cancer*, it lacked that book's vitality. 'It is . . . flapdoodle, great cadenzas of it – of a cathartic sort, for this is a chronicle of "the English death", but flapdoodle all the same.'[14]

Durrell was not always comfortable in the respectable roles he was called upon to perform. On 28 April, he and Ghislaine left London for Cannes, where he was to serve as a judge at the Film Festival with Ingrid Bergman and Sydney Pollack. To a journalist who expressed surprise at this he said, 'I am becoming an elder of the established church.'¹⁵ Interviewed for the Festival *Bulletin*, Durrell was asked what kind of youth he had been, and replied, 'The teenager is long gone . . . I would rather be a very dignified but rather aged old gentleman of 61. *Hurray! Mummy, daddy, it's me, I'm at Cannes with Freud!*' And asked, inevitably, about sex, he said, 'The only thing which has value and a spiritual density is that tragic episode in everyone's life: love. To love is to understand one another, and to understand is to imagine everything . . . Sexuality is as fragile as life itself, and twice as interesting.' And he promptly invited the woman interviewer to the cinema.¹⁶

Then, when he and Ghislaine had an argument, he slapped her face and she immediately threatened to return to Paris. The following day he came to her in tears to apologize, telling her he was very nervous in Cannes with all the high-powered people he had to meet, and what with smoking all night long. Would she marry him? This she could not resist, and so she stayed on with him.

Ghislaine moved in to the house at Sommières. At almost the same time, Larry's new volume of poems appeared – *Vega*, dedicated to Claude Kieffer.

Although Durrell had made his intentions clear to Ghislaine in speaking to her of marriage, his mind was elsewhere. Wrestling with *Monsieur*, embroiled in writing it, and wondering whether he could extend it into something grander, he had finally conceived of a shape for it – a quincunx, a sequence of five books, related poetically rather than chronologically.¹⁷ Sometimes, to relax and to calm himself, he took laudanum. Ghislaine who was aristocratic, temperamental and twenty-five years younger, found him very difficult, as he was drinking heavily and becoming almost violently irritable. So she told him, 'Maybe it's better if we don't get married; people do just live together, you know.' However, he was always contrite, saying, 'No, no, darling, you see, when I am your husband I will be absolutely different. If I get nervous with you it's because I'm not sure that you won't escape.' Being in love, she went along with this.¹⁸ But he was well aware of what she was experiencing

– the 'creative madness' which he felt he had to induce to fuel his genius.

His anxiety and tension were not evident to visitors from outside. The Thomases came to stay, and Durrell and Ghislaine entertained them in leisurely style – sunbathing, swimming in the pool, eating good food with wine, dining out in the wild garden at evening beneath the trees and the hooting owls. Meanwhile, Sappho had graduated and moved to London after living through three unsettled years at university when student revolution was in the air. She had emerged from it as something of a hippy, settling with her boyfriend, Simon Tompsett, in a squat in London and taking a job as a junior editor with Weidenfeld and Nicolson, while he worked for Unilever.

When Durrell became absorbed in a novel he lived inside it. Now he was feeling unsatisfied with it because it was not wide enough in scope to satisfy his desire to create something big. But a cheerfully optimistic letter from Miller, who had had a further artificial artery operation and lost the sight of one eye, raised his spirits, especially the news that the old libertine's affair with his Chinese actress was still going strong. Ghislaine de Boysson had been living with him in Sommières for five months when one day – a day, it so happened, when a strike had closed all the bistros – Durrell said, 'Today maybe you can wash your hair and put on a nice dress, because we are going to be married tonight.' It took her completely by surprise, but she said, 'OK,' and that evening they climbed into *L'Escargot* and drove to the Mairie. A local tart and a local drunk were witnesses. Afterwards, Durrell invited everyone back to the house for a drink. The drunk asked Ghislaine what she thought of 'the pink ballet' (an orgy with little boys); the tart took off her high-heeled shoes and smashed him on the knee, then proceeded to expand on her sexual adventures. Ghislaine was bemused. What kind of a weird world had she let herself into? she wondered. It was like living in a Durrell novel.

The following day, Durrell insisted she go immediately to her flat in Quai Voltaire in Paris and clear it out. He did not want her things at his house, so she sold most of her possessions. While she was in Paris Durrell telephoned and said, 'Darling, you are my wife now and don't be angry, but there is a woman here with me.' He had invited someone he had met in Cannes to visit the fair in Nîmes with him and then stay over at the house, which was why he had got Ghislaine out of the way. When Ghislaine returned to Nîmes, he was waiting in *L'Escargot* with a bottle of pink champagne, and said, 'Darling, nothing happened between me and that woman. She said I stank and wouldn't sleep with me.' Ghislaine fell ill with a high fever, and was unable to see anyone. Later, Gerry came to visit, took her for a walk in the garden and said he was sorry he had not had much of a chance to talk to her before. 'I was going to tell you not to marry Larry,' he told her.

Her new husband, she found, was very jealous of her friends, and refused to allow them to visit her. One who did come he insulted so badly that she left next morning. Nor was she allowed to work. When *Elle* invited her to act as their correspondent in Montpellier, he objected so strongly that she turned it down. She was expected to cook and to entertain his friends, though at least not to have to clean the house. Marcelle had departed and her place had been taken by a Mme Mignon, an Alsatian woman, who arrived at 6 a.m. and worked at such speed that Durrell christened her La Bonne Atomique.

Now that he was in the throes of composition, his writing regime was as ferocious as ever. He rose at 5 a.m., and drank a thermos flask of very weak coffee. After that, he did an hour of yoga. At seven he settled down to work, sometimes with a little red wine, until midday. Before lunch he would go for a swim, walking along the broken stone path from the house to the swimming pool in ill-fitting shorts, often with his balls showing, wearing sunglasses and a beret. Why did he make himself look like that, asked Ghislaine? 'To frighten the snakes,' he replied. After lunch they would go for a walk together, returning at 3 p.m., and he would sit in the kitchen with the bottle of red wine at his elbow. According to Ghislaine, 'He sat like that, at the table beside the window, with the bottle, a glass of red wine and a little lighted candle, from 3 p.m. until 7 p.m.'[19] Sometimes he would put on a Mozart record and play it over and over again all day long; sometimes he would settle down to play jazz at the piano, or perhaps he would paint.

Ghislaine was amused to see the trampish way he dressed and the funny hats he wore. Asked why, he replied, 'When you have a nose like mine it's better to have a funny hat on your head because it distracts people from the nose.'[20]

In 1972, Durrell had been invited to give a series of lectures at the Californian Institute of Technology, but had been unable to go. Now he accepted to give the lectures in the new year. Hearing that Larry was coming to Los Angeles to teach at Caltech, Anaïs wrote, saying how she hoped to meet him, and to clue him up on her complicated life. She asked him please to not contradict what she said about her marriage to Hugo – that she was not brought up in Palace Hotels, was never wealthy nor owned a Henry Moore. Unless she could be sure he would not embarrass her with his over-imaginative allegations, she was hesitant about asking him to her home, she said. The preface which had offended her still rankled.[21]

On Christmas Day, the Durrells left La Bonne Atomique in charge of the Vampire House and flew to Los Angeles for Larry's stint at Caltech, which was to run from January till March 1974. Ghislaine was surprised to find how afraid her husband was of flying; on the plane he behaved like a scared little boy. At the Caltech campus in Pasadena, friends were waiting with a huge case of champagne. They were put into the quarters in which Einstein had lived when he was at Caltech – very appropriate for the man who put the theory of relativity into literature. But Durrell felt intimidated by the academic environment, fearful that he would be exposing himself to a very high-powered audience; Caltech, after all, had produced twelve Nobel Prize winners. The apartment had a large terrace and a fridge, and, having brought their camping equipment along, they decided to cook for themselves. When Ghislaine prepared a meal with garlic and onions on their camping stove, a governor of the College came along in high dudgeon and warned them that they had no right to cook in their rooms. 'It stinks everywhere,' he complained. 'You have to take your meals in the big restaurant downstairs.'

They now felt uncomfortable in their quarters, and when a friend of Ghislaine, the daughter of film director William Wyler, offered them a beach house at Malibu they moved there. It had the advantage of being close to where Miller lived. Wyler's wife said, very generously, 'Ghislaine, it's our wedding present – from Willie and me.' So except for two days a week when then moved back to Caltech for Durrell to give his lectures, they lived on the beach for three months, the perfect place for Durrell, and here he had the peace and quiet he needed to complete *Monsieur*.

There were frequent visits to Miller, still in love with his Chinese actress, Lisa Lu. But Durrell's 'creative madness' was always enhanced when he drank. One evening after Miller had gone to bed (he was still recovering from his second artery operation), Durrell slapped Ghislaine's face in front of Miller's children. She was so humiliated that she refused to go to Miller's house again. But Miller phoned, saying he wanted to speak to them both, so she went. He was in bed and called them in. Ghislaine noticed that, in front of him, Durrell stood like a naughty schoolboy facing his headmaster. 'Larry,' said Miller, 'I love your wife, she's a good nurse, and if I once more hear of you doing what you did in my house I'll never see you again in my life.' When Cathy Wyler came from New York to visit Ghislaine, Durrell said in front of her, 'I don't want to meet your bloody friend!', which, considering that it was through Cathy that they had the house, Ghislaine thought unforgivable. She asked her friend at least to stay the night, but Cathy flatly refused. There was one woman who would not throw herself at the master's feet.

On Durrell's sixty-second birthday, there was a grand reunion of the Three Musketeers – Miller, Anaïs and Durrell. Over dinner they began to reminisce. Miller asked Anaïs if she remembered something which happened in Paris, and she asked him if he remembered the dark velvet dress she wore for her father's concert, then Durrell pitched in with his memories. Ghislaine realized they were not listening to one another, but talking about themselves and seemingly *to* themselves. She found it strangely unreal. And, while she liked Anaïs, who, despite her reputation, had a strangely virginal air, she thought Miller's views were appalling: he acted the puritan and complained if she swore or wore a low-cut dress, but was at the same time sex-obsessed, and spoke of women as 'holes – holes that move' – good for nothing but sex.[22]

Durrell's seminar lectures at Caltech dealt with Virginia Woolf, Joyce, Ford Madox Ford and D. H. Lawrence, approaching them through ideas which were the key to his own thinking – Time, the disintegrated personality and the male–female split – referring also to Freud, Einstein and Wyndham Lewis. As in his Argentinian lectures he was trying to trace out, in his own fashion, the spirit of the age as it infused certain key texts. Anaïs came along to his final class on Lawrence's *Sons and Lovers*, and apparently made as great an impression on the students as Durrell. While in California he also gave two speeches, one at Claremont College and one at Caltech, which Miller enthused over so much that he had them published, under the title *Blue Thirst*. One was about his life in Corfu, the other about his time as a diplomat and would-be spy in Greece, Egypt and Yugoslavia.[23] Ghislaine remembered how nervous he was on the platform at the first lecture, a small man dwarfed in a big chair, but how, after a stumbling start, he mesmerized his audience with his relaxed manner and lyrical fluency.

By the time they returned to France, Durrell had sent off the manuscript of *Monsieur* to Faber. In *The Avignon Quintet*, as in *The Black Book*, there is an overriding obsessive theme of death, as if the solution to the mystery of death represented the solution to the mystery of life. And of course one strand of his thinking inherited from Fraenkel was that death is the necessary precondition for rebirth. In addition, his expressions of Gnostic doctrine pronounced the death of Christianity, and the search for the Templars' treasure symbolizes the never-ending pursuit of that mystery. As in his previous major fictions, the complex narrative involves a number of friends who live through important formative years together and finally are scattered, though in retrospect their lives are made sense of through one or other of them reconstructing their story in some meaningful fashion. The action shifts from one country to another – France, Egypt, Switzerland, Germany; and Alexandria is seen through Durrell's telescope from Europe, rather than the other way round as in the *Quartet*. Here he begins to explore his overriding themes: the quest for wholeness through sex and art and, faced with the disintegrating ego and a world gone mad, the confrontation of death and the coming to terms with it.

The structure of the novel sequence is the quincunx – a five-pointed figure laid out like the points on a dice, or of a pyramid viewed from above, the centrepoint of which was considered by the ancients to be sacred ground, fit only for the burial of monarchs. It was also, Durrell liked to add, the form of an Elizabethan dance, and this first novel begins his dance through its five ludic phases. The number five was thought to have mystical and healing significance. He also likened his quincunx to a traditional puppet play in which there was a confusion of authorship. The authors involved are Durrell and his creation Blanford and *his* creation Sutcliffe and *his* creation Bloshford. *Le Monsieur* is the novel being written by Blanford and *Monsieur, or the Prince of Darkness* includes elements of the longer draft which preceded it. (To confuse matters even more, Durrell's Sutcliffe also appears as his own and as Blanford's creation.) The characters we meet, therefore, are fictions created by a fiction, and might in future be reinvented (that is reincarnated or reconstituted) or disposed of at the author's whim or that of his invented author. As Durrell later said, half of the characters existed only in the minds of the other half.

Monsieur concerns Bruce, a doctor, Sylvie, his wife, and her brother Piers, a French diplomat. These three had enjoyed a *ménage à trois*. But Piers is mysteriously dead and Sylvie gone mad, and Bruce, typical of a Durrell novel, is trying to make sense of a fragmented past. The Monsieur of the title is the Gnostic Prince of Darkness, who rules this material world to the exclusion of God. This faith was expounded to the three lovers and their friends, Toby and Sutcliffe, by Akkad, the Egyptian mystic, who won over Bruce and Piers (a descendant of the man who betrayed the Knights Templar to the Inquisition). To Gnostics, Monsieur's world of appearances is an evil one peopled by forces of disintegration. Gnostics seek wholeness and spiritual fulfilment by renouncing this world and embracing death, so to them suicide constitutes an act of redemption. In Akkad's sect an inner circle arranges the suicide of members, who are informed so that they can prepare for death, but the 'when' and 'how' of their despatch are kept from them. The sect considers the Serpent, who seduced Eve with 'knowledge', to be a symbol of good – the basis for a mystic philosophy of sex (for what is unknowable through reason may be knowable through the mystique of orgasm), knowledge and pleasure simultaneously communicated by penetrative sex. The secret is to be highly conscious of the orgasm, to cling to its fleeting delicacy. Love, like death, is a means to defeat the Prince of Darkness, and is symbolized by the snake (Ophis), who plays a key part in Akkad's desert initiation of Piers and the others.[24] Since the ikon of material culture is gold which equals shit (*merde*), the Gnostic aim is to replace the *merde* culture with a *sperm* culture.

The unbelieving Sutcliffe collapses mentally and is driven to suicide when his wife Pia becomes a lesbian and leaves with a black woman, Trash. (The double-sex idea of Freud had fascinated Durrell since watching Gerald's insects in Corfu.) Toby, the Oxford-educated historian researching the extermination of the Templars, resists Akkad's Gnostic vision; Piers, with a less conventional mind, accepts instantly. The Gnostic idea runs through the novel and highlights what happens to all the main characters. At the end, the world of the friends disintegrates, the château falls into decay, Bruce and the mad Sylvie are worlds apart. They are also (like Piers, Sylvie and Sutcliffe) revealed to be creations of the novelist Blanford (who is, of course, Durrell's creation), so their reality (and Durrell's) is undermined – for if the world of appearances is unreal, it may be recreated according to taste. In fact, most of the characters will go on into future novels, transmogrified or reconstituted as the kaleidoscope of Durrell's imagination is shaken yet again. One reality will give way to another as fragments of it are reassembled by Blanford or Sutcliffe or Durrell. Blanford, shattered by war, imagines himself (and therefore this is a fictional Blanford) with an old love, Constance, and, Gnostic-fashion, awaiting the letter which will signal his suicide. But Blanford, the author who is imagining this, is able, like Darley in the *Quartet*, to turn to the healing influence of art and love to recuperate from the destruction which the war and the Prince of Darkness has wreaked upon him. As in the *Quartet*, Durrell is suggesting possible alternative endings to the story. After all, as he said, his readers composed his novels as they read them. By the time he had finished *Monsieur* he thought he had developed a new kind of timeless prose – the *flou* style (diffuse and woolly) of the *Quartet* again, but even more so.

That one character may become another who in turn becomes another is Durrell's way of portraying the world in which the creator of fictions lives. He reveals the process whereby the author transforms one reality into another, one fiction supersedes another in the creative conscious and ends up some way removed from the original model. Durrell claimed that his characters were not based on individuals, but he did observe and focus on individuals (as he admitted). This exercise in fictionality shows how conscious he was of the process. He was also raising questions about the nature of reality. If, as Gnostics maintained, we live in a world of fictions, then which fiction do we choose to call 'reality' and why?

The *Quartet* had been conceived as a cycle of novels linked through a word continuum rather than through chronology. The quincunx was more an arrangement of associated ideas based on the quinx, the basis of that old Elizabethan dance. So figures in one novel would move in and through the others, much as they did more casually through his other novels. However, this time they were there because they were conceived of and written about by surrogate authors of his own creation.

Durrell spent the summer working on *Livia*, the second book of the quincunx (he had completed fifty pages by the end of September), and correcting the proofs for *Monsieur*, which Faber planned to bring out in October. Before the autumn arrived, Curtis Brown had sold it to Viking Press in America (of which Dutton was now a part) for an advance of $50,000 and had sold the foreign-language rights in eight different countries. Even Gallimard, notoriously cautious, had bought it promptly. When Miller read an advance copy, he hailed Durrell as maestro of an ever-changing carnival. But he also said that after the desert scene with Akkad and Ophis the book appeared to disintegrate, unresolved complications were added and the Templar theme seemed to contribute nothing to the main theme.[25] However, Durrell had anticipated this reaction; much the same had been said when *Justine* and *Tunc* first appeared. Yet he valued Miller's comments, feeling now, with Eliot and Seferis dead, that the American was the one surviving surrogate-father he wanted to impress.

The problem he faced in wrestling with *Livia* was how to extend the first novel with the whole quincunx in mind. The psychological stress of this brought out the Durrell which Ghislaine had only glimpsed in California – the drunk and violent Durrell, apt to explode without notice. One evening, he took her through his tortured childhood – forced to drink the blood of a freshly killed chicken by Indian servants, seeing the bleeding Christ in the chapel at Darjeeling, being bullied and sneered at at school because of his size and because he was a *pied noir*. Then suddenly, having aroused her sympathy for his suffering, he picked up the table, overturned it on her and stamped off to bed. She was furious, but cleared up the mess and wiped up the spilled wine. Then she went into the bedroom where he was snoring loudly. She called his name and when he sat up she hit him in the face, then took and bit the index finger of his right hand, the hand he needed for writing. In a rage, he leaped out of bed and hit her hard, so that she fell backwards, striking her head against the chimneypiece. She was out cold. Next day he did not apologize, but simply said, 'You win, Bubool.'[26] She felt she had found a strength in herself that she had not known was there. But the demons which seethed beneath the often congenial exterior of her husband had revealed themselves. He could be dangerous.

When Sappho came that summer Ghislaine was very taken with her – beautiful, highly intelligent and with a kind, generous spirit. But Sappho was also highly strung and liable to become stressed, especially when Durrell said cruel things to her, which he often did. She was trying to write, but when he read her work he told her it was shit, and she became too upset to eat. Her friend Simon was also treated appallingly. Durrell never spoke a word to him. At one point Sappho took Ghislaine aside and warned her, 'You must leave! He is going to kill you!' But Ghislaine told her, 'I am in love with your father. I can't leave him.'

But Durrell talked all the time of his dead wife Claude and taunted Ghislaine about her cooking, saying, 'Claude is looking down at you and laughing at you.' When he began to smash things up, she cleaned up because she did not want La Bonne Atomique to know the state of her marriage. When he got drunk he turned violent. His plunges into 'madness' were calculated, because he did not believe that a sane person could write really creatively.[27] He told Ghislaine that when he had got that way with Claude she used to break plates on his head, and he advised her to do the same. But she found her own way of dealing with him. She took to drinking whisky. If he threatened to get violent she threw the whisky in his face. He sobered up instantly. 'Whisky is so expensive,' he would say angrily. 'How could you!' It touched his mean streak, and always worked.

The private, obsessed Durrell at Sommières was easily transformed into an extrovert public performer on the wider stage – like one of his own characters being reconstituted as another. In October he went to London for the publication of *Monsieur* together with Ghislaine, to whom the book was dedicated, and they stayed as usual with the Thomases. He did the book-signing round of bookshops, appeared on Michael Parkinson's television talk show, and then on the BBC arts radio programme, *Kaleidoscope*. The shifting fictions in the book, he said, were there to challenge readers who generally were fed so much pap.[28]

Interviewed by the *Guardian*, he defended his style with his usual vigour. 'I hate corrugated-iron prose, and American slop-slap. Why not some colour, why not some energy? Why the hell should one be frightened of that? . . . A novel of the purest schizophrenia is developing. If only one could bring the damn thing off . . .' He was touching wood, hoping that the stereoscopic effect he was aiming at would work; if it did, it might have a claim to being an original form in English literature. It was, he thought, more ambitious than the *Quartet* – a bit more *flou*. 'The *Quartet* was rather rigid in its way because it was limited in its four-dimensional notions. This is much freer. And more full of dangers. At what point does the reader yawn?'

(Sometimes, of course, Durrell's experiments were a source of unintended amusement. Hugh Herbert, his interviewer, recalled that when, in 1962, the *Guardian* had published a parody, supposedly an extract from the fifth volume of the *Quartet*, called *Voluptia*, Faber were overwhelmed with orders, prompting them to write a denial to the paper that such a book existed.) He was contemptuous of the fashionable 'suburban novel' and waxed eloquent about sex.[29] The British reviewers could not agree whether he was about to deliver a work as satisfying as the *Quartet* or had descended to trickery. In a *Sunday Times* review, Ronald Blythe saw in *Monsieur* 'undertones of Waugh' and 'an extravagant extension of the Alexandrian scene'. Christopher Wordsworth in the *Guardian* detected dark magic. 'This latest sumptuous box of tricks has the usual false bottom, two-way mirror, ravelled identities, and osmotic chronologies ... Self-indulgent necromancy, maybe, but there's a sucker born every minute, and for splendid flummery count me one.'[30]

In November his new Epfs exhibition opened at Marthe Nochy's bookstore in Rue de la Seine – mostly watercolours. The *vernissage* was an excuse for Durrell's Parisian friends to congregate to greet him. Ghislaine was there to meet some of them for the first time. One visitor to the exhibition was a dark, intense girl, with Slavic looks, who obviously found Durrell fascinating. A critic who had seen his earlier work claimed that his paintings had now ceased to be anecdotal and 'touched the deepest part of the subconscious'. Asked if poetry was the closest he came to Epfs, Durrell said, 'I would like to be able to "feel" the poem and the painting in the same way. But the medium dictates everything. Form is largely dictated by the presence of language, and colours are Epfs's language.'[31]

The year ended on a pleasing note, when Paul Scott in *The Times* made *Monsieur* one of his choice books for 1974, referring to it as 'vigorous and inventive'. Having had compliments from three practising novelists for the books that year – Ronald Blythe, Paul Theroux and now Paul Scott – he could reasonably feel that his *Avignon Quintet* had been launched.

Durrell and Ghislaine had celebrated the New Year in

Switzerland with the de Rougemonts. There Durrell wrote a poem, 'A Patch of Dust', and announced 'This is for the tart I married.' (This nostalgic poem contains a vivid reference to 'the French whore' he was living with.) When they got back to Sommières, Durrell said to her, 'I want a divorce.' She was astonished. 'You must explain why,' she said. 'Because you are a lesbian,' he told her, to which she could only reply, 'If you say that in Paris everybody will laugh at you.' But it was obvious to her what he was doing. In the throes of writing *Livia* he had turned her into his own character – a beautiful wife who leaves her husband for a black lesbian lover.

After this she tried to escape whenever possible to her flat in Paris, and return for weekends.

The mixed nature of his reviews in England and America (where *Monsieur* was published in January 1975) show how Durrell suffered under the weight of his past reputation, something of which he must have been acutely aware, and one of the reasons why he found continuing with the *Quintet* so very taxing. But there was news to cheer in March 1975, when he was awarded the James Tait Black Memorial Prize, and in April when *Monsieur* was declared a Literary Guide book choice. Diana Menuhin wrote to take him to task over the humourlessness of his women characters, who seemed to lack gaiety or fun. He had a great sense of humour so why not use it to create a woman – an outrageous Restoration character, for example, witty and quick of tongue? Had all his wives been as dull and lacking in gaiety as his characters? she wondered. Claude, the only one she had met, seemed to her quite the reverse.[32]

By the end of March, *Livia* had grown to 100 pages and the multiple narratives were beginning to meld together, characters from one reality were beginning to obtrude into the lives of those from another. Ghislaine and Durrell were now getting on well again. She had returned to stay in Sommières for a few months, and was considering offers of work as costumier on a number of films.[33] There was also, for him, the prospect of making a film in Greece in the autumn.

In April, he suddenly asked a visiting academic, 'Would you like to see my grave?' and he took the bemused professor in

L'Escargot to the little Romanesque church of St Julien de Salinelles out along the Quissac road to show him the plot he had picked out for himself, marked by a dog-rose. He had bought the plot, he said, much to the annoyance of the local mayor, who had had his own eye on it.[34] But by now he had the purchasing power, claiming later that 1975 was the year in which he had first become a millionaire,[35] though whether this meant a franc millionaire or a sterling one was not clear.

Sometimes his unpredictability was less amusing. Ghislaine once suggested that they go camping on the coast in *L'Escargot*. They drove down to Saintes Maries de la Mer to have dinner with Cathy Aldington, and afterwards Durrell, the worse for drink, drove the camper to the town carpark. 'Are we going to camp here among all the other cars?' she asked. 'Yes, here,' he said. 'OK,' she replied. 'You stay. I'm going back to sleep at Cathy's place.' 'Well, where do you want to go?' 'On the beach,' she said. So he drove *L'Escargot* on to the beach, as far as it was possible to go. There they bedded down for the night. Next day it took them hours to retrieve the camper. It had stuck fast in the sand.[36]

Because *Livia* was taking longer than had been hoped, and to keep his name in print, Durrell was commissioned by his American publishers to write another island book – this time on Sicily. Ghislaine was furious when he refused to take her with him. He merely asked her to find pictures for the book, then asked another woman to do it instead – a married woman with whom he was having an affair, and whom Ghislaine nicknamed 'La Gioconda'. But, in spite of her anger, she drove him to Marseilles, where he caught the plane to Sicily.

If *Sicilian Carousel* is the least satisfactory of Durrell's island books, it is because it fails to satisfy his own specifications. He'd lived in Corfu, Rhodes and Cyprus. Now he booked up for a two-week tour and went around Sicily on a bus. (The 'Sicilian Carousel' of the title was also the title of the tour.) Again, as in *Reflections on a Marine Venus* and in some of his other travel writing, he invented a 'straight man' – an ex-colonel in the Desert Rats who shared his war experience in Egypt and Cyprus (his public service *alter ego*, perhaps) and his condescending attitude towards the other tourists – a suitable character for Durrell to engage in witty and civilized conversation. But he allowed himself to write about the Languedoc and Cyprus and Greece (especially Rhodes) as if, while in Sicily, his mind was constantly wandering to other places where his spirit was more in tune. His final stop, in Taormina, enabled him to visit Lawrence's house and reflect on Norman Douglas, whose writing on the Mediterranean had so influenced his own.

The pull of Greece drew him away again in September, when he went to Corfu with BBC producer Peter Adam, to make a film called *Spirit of Place: Lawrence Durrell's Greece*, a co-production with Germany and France. Returning to Corfu and being cast into a reminiscent mood prompted an eloquent response from him. He was back on Prospero's enchanted island. His smooth, coherent, lyrical presence, brimming with curiosity and sensibility, concealed the violent confusions of his personal life. They visited Kalami and the White House, and the little shrine to St Arsenius, and Durrell spoke to priests and villagers, swam and messed about in boats. Later, in Rhodes, he revisited the Villa Cleobolus and the little Turkish graveyard where he and Leigh Fermor and Xan Fielding had passed the hours talking hopefully about the post-war years to come. His old friend the Mufti had died the year before, and was now no more than a shade among the toppled gravestones. The final shot of the film had him floating in the sea off Rhodes in the lotus position.[37]

Before returning to Sommières, he spent three days in Athens with Katsimbalis, whom he found in a wretched condition, bedridden with arthritis and prostate trouble (the result of an old untreated case of the clap, he told Durrell), fearful of an operation, unable even to entertain because he had to pee every five minutes or so, and because he felt his life was over. Durrell wrote to Miller asking him to call up his old friend in the hope that it would give him the inspiration to rise from his bed and seek treatment.[38]

A strong literary debt to Cavafy took him to London in November to unveil a blue plaque from the London Hellenistic Society dedicated to the poet at the Bayswater house where he had lived from 1873 to 1876. *The Times* caught up with him at the plaque unveiling and found him looking well and bouncy but affecting a profound pessimism. At a cocktail party in the nearby Royal Lancaster Hotel he described his Sommières house as 'like a recherchè lunatic asylum', and said gloomily that recently he had been unsettled, moving around 'from pillar to post'. He was two-thirds of the way through his next novel, which he called *Buried Alive* – exactly as he felt. He was the centre of journalistic attention and when someone asked if he would be prepared to be nominated for the chair of poetry at Oxford, he declined, saying 'I'm not a good critic. I've already turned down a series of lectures in Cambridge. And anyway my publisher is letting my poetry go out of print.' And he sighed as if fated to be a disappointed man.[39] Two days later, he met Alan Ross in the World's End pub, close to the Thomases' where he was staying, to discuss the shape of a new *Selected Poems* which Ross was to edit.

He was back in Sommières by the end of November, still in pessimistic mood, having to cook for himself, and dwelling on the humiliations of old age. Ghislaine had accompanied him neither to the Greek islands nor to London. She now spent a lot of time in Paris.

Ghislaine was well aware that Larry was seeing other women, but continued to love him. On one of her visits to Sommières, sleeping separately from him, she had a bad dream. She dreamed that Claude, whom she had met and liked, came to the house and collected up all Ghislaine's things and threw them out of the house telling her to 'Go away.' Next day she told Durrell about this, saying 'I think Claude is furious with me,' and he replied, 'But, darling, you are sleeping in the room where her ashes are.' Nine years after her death he still had his wife's ashes in a little Air France plastic bag in the cupboard. Ghislaine was shocked and told him he had to see Claude's remains properly disposed of. 'OK,' he said, 'I'll put her in the garden.' 'No, no,' she protested. 'She would be annoyed by that.' He had that plot marked by the dog-rose, all picked out for himself in the graveyard at the little Romanesque church of St Julien de Salinelles, set in a beautiful landscape of vine-yards. That, she told him, was where the ashes belonged. He said nothing for some days, then one morning she found him all dressed up in a grey suit. 'I am waiting for the man from the Mairie to go and bury Claude in my cemetery,' he told her.[40]

And so Claude was finally laid to rest.

CHAPTER 17

The Avignon Quintet:
Cruel Fiction (1976–1980)

The monsters exist in every one of us.

Lawrence Durrell

Early in 1976, Durrell was visited by a Chinese Taoist philosopher and sexologist, Jolan Chang, with whom he had been corresponding. Chang, who lived in Stockholm, descended on Sommières for a weekend of frank and fearless talk with Durrell about health and diet and sex – all wrapped in a cloak of Taoism. Apart from eating correctly and forswearing alcohol, the secret of happiness and longevity for men, said Chang, was prolonged intercourse stopping short of ejaculation. He lived in Stockholm with seven Swedes with whom he claimed he made love ten times a day with the greatest of pleasure and the minimum of fatigue, ejaculating only once in every 100 acts of coition. If one followed his regimen there was no reason why one should not live to be 150.[1] At Durrell's suggestion, he visited Ghislaine in Paris. On arriving at her flat he began to feed her his line about good eating and prolonged sex. She regarded the whole thing as a strange joke – no doubt a cryptic communication from Larry. Afterwards, Chang wrote to Durrell to say that he now realized what lay behind his deep melancholy – too much ejaculation: 'Après coitus triste'. Without ejaculation he would be saved the sadness from which he so obviously suffered. Alcohol, too, was a depressant which only plunged one deeper into gloom.[2]

Peter Adam came to visit in early January to gather more interview material for Durrell's TV programme about Greece.

He found him living a shuttered and reclusive life in the gloomy old house. As usual, he was saving money, and only the kitchen and one other room were heated, plus a black bathroom, which Durrell called 'Hollywood'. The place was just 'ten rooms of junk', he said. He took his visitor over the Vidourle to meet local friends, including Ludo Chardenon, who now had a shop there. Adam was impressed by the simple country life he lived.[3] His life may have seemed simple and idyllic – a wealthy writer with all the freedom in the world – but Durrell was often alone in his Vampire House, with his ghosts and memories. He was constantly gnawed by the fear of poverty.

He had decided that married bliss was incompatible with work – the state of frenzy he required to create made him impossible to live with. What Claude had been prepared to endure, Ghislaine was not. He had found her charming and was taken by her aristocratic beauty, but he discovered that she had too much steel in her spine silently to suffer his cruelty and violence. Now he was alone, he enjoyed cultivating the image of eccentric old curmudgeon. James Heilpern, who went to interview him for BBC's *Radio Times*, found him looking 'unkempt in baggy jeans and battered suede shoes', giving the impression of an ex-boxer, with his stubby fingers and blob of a nose – 'sign of the drinking man'. And 'when drinking and talking, he has an unstoppable quality, tending to steam like a hot stew'. He struck Heilpern as 'an old-fashioned English reactionary', something of a Colonel Blimp – more English than the English, as colonials often are. He talked about his childhood and the drive he had inherited from his father, whose wish to send him to university he frustrated, and quoted Eliot about starting early in the morning 'to beat the others'. His yoga exercises, which had seen off several minor ailments, he said, now stretched to standing on his head for forty minutes every morning. Asked why he wrote, he replied, no doubt in suitably self-mocking tones, 'There is an inner voice which cannot be silenced.'[4]

The BBC continued to be kind to him. They transmitted not only *Lawrence Durrell's Greece* in March, but also a radio dramatisation of *The Dark Labyrinth* in April. Ghislaine, meanwhile, was trying to set up a film version of Anaïs's *House*

of Incest, which Durrell would script. Nin, who was now
fatally ill with cancer, was extremely keen on the idea, saying
she would be proud for him to do it.[5] He considered her and
Miller (one leg useless and one eye gone) tremendous examples
of fortitude in the face of suffering; they remained cheerful and
continued to inspire him.[6]

His isolation and 'creative madness' made him more and
more difficult to live with. That summer, Ghislaine came down
to stay, and Sappho was also there with Simon. Once again
Durrell studiously ignored Sappho's boyfriend. Sappho may
have sensed her father's dark animosity more than others. One
day, after dinner, while they were swimming in the pool she
again urged Ghislaine to leave him.

Sappho later complained that her father practised his psychological cruelty on her by turning her into Livia (much as he
had Ghislaine), taunting her that she was a lesbian, as her
name suggested. The burden of having a famous father who
crushed her literary ambitions, yet who loved her as she loved
him, was a trap from which she could not easily escape. Since
Claude's death, she claimed, he had treated her more and more
like a wife, refusing to give her the space she needed to be
herself and becoming more and more destructive towards her.
He told her that sex was sadism and men had to treat women
cruelly because their sexuality was so disgusting. He argued
with her about the slightest thing and she could never do
anything right. She was convinced that he was out to destroy
her because he had to destroy those he loved. But her implied
story of childhood incest is questionable; more likely, he wove
her so closely into his fiction-making that what she called
'mental incest' took place, with obviously painful consequences
for her.[7]

Durrell himself hinted at the other side of the relationship –
that she regarded him as a lout who cared nothing for politics
and the good of the world, and told him so. He told a reporter
that she was one of the young writers of the future who would
pick up where he left off, considering the destruction of the
ego since 1900. He felt, he said, like an old man picking
through the ruins of battle. 'I pick certain elements that might
make a useful point of departure for other people (like my own

daughter), who want to see if they can fabricate some kind of wigwam out of all this mess.'⁸ He obviously saw Sappho as a serious writer wanting to reconstruct what a century of science and psychoanalysis had destroyed. But as he believed that a true writer must suffer to be able to write anything worthwhile, this opens the possibility that he deliberately made her suffer on some far-fetched theory about creativity. Certainly he put value on his own self-confessed and self-induced periods of derangement, and reiterated to Sappho his belief that for him analysis would destroy the creative spark on which he depended.

News came that the enduring Miller, whose liaison with Lisa Lu had finally ended, had now taken up with the ex-beauty queen and film actress Brenda Venus and was in the throes of yet another massive exchange of love letters. Venus was from New Orleans, a dark beauty of part-American Indian extraction, and was to become Miller's final lover. One of the earlier ones, Anaïs Nin, died on 14 January 1977 at Cedars of Lebanon Hospital in Los Angeles.⁹ Durrell wrote a eulogy to be read at her funeral, but it arrived too late. However, Christopher Isherwood and Stephen Spender were there to read from her work accompanied by a 'low-key jazz combo'.¹⁰ Miller was too ill to attend, so no other musketeer was there to bid this strange and gifted woman farewell. Durrell duly added her name to his death-map, along with Patrick Kinross and Alan Pringle, who had also recently died. And he soon had to add yet another when, in March, Robin Fedden died of cancer after returning from one last mountaineering expedition with his friends Leigh Fermor and Fielding.

Reactions to *Sicilian Carousel* were negative; the book was simply not up to Durrell's own high standard. Nevertheless he accepted yet another commission to produce a money-spinner, which he hoped would fund him for a whole year – a coffee-table book about the Greek islands, which he was hoping to have finished by August. At the same time he was trying to restart *Livia*, which had been stalled by work on the Greek book. This, however, required more thought after the delay, because on it depended the shape of the *Quintet* to come. If he got this book right the rest, he thought, would follow.¹¹

When Diana Menuhin saw the first chapter of *Livia*, published in the *Malahat Review*, she sent him a typically forthright reaction. She found it meaty but rather stifling as if he was talking to himself, she wrote. In her opinion, he should remove himself from the insane mythological world of Provence and return to the less complicated and less suffocating myth of ancient Greece, a lighter, more healthy and more congenial atmosphere. Intuitively she had detected something unwholesome in Durrell's work and put it down to his isolation in Sommières.[12] If his female characters were unrecognizable to women, as Diana intimated, what he created was maybe what he wanted, creatures who were vehicles for his own ideas and sex objects for his pleasure, his own invented women, about as real as Julian's Iolanthe.

The isolation was getting him down. He rented a small worker's flat at Grau du Roi close to Aigues-Mortes by the sea, and asked Ghislaine to come down and look after the house for him. Gerry, who was being sued for divorce by Jacquie, would also be around, having decided not only to buy the mazet but to rent a flat at the Sommières house. Ghislaine, however, suspected that Larry was taking a woman to Grau du Roi with him. La Gioconda, Mme Lestoquard, had contracted cancer and withdrawn from the world, but Durrell had begun an affair with a Marlene Dietrich lookalike, a rather well-built woman whom Ghislaine had christened Two Ton.

The ocean, and whatever other comforts he found at Aigues-Mortes, seemed to work for Durrell. In his quiet seaside flat, he finished *The Greek Islands* and by early August was about forty pages from the end of *Livia*. Now the characters from one story, Blanford's, were moving into the lives of characters from another, Sutcliffe's. It was a delicately balanced time for the whole *Quintet*, a tangle of interwoven texts which would have to be handled with great finesse if the trick was to be brought off successfully. It was all about the instability of the ego and the slippery nature of time. He knew that the next volume was going to be torture.[13]

Ghislaine found herself alone in the Sommières house, Gerry having taken off. Larry came back from the seaside each weekend to pay La Bonne Atomique and pick up his mail, and they would lunch together. She was still deeply in love with him, and extremely jealous of his many women, but had come to terms with the idea of remaining his wife on the basis of a loving friendship. Feeling nervous about being alone, she invited a Mexican girlfriend to stay with her. One day when they returned from a swim, there was a letter from Durrell asking for a divorce. If she stayed she would have to rent a flat in the house, he said. She was astonished; he had given her no hint of what he had in mind. When he returned he flatly refused to speak to her and for the next three months all she met from him was silence. She thought it was the worst thing that had ever happened to her.

Then one day she saw a letter on his desk from his lawyer saying to him 'Don't you think that 2,500 francs a month in alimony is an enormous amount?' So she immediately hired the same lawyer to handle her side of things too, something which in France cannot be refused in the case of a divorce, and over their next silent dinner she said, 'As we now have the same lawyer he cannot say to you that you are offering me too much money.' Durrell choked and demanded to know how she knew what was being discussed between him and his lawyer. She told him she had read the letter on his desk. At that, he leapt up, ran to the bedroom and returned brandishing his revolver. 'Go on, do it,' she said. 'Tomorrow I will be happy and you will be in a lot of shit!' Faced down, he retreated back to the bedroom.

This marriage, he reflected, had been a costly mistake, and he told Miller that it was not Ghislaine's fault; the failure was entirely his. Strangely enough, at the very same time, Miller was also going through a divorce, from Hoki.

Durrell's inner life must have been in great turmoil because of the breakup of his marriage and because of his anxieties about his quincunx. But in October he set off with Peter Adam for Egypt, there to retrace his steps in the country which had given him his *Alexandria Quartet* and his literary fame. They flew first to Cairo, and the following day he was sitting in the Cecil Hotel in Alexandria talking to a camera about wartime encounters – with Gide, Seferis, Leigh Fermor and Diana Gould

– and about how the wearying and tense atmosphere of the war had been strangely conducive to living just for the moment. He wandered around the city 'aimlessly', in accordance with Forster's advice, spotting places once familiar to him, including a Greek bookshop and Eve's father's café. They found the house where he had lived with the Gotches, and the tower where he had worked, and he met a woman who had known Clea Baduro, now dead. They went to Cafavy's house, where Durrell sat at the poet's desk and wrote a short letter to Miller. He faced the camera, submitted to interviews and read his own translation of Cafavy's 'The City'. They were entertained by elegant ladies whose inane questions Durrell answered politely, stifling his boredom. To him, these beautiful Alexandrian women were just as empty-headed and just as desirable as they had ever been during the war.

He met a woman who was Justine's double, who asked him to sign her copy of the book, stirring in him a strong sense of *déjà vu*. After eight days in Alexandria the crew moved to Cairo, but he was by now fed up. He drank heavily and, according to Adam, his mood of gloom and boredom threatened the whole enterprise. He complained about the world being too full of talk, and said that, for two people in love, often silence descended.[14] He was disappointed that belly-dancers were no longer able to dance bare-breasted. They visited a Coptic monastery and met an eighty-five-year-old Egyptian architect who talked fascinatingly about the shapes of minarets, but Durrell seemed hardly moved. Adam concluded that he no longer relished intelligent conversation, and that his isolated life style had made him introverted – much the conclusion Diana Menuhin had reached from reading the first chapter of *Livia*. Compared with the old architect, he seemed used up. His mood worsened when they filmed at a village just outside Cairo. But then suddenly, within a couple of days, at the beginning of November, his mood had changed. He had stopped drinking and was on the top of his form.

They flew to Aswan and filmed at the old Cataract Hotel, where he had once stayed during the war. He spoke lyrically about the hotel and the train journey down from Cairo, and the Nile provoked him to new heights of poetic eloquence.

They met the cast of *Death on the Nile*, filming near by, and Durrell was thrilled at being photographed with Mia Farrow and Lois Chiles. Seeing how seriously he haggled with pedlars over cheap necklaces, Adam decided that he was a man with very simple needs.[15]

If Egypt reminded him of his faded youth, the appearance of Alan Ross's *Selected Poems of Lawrence Durrell* perhaps reminded him of a dulled poetic spark. The reviews were mostly friendly. 'A timely reminder', said *The Times*, 'that whatever Durrell's fame as a novelist and charm as a writer about Mediterranean places it is principally as a poet that we ought to consider him.' The reviewer especially liked the beauty and lyricism of poems like 'To Ping-Kû, Asleep' and 'Nemea'. And 'A Ballad of the Good Lord Nelson', it said, could have been written only by Durrell. 'It is hard, bawdy, witty, dashing, dashed-off, and brilliant. I wish he had written two dozen things like it, to dismay the academics.'[16]

In *Livia, or Buried Alive* we meet the characters in whose minds those of *Monsieur, or the Prince of Darkness* are to be found. They are Durrell's creations, but that book's 'originals'. The manuscript of Blanford's novel *Monsieur*, based on his own life, is recovered by its author from the library of Constance, Duchess of Tu, after her death. The setting is Constance's château, Tu Doc, before the war, where she, her brother Hilary and their friends Sam and Aubrey (Blanford) spend an idyllic summer. The movement of the whole book is towards disintegration; typical of Durrell, at the end the friends will all disperse as war approaches. Nearby Avignon embodies the spirit of place with which his characters are most in tune, but it was also the setting of papal authority during the fourteenth century (symbolized by the ugly Palaces of the Popes – monuments to Mammon and the *merde* culture), and part of a heraldic landscape speaking of a pagan past which Judaeo-Christian culture and the Inquisition had obliterated. Now, as war looms, the arrival of a new Inquisition is threatened, in the form of the Nazi occupation, and the extermination of the Templars will be paralleled by the extermination of the Jews. All are expressions of the death-culture of the west.

Against that, epitomizing life against death, stands the blonde, beautiful, feminine Constance. She also stands against her sister Livia, dark and masculine, who prefers to live in Germany rather than France. Livia is the man–woman against whom Durrell wrote in his notebooks (perhaps in the person of one of his characters) with such passionate hatred. Blanford's psychological deterioration begins with his marriage to Livia, who inexplicably he chooses over the delectable Constance. Symbolically he has moved from light to darkness, like moving between the saintly Laura (Petrarch's Muse) and the diabolical Marquis de Sade, whose manuscripts are shown to him by Livia in the Avignon Museum. When Livia enthuses about Nazism, the connection to de Sade is obvious. Livia is perversely attracted to her sister Constance, and marrying Blanford, against her own deepest instincts, is a way of keeping her from him. She leaves Blanford for the black lesbian Thrush, and as a result of this deeply corrupting experience he comes of age both psychologically and as an artist. As in the *Quartet*, with Darley and Clea, Blanford will discover the healing properties of art, but not before being driven close to madness and suicide. In this he epitomizes Durrell's belief that to be great the creative artist must suffer. As the new age of the Prince of Darkness is about to descend on Europe, the Egyptian Prince Hassad holds a drunken revel beneath the Pont du Gard, complete with wild entertainments, whores and orgiastic junketing. If Aubrey Blanford and his friends and the whole of Europe are about to be buried alive, this is one final frail gesture against the encroaching darkness.

Larry was quite pleased with *Livia*, feeling that it had ironed out many of the questions left unanswered in *Monsieur*, and that it paved the way for the third of his five volumes, to be called *Constance in Love*. For the first time now he referred to his quinx as his *Avignon Quintet*,[17] or a *roman gigogne*, after the French word meaning a nest of small tables. At the same time he felt dissatisfied with the state of France – taken over by the petrol engine, wrecked by modern architecture and the sprawling, badly-constructed holiday apartments disfiguring the Mediterranean coastline, the growing swamp of tourists, the rising crime-rate, and, he complained, Paris dominated by Jewish intellectuals. England was no more attractive – exhausted of money and ideas, thanks to 'the people' having got too much above themselves.[18] He envied Miller his Brenda Venus, but comforted himself from time to time with young ladies who visited him to research his work or ask his advice. The author of *Justine* was still much sought after, and the line in poetic seduction continued to be persuasive.

The appearance of *Livia* in September brought careful and perceptive reviews in England from Richard Holmes[19] and Julian Barnes,[20] writers of a younger generation with a taste for Durrell's formal experimentation and literary versatility. And if reviewers had complained so often that Durrell revealed little of himself in his work, one reviewer, Keith Brown in the *TLS*, observed perceptively that in this new cycle of novels he was trying to cram into it every facet of himself and, without morbidity, to summarize everything from the viewpoint of death.[21]

What these reviewers had spotted so well were the retrospective and personal nature of the project, the confusion of realities, the confidence (despite his protests to the contrary) and professionalism, the sometimes tiresome devices and recognizable stereotypical characters, the jokey games-playing element, the rich outlay of language and the fascination with place – all achieved with a degree of magic and alchemy rare (certainly at that time) in fiction writing. All these things were there, not just in his work, but in his own character. However, the dark side of Durrell was also there, and Sappho is said to have reacted badly to it, believing that her father had taken her as his inspiration for Livia, the dark-haired lesbian who marries an English writer (discovered in a later volume of the *Quintet* to have hanged herself).

George Katsimbalis, the Colossus of Maroussi, who had been ill for a long time, finally died in October. Ironically, just before he died, this man, who had lived in modest circumstances most of his life, had sold his Athens house in Syntagma Square to a bank for such a vast amount of money that the income from the capital alone had, he told Durrell, been worth 'a Nobel Prize every year'. His name was duly inscribed beside that of his wife on Durrell's death-map, and he lamented that so few of his friends from the old days in Athens and Cairo now survived. The Nobel continued to obsess both him and Miller. It was awarded in 1978 to Isaac Bashevis Singer, a writer whom they both admired. Durrell told Miller that a man from the committee whom he had met in Hamburg had told him that they had to wait until Miller became respectable.[22] Miller told Durrell not to worry; he was planning his application for the following year.[23] In any case, one of the committee now was Artur Lundkvist, the Swedish poet, who had appeared in the *Booster*, but who Miller believed he had offended in some way.

Despite his strangely cruel relationship with Sappho, and his apparent dislike of Simon, Durrell put up half the money, together with the young man's father, for them to buy a somewhat dilapidated house at 39 Loraine Road in north London, which they planned to renovate before renting out rooms to friends. In the following year, Sappho gave up her job at Weidenfeld and went freelance as a book editor. It was a difficult time for her, and this is where, friends believed, her problems began. The squalor of the house depressed her and she was unable to write. A neighbour, Barbara Robson (a researcher for the right-wing Institute for Economic Affairs), would visit her, bringing her work along; but Sappho preferred to gossip rather than work. She had four abortions in the following eighteen months, according to Robson, who added, 'First of all she didn't want a child, then she switched to desperately wanting a child.'[24] Simon believed that it was at this time that 'she began to crack up'.

The end of Durrell's marriage left him feeling even more bitter about women, especially in an age of feminism, and he was determined not to marry again. The sexual freedoms he and Miller had always advocated had not necessarily meant equal freedoms for women. If Sappho came to blame her father for her mounting difficulties, she took her revenge a year later by telling a Paris newspaper that it was because her father worked so compulsively that all his wives had fled from him.

In March 1978, there was court hearing to fix the amount

of alimony he would have to pay Ghislaine. As they left the building, Ghislaine noticed that he was crying, and she said, 'Please, Larry, don't cry. It'll be better like this. I'm sad, too, but we'll try to be good friends.' And he said, 'I'm not crying about divorcing you. It's the alimony I'm going to have to pay you that I'm crying about.' To her surprise, she found herself laughing.[25]

Faber had now told him they wanted a new *Collected Poems* from him, a true 'collection', and he was thrilled. He had always felt more pride in his poetry than in his fiction. But the novels had eclipsed his verse, and now he felt they could be brought right out of the shadows once and for all. When that was done, he thought, he would take his time, but focus all his efforts on finishing his quincunx. At sixty-six, he felt that his system was slowing down, though he could sustain a good head stand at yoga for up to an hour, and had kicked smoking, if not the local *vin rouge* which he enjoyed so much. He could also spare more time for his brother, Gerry, who was busily renovating the mazet, and hoping to marry a young American, Lee McGeorge, whom he had met on a visit to an American university and lured to Jersey on the pretext of her doing research there. Gerry continued to travel and write, though the book he was about to publish, *The Garden of the Gods*, was another fond look back at the family's years in Corfu. Of the rest of the family, Margo was still living in St Alban's Avenue with her two boys, planning to visit Gerry at the mazet, and said to be writing a book; and Leslie was acting as a janitor in a block of London flats at Marble Arch, no longer on Larry's or anybody else's visiting list apparently.

In Paris that autumn, Durrell was pinned down and interviewed for the *International Herald Tribune* at the Café Dôme in Montparnasse. He said that like Miller he was uninterested in politics, and held to the Gnostic view that emphasized 'the superiority of evil forces over good in the material world and the secretiveness of salvation'. Of the quincunx, he said, he hoped to complete *Constance* during the coming winter and wanted to achieve novels where 'it wouldn't matter if bits of the narrative stopped suddenly'. 'It would be planned of course – all art has to be planned – but

it would be non-deterministic in the Einsteinian sense. It might
be a new form, a new animal, in any case it would breathe.' The
analogy to breathing was important to him, he said, because he
suffered from asthma, though yoga gave him a great deal of
relief, and had even helped him give up smoking. But a novelist's life was monotonous, and (perhaps here he was trying to
gloss over Sappho's comment on his marriages) that was why
his wives ran away – they could not stand the monotony of
the novelist's life. He talked a lot about getting old and about
time running out for him, and admitted also that *Constance*
was weighing him down somewhat. Afterwards he wanted to
write a comic novel. The prospect of that comic novel seems
to have been, as yoga was to his breathing, a help in bearing
the pressure of intense creativity. He would like the resolution
of his quincunx to be a celebration.[26]

To break out of the monotony of novel writing and the
melancholy of living alone in the haunted house with the owls,
he went to spend Christmas with Gerry and Lee. After that he
went alone to Paris and checked into his favourite Room 13
at the Hôtel Royale at Montparnasse. He saw the New Year
in at the Coupole on the same bar seats he had once shared
with Miller and Perlès. Ghislaine joined him for champagne at
midnight; and afterwards Buttons, his old flame of ten years'
standing, spent the night with him. He had hopes for a young
Arab Canadian whom he had already bedded but who had
been dragged off by her boyfriend. North American girls, he
thought, were so brutalized by their men that they were grateful
for the slightest show of sensitivity and kindness, though they
made oversentimental, robotic lovers. There was also a twenty-
year-old French concert pianist.[27] Ironically, one of these
'younglings' he took to bed in Paris wore a haunting perfume
and, asked what it was, said it was called 'Anaïs'.

Miller, eighty-seven on Boxing Day, reported himself still
insanely enamoured of Brenda Venus – they were so compat-
ible. He was sorry that Durrell was feeling melancholic, and
quoted Wallace Stevens to him: 'Death is the mother of Beauty.'
That obsession, which Durrell more and more reiterated, about
falling apart as age encroached, was something he knew all
about. But, as for Durrell, he was a mere stripling.[28] However,

when Durrell wrote in the new year listing some of his young conquests, Miller expressed surprise that he was still avid for 'cunts' and hazarded that he was still proving his manhood in some way. When, he wondered, would his young friend start searching for something more permanent?[29]

The melancholy which Miller had detected was a life long sensation with Durrell. Sometimes he succumbed to it with sentimentality, at others he displaced it by aggression, literary as well as physical. Having some deep cysts removed from his back by a surgeon under local anaesthetic in Geneva (the surgeon who had done the final operation on Claude) he was led to remember the roses and oleander which Claude had planted at the mazet. They had somehow taken root in the rather stony soil around the house, and Gerry was intent on reviving them now he was buying the place. It led Larry to think of Miller's last visit there when they both over-indulged.[30] But his mood was not all nostalgia; in March 1979 he wrote a tirade against what Perlès called their grovelling 'coprophagous' writer contemporaries.[31] He was still out of step with the scribes and critics of Pudding Island.

While Larry worked at *Constance*, Sappho had a nervous breakdown and was in hospital for a week. It was so dramatic that Simon suspected she was schizophrenic, later recalling that 'She had visual hallucinations. She couldn't go outside the house because people appeared to be animals biting at her.' In April, shortly after her release from hospital, she began a series of sessions with a Hampstead psychoanalyst, Patrick Casement. From the notes she made during her course of treatment, it is evident that she was focusing all her anguish on her relationship with her father, implying something unhealthy in it, frequently referring to 'incest' – either metaphorical or mental. To Simon and some of her friends she said she had a 'buried' memory of incest.[32] Later she told him it was more 'psychological incest' than the real thing. Meanwhile the subject of her anguish visited Vienna and no doubt paid homage to Freud on the way through. Exactly how he felt about Sappho's breakdown is not clear, except that his letters to her seem less than sympathetic, and were often cruel, as if, as in the case of Eve earlier, he could nurse his own madness, but entirely lack understanding for that of others. It is likely that what he saw happening to Sappho presented him with an image of himself, and he found it extremely difficult to cope with.

Metaphorical incest was the theme of at least one of the reviews of *Livia* when it came out in America in the spring. Some reviewers admired the way he had disarmed his critics, making their own points for them by citing them against his own fictional authors. And despite finding lamentable his procession of sexual deviants and grotesques, better left perhaps to Fellini, they felt that Durrell remained irreplaceable as a master of English and European literature.[33]

Itchy feet took him off to Greece again in his camper that spring – no doubt in search of romantic adventures. Meanwhile Sappho was telling her analyst that her relationship with Durrell had been 'fucked up' after Claude's death, when her father had substituted her for his wife. Before, he had accepted that she was 'different' when she withdrew; afterwards he turned his aggression on her with 'hostile silences' and bitchiness, knowing just how to destroy her psychologically. She thought that as his life became more empty he could not stop getting at her. She was scared of him physically, and referred to something mysterious which had happened to her in Greece in 1965, when she was fourteen. On 9 May 1979, she recorded in her diary that she had had a miscarriage. She also recorded her father's equating sex with sadism, and his calling her 'a monstrosity'. Although she had played at lesbianism, she affirmed her heterosexuality, yet felt that neither was for her and she was reduced simply to flirting. Because her father was sleeping with women of her age and younger she felt threatened, but recognized that she had difficulty separating myth from reality. She blamed her parents for giving her a name which encouraged the belief that she was a lesbian, even though she had sometimes encouraged other women.[34]

Sappho must have been lecturing her father about morals, because she mentions him referring to her having the super-ego of a rat. But she had developed a political conscience over the years, and when the Conservatives were elected under Margaret Thatcher in May 1979 she observed that the Pudding

Islanders had signed their own death warrants. Despite her feeling of intense antagonism towards her father, she seemed to want to spend time with him in Sommières even though she probably knew there would be confrontation and he would leave her feeling wretched.[35] In mid-June, she went on what she called a 'Cold Turkey weekend' where she talked to other 'sufferers' and to therapists about her problems with men. Because she was terrified of them she felt drawn to anyone who was traumatized by sex (like the characters in *The Alexandria Quartet*). The fact that her father slept with prostitutes and very young women while being simultaneously puritanical and prurient about female sexuality outraged her. He was, she wrote, 'a creep'. There was a malevolent father and a benevolent one, one of whom wished to destroy her – perhaps by dragging her with him in a suicide – because, in her female aspect, he had to destroy what he loved and because, in her male aspect, she was a threat he had to eliminate.[36] In July he told her that she was attempting to develop a male appendage.[37] She believed his letters were cryptic and wrote over them, adding her own interpretations, as if he were sending her aggressive or self-pitying messages concealed in them, even seeing a sexual connotation to his writing about cysts, goitres and cancers in men.

During October, while still undergoing analysis with Patrick Casement, Sappho drafted her will in her diary. Her share of the house in Loraine Road and her books were to go to her mother, and if that were not possible, then to her boyfriend, Simon. A few things she left to the children of her neighbour, Barbara Robson. She asked to be buried in the churchyard at Steep, a small village close to Bedales, her school in Hampshire. Then she began to read papers on father–daughter incest with the aim, she said, of writing an article on the subject for the feminist magazine *Spare Rib*, under the pseudonym Vivien Gantry. She was also writing for *Time Out* under the names Frances Duarte and Mr Latimer. She considered training to be an analyst herself and became a secretary at the Psychiatric Rehabilitation Association, later taking on responsibility for disturbed teenagers. But office politics upset her and she left. Thereafter she got work reviewing plays for *City Limits*.

Although she visited Sommières in December, she did not, it seems, stay for Christmas.[38] *Constance* was proving an awkward child to deliver, and perhaps her father was not easy to be with. He said a little later that writing made him grouchy; from Sappho's side of the equation it made him cruelly determined to destroy her as a person and a writer. In January 1980, she applied for a booklet giving details of the Society for the Right to Die with Dignity, and disappeared to a Carmelite retreat in the guise of Vivien Gantry for a period of contemplation.[39] If he knew of her agonies there is little evidence that he lost any sleep over them, probably putting them down, as he had with Eve, to religious hysteria or reading some cold Freudian message into them.

Durrell spent Christmas in Paris again, this time with a thirty-one year-old French doctor called Nicole, whom he had met at a music festival in the summer. She was an intellectual, with a tormented look, and in bondage to 'black psychiatry' – her only fault, he thought. If there was any psychiatry going around he wanted it to be in his own hands. But, as he was in the throes of writing *Constance*, about his own slave to psychiatry, his young French intellectual must have been a valuable subject to draw into a degree of creative symbiosis. They spent most of Christmas day in bed together – no doubt in Room 13 of the Royale.[40]

As a rest from his own act of 'black psychiatry' – writing the quincunx – he had written a book about his association with Jolan Chang, coupled with a cryptic account of a perfect Taoist love affair with a mysterious woman he called 'Vega' – almost certainly Claude Kieffer. The book, called *A Smile in the Mind's Eye*, was published in London by Wildwood House in the following year, and also contained a very moving account of the death of his wife Claude – the presence that continued to haunt.

The survivors of the *Personal Landscape* days were now very thin on the ground, and became more so when G. S. Fraser died on 3 January. Meanwhile Miller, inspired to keep going by his love for Brenda Venus, felt able to be blunt with his old pupil, saying that his trouble with women was, he suspected, an inability to fulfil himself through right and faithful love; being tolerant, not scolding or carping. Did that, he asked, strike a chord? No doubt it did, though whether Durrell heard it is questionable.[41] The American was, in fact, remarkably aware of his own approaching death, and was able to write about it dispassionately. When Durrell told him he was going to Greece in the spring, Miller wrote implying that *he* was heading in a different direction. In fact he had allowed a French television crew to film him on his deathbed, where he gave a lively, defiant but moving performance. He wrote telling Durrell about this, hoping that he would get to see the last watercolours he had painted. That was on 8 May. It was his last letter to Durrell. He died a month later on 7 June.

There can be no doubt of the major role which Miller played in Durrell's career. Discovering *Tropic of Cancer* was probably the big turning-point in his life. The American's freewheeling, untrammelled, bawdy imagination gave him a model even more unlaced and pugnaciously rebellious than D.H. Lawrence. If *The Black Book* was to a degree parasitic on Durrell's new-found father-surrogate, it also enabled him to find his own voice and gain self-confidence as a writer. Thereafter he developed and matured in a way that Miller did not, so much so that Durrell could brutally criticize Miller when he found *Sexus* deplorably obscene. And although Durrell himself later wrote passages of extremely graphic and often sadistic sex, he continued to disapprove of what he considered cheap and crude titillation. But Miller was more than just an influence on him, he was for some forty-five years his confidant and unfailing supporter, and helped him, with his publishing contacts, to enhance his reputation. Not having Miller there would leave a great gap in Durrell's life, and his death brought to an end one of the most sustained and remarkable correspondences in modern literary history.

CHAPTER 18

The Avignon Quintet: The Mystery of the Quincunx

(1980–1985)

I advance trembling as in a darkened cave
and I am frightened of losing my reader,
my editor, everything.

Lawrence Durrell, 1984

By the summer of 1980, Durrell was back from Greece, but probably still had not hauled *Constance* fully out of the bog. So when Sappho phoned to talk about a possible visit to Sommières with some friends who were bound for India, she complained about his being cantankerous with her and talking to her in a form of code which only made her feel more agitated. As he hated visitors (except those close to him) he was no doubt trying to discourage her from bringing a group of her hippy friends to the house. However, he was due in London in September when his Taoist book and his *Collected Poems* were to be published, so she asked him to keep at least one evening free for a liquid supper with them at 39 Loraine Road. His agent at Curtis Brown, Anthea Morton-Saner, had arranged for him to have a friend's flat during his visit, but Sappho said if that fell through he was welcome to stay with her and Simon, even though they were knocking walls down and in rather a mess. She hoped that he would bury all his hatchets for good and try to make a phonecall from her sound at least agreeable to him. He seemed not to realize how hurtful she found his attitude towards her.[1]

She told her analyst about extreme feelings of destructiveness which she did not know how to contain, and hoped that when she got a more lucrative job, she would be able to afford more thorough analysis. However, she felt rather better than she had the previous year, she said.[2]

Durrell would have known all about his daughter's feelings of violence; he could generate them at will. He continued to follow the same old routine, rising at 4.30 a.m. The only exception was when Gerry came over from the mazet for a convivial evening, and they stayed up late. Mostly he got to bed at nine. He told the *Sunday Times* in October that first thing in the morning, he did his stint of yoga – the lotus position in headstand usually – then a shave and coffee before looking to see what he had written the day before and putting his notes in order. Then he sat down to watch the sun come up – something he had done for the previous fifteen years. He went out at 6 a.m. to get his croissants hot at the boulangerie, and at 8.30 a.m. collected his mail, returning to the house to answer it. His cleaner, now someone called Ellen (a singer and pianist, he said), arrived at nine and left at midday. When he was busy writing, as he was most mornings, she would make him some rice to which he would add vegetables and eat camping fashion. He was not exactly a vegetarian, but through yoga he was able to control his passion for meat. He had also managed to cut down on alcohol – except red wine. After lunch he would take a walk on the garrigue or do some gardening, though he preferred his garden to be a jungle to remind him of Darjeeling. At other times he would paint or compose jazz at the piano.

He had now set himself a daily total of a thousand words, aiming to build up the first draft of a novel in two months. After that, he settled to cutting and polishing. Novel writing, as always, put him in a bad temper, but *Constance*, which he was halfway through by mid-September, was a crucial book for him, being the centre-point of the whole novel cycle.

For the past few years, he said, he had tried (not always successfully) to get to Greece in his Volkswagen camper *L'Escargot*, and to England twice a year, staying with one or other of his daughters – for just long enough not to incur tax there.

(Penny was now Penelope Durrell Walker, married to a sculptor and living some of the time in Ireland.) In summer he was on the move, doing his research, trawling and note-taking. He went to Paris every two months to give interviews and see friends. 'When I come back, it's rather my Diogenes' tub', he said. Diogenes the Cynic taught moral freedom and liberation from desire, and the idea of living in a tub, like Diogenes, would have appealed to him enormously. In fact he claimed to be 'addicted to solitude', and was pleased that 'the inhabitants of the village protect me by misdirecting people who come here to see me'. When he had a chance to read – usually in bed at night – he studied mostly philosophers and scientists. 'The *Scientific American* should be on every poet's desk', he said. He read little fiction, though he admired Saul Bellow and John Fowles, but he did not have television – 'like having a sick child in the house'. Going to bed early was to make up for abusing himself by staying awake all night as a young man.[3]

On 13 September, Sappho got married to Simon at Islington Town Hall. It was later implied that she married in the hope of keeping together a relationship which already showed signs of falling apart. Simon even commented, 'It was a goodbye present'. She had spent the preceding months dieting to get her weight down to look trim, and wore tight-fitting red jeans with a matching silk jacket; the wedding party was held in the garden at Loraine Road. Her friend Mrs Robson's husband acted as best man. Neither of her parents attended.[4] However, she saw her father for that liquid supper when he visited London on the 18th for the publication of *A Smile in the Mind's Eye* and his *Collected Poems*, and thought he looked on top form – probably healthier than she was. She seemed quite cheerful in October, responding to an unsympathetic letter from him telling her that her illness was simply *her* trying to replay and exorcise her mother's previous crackup in Belgrade. There was no suggestion of her having to re-enact *his* previous crackup in Argentina. However, she thought his letter was charming and affectionate. When he wrote to her describing his ideal woman, a cross between 'Madame Mignot' (Mignon, La Bonne Atomique) and Xanthippe (Socrates' wife, renowned as a scold), to keep him upright and feed him in his

Diogenes tub, she asked where he would find this paragon – perhaps among his many dazzling female correspondents? In any case, she gave him an invitation to stay with them for Christmas, though more in hope, it seems, than in expectation.

Despite Sappho's invitation, Durrell spent Christmas in Sommières, visited once by Paddy Leigh Fermor and his wife. In the New Year he could look forward to the publication of another correspondence – this time letters between himself and Richard Aldington. It is striking that so much of Durrell's correspondence survived, no doubt because that bubbling mind spread itself with such force and vividness upon the paper that the recipients felt the letters were worth preserving. The Aldington–Durrell correspondence, published as *Literary Life-lines*, reached back in a tenuous way to that youthful letter of enquiry to his literary hero in 1933, quizzing him about the Imagists, Lawrence and Pound, and to Aldington's reply which begins the collection.[5]

The Americans saw the collection first, in May 1981, and seemed to think it 'quietly moving' and 'satisfying'[6] or 'hugely entertaining' and 'funny'.[7] In Britain in June, critics took both men to task for their elitism, their bragging and their corroded prejudices, especially Aldington. In the *Sunday Times*, John Carey wrote scathingly that 'Aldington comes across as a man so charged with venom that it would be risky to let him out of doors lest he blight the crops'. He could only suppose that the 'exemplary tact' which Durrell displayed in responding to 'this rancid flow' was due to his diplomatic training.[8] A kinder note was struck by George Hill in *The Times*, who said, 'These letters are less self-interested than most . . . It says much for Durrell that the friendship survived the test of his own rise to a success greater than Aldington had ever enjoyed', and he was amused how these impoverished authors alerted one another to 'the excellent new wheeze of selling old papers to the American scholarly industry'.[9]

The French love affair with Durrell continued, and in March Ghislaine was told by a friend that Larry would be lecturing at the Pompidou Centre in Paris. Jean Fanchette was in the chair, and it turned out to be an odd occasion, at which Durrell gave a lecture entitled 'From an Elephant's Back' – an idea taken from the story of Ramon Gomez de Serna told him by George Seferis in Cairo in 1942. From that perspective, he lectured about his Indian childhood and early life, illustrating with slides as he went along. When he announced a slide as, say, 'This is me as a boy in Darjeeling', up came a picture of Durrell drinking. At first the audience thought it was a mistake. But the next slide ('And this is me with my ayah in Jullundur') was another picture of Durrell drinking. Now it was an amusing bit of self-mockery, not unappreciated by the audience. Afterwards, outside the lecture hall, he caught sight of his ex-wife. 'What the hell are you doing here?' he asked furiously. 'I'm sorry', she replied, determined not to be worsted. 'I thought William Styron was speaking'.[10]

Sappho continued to be unwell, complaining to her diary in June about the sickening egocentricity of men. Only a few homosexuals and poets escaped her contempt. This seems to have been prompted by a falling out with her husband, about whom she felt, for the time being, bitter.[11] She was still not feeling good about her father either, and on 6 July, during a visit to Sommières when he must again have savaged her nerves, she wrote in her diary that, if her father ever asked to be interred with her, his request should be refused.[12] On her return to London, however, she was thanking him for an enjoyable and invigorating time, and regretted not being able to stay longer. Her mood seemed buoyant, and she recommended him to read Salman Rushdie's *Midnight's Children*, and to get a recording of Mozart's *Cosi Fan Tutte* with Karl Böhm and Elizabeth Schwartzkopf.[13] In the autumn he sent her a package of press reviews of his books, letters from family members, and love letters from fans – all of which she found very embarrassing.[14]

In Paris in August for the publication of the French edition of *Livia*, Durrell was cornered at the Café Dôme by a French journalist, Eric Ollivier from *L'Express*. Ollivier thought him large and colourful, like a Holbein portrait, yet 'blond, tough and agile ... like a man of action, a robust countryman with large hands'. His French, he thought, was perfect, but with an English accent mixed with southern intonations. He looked to him like the ideal European, and yet, sitting there at his table, he was unstylishly dressed, like something from pre-war Paris – and he carried his possessions around in a string bag. Montparnasse, said Durrell, was one of his favourite villages, and when he came he stayed always at the same hotel, Room 13. He said that 'all artists are hysterics, hence the alcohol and the rest, because, if one were well-balanced one would write nothing'. Now, he claimed, he had learned to live independently of women and was celibate; he had even given up his legendary feasting and drinking, except for good glassfuls of red wine. Of his complete oeuvre he said, 'After my death the whole collection of my books will have the air of a family, the characters wandering from one novel to another.[15]

The Durrell industry, the academic interest in him which had begun at least with Lawrence Clark Powell in the 1940s, had gathered momentum over the years. There was now a Lawrence Durrell Society and a *Lawrence Durrell Newsletter*, about to become *Deus Loci: The Lawrence Durrell Quarterly*. In April 1980 a first Lawrence Durrell Conference, entitled 'On Miracle Ground', had been held in New York. Now in the fall of 1981 a Lawrence Durrell Conference was to be held at the State University of New York in Albany to which Durrell was invited. He excused himself saying that he had to go to Vienna to complete a 'think-piece' for *The Times*. His feelings about academics were ambiguous. He had little respect for them, but sometimes they impressed him. He joked that they were trying to make him posthumous before his death and that they seemed convinced (unlike him) that he was going to bring the *Quintet* off. One scholar had discovered some of his many sources, he told David Pryce-Jones. 'Apparently I've put into the novels bits and pieces borrowed from here, there and everywhere, without knowing where it comes from. There's a word for it, cryptamnesia, I think. Now these two chaps come along and tell me what I've pinched.'[16] With *Constance* still unfinished, probably the last thing he wanted to do was to divert to North America to meet so many enthusiasts. Gerry, on the other hand, had recently gone happily to America to marry his American, Lee, in Memphis, Tennessee 'on a carpet of wild strawberries and violets'.[17] But America would not be starved of brother

Larry altogether. Over December and the New Year, KPFA, the North Hollywood radio station, devoted seven days of radio to Durrell and *The Alexandria Quartet*.

Rather than Vienna, it was to Greece that he escaped from the toils of the *Quintet*. He took off in *L'Escargot* for Corfu again, leaving his address as 'post restante', which Sappho complained made it sound as though he owned the whole island. By returning to Prospero's Cell he became something of a tourist attraction himself and was considered attractive by enough young holidaying women to satisfy his ever-present lusts. When necessary he could also find the solitude to work on his novel. And he did not need to use hotels, although he had a favourite one in Corfu town. The camper was his home when he needed it, and he was happy to live the gypsy life. For him it must have been very much as it had been in the late 1930s, except that he now worried about his failing strength and talked not about having asthma but of having emphysema – something far more deadly. Perlès thought it was psychosomatic (a good Groddeckian diagnosis) and wondered why all such diseases had Greek names.[18] But in February 1982 Durrell had reached seventy, and, whatever the state of his health, he was able to continue sending news to Perlès of his most recent amatory adventures, so that his old friend wrote asking whether it was his yoga exercises which gave him his incredible erections.[19]

After his Greek trip, work on the quincunx kept him occupied well into the year. As he drove the complicated and lengthy *Constance* towards its conclusion, notions of madness and death loomed large in his mind. He was struck by the familiar graffito written on a wall in Nîmes near the Amphitheatre, reading, 'Skinheads rule! . . . Yes! Yes! Madness reigns! . . . Kill everyone! Yes! Yes!' The exterminatory message he would have found appalling to contemplate, but the comment on the mental state of the world he would probably have agreed with.[20] However, that year, the British had become briefly sane and included him in the top twenty contemporary writers in a Best of British exhibition in London.

By the spring, Sappho's husband Simon had taken a new job in York, and came home rarely, finding her more and more difficult to cope with. Now she was (like her father before her) advertising in lonely-hearts columns: in *Time Out*, the London listings magazine, she stated her interests as 'theatre, poetry, cinema, psychology, writing . . . classical and some contemporary music, dance and some opera'. But she was very clear that with men over forty she could only contemplate friendship. She signed herself Vivien Gantry.[21]

Suddenly Durrell became aware that, in trying to bring his quincunx to a satisfactory conclusion, he was drinking too much – as much as a bottle of whisky a day[22] – which brought on a series of 'grave hepatic crises' or black-outs,[23] probably the onset of drink-induced epileptic seizures from which he suffered more as time went on. He realized that he was in danger of killing himself before his task was completed, so he consulted a Victnamese doctor who practised acupuncture. She stuck 'drawing pins' all over him, he said, and he was cured. For stretches of a whole year he claimed not to have touched a drop of alcohol, though, while he might have kicked whisky, he did sometimes turn his spring water into wine.

That summer of 1982, a journalist from the *Sunday Telegraph* visited him and strangely Durrell declared himself 'separated' from Ghislaine rather than divorced from her. The new sequence of novels, he said, was 'a whodunnit, an everyonedunnit, using every sort of cunning thing I can lay my hands on to do a progress of the soul in the 20th century'. All the grotesque scenes – eating dry mummy flesh, heads in boxes – were all 'pure pantomime', Dickensian fustian, just to have some fun. Then, as if to comment on that scholarly interest in his work, he added, 'As with Joyce, there's not a serious word in it.' He thought that he had about three or four working years left in him. And after Gerald's various books on the family, he said, both Leslie and Margo were planning autobiographies. 'We're the poor man's Brontës.[24] But sadly, if Leslie had had a book in mind, he would never write it. On Friday 13 August, Durrell's gun-toting Prodigal Brother, the Kenyan settler and self-styled civil engineer, prone to confidence trickery, who had been living near Notting Hill Gate for the past five years, died suddenly of a heart attack in a pub close to his home. He was sixty-five. The names on the death-map were crowding in on the obsessive author.

By this time, Durrell had finished *Constance, or Solitary Practices* and Faber were trying to rush it out in October to be in time for the annual Booker Award.

Avignon under the Nazi occupation is the background to *Constance, or Solitary Practices.* Here Durrell put to use all he had gleaned from his friends at the city's lunch club, to produce as convincing a portrait of those times as one might find. Despite his inclination to wallow in details of sadistic cruelty, here we meet Durrell at his most humane, for it is evident which side he is on – the side of life and light against death and the realm of Darkness. The Nazi philosophy, expounded by the ideologist Smirgel, is, like Gnosticism, directed against conventional Judaeo-Christian culture, but offering instead unrestrained evil rather than a life-enhancing philosophy of light and love. In the book, Hitler has set out to recreate the order of Knights Templar, but as a black rather than a white order. And Nazism is *merde* culture taken to its evil utmost, its sexuality expressing itself in the sadistic rather than the celebratory orgasmic terms of the Gnostics. The German General von Esslin and the Gestapo Chief Fischer are embodiments of this destructive philosophy.

In dealing with the Nazis in the novel, and by contrasting them with characters like Nancy Quiminal, who exchanges sex for the lives of her children and others, Durrell is able to imply the kind of society of which he approves – one in which the horrors of Nazism are forever banished and which works against the *merde* culture of capitalism (the realm of the Prince of Darkness) in favour of a *sperm* culture where human happiness is achieved through health-giving sex. The doctor he once hoped to be now expressed himself through grand prescriptions for human welfare, through the alternative perspectives of heretical religion and mystical sex.

Von Esslin is blinded, Sam, Constance's husband, has been killed and Blanford's legs are paralysed in an accident in the Egyptian desert, while Constance escapes to work for the Red Cross in Geneva. As a Red Cross worker she returns to France and her old château, where she meets her sister Livia, now working as a nurse at the nearby asylum. Livia, who has lost an eye in a failed suicide attempt, hangs herself. (We learn later that she has had an incestuous affair with her brother Hilary, who is guillotined in front of her.) Constance returns to Geneva and meets Affad who introduces her to the ecstatic mysteries of Gnostic sex and his theories about a civilization based on sperm rather than excrement. It is oriental thought advancing upon western scientific philosophy. She, the Freudian analyst, has somehow to accept it into her scheme of things. It is Lawrence, de Rougemont and Chang in three dimensions, perhaps five, since this is a quincunx. It is no accident that his heroine-initiate is called Constance, nor that the lady's lover embraces a mystical belief in sex. But Affad and Constance are unable to achieve what the theory demands – the fusion of opposites, and in their solitary practices find themselves engaged in a struggle for control. Durrell seems to be saying that a return to sexual innocence is unachievable in the west. And, as if to confirm this, as Avignon is liberated, the tragic Nancy Quiminal (her sacrifice unknown) is executed as the lover of a Nazi and her true sacrifice is swamped in a wave of revengeful bloodlust.

To his delight *Constance* was shortlisted for the Booker. Claire Tomalin, reviewing all six finalists in the *Sunday Times*, counted in it three female suicides, two by women whom the reader knew only through their performances in bed, and one horrible murder of a woman – Nancy Quiminal, mistakenly thought to be a collaborator. The evident sexism of the book was left for the reader to deduce, but Tomalin judged it yet another repeat performance. 'Durrell, now 70, is a magician, who has plucked his multi-coloured silk scarves out of the air many times. But we have seen it before, and are not fooled for a moment that it is more than a skilfully repeated trick.'[25] Thomas Keneally's *Schindler's Ark* won the £10,000 prize. Alf Perlès wrote, saying that Durrell's book was 'too good for the Booker'. He also wrote just after Christmas to declare that there was really only one musketeer, and that was Durrell. Old 'Joey' was doffing his hat to the 'magician'.

One day, early that winter, Durrell and Jacques Lacarrière were driving aimlessly around the French countryside in the heart of the Morvan mountains, discussing the Tibetan poet Mila Repa, when down a country road they overtook two Buddhist lamas, making their way to the Château de Plaige near Dijon, a Buddhist study centre since 1974. The monks were offered a lift, and the two men were invited to see the place – christened Kangû-Ling by its founder, the eighty-year-old Abbot, Venerable Kalou Rinpotché, a 'master of the higher insight', based, of all places, in Darjeeling. Finally, it seemed, those mysterious peripatetic Darjeeling Buddhists whom Durrell had watched as a child had ended their journeying and arrived in much the same place as himself. Highly symbolic – even heraldic! There they met Lama Sherab, the Tibetan lama in charge, and yet another strange fact emerged: the Buddhist teaching at Kangû-Ling was inspired by Mila Repa. Durrell was delighted. The atmosphere was very much to his taste: the ghost of Original Sin, it seemed, had been thoroughly exorcised by these gentle people. He became a not-infrequent visitor to the place, imbibing their teaching and coming to see himself as more of a Buddhist than anything else. And he began to see his quincunx as an expression of Buddhist thought.

Gerald was awarded the OBE in the New Year's Honours List, and, unlike his eldest brother, happily accepted. If there was to be no honour for Larry in Britain that year, there was one for him in France that April when a *Hommage to Lawrence Durrell* was mounted in Lyons, which included paintings by Oscar Epfs, photographs of his *alter ego*, Durrell, and paintings by other artists inspired by his work. And if monetary value can be regarded as an honour, then his manuscripts were certainly honoured in the market place. In early 1983, the University of Southern Illinois paid $6,000 for seven Durrell letters.

Less happily for Larry, the first six months of 1983 brought three deaths to add to his death-map. Theodore Stephanides died in April, and both Nancy and Tambimuttu died in June. In one fell swoop he lost his last surviving father-surrogate, his first wife and a favourite editor. Later that year he almost lost someone even closer to him. That autumn, Sappho became ill again, in November taking an overdose of sleeping pills. But she phoned her mother and was quickly taken to hospital and had her stomach pumped. She told Barbara Robson, who visited her, that she knew she had been silly and would not do it again because she had to go on living.[26]

The fourth of his five Avignon novels was shorter than the previous three, and written at speed. Its style was sparer than that of the others and the form simpler, more chronological. By now he probably saw where the whole thing was leading, and so *Sebastian, or Ruling Passions* smoothly embraced at least two new themes and set the scene for the conclusion of the whole cycle. The eponymous central character is the Egyptian Gnostic Akkad in *Monsieur, or the Prince of Darkness* transformed into Affad in the subsequent parts of the *Quintet*. It is his renunciation of his Gnostic membership under the influence of his love for Constance, followed by his change of heart, which precipitates the crisis at the centre of this novel. He has resigned too late; the letter announcing his death has already been despatched, his executioner given his orders. He pleads to be reinstated, and is assured that his Gnostic suicide, for which he now lusts, has been restored, and he is happy. But he may not say his farewells to Constance and is riven by the two ruling passions of love and death. He does return to Geneva and Constance, but the rigidity of his beliefs now makes it impossible for him to abandon himself to what is natural and spontaneous. Constance has had a disturbing influence on him, as she has on Mnemidis, a paranoid-schizophrenic she is treating, who sets out to kill her, thinking she has poisoned him. Just as Affad rejects Christianity on Gnostic grounds, so too does the sadistic madman Mnemidis, bringer of death and darkness like the Nazis.

Lord Galen, the Jewish tycoon who first appeared in *Monsieur*, naively bankrolling Hitler, is now the designated Co-ordinator of Co-ordinated Cultures in search of the cultural cornerstones for the reconstruction of western civilization – much as others have been, throughout the *Quintet*, in search of the hidden treasure of the Templars for their own ends. He seems to suspect that Joyce's *Ulysses* is anti-semitic. But Blanford sees the novel as a true cultural cornerstone insomuch as Leopold Bloom is there given the role of desecrating the death-oriented, blood-worshipping Christian Church (so destructive of sexual tenderness). Galen's ludicrous effort to sample western culture in the flesh, in a brothel orgy, culminates in his mock crucifixion, symbolic of decadent occidental sexuality.

If finally Gnosticism offers only suicide, if Galen has no answers, then nor has psychoanalysis in the persons of Constance and her colleague Schwarz. Schwarz's wife is about to return from a concentration camp, and his feeling of guilt about her suffering leads to his suicide. Constance has no cure for Mnemidis (who kills Affad in mistake for Constance – more echoes of the *Quartet*), although she does cure Affad's young son of autism – by accident rather than by psychoanalytical design, when he smells her perfume, the one his mother also wore, 'Jamais de la Vie', the perfume worn by Justine in the *Quartet*. The cure comes about, therefore, not through western science, but through an accident of nature – the very force to which Durrell believes the western mind should be ever open if it wishes to save itself. Accepting such possibilities is also Constance's salvation. It is worth remembering that at the time he wrote *Sebastian, or Ruling Passions* he was rediscovering Buddhism. Now the dominant presences in his thinking were Freud and Lawrence and an oriental philosophy of acceptance.

Sebastian was given a good reception in Britain. It was as if the serious critics now realized that they had in the offing yet another, and doubtless the last, major work from Durrell. Nicholas Shrimpton in the *Sunday Times* thought something momentous was coming from Durrell. 'He overwrites. He sentimentalises. He has a weakness for theories (particularly about sex) of an almost Lawrentian looniness. As if this weren't bad enough, he works in a form – the *roman fleuve* – which is supposedly outmoded. The awkward fact remains that Lawrence Durrell now seems to be four-fifths of the way through one of the greatest novels of our time . . .'

Durrell woke one day, he said, and saw Buddhist lamas in his garden. His friend Lama Sherab from Kangû-Ling had arrived to ask his help to raise funds to complete the temple they had started to construct on the wish of Kalou Rinpotché in Darjeeling. Durrell agreed to set up a committee to help, and roped in brother Gerry and Jacques Lacarrière. They came up with a few gimmicks for raising money, such as encouraging people who gave money for the temple to plant a lotus flower bearing the name of a loved one. Also Durrell, somewhat against the miserly grain, contributed funds of his own. It was joked later that he probably put an extra zero on the cheque by mistake.[27]

At work now on the final volume of the quincunx, which he called *Quinx or the Ripper's Tale*, he was as usual uncertain if he would bring off the completion of so ambitious a work. Under the pressure of creative madness, but with nobody to take it out on, he laboured under the melancholic weight of increasing age and the feeling at times of being unable to breathe. Oxygenation was the cure, plus yogic meditation.

In February 1984, the British Marketing Council published its list of Best Novels of Our Time, books which were then promoted in British bookshops. No Durrell novel was on the list. But the promotion prompted a number of rival listings, and in Anthony Burgess's list of the Best 100 Books, the *Alexandria Quartet* justly takes its place – strange when one considers Burgess's earlier dismissal of his work as 'sadistic-sentimental exotic escapism'. But Burgess's changing literary tastes also reflected a change in the kinds of novels which were coming from a younger generation of British novelists. The realism was becoming more magical and moving closer to Durrell's own Heraldic Universe. And something which no doubt delighted him was a review of the *Avignon Quintet* so far, comparing it favourably to Umberto Eco's *The Name of the Rose*, in the *British Medical Journal*.

Both before and after divorcing Ghislaine, Durrell had lived a life of wild debauch, sleeping with whatever young woman he could persuade into his bed. But, as his powers failed, that avenue of self-fulfilment was gradually closed to him. At this low point, into his life came the last of his great loves. When the two hippy girls taking care of him left, a woman who was running a restaurant in Sommières, Françoise Kestsman, offered to look after him. She was a striking-looking woman, tall and dark, a Slav émigrée with a young family. Before long they were powerfully drawn to one another, and Françoise became his last companion, dividing her time between the house in Sommières and her family. They had vaguely met before. This was the young woman who ten years earlier Ghislaine had noticed staring at him during his 1975 Oscar Epfs exhibition at Marthe Nochy's bookshop in Paris.

Whatever the acupuncturist had done for him, Durrell seems to have tottered gently off the wagon when he was interviewed by Michel Brandeau of *L'Egoïste* that summer. He began by explaining that not having drunk for at least five days he felt he needed a shot of dry white wine before he could get going with the interview. 'Alcohol, I think, is a form of hysteria. I force myself to control it with yoga, because at my age it isn't a good idea to have black-outs, like those I've just had. In the end it's my Irish side that comes out; alcohol greases the machine, the ideas come more easily.' It also, he said, kept out the solitude in which he lived, although Gerry came over from the mazet to get drunk and yell at him from time to time. Asked about the overall conception of all of his work, he pointed out how he had kept to the plan for 'the three Gnostic stages': *The Black Book* was his agon (the struggle), the *Quartet* was his pathos (acceptance of experience) and the *Quintet* would be his anagnorisis (reconciliation of opposites and acceptance of reality). Now, too, for almost the first time, he spoke about the quincunx as an oriental conception; it was the Buddhists, he said, who had inspired it. Comparing the *Quartet* with the *Quintet*, he said: 'I wanted to produce a book to celebrate Einstein and his four dimensions; and another for Tibetans and the number five (after the five skandas of Chinese Buddhism), since in their country there is no conscious and unconscious.' The individuals in his 'boxes within boxes' novel, he said, were not consistent and linear, but unfocused, and corresponded to the Tibetan. He added, 'I'm not sure that this is not a damned stupid mistake that I am making, and I am fearful of losing my reader.'[28]

If he had lost some readers he had gained a religion which was in tune with his own thinking as it had evolved over the years. Reflecting on his yoga, he told another journalist, Jean Montalbetti, that he linked this to his Buddhist beliefs. From the Tibetan viewpoint it was possible to detach oneself from the carnal body through correct breathing. He was therefore able to detach himself from his own dying body and so become 'the living dead'. 'I suppose', he said, 'that one begins to die with one's first breath and the moment of birth.' Developing an awareness of death brought equilibrium – 'the moment when one can live death peacefully because it has always been there'.

> You have to be a Christian to be anguished about death. Inevitably since for Christians death is the end of everything; there remains only Hell and there you are! With all that stupid notion of sin. The idea of the Ancient Greeks is much more spacious. That of the Indians also where one comes back to expunge the error. One remakes one's life until it is perfect. You have all the centuries before you. The only sin that exists is firstly ignorance and then sloth.[29]

If he had the secret of humanity's ills, he had failed to communicate it to his unhappy daughter, Sappho. Her marriage over, she had continued advertising in lonely-hearts columns in the hope of finding a suitable man to father a child. Then in September Durrell put up the money for her to take a trip to Australia. Before leaving she arrived at Barbara Robson's house with four carrier bags full of her writing, asking her to be the executor of her will and to publish her writings if she died – but not before the death of her father. 'I don't want the old fart to interfere in any way,' Robson reported her as saying.[30] If Durrell knew of Sappho's hostility towards him, he gave no evidence of it.

Quinx was now finished, and scheduled for publication in the spring of 1985. Faber were, of course, aware that the completion of a major work would be a notable literary occasion. The blurb they produced was suitably eulogistic; 'a fascinating jig-saw puzzle' – the *Quinx* being the last piece in the whole mosaic – and stressed the inventive, 'free-floating' and evocative nature of the whole enterprise.

The scene in *Quinx, or the Ripper's Tale*, shifts back in the aftermath of the war to Avignon and the search for the treasure of the Templars, which is said to be hidden deep underneath a quincunx of olive trees. Sabine, the rich Lord Banquo's daughter who has turned gypsy, challenges the remaining group of friends who return to the city, to solve the riddle of the Quinx. The key is the power of five – the five skandas of eastern religion which correspond, as Constance suggests, to the five parts of human existence: the two arms, two legs and the kundalini – the yogic source of spiritual enlightenment seated at the base of the spine. The heart of any reconstructed insightful human being capable of solving the riddle, therefore, is the sexual part of our bodies, which provides the path to understanding. Money, too, like the Templar treasure, stands at the heart of the quincunx, for the base of the spine is also the point of excretion. And symbolically, buried beneath the Pont du Gard, until the Germans desecrated the site, were part of a fertility cult, the embalmed legs of Julio, a gypsy who, with his extremities severed, developed an enormous snake-like phallus. Sabine says that without the legs the tribe has lost its powers of procreation. The body must be brought together, made whole again. While others seek the Templar's treasure in a quincunx of caves beneath the bridge, the gypsies seek Julio's embalmed legs. (The parallel with the impotent and legless Clifford Chatterley has been well pointed up by scholars.) The ambiguities of the quincunx thus proliferate to encompass many aspects and angles of Durrell's eclectic metaphysic.

Whatever the mystical secret of human happiness through the electric current of sexual attraction, in a dangerous and cruel world humans may opt for money to protect themselves against the threats of their fellow beings. Instead of the mutually loving couple standing at the base of the social quincunx, protected by its divine power, in the world of material man stands dominating wealth, and the bank, the palace erected to money. In thus playing with dystopias and utopias Durrell is revealing himself to be a man of the 1930s and 1940 – a Huxley or an Orwell – but also a Freud and a Lawrence, attempting to create a vision of the future, yet leaving it open, so that what emerges may be seen not as predetermined, but as the outcome of human efforts towards wholeness – and, of course, of natural accidents.

The fragmentary style of *Quinx* can be seen as a literary representation of a chaotic, entropic universe and the fragmented ego. But the Quinx can also be seen as standing for wholeness, adding yet another level of ambiguity to it. The futures of Blanford and Constance are open to speculation – even though the use of Blanford's legs, and consequently his creativity, are restored by Constance; the outcome could be tragic, it could be a happy one. The same goes for the remaining characters. The important thing about the riddle of the Quinx, indeed of the whole quincunx, is that it is a riddle. At the end it is announced that something completely unpredictable has started to happen. The reader must compose his/her own ending just as he/she has composed the story so far in reading it.

Through the pages of the *Quintet* wander the shades of characters from the *Quartet* – Pursewarden, Melissa, Justine, Darley and Clea, and perhaps, in the shadows of the Gnostic cult, Balthazar too. The characters in the *Quincunx* itself wander back and forth, sometimes in and out of one another's minds like ghosts. Durrell is here saying something important about fiction – not just the fiction created by novelists, but the fictions created by us all. We appear different from different angles, from time to time we may reinvent ourselves and reinvent others. But, even knowing this, the search for personal integrity goes on, and the search for a stable healthy society goes on. In the end reality is made for us, though we have a part in its making. Durrell's genius is that he not only sees this but is able to embody it in a series of highly compelling novels. We may find ourselves not caring very much about his characters and their fates, but we would do well to pay attention to Durrell's ideas and ponder our own destinies.

Meanwhile *Constance* came out in Paris and the French journals continued to seek him out for interviews. In October he told Robert Briatte of *Dolines* that now that he had finished *Quinx* he had finally given all he had left in him; from now on there would be no more novels. *Quinx* appealed to a definitely anti-Freudian psychology; more to Hindu or Buddhist philosophies where the individual does not exist. Of the *Quintet* as a whole he said:

> As a novelistic intention it is very dangerous, but if I succeed in
> handling it correctly, I will have created an Indian novel, adjacent

parts linked to each other and inter-penetrating through their characters. To tell the truth, I gave up worrying about the question of the value of the whole thing: for me, it is to do with being able to breathe. I have to do it that way or die, that is all.

He had absolutely no pretension about being original, he said, and had ferreted around a lot, drawn from texts here and there and adopted what seemed to bring answers to his own problem. 'I am a thief, a gambler. I am not a great philosopher – I do not have a rigidified philosophy, ready for offering: I simply tried to become a contemporary, through our cosmology and the preoccupations of our era. I have the impression that if we want to do something of value, it has to be strictly contemporary.'[31]

Reviewing the French edition of *Constance*, Claude Fleury called the *Quintet* 'magic', but thought that a series of books which abandoned all resemblance to truth or rationality was impossible to define.[32] *France Soir* described *Constance* as 'a torrent of images or words and ideas'.[33] Bruno de Cessole of *Temps Libre* wondered whether the inventor of Blanford, the inventor of Sutcliffe, was not someone else's invention. But, after interviewing Durrell, de Cessole decided he did exist and that perhaps in finally shedding the work 'like a snake's skin' he had fulfilled what Darley hoped for in the *Quartet*, to fulfil himself in art through art.[34]

In December, the newspaper *Libération* brought Durrell together with Perlès for a tour of their old resorts in Paris. There was also a reunion with David Gascoyne, just winding down from a lecture tour of European universities. They met for an evening at the Coupole – Durrell, Gascoyne and his wife, Alf and Anne Perlès. Gascoyne was so moved by the occasion that he wrote that at any moment he expected Miller and Anaïs to walk in. Durrell impressed the Gascoynes immensely with his abstemiousness, sticking religiously to Perrier water all evening – and this the man who could once drink everyone under the table with no apparent ill-effects. At Gallimard, Christine Gallimard and one of her editors Christine Jordis, having read *Constance*, were of the strong opinion that Durrell was a 'male chauvinist' with a pretty low opinion of women. But, according to Gascoyne, during that visit to Paris, he completely charmed them and changed their minds about him.[35]

Sappho returned unexpectedly from Australia to spend Christmas of 1984 with her mother. Afterwards, she was more depressed than ever and spent a lot of time sleeping in her room. Then one of her tenants, Andrew Travers, a sociologist, cajoled her into going out for dinner one evening with another tenant Rosie Blair, an actress. Over the meal she got bitterly angry with Travers, accusing him of 'sexism' and seemed to him to want to annihilate the whole male sex. Walking back afterwards, along the Holloway Road, she suddenly dashed out into the traffic and was just pulled back before she could be run over. She then hid herself in an upstairs room at Loraine Road for a couple of weeks and, around 24 January, her two lodgers discovered her locked in her bedroom contemplating a lethal cocktail of drugs. They made her flush it down the toilet, and promise never to try such a thing again.

A week later, on the 31 January 1985, Sappho hanged herself with a pair of tights from the skylight of her bedroom in the attic. She was four months short of her thirty-fourth birthday. At the inquest, held on 2 April, the verdict was that she had taken her own life 'on account of her illness'.

CHAPTER 19

Out of Breath (1985–1990)

> I have scaled the peak and found no
> shelter in fame's bleak and barren
> height. Lead me, my Guide, before the
> light fades, into the valley of quiet where
> life's harvest mellows into golden
> wisdom.
>
> Rabindranath Tagore

There was no doubt that Durrell loved his daughter. When he heard of Sappho's death he was plunged into a state of deep mourning and told Alf Perlès that he simply did not wish to see anybody, and was thinking of disappearing off to Greece for a while. Perlès told him that he could never get away from people; he was too attractive. No doubt he was able to take consolation from the Tibetan attitude to death and reincarnation.

However, in this life, words continued to define and determine his being. When *Sebastian* appeared in French translation in May 1985, *Le Monde* declared it a manifesto of Durrealism.[1] Meanwhile London braced itself for the publication of *Quinx* on the 27th. The *Bookseller* announced that the author would be in England for ten days.

The completion of *The Avignon Quintet* was a major moment in his life and a moment to mark in English literature, for which the media was well prepared. The serious press gave it much attention and interviewers queued up to talk to him. He was also much cosseted by Faber and Curtis Brown. 'It's . . . marvellous,' he said, after a couple of days in London. 'Like

being in the cradle again. Dozens of pretty girls from my
publishers and my agents doing nothing but please me.'[2]

One of the first notices appeared in the *Scotsman*, where
Allan Massie gave a thoughtful but finally triumphant greeting
to the whole project. He wrote with the enthusiasm of a
convert, having, as a youth, considered Durrell's *Quartet* 'over-
written and pretentious', but now feeling more sympathetic to
what he called 'a splendid eccentric in whose novels the absurd
and incompetent is strangely mixed with the glorious and even
the sublime'. He could think of no other post-war writer who
had achieved two novel sequences, something which had obviously demanded 'an extraordinary effort of concentrated
imagination, invention and virtuosity . . . [and] in his work
at its best . . . an illumination and excitement that is rare in
contemporary fiction'. In English literature he had most in
common with Malcolm Lowry, using fiction 'not as a means
of explaining life, but in order to try to understand it'.[3]

Slightly more sceptical was a columnist from the *Sunday
Telegraph* who arrived to interview him at the Shepherd's Bush
house of his agent, Anthea Morton-Saner, with whom he was
staying. (He said that Faber had wanted him to stay at the
Connaught, but he preferred somewhere where he could
potter.) The columnist (pseudonym 'Mandrake'), having read
the *Quartet* and some of the *Quintet*, expected a tall, spare,
aloof man shooting out abstractions and shafts of insight. But
the man he met was 'a small, stout, twinkling man' who drank
instant coffee from a plastic mug and chuckled a great deal –
the kind of chap he thought he might once have come across
in the Planters' Club. But colonial though he was, and Blimpish
though he claimed to be, he talked in a very unBlimpish way
about yoga and Buddhism. He said he thought the English
critics tended to snipe at him because of his earlier success with
the *Quartet* and because of his 'self-indulgent' prose. However,
he admitted to having created an unreal Alexandria, adding,
'They're full of lies, my books.' He said he was amused by
Americans becoming obsessed with the details, religiously
trying to trace the asylums he had written into the *Quintet* –
he had taken real asylums but put them in the wrong places.
Despite his recent bereavement he was singularly optimistic.

I still think the world is bliss, but . . . there's confusion in our vision . . . What's wrong? . . . My novels are rather like the geese quacking in the Capitol, I can't provide the answers. That would be like deciding I was God or Buddha. I'm not. I'm poor, poor, poor Durrell.

This is a far cry from the Durrell of 1937 who agreed with Miller that artists were gods. (And, perhaps overwhelmed with all the attention he was receiving, the 'poor, poor, poor' Lawrence Durrell let slip that he had been a millionaire since 1975 – or joked that he had.)[4]

Desmond Christy of the *Guardian* went to the house in Shepherd's Bush and found Durrell wearing a little woolly hat which made him look as though he wanted to sell you onions rather than his novels. 'What you notice is that he looks his 73 years and that he's grown as corpulent as his prose.' He admitted that his idea of a Tibetan novel was a retrospective notion. 'Looking back now on the whole thing I think what I was after was one occidental novel and one oriental.' He hoped that eastern and western philosophies could be joined in some way to make a one world viable – the old search for wholeness. The answer to world chaos was not military but philosophical. But, as Durrell expounded the philosophical message behind his work, Christy was not the first English critic to become puzzled. 'You begin to wonder if he's really describing the five novels you've just enjoyed reading so much. Here's a fellow who would make the *Alexandria Quartet* sound like a cross between the Special Theory of Relativity and the complete works of Sigmund Freud.' Noting how often madness and suicide featured in his work, Christy asked Durrell why he thought his daughter had taken her own life. 'I don't know,' he said. 'I don't think anybody knows. It's another mystery. She went through a very bad period – her husband left her . . . It's been an enormous thump.' His own home life had lacked consistency for the past ten years, he said, and as for psychoanalysis, 'I've never been treated but I can't deny that there have been times when I needed it. If an analyst had been possible I would have asked for help. I've been terribly neurotic.' But he could now hope to be released from the painful mental state he thought he needed to complete the great cycle of work. He talked of returning to poetry, and if that did not come he had his yoga. However, 'I've had trouble with breathing, old age takes a whole new technique – like adolescence does. You get everything but spots.' After the interview, he went off to see a Francis Bacon exhibition – suitably gruesome for his taste, thought Christy.[5]

He bumped one day into his old friend Richard Lumley, Lord Scarborough, telling him to come along to the booksigning at Hatchards at 12.30 p.m. When Scarborough got there he found a long queue of readers eagerly awaiting the author and his pen.

> A rather harassed-looking man came up to me and said, 'Are you Lord Scarborough?' so I said, 'Yes.' And he said, 'Oh, Larry wants to see you upstairs.' So we went up. And Larry was refusing to come down until he had had a) a bottle of red wine, and b) me. He was being very difficult, and he then said, 'I want to talk to my friend, Dick, so go away.' And he slopped wine all over the book and signed it, and they were getting more and more harassed, and the people downstairs were getting more and more angry about waiting for him. And that was the last time I saw him.[6]

Sober, at the book-signing at Turret Books, he was reunited with Bernard Stone and Alan Thomas, now with a taste in eccentric costume to rival Durrell – broad-brimmed black hat and cloak which, together with the Charles Darwin beard, outrageously upstaged Durrell in his onion-seller outfit.

Interviews with the press sounded like premature auto-obituaries as he reflected ironically on his life and work, and pondered his death. He told a reporter from the *Liverpool Daily Post* that the neurosis necessary to create a work like the *Quintet* and 'talking in the bath and mumbling to the walls' had contributed to the problems in some of his marriages. He linked his obsession about breathing to religion, saying, 'Anybody who uses oxygen must be religious . . . In fact, I think it is a religious act to be breathing.' If he had not won the Nobel Prize, he had certainly won the love of many women. 'I've always chosen countries and girls that nourish me. I know that sounds like cannibalism, but I've given women everything. If you really worship women, they'll forgive you everything.' But he would never marry again. 'It's affecting my oxygen and cash flow far too much.' He did not expect to live very much longer and would rather like to be embalmed. 'I once heard of a French publisher who created a stir through throwing a party after his death, sitting upright with a cigarette lodged in his lips. Every so often his authors would come up to the corpse and reverently give it a light.' As to the *Quartet* and the *Quintet* – they constituted his own inner autobiography and that was all there was to be said about them.[7]

Interviewed on BBC's *Woman's Hour*, he said that his concern about women's liberation was that men were not up to it. And, with a passing swipe at Mrs Thatcher's Britain, he added that in a false consumer society, based entirely on making money, ordinary human sensibility, and especially sexual sensibility, was impoverished. It was what he had written about in *Tunc/Nunquam* – the firm had us all in its grip. Woman was much harder hit by this money-obsession which drained away all sexual and affective life, because through her sensibility and sensuality, her judgments and evaluations, she constructed the future – but that future was already diminished. It all sounded very Lawrentian.[8] On the World Service's *Meridian*, he told Edward Blishen that ideally he would like all his characters to be one character. Time was just a convention, and oriental thought put causality deeply into question. He hoped before he died to forget everything. In any case, the erudite knowledge that he enjoyed putting into his books was stolen, and the Mystery of the Templars was pure Grand Guignol.[9] As he left the World Service studios, the radio producer said to him, 'I think your zoo is wonderful,' to which he replied, without batting an eyelid, 'Yes, I'm very proud of it.'[10]

Women still fascinated him and were fascinated by him. He was interviewed over lunch in a smart London restaurant by a writer and fashion editor from *Vogue*, joined for the occasion by his daughter Penelope. However, he made no concession to style and turned up in an old duffle-coat and his onion-seller's knitted hat. They questioned him about Justine. 'She is very typical of the Mediterranean; she's all over Cannes. I didn't invent her – she's there.' Anouk Aimée was ideally cast in the film, though that had been a mess ('Peyton Place with palm trees'), thanks to the inferior people whom the cinema attracted. His novel-writing career was now over, he said, and there was nothing much more that he wanted to do. 'I think that's the only reason that suicide stares me in the face. I've done everything that I've wanted to do.' Now he was reading a lot of eastern texts and being taught by the Buddhists. 'I think I'm more a Buddhist than I would have believed. It's the only religion that's demonstrable.' Christianity meant signing up for 'a mass of protocols which don't make much sense. Whereas with Buddhism, if you do your breathing exercises and yoga correctly, the state of mind you can achieve are all they promise. It's as honest as ice-cream.' However, as to life's certainties, 'I've become less and less certain about things until I'm so uncertain that I have to wear braces.'[11]

Perhaps his most sympathetic and perceptive notice came in the *London Review of Books* from Patrick Parrinder. Parrinder spotted one aspect of the novels which seemed to reveal a crucial part of that 'inner autobiography' that Durrell claimed the quincunx to be. It was, he said, an aspect highly appropriate for a banned writer of the 1930s and former associate of Henry Miller – one of ' "love-lore" or the secrets of sex'.

> These, which have something to do with 'dual-control' in the love-act and simultaneous orgasm, are passed down from master to mistress to hand-picked pupil in certain rare and long-delayed bouts of sexual intercourse . . . The characters of Durrell's charmed circle work through many of the possible erotic combinations with one another, but only the favoured few join the inner ranks of the sexual magi.

What 'liberated' young woman could resist an offer of initiation from the author of great works about female love such as *The Alexandria Quartet*?[12]

His final London interview was with the *Sunday Independent* – amusingly billed as 'a rare interview' – in which he was hailed as 'a man of outrageous contrasts with more than a touch of Irish'. He admitted that the Irishness was merely 'a touch' and to pretend otherwise was whimsical. (When he spoke to the French press he was decidedly whimsical on this point.) After what he had so far achieved, he said, the honourable thing to do was to shut up, 'But who wants to shut up?'

He might, however, go back to verse. 'I've a poetry book full of leads. Slogans almost. Reading it is like travelling on the top of a London bus.' He said that age was an illusion (he hoped to phase himself out gradually in the lotus position) and life a complete lie. 'I like to throw it into doubt in the interests of good fun.' Sex may have been coming of age with the freedom of women, but he was dubious about the approaching 'sperm-bank civilization' – 'the taming of the screw', he called it. All he was faced with now was second childhood, he said. 'I don't have any plans apart from writing a travel book as a thank-you to Provence. I'll see how my oxygen supply holds out.'[13]

Durrell could be well pleased with the critical reception of his final major work. Few thought the *Quintet* was as great as the *Quartet*, and some were dismissive, seeing him as a clever charlatan, selling the same story over and over – a judgment he was often happy to agree with. Most thought it a considerable achievement, a work of great intelligence and awareness of how words work and how narratives display versions of reality and identity, like an ever-shifting kaleidoscope in which dream and fantasy and hallucination and mirage and various emanations of the unconscious weave themselves to produce an illusion of stability without continuity. By destroying time he could demonstrate the way in which the great creative art of self-delusion operates. Most perceptive critics saw Durrell for the pioneer he was in constructing this type of text, though whether this made him a brilliant novelist or a philosophical games-player with an unusual command of the way meanings and identities are invented, was a matter on which there was no critical consensus.

The effect of all this media attention was to push *Quinx* into the best-seller list. By the end of June, Heffers, the Cambridge bookseller, placed it at number one in its list, and on 7 July the *Sunday Telegraph* placed it at number three behind Barbara Pym's *Crampton Hodnet* and Antonia Fraser's *Oxford Blood*. Faber had ensured that all the four previous novels in the quincunx series were available in paperback. Before the end of the year another *Antrobus Complete* would also appear.

In April 1986 Durrell was finally prevailed upon to visit America, to attend the Fourth Lawrence Durrell International Conference put on by mostly US scholars at the University of Pennsylvania. It was more than ten years since he had last visited the country, when he had lectured at Caltech and had had Ghislaine with him. No doubt he was pleased to get away, after the past decade slaving over his *Quintet*, and he was now also beginning to fret about high French taxes. In London, *en route* for New York, staying again in Shepherd's Bush, he was tracked down by Cécile Wajsbrot, who interviewed him for the Paris journal, *Les Nouvelles Littéraires*, in anticipation of the publication of *Quinx in France*.

Wajsbrot found him in a merry mood, winking at her a lot, but talking seriously about his *Quintet*, and his obsession – to repair the short-circuit between the orient and the occident. He talked rather more lightly about his visit to the States and the veneration he received from the Lawrence Durrell Society, but reserved his coldest remarks for the English, who, he said, did not like ideas and abstraction, and many did not understand his work. His whole life had been a means of recovering his Indian childhood, he said, and having swum in the Mediterranean he had begun to reconstruct the link between Greek philosophy and India. Creating a work of art was a way of reconciling the two. That was what had given birth to *The Avignon Quintet*, which was above all a novel about writing.

> All these writers [in the books] are variations of myself. There is someone who went much further in dissociation, that is Passoa, who invented five poets and published poems under these five names. The *Quintet* is composed of puppet books. In the same fashion each of the authors is an aspect of the other, just as if they had been given a separate identity.

The only modern English writer he had good words for was John Fowles, though he was always rewriting the Victorian novel. Authors who had not read Freud could not write about modern times. 'We are not the same since Freud. One cannot imagine now the shock which was *The Interpretation of Dreams*.' Psychoanalysis could never leave him, and he practised it by proxy in his novels, treating mental illness and suicide with Constance, his psychoanalyst character, and using them as recurrent themes in the books of his various writers – Blanford, Sutcliffe and even himself.[14]

In New York on 14 April, Viking Penguin threw a party in his honour at the Gotham Book Mart, and shortly afterwards he travelled to the University of Pennsylvania where he delivered an apparently impromptu talk – full of wit and self-depreciating humour – about his life, his penchant for alcohol and his impending death. It was 'three days of sizzling creative play', he said later. 'I fell in love with myself all over again.'[15] He was thrilled to be the centre of devoted attention. In New York just afterwards, a reporter from the *Boston Globe* found him 'almost childlike in his delight at having dazzled the scholars' with his *Avignon Quintet*.

> The reception was tremendous. It wasn't just a sort of intemperate, typical exhibition of American generosity . . . it was very thoughtful. All the 20 papers were different, and all of these guys have a list of critical books as long as your arm. I was more and more humbled as the conference went on. And they were reading my stuff! I just can't tell you . . .[16]

He had now given up all pretence of abstinence, referring jokingly at the conference to 'a drunkard like me'.[17] Interviewed by David Lida, he began proceedings at 11 a.m. by uncorking a bottle of Californian chardonnay with the comment, 'I thought you might be thirsty.' He had been on the wagon for eighteen months, he said, 'but abstinence just disintegrated with fatigue from travel – I need the alcohol'. Challenged that back in the 1960s he had predicted the end of the world within a decade, he laughed, saying,

> The world has ended. All the fun's gone out of it. Look at this immense city. It should be the Samarkand of our culture. People are terrified to go out and post a letter. This alienated behaviour is a ludicrous position to be in. Women are acting more like men and vice versa. Our sex lives are enormously compromised. The tabloid which I bought yesterday reported Americans have invented some sort of snuff which will prevent conception. And there's a dipstick which you can dip in your girlfriend's urine and assure yourself you won't get something terrible from her. Marvellous! It's the beginning

of the end; all these considerations are going to inhibit sex enormously. I'm so glad to be so old.

He was using smelling salts ('like an old Victorian whore'), which he claimed were good for his emphysema, and said that at seventy-four things were beginning to fade. 'I think I'll croak in a year or two.'[18]

He found the city oppressive and complained about the effect of the Manhattan air on his emphysema. 'For the last two or three years,' he told yet another interviewer, 'I've been plagued by bad health, which has disgusted and surprised me. I was always healthy like an athlete. Suddenly, in my old age I've toppled into emphysema and no longer can travel or stand on my head or do anything enjoyable except drink.' Of his 'hepatic attacks' he said that an American girlfriend had given him a bottle of Vitamin E tablets and since taking them he had suffered no more attacks. It was 10 a.m. and he was on his first glass of white wine.[19]

On his return to Sommières, he was still quite excited about his time in America among the scholars, telling a journalist from *Le Matin*:

> [It was] ideal country in which to check the working of a mechanism. They analyse a poem like a kitchen implement. I was reassured, they called me the new Einstein. Each character from *The Quartet* and *The Quintet* produced its own fan-club. I was questioned on Justine and Sutcliffe as I would be on an uncle. And the students exchange epigrams they read dotted around in *The Quintet*. These same poems have become samizdats in Moscow, I get letters from young Muscovites, it's wonderful!

Now, he said, for the first time in his life he felt like a saved soul. The entire work was finished. When he was polite enough to depart he hoped that his work would be regarded as a sort of 'bouillabaisse' of his ideas and concerns about love – a series of Chinese boxes in which all the personalities would conceal his own. 'Russian dolls really is what defines the best that I have written.'[20]

He was still in touch with Fanchette and also, at the beginning of 1987, with Cecily Mackworth, who had written an

autobiography, *Ends of the World*, one chapter of which dealt
with her time in Paris in 1937 when she met Miller, Perlès,
Durrell and Nancy at the Villa Seurat. She sent Durrell a copy
for his seventy-fifth birthday in February. It found him in bad
health and feeling gloomy about the death of so many of his
friends. Reading it filled him with nostalgia and melancholy,
so much so that he hoped she would visit him. She only had
to phone and he and his last (he hoped) madonna, Françoise,
would crack open a bottle.[21]

In the summer, Penelope, who was about to remarry, came
to the house to inspect the small library of books which Durrell
had chosen to give her as a wedding present – mostly modern
novels and poetry. She also helped to clear his decks by helping
to sort through his archive, which he had a mind to have
auctioned at Sotheby's. Meanwhile, with the income tax situation under the Thatcher government in England now more
advantageous for the rich, Durrell had once again altered his
tax status from 'resident' (he had to revoke his 'permit de
Séjour de résident-permanent') to that of simply 'tourist
residing in France as a member of the European Economic
Community on a British passport'. Technically he had departed
from France on 1 June. The exile, if only technically and for
tax purposes, had returned home.

The stream of visitors continued to pass through his house.
That summer, Paul Hogarth spend four days in Sommières with
the writer Robin Rook, gathering background and a comment
ary for a proposed book of paintings of scenes from his novels.
And Artemis Cooper, writing a book about Cairo, came in
August to gather his memories of the war years there and
in Alexandria. In August, too, there were celebrations at
Kangû-Ling (at the Château de Plaige in Burgundy), where the
Buddhist temple, for which he and Jacques Lacarrière had
raised funds, was finally finished, and Durrell was invited by
Kalou Rempotché to consecrate it. 'It's fascinating,' he told *Le
Matin*, 'not as a parochial affair, but because Buddhism has
just planted a foot in the European context.' And again he
expounded his view of the west's malaise.

I'm a philosopher. It is too painful because I see reality. What one calls the principle of indetermination remains at the heart of our Cartesian philosophy. That produces troubled, stressed and hysterical spirits which eat each other. It's that incomplete, stunted spirit from which we suffer in Europe. Happily, through psychology, thanks to Buddhist philosophy and above all thanks to yoga, one is able to relax oneself. In a sense, all misadventures, all passions which fill my novels, are a kind of badinage; they are not reality.

He hoped that the whole continent would convert to Buddhism, because with that religion, 'it is necessary to live it instead of talking about it, as you are. Europe is full of believers, not practitioners.'[22]

Durrell and Françoise took the opportunity to go through a Buddhist 'marriage' at the temple, over a bottle of *morgon consacrée*. It seemed to put the final imprimatur on him as a believer and practitioner, though he required a dispensation for his drinking – duly afforded him for his part in raising the cash for the temple.

A less Buddhist image of Durrell appeared in Pudding Island in October, when BBC Television began a ten-part serialization of Gerald's *My Family and Other Animals*, filmed in Corfu. Gerald was impressed that the BBC team had managed to find bits of the island as lovely and peaceful as they had been in 1935, and not wrecked by tourists. Durrell thought that watching himself depicted as a twenty-three-year-old rivetting, though somewhat eerie.[23]

His homage to Provence was now consuming most of his time, but in the autumn he took time off from it to travel to Lyons, where a performance of Jacques Temple's 1976 translation of *An Irish Faustus*, starring Eleonore Hirt, ran from 10 to 29 November at the Théâtre des Célestins. *Figaro* declared him 'an alchemist of writing' and his *Faustus* was judged 'different'.[24] After the show he was persuaded to talk a little about his Provençal book. It was almost finished, he said, but when he was within twenty pages of the end he realized that Provence was as impossible a place as Los Angeles – it had no centre. Its colours, absurdities and past atrocities made it difficult to write about.

In some parts it's a powerful, brutal and malevolent country, and all benevolence in others. Alchemically speaking, the emanations are on the dark side, the side of Montségur with its history of the Albigensians and the Templars, but there is also a totally innocent aspect to it. Then again, the contours of the country change all the time; it is unstable, so I am obliged to do the book in small morsels. If it's sufficiently well written it will be read, I expect. Biographically now I am beginning to interest people, not simply because I am doing a book, but because it comes into the category of a biography: people are wanting to know what was he doing during these years . . . so I think it will sell. If not, I'll commit suicide . . . I am almost dying, you know, it's terrifying to be asked to explain these things [about my work] which I hardly know . . . I am old, easily fatigued, I take it easy, perhaps write several poems. I feel that I am a very great fraud. You understand, in reality I detest novels. I would rather be a poet.

He would have been a poet, he said, if he had not had to pay for the luxury of a woman, children and a house. 'One is obliged to write novels, but I feel a bit of a renegade. But I should not say this, especially to the Americans, these amusing Americans.'[25]

He was still talking himself down as a novelist in an interview early in the new year, saying that he had never really been a novelist. 'I've always despised the novel. I was bored stiff with the British novel as it existed. I wondered if I couldn't give it a dent or two or shove it a little bit out of frame to let in a bit of light, because it seemed to me the cinema was doing better than the novel in its account of reality.'[26]

However, 1988 was to be a year of letters for him. Jean Fanchette published some of Durrell's early letters to him, mostly about the *Quartet* and about *Two Cities*. Then, when Durrell's archive was finally unveiled at Sotheby's in July, the letters between him and Miller's wives, Hoki and Brenda Venus, brought a slightly scandalized response in the *Independent* – especially as they revealed how Durrell had cuckolded Miller in his own house in 1967.[27] The sale of the archive was a disappointment. Originally valued at between £60,000 and £80,000, the bidding failed to pass the £20,000 mark, and the lot was withdrawn. Interest in Durrell was, for the time being, in eclipse. The mystical 1960s had long been overtaken by the materialistic 1980s. The archive was later purchased for an undisclosed sum by Southern Illinois University, which had made itself the home of many of Durrell's important papers.[28]

But the letters which did bring Durrell briefly back on to the literary front pages in July were *The Durrell–Miller Letters: 1935–80*, edited by Ian McNiven, a revision and extension of the edition edited by George Wickes in 1963. Yet the 500-odd pages contained only around a third of the letters exchanged by these hardy long-distance correspondents over that forty-five-year period. It gave reviewers an opportunity to sum up each life in relation to the other. Not untypical was the review in the *New York Times*:

> Energy, high spirits, tender regard spill from these letters: and for a remarkably long time. What is missing from them is ideas, wisdom, a sense of developing experience. Knowledge is tempered over the years, but not transformed. What each one knows in the late 1970s he knew in the mid-30s. Neither Durrell nor Miller ever sees himself differently; or the world around him differently. Other people do not become real to them. That's why each one wrote the same book over and over again.[29]

Anthony Burgess was fierce in his condemnation, concluding that 'We are reminded that some books have to exist, even if some of us don't want them. This is such a book.'[30] To round off the year of letters Anaïs Nin's correspondence with Miller appeared, and the memoirs of his friend Diane Deriaz, *La Tête á l'envers: souvenirs d'un trapéziste chez les poètes* (Head Upside Down. A trapeze artist among the poets), which Durrell had long encouraged her to write, was also published.

That same year, 1988, mindful that a whole literary generation was about to pass away, a French TV crew came out to Sommières, having already filmed Alfred Perlès. The final programme (produced by George Hoffman) also used footage of Miller, filmed on his deathbed by a German television crew in 1980. When they had all met up in Paris, Durrell said, he, Miller, Perlès and Anaïs were unknown. 'All ideas were based on the idea that we were not ordinary human beings but aristocrats.' He went on to express, in more crystallized form perhaps, a view of himself towards which he had been slowly moving through the residual melancholy which followed the death of Claude:

I never enjoyed anything in my life. I have been bored ever since I crawled out of my mother's womb, and never found anything that really pleased me, so I've always been making do with second best . . . I've always been conscious of being dead-born – still-born we call it in English – and I feel always very posthumous but very gay . . . I shall have to die in the middle of *Hamlet*. It's so fatiguing, and I hate the play.[31]

In the wake of the successful televising of *My Family and Other Animals*, Gerald was happily collecting honorary doctorates – at the University of Durham in 1988 and at Kent in 1989. Larry, on the other hand, having turned down an OBE back in 1962, was now claiming to have also turned down the more prestigious CMG on the ground that he could not be honoured by a country which still retained possession of Greek treasures such as the Elgin Marbles. Drawing a distinction between his brother and himself, Gerald is reported as saying, 'My brother writes for posterity, but I write for money. It provides me with the wherewithal to do what I really like doing.'[32] Of course, he was not to know that Larry also confessed to having been forced to write for money to have what he really liked – women, houses and children.

More reminders of his own mortality came with the death in January 1989 of Audrey Beecham, and a birthday greeting from Alf Perlès (himself on the way to becoming ninety-two) on his seventy-seventh birthday in February. In August, *Le Figaro* published a piece on him under the headline 'Le Vieux Sage', but by now Durrell was more old than sage. He was subject to absent-mindedness, and those epileptic-type attacks had returned. Sometimes he would seem to blank out and sit staring into space, oblivious to everything around him.[33] When, in September, he sent Perlès his own birthday greetings on his ninety-second birthday, plus £100, Perlès was overwhelmed that their friendship had lasted as it had done. It had nothing to do with literature, he wrote, and everything to do with a total empathy – very rare between people even of the opposite sex. 'I hear that you're drinking yourself to death and am amazed you don't give it up. But I'm not amazed and don't advise you to give it up.'[34] Durrell took Perlès at his word. David Gascoyne, who visited Sommières in November found him drinking white wine from dawn until dinnertime, and practising Buddhist meditation at the same time.[35] On 23 November, the *Chicago Sun-Times* ran an article entitled 'Novelist Durrell Frail, But He Writes On'. *Caesar's Vast Ghost* had to be finished, and he had been encouraged when earlier, on 3 November, he was awarded a Provençal honour – the Grand Prix Littéraire International awarded by the town of Antibes.[36] By the end of the year he had finished his book, but was worried that some of the new poems he had included might not stand up, and that Faber might not want them to stay in. But by the spring of the next year, 1990, the text had been approved and publication was scheduled for the autumn.

As 1990 dawned, Durrell was suffering occasional black-outs, and lapsed into occasional states of oblivion. He had hoped that Penny would be able to come out for the summer for a belated celebration of her fiftieth birthday, but she was unwell and felt unable to travel. However, he did not want for company – there were many local friends to visit, and (although his literary star was perhaps not as bright as it was even a few years earlier), as ever, journalists wanting to talk to him. Michael Dibdin of the *Independent* visited in the early autumn, ahead of the publication of his book, and was surprised to find the 15 Route de Saussine looking so gloomy, the outside shuttered, steps weeded over, paint peeling, the interior with 'all the charm of a mausoleum'. The upper floors had, he wrote, been 'abandoned to rats, bats and that odd nocturnal prowler, the Mediterranean loris'. No wonder Durrell had said in a poem that of late he had come to regard the house as 'something poisoned', the beauty of the place masking 'pure grief'. Dibdin found Durrell dressed in heavy peasant clothing – 'thick blue corduroy, near-white shirt, dark heavy-duty trousers, slip-on shoes splitting apart like over-ripe fruit'. And he looked the part of the aged peasant too. 'His back was bent and his legs slightly bowed, as though by a lifetime of physical labour. From this frame, astonishingly, issued the patrician accents of a Gielgud.' He said that he felt 'frightfully *posthumous*', having had a recent attack from which he thought he would 'croak'. 'When the doctors said I had another few years to go I felt slightly disappointed.' But he was, reported Dibdin, being 'fiercely' protected by Françoise and owed his surviving these last few years to her care. But fiction no longer interested him. 'I am far more interested in philosophy and Buddhism,' he said.

He was still talking about future books – one on tramps, inspired by Blanco, the *clochard* he had built his film *The Lonely Roads* around with Diane Deriaz – and even about a new Oscar Epfs exhibition in Geneva. He showed off some of his latest Epfs paintings – according to Dibdin, 'dense, colourful, acrylic doodles whose anarchic innocence may be sampled on the end-papers of the new book'. The Epfs name brought up the question of his use of pseudonyms, and he explained that he had been 'condemned' to role-playing by his background – neither Indian nor English, and so a complete fake. Durrell and Françoise took Dibdin out to lunch and ate baby squid and drank good white wine followed by *arquebuse*, the local liquor which had once defeated Nigel and Beatrice Dennis and excited Miller. They then went to visit Ludo Chardenon and his wife. Although *Caesar's Vast Ghost* was not yet due out, Dibdin had brought along a newly minted copy, which became a point of heated discussion when Ludo's wife objected that he had included Sommières (in Languedoc) in his picture of Provence, and even his explaining that he was focusing on the Roman *provincia* rather than the modern Provence did not quieten her fierce sense of local loyalty. Back at the Vampire House the mood grew gloomy again, and, as Didbin departed, Durrell said, 'Growing old is awful.' Then, as he saw his visitor to the door, he pointed to the bags of rubbish that had blown across the steps and said, 'Mind you don't trip on all the French letters.'³⁷

It was his last interview.

Although the death-scene had been a long one, the end came suddenly. On 7 November 1990, Françoise came back from shopping to find him dead in the bathroom. He had died of a cerebral haemorrhage combined with a pulmonary embolism. On the 9th, he was cremated at Orange. Françoise and Penny were present, and some of Françoise's children. Margo, and

Gerry, who was on an expedition to Madagascar, were unable to get there at such short notice. Françoise returned with his ashes to Sommières.

So what is the last resting place of the spirit of Lawrence Durrell? Is it at the Vampire House, where he spent his last years? Is it at the mazet or pacing across the wild garrigue? Has it returned to the Tibet he saw as some kind of Shangri-la? Has it joined the Buddhists at Kangû-Ling? Or is it beneath that dog-rose in the cemetery at the tiny church of St Julien de Salinelles where he had wished to be laid to rest? It is appropriate that his life should end with an enigma. Just as his characters in the quincunx spent years searching for the treasure of the Templars, and he himself spent his life in pursuit of wholeness, so Durrell's admirers will try to discover the secret (possibly never revealed even to himself) of where his genius rested.

The Buddhists may have the last word. It is said that a lama has reported him already reincarnated and living as a keeper of a vineyard in Burgundy. So perhaps his spirit is to be found in the sunshine among the vineyards or even in one of the finer vintages of good French Burgundy.

CHAPTER 20

The Bubble Reputation

(1990–1995)

In the end is my beginning.

T. S. Eliot, *East Coker*

The end of life is often the beginning of biography. It is only after a death that certain things come to light and it is possible to view a life more in the round, in all its complexities, its shades of colour, of dark and light, rather than from one point of view. The biographer, faced with the scattered fragments, the shards and relics left behind, sets out to construct a meaningful narrative, as Darley did in *The Alexandria Quartet*. There is, as Durrell saw clearly, a desire for wholeness; we try to integrate lives (our own and others') in order to give them meaning. Not only are lives, and reputations, worked over in this way, but the biographical process is one of continuous revisions, writings and rewritings. And, of course, the appearance of previously unpublished work, and new revelations which post-date the death of the subject, often leads to the reassessing and reinterpreting of a life.

Obituaries are often the first gloss on a life – thumb-nail biographies – and Durrell's were prominently printed in the major newspapers of Europe and America. Some of his friends were given the opportunity to reflect on the man as much as the work. For David Gascoyne, he was 'one of the most sophisticated intelligences of his generation', and he praised his loyalty and generosity, recalling the time that he and Nancy

fed him when he was a starving poet in Paris in 1937.¹ Paddy
Leigh Fermor remembered him being described as 'a man who
pumped oxygen back into the air',² and Erica Jong, who had
befriended Miller in his final years and had visited Durrell the
previous year, recalled his 'beguiling modesty' and applauded
his courage, a courage she now thought lacking among writers.³
Those critics who had been less than friendly during his lifetime
were no more friendly at his death. Anthony Burgess, for
example, thought that his verse was 'good but little of it was
memorable', and considered the *Quartet* gimmicky rather than
innovative. Although there was fun in his Antrobus stories, his
novels were generally humourless. However, the French
thought highly of him, and, said Burgess, 'French aesthetic
judgments have to be respected.'⁴ Kenneth McLeish, while
finding him 'one of the century's great literary pyrotechnicians',
thought his island books and the *Quartet* were his finest works.
Later, however, 'he succumbed, in print, to the persona he had
assumed in life from adolescence – the bombastic portrait of
Lawrence in his brother Gerald's *My Family and Other
Animals* is not just farce.'⁵ Some obituaries dubbed him 'the
poor man's Proust'.

Defending him against his detractors, Philip Howard, literary
editor of *The Times*, applauded him as the last of the modern-
ists. 'We are not so rich in innovative and complex and fluent
novelists that we can afford to put them down for not being
Proust. Quite a lot of the criticism is insular jealousy of the
foreign and the strange. The French are more adult about
fiction than we are.'⁶ In fact, the French bade goodbye to their
favourite English writer with headlines such as 'Sir Larry de
Sommières' (*L'Humanité*) and 'Durrell, Lawrence d'Alexan-
drie' (*Libération*), though in America he was portrayed mainly
as a writer whose talent had faded following the *Quartet*.

At the end he had captured again that sense of light and
music in *Caesar's Vast Ghost*, his literary swan-song. It is a
guide book in the very best sense – as only he could do it –
blending personal anecdotes with the recalled shades of gen-
erals, poets, baleful saints and lustful pagans, all richly
illustrated with photographs of such landmarks as the Pont du
Gard, the Maison Carrée Temple in Nîmes, old castles at

Aigues-Mortes, as well as emblematic local sights such as bull-fights and stampeding wild horses of the Camargue – in fact the very landscape and the very spirits which are the backdrop and chorus to Durrell's last novels. This final book, together with *The Avignon Quintet*, provides the literate traveller with the ideal reading to take on a visit to the ancient Roman province. It is also a beautifully written last act to Durrell's own poetic drama.

When the book (dedicated to Françoise) appeared shortly after his death, reviews of it were often combined with obituaries and obituaries with reviews. David Hughes, writing in the *Mail on Sunday*, saw it as 'the last word in famous last words'.[7] Roger Clarke, in the *Sunday Times*, read it as 'an elegy to ruins and lost friends... both an introduction to the life of Lawrence Durrell and a numinous farewell'.[8] For the *New York Newsday* reviewer, too, it drew a line under a life – 'it sums up Durrell himself as both a sybarite and a man of great tenderness contemplating the end of his life'.[9] And for Nicholas Delbanco in the *Detroit Free Press* it was a lamentation, 'a long-postponed love-letter to [Durrell's] final home'.[10]

Hardly had the sound of eulogies at the time of his death died away than, on 26 May 1991, the story of the charge of incest against him broke on the front page of the *Sunday Telegraph*. The allegation was that because his fiction was obsessed with 'violence, death, magic, the occult, incest, child abuse and sexual perversion', Sappho's journals with *their* obsession with sex, violence and incest confirmed that he had engaged in incest with her. This, it was suggested, was the cause of her psychological problems and ultimately her suicide.

Barbara Robson, from whom the story came, and who had been studying 'corruption in the inner city' for the Institute of Economic Affairs and the Centre for Policy Studies, claimed that Sappho had told her what had happened. The article also mentioned Sappho's request not to have her father buried with her, and stated that Robson planned to publish her journals and letters now that Durrell was dead, and as Sappho had requested.[11] The rest of the press took up the story and ran with it. Eve and members of Durrell's family were doorstepped and questioned, Sappho's husband Simon was quoted, as were old schoolfriends of hers. Some newspapers ran lurid headlines which already carried the assumption of guilt.

The story was fiercely defended by Robson and a few others, and was adamantly denied by Durrell's friends. Anthea Morton-Saner, Durrell's agent, pointed out that Sappho was unstable and that the Durrell known to his friends was incapable of such a thing. Robson, who was convinced of the truth of the allegation, pointed to Durrell's novels and his obsession with incest and the parallels between Sappho and Livia, the dark incestuous lesbian, in the *Quintet*. However, while one schoolfriend said that Sappho had told her the same story of incest, her 'best' schoolfriend said that she had never heard of the allegation, and Simon Tompsett was reported as saying, 'I was never really sure how much of it was a genuine remembrance and how much of it was Sappho's attempt to understand the feelings and disturbances she was going through at the time. There was a deep bond of affection certainly, but if you ask me if a physical relationship existed, I think perhaps not.'[12] Later, the literary magazine *Granta* agreed to publish Sappho's journals, but Robson's plan to publish was challenged by Sappho's mother Eve, who took the matter to court, claiming copyright on her daughter's notebooks. The court, however, gave *Granta* the right to publish the material, leaving the question of copyright to be settled later.

Sappho makes no specific allegations in the journal extracts published. The theory of suppressed memory of childhood incest was highly fashionable at the time but has since been called into question. She was undergoing psychoanalysis when she wrote about this in her diaries and even planned to write something on the subject for *Spare Rib*.

Certainly Durrell was capable of living inside the novel he was currently writing, and he was also known to transform people close to him into his characters. (Ghislaine experienced it, and Françoise noted how one felt that he was watching and planning to write one into his next book.)[13] Doubtless, because he thought of her as a creative writer with potential, he drew Sappho into his literary fantasies, and, since these involved lesbianism and incest, he may have affected her perception of what occurred between them. That she told her husband Simon that it was probably 'psychological' incest adds credence to this scenario. Durrell was undoubtedly a difficult man to live with, especially when 'madly' creating, and for a young woman growing up this could have been hard to take. His wives could divorce him, but she must always remain the daughter of Lawrence Durrell. On the charge of incest with his daughter, Durrell must be declared innocent until proved guilty.

On Sunday, 7 July 1991, with the cloud of the incest allegation still hanging over events, a 'tribute' was held in his honour at Stratford-upon-Avon. Although, sadly, Gerry was unable to get there, Penny, Eve and Françoise attended, and there were readings from Durrell's work. It is to be hoped that the readings included one of the marvellously rapturous letters he wrote to Henry Miller and Anne Ridler about visiting the home of the Bard in 1939, and no doubt the debt he owed as a boy to Shakespeare's inspiration was given due weight on the occasion.

Granta published Sappho's 'Journals and Letters' in the autumn issue of 1991. That November, Françoise opened the house in Sommières as a Study Centre for research into Durrell and his work. She was translating *Caesar's Vast Ghost* into French for Gallimard, and found herself in charge of the Pléiade edition of Durrell – something he would have savoured, valuing the respect of the French above all others as he did. In 1994, Margo's book, written in the early 1960s, stored away and left undiscovered for thirty years, was finally published. *Whatever Happened to Margo?* is a beautifully comic account of her life keeping a boarding house at 51 St Alban's Avenue, with eccentric lodgers and eccentric Durrells (including ancient aunts, louche brother Leslie, Gerry and his animals, Larry with his mordant wit and the long-suffering Louisa) among the cast. On 30 January 1995, one of the cast, Gerry, died in hospital in Jersey, eighteen months after a liver transplant from which he never fully recovered.

Lawrence Durrell's place in English literature is not as secure as it ought to be. He was the victim of his own achievement. The huge success of *The Alexandria Quartet* in the late 1950s

and early 1960s brought him great celebrity, but he had caught
the mood of the time, a period when more cosmopolitan attitudes were awakening in the Anglo-Saxon world. The
loosening of morals made Durrell, with his fascination with
the erotic and the sexually deviant, a guru to whom to turn
for enlightenment and justification for a new, sensually aware
lifestyle. It was even said that during the 1960s Flower Children
could be found carrying copies of *Justine* in their knapsacks.
But as moods changed and as he had difficulty living up to the
expectations of readers in his subsequent novels, his position
as a literary luminary and creative genius declined. Though all
of his major works are in print in the mid 1990s, his star has
waned somewhat, and it is still questionable whether even *The
Alexandria Quartet* will survive as a classic – as it should.

It is difficult to think of another English writer who evolved
so intricate and self-conscious a literary mode, and succeeded
in producing two great novelistic cycles. Of course, his novels
were not novels in any conventional sense, but fictional vehicles
for a wide variety of ideas – not his own but brought together
in a unique fashion. He was among the most Freudian of
creative writers, and his overall project was ameliorative and
therapeutic – though not in line with any orthodox social
philosophy. Rather, he believed that it was through personal
experimentation and psychological wholeness that human happiness was attainable, and this emphasis on practice rather
than belief is what attracted him to Buddhism. If he had a
wider solution it was a negative one – against scientific rationalism and the depredations of modern technology, against
materialism and the power of money, against the destructive
force of monotheism – against all forces in the world leading
to the fragmentation of society and of the human psyche.
Insofar as he saw sex as an antidote to many of these evils, a
view he shared with D. H. Lawrence, he went further, as did
his mentor Miller, in shedding any sense of religiosity or guilt
about it. Sex, even sadistic sex, was fun to him, and could only
have beneficial results (though not every woman he slept with
agreed with this). His fascination with sexual deviation – incest
(Pursewarden and Liza, Julian and Benedicta, Hilary and
Livia), prostitution (Melissa, Iolanthe, Sabine), lesbianism

(Clea and Justine, Constance and Sylvie, Pia and Trash, Livia and Thrush), paedophilia (Prince Hassan) had a strong anti-Christian, anti-Anglo-Saxon motivation. And his exile from England was as much a rejection of its artistic and sexual mores, as much a search for a more congenial spirit of place, as it was a mere desire to travel and see the world.

Durrell said a lot of profound things about the craft of literature to which he was so committed. His novels all question the nature of the creative act and the kinds of reality fiction creates. *The Alexandria Quartet* is a brilliant exploration of how history and biography are constructed (so questioning the nature of chronological time); *Tunc/Nunquam* relates that to the power of great impersonal commercial organizations and their need to impose one version of reality for their own ends; and in *The Avignon Quintet*, by composing and decomposing characters, he shows how authors try to achieve whole characters out of disparate psychological fragments, and how the stable psyche begins to disintegrate the moment it is constructed. The instability of the ego, the instability of time, the instability of reality are great themes in Durrell's work, which anticipate modern philosophical critiques and exemplify them superbly. It would be in this that I would place his greatest claim to literary stature, after his magical power over language.

He had probably been justly accused of representing women in an unnatural way. Diana Gould/Menuhin was highly censorious of him on this score, and other women critics noted how women characters were often used only as sexual objects and as victims of violence. He seems to have remained unmoved by these criticisms and continued to present them as he always had, even to the end; but he did make women important vehicles for ideas (Constance), and even of anti-male rebellion (Iolanthe). He may have thought that puritanical women lay behind the restrictiveness of pre-war English life, and in presenting them as unlaced sensualists and willing objects of male desire he was out to shock and sting his Victorian aunts – Prudence, Patience, Norah and company.

Durrell's status as a poet is difficult to judge because of the breaks in his poetic career, especially the period after 1956 when he turned his attention almost completely to fiction. G. S.

Fraser judged him 'a minor poet, though of a very distinguished sort'.[14] Durrell declared himself to be not a great poet because he had written too much, something which Eliot had counselled him against. Often he wrote from within his own private country, and he appears at times to be wilfully obscure, but the pure lyrical tone of his voice lent itself to producing haunting love poems and poetry of landscape which, after Wordsworth, are probably the subtlest in the language. And his comic poetry. 'A Ballad of the Good Lord Nelson' for example, shows him, in Rabelaisian mode, to have been one of the wittiest poets of our times. But it was a vein he rarely tapped. If his power decreased in the second half of his life, it could still surge to give us some of his later, sadder poems such as 'Vega', and fine nostalgic poems of mood and atmosphere such as 'Certain Landfalls'.[15]

However, the poetry that infused his prose is what makes it lift off the page, and his descriptions of Alexandria, of the Nile and of the Egyptian desert, and the great set-pieces which he wrote with such facility, radiate from the page like displays of cut and polished jewellery, and can leave the reader breathless with admiration.

There were faults with Durrell the poet and novelist, as there are with any writer. He was inclined to overindulge his rich vein of fantasy and the lusciousness of his prose, and occasionally he could become boring, especially when his characters expound their pet philosophies to one another. And to the prosaic mind the kaleidoscopic view of the personality and of external reality could read like nonsense – as the reactions of some critics remind us. But at a time when the Anglo-Saxon novel was constricted by parochialism, and experimentation was frowned upon, he went against the literary grain and helped pave the way for the magical realists of a later generation.

His position as an exile was probably crucial to his ability to do this. From the perspective of the Mediterranean, with its classical and pagan inheritance, he was able to weave an alternative literary reality which was still recognizably English. His colonial and Irish background, however blown up, helped him greatly to carry off his experiments. The only other English writer, also an exile, who can be compared to him in pointing the way forward for the intoxicated imagination in the novel is Malcolm Lowry, whose *Under the Volcano* was equally rich in poetry and equally experimental with reality. Lowry used the unstable vision of the alcoholic as his vehicle, while Durrell used the shifting vision of the creative writer.

Durrell probably never recovered from being expelled from India as an eleven-year-old. He was pitched into an alien society where, as an undersized 'colonial', he was marginalized and at the same time bereft of maternal care and comfort. He occasionally hinted at the excruciating pain of solitude which he had endured throughout his life and which he was never able to throw off. Faced with a hostile England, and cast into a despised role, he had acquired a series of *alter egos*, of masks with which to face the world. This gave him a mastery of the puppet-theatre of multiple personae which he exploited so brilliantly in his novels, but it constituted no solution to his own feelings of confusion and pain. Throughout his life he searched, often in odd corners, for philosophies of integration, and the quest for wholeness became the overriding theme of his creative work.

The protective mask and the theatrical act probably left him with the feeling that, behind all that, he was empty, and he hinted at that when he spoke, as he sometimes did, about not existing or about having been born dead. This meant that on the outside he could be the effervescent personality, imbued with *joie de vivre*, an indomitable wit and an unquenchable charm. Inside there was gloom and pain and suffering. With his men friends he showed them mainly his glittering exterior; to women, in the intimacy of love, he became the unrestrained child – lustful, irresponsible and violent. He felt cheated and abused by women – the woman who had abandoned him to his lonely childhood exile, the wives who had left him or taken his daughters from him – and he seems to have directed a great deal of anger against them. The love–hate he showed towards his daughter Sappho was probably the same love–hate he showed towards many of the women he drew into his own orbit. First he needed to be loved and then he needed to hate the loved one.

By association, he hated England, the country to which he

had been sent, away from what he had grown up to love. Like many alienated young people he inverted the values he despised. If death was to be feared, as it was by Miss Farrell and by Big Granny, then he would embrace death as a theme and learn about it in all its aspects, almost wallowing in the goriness of it and the body's decay. If the hated English were screwed up about sex, he would abandon himself to it in all its perversity. If gentlemanly restraint was the British order of the day, he would erupt with Rabelaisian outrageousness. If they favoured sober self-discipline, he would smoke and drink and use the English language to excess. If they were somehow bound into their medieval social system by a medieval Christian Church, he would become an atheist and then turn to some alien religion – to Gnosticism and to Buddhism. And if his generation embraced socialism he was happy to declare himself a monarcho-fascist, though this was probably as much a gesture as a deep-rooted belief. But, whereas rebellious youth often grows out of all this, Durrell retained his youthful passions and hatreds. Out of necessity he crammed himself into a suit and tie and took on the role of teacher or diplomat, but at every opportunity he subverted the role – played the non-establishment figure or the loose cannon – and once free from all such restraints allowed his wild side full rein.

Writing, to him, was a drug which anaesthetized him to the pain of a world into which he thought he had been born centuries too late. He would have preferred to have been born an Elizabethan, and it was to the unlaced rumbustiousness of the Elizabethan writer that he turned for much of his inspiration, as well as to Rabelais and to de Sade, to whose intellectual justification for cruelty he found himself drawn. By taking on the Gnostic belief that we live in the realm of the Prince of Darkness in which evil reigns, and the Buddhist idea that the 'reality' in which we live is in fact a dream and a delusion, he was able to give further legitimacy to his often sadistic appetites. Freud and Groddeck provided for this a modern gloss, for ironically wholeness and health could result from unrestrained and uninhibited conduct, personal disintegration and disease could result from self-denial.

Durrell's lack of restraint, however, also had its less than wholesome side in strong ethnic prejudices. About Jews, for example, he was highly ambiguous, and his anti-semitism cannot be stereotyped. It expressed itself in the caricature Jews who appear in his novels – the rapacious Noah Silverstein in *Panic Spring*, the wife-seducing Coréze and Campion in *Cefalû*, the monied but ignorant Lord Galen in *The Avignon Quintet*, and the nymphomaniac Justine in the *Quartet*. His friends and mentors, Miller, Eliot and Aldington, held anti-semitic views of greater or less virulence, and he caught from Miller his contempt for Jack Kahane, the 'Manchester Jew', who nevertheless published *The Black Book*. However, Durrell was not anti-semitic on racial grounds (though he may have been somewhat so in the pre-war period); rather he was anti-Judaist on religious and intellectual grounds. He was appalled by the Holocaust, but blamed Jewish thinkers for the monotheism which had been such a murderous force throughout the world, and for materialist science which wrote off metaphysics. At the same time he found Jews attractive. Two of his wives were Jewish (including Claude, to whom he was so devoted) and he greatly admired the religiously tolerant Israel which he found on the kibbutzim. However, Durrell took little care to hide his prejudices. He had contempt for Pudding Islanders, and referred to Egyptians as begowned apes. The Greeks, French and Tibetans, on the other hand, could do little wrong.

This dark side of Durrell was complemented by a humanistic one which, in its Gnostic mode, recognized threats to human values in the perverted science of Nazism and the perverted application of science through powerful, unrestrained big business. And on a personal level, despite a strong mean streak deepened by a fear of poverty, he could be generous in helping others – Gawsworth, Bernard Spencer's widow, Perlès, the Buddhists of Burgundy and even his old school in Canterbury benefited from his benevolence.

In his violent explosions with Ghislaine and his other wives, he revealed briefly and dramatically the fears and terrors which tormented him, those same demons he conjured from his Freud-haunted subconscious when he wished to induce a creative madness. These were the raw forces which powered his creative genius. Having revealed them, as he never revealed them in his work or to his other friends, he had to destroy the moment and attack the recipient of these secrets. And, as he admitted, he had become more disembodied in his personal relations over the years. Where he attacked his wife or was cruel to his daughter, he was doing it not to them, but to one or other of his own characters. Finally, with Ghislaine, he would have to erase her from his life.

He was also quite capable of visiting his inner violence on other women who got close to him – his casual lovers and even one of his daughters. Penelope, his eldest daughter, seems to have escaped much of this. She had never lived as close to her father as had Sappho. When she was young, her mother Nancy had not been keen for them to spend time together. And, although she visited him as a teenager, it was in the happy days of his marriage to Claude. When Durrell disintegrated following Claude's death and descended into wild debauches, it was fourteen-year-old Sappho, at her most vulnerable, who had to deal with his violent moods – the moods which Claude had previously handled. The tall, cool Penny was able to view him in a more detached way, from a distance. By the time Claude died, Penny was a married woman with a life and career of her own. Those who have favoured a textual analysis of Durrell's attitude towards his daughters have seen it in his portraits of the two sisters in the *Quintet*, Constance and Livia – one blonde, cool and feminine, the other dark, unfathomable and masculine. The fact that Sappho expressed confusion about her sexuality, and hanged herself in her own attic bedroom, as did Livia, certainly suggests that she saw herself portrayed there. The fact seems to be that Durrell was a difficult and dangerous man for any woman to get involved with. That said, most of Durrell's friends agreed that Françoise and he were particularly well suited – a strong woman with a feel for the French language and for good living.

To his friends Durrell was sparkling 'champagne', the man who oxygenated the atmosphere. He showed them his brilliant exterior – the pyrotechnician expressing himself through a firework display of words, verbal brilliance and wit – which kept him alive and drove him through his social life as a highly congenial companion. But the small child shivering inside this shell he rarely allowed others to see – the lonely boy making his way through miserable, deserted, fog-bound London streets when he might have been shining beneath Tibetan-blue skies or skirting the rich edges of the Burmese jungle, rubbing shoulders with saffron-robed Buddhist monks, like his youthful hero Kim. The little boy haunted by fears of death and decay, and of suffocation, being forced to drink the hot blood of chickens, oppressed by gloomy religion with its cannibalistic and vampiric rituals – all that steaming brew could erupt when he was drunk or trying to drive on a highly convoluted and over-heated work of fiction. But mostly it was kept bottled up, in good Victorian style, and channelled into his writings.

Durrell was a writer of dazzling virtuosity, a man of huge appetites, and a celebrant of life over death. To be able, as it appears he was, to move from one reality to another with such facility – even into madness and out of it at will – gave him a means of creating formidable fictions which could stir the mind as well as the senses. His power over language was daunting, and for a language and culture to survive in the new world of cyberspeak we need more like him – poets on the side of life – not fewer. The book on Lawrence Durrell can never be closed.

Select Bibliography of Durrell's Work

Novels

Pied Piper of Lovers, Cassell, London, 1935
Panic Spring, Faber & Faber, London, 1936 (under the pseudonym Charles Norden)
The Black Book: An Agon, Obelisk Press, Paris, 1938; Faber & Faber, London, 1973
Cefalû, Editions Poetry London, 1947; as *The Dark Labyrinth*, Ace Books, London, 1958; Faber & Faber, London, 1961
White Eagles Over Serbia, Faber & Faber, London, 1957
Justine, Faber & Faber, London, 1957
Balthazar, Faber & Faber, London, 1958
Mountolive, Faber & Faber, London, 1958
Clea, Faber & Faber, London, 1960
Tunc: A Novel, Faber & Faber, London, 1968
Nunquam: A Novel, Faber & Faber, London, 1970
Monsieur: or The Prince of Darkness, Faber & Faber, London, 1974
Livia: or Buried Alive, Faber & Faber, London, 1978
Constance: or Solitary Practices, Faber & Faber, London, 1982
Sebastian: or Ruling Passions, Faber & Faber, London, 1983
Quinx: or The Ripper's Tale, Faber & Faber, London, 1985

Books for Travellers and Isolmanes

Prospero's Cell: A Guide to the Landscape and Manners of the Island of Corcyra, Faber & Faber, London, 1945
Reflections on a Marine Venus, Faber & Faber, London, 1953
Bitter Lemons, Faber & Faber, London, 1957
Spirit of Place: Letters and Essays on Travel, Faber & Faber, London, 1969,
Sicilian Carousel, Faber & Faber, London, 1977

The Greek Islands, Faber & Faber, London, 1978
Caesar's Vast Ghost, Faber & Faber, London, 1990

Plays

Sappho, Faber & Faber, London, 1952
An Irish Faustus: A Morality in Nine Scenes, Faber & Faber, London, 1963
Acte: A Play, Faber & Faber, London, 1964

Poetry

A Private Country, Faber & Faber, London, 1943
Cities, Plains and People, Faber & Faber, London, 1946
On Seeming to Presume, Faber & Faber, London, 1948
The Tree of Idleness, Faber & Faber, London, 1955
Selected Poems, Faber & Faber, London, 1956
Collected Poems, Faber & Faber, London, 1960
Selected Poems, 1935–1963, Faber & Faber, London, 1964
The Ikons, Faber & Faber, London, 1966
Collected Poems (revised), Faber & Faber, London, 1968
The Red Limbo Lingo: A Poetry Notebook, Faber & Faber, London, 1971
Vega And Other Poems, Faber & Faber, London, 1973
Selected Poems (Selected and Introduced by Alan Ross), Faber & Faber, London, 1977
Collected Poems 1931–1974 (edited by James A. Brigham), Faber & Faber, London, 1980

Essays

Key to Modern Poetry, Peter Nevill, London, 1952
Blue Thirst, Capra Press, Santa Barbara, 1975

Comic Stories

Esprit de Corps: Sketches from Diplomatic Life, Faber & Faber, London, 1957
Stiff Upper Lip, Faber & Faber, London, 1958
Sauve Qui Peut, Faber & Faber, London, 1966

Notes

Published correspondence is indicated by the abbreviation 'Ltrs'. This formula applies to the following published correspondence:

Ian MacNiven and Harry T. Moore (eds.), *Literary Lifelines: The Richard Aldington–Lawrence Durrell Correspondence*, Viking Press, New York, 1981

Ian MacNiven (ed.), *The Durrell–Miller Letters 1935–80*, Faber and Faber, London, 1988

Gunther Stuhlmann (ed.), *Henry Miller – Letters to Anaïs Nin*, Peter Owen, London, 1965

Paul Ferris (ed.) *Dylan Thomas: Collected Letters*, Dent, London, 1985

The archival sources of letters and manuscripts are indicated as follows:

Bodleian: Bodleian Library, University of Oxford
Iowa: University of Iowa
NLC: National Library of Canada
NLS: National Library of Scotland
PRO: Public Record Office, Kew, London
SIU: Morris Library, Southern Illinois University at Carbondale
Sommières: Centre d'Etudes et de Recherches, Sommières
UCL: University College, London
Victoria: McPherson Library, University of Victoria

In reference to Lawrence Durrell's works; one-word titles (e.g. *Justine*) are given in full, but others are abbreviated as follows:

BB: *The Black Book*	PPOL: *Pied Piper of Lovers*
BL: *Bitter Lemons*	PS: *Panic Spring*
BT: *Blue Thirst*	QF: *Quaint Fragment*
CP: *Collected Poems, 1980*	SITME: *A Smile in the Mind's Eye*
CVG: *Caesar's Vast Ghost*	
KTMP: *Key to Modern Poetry*	SOP: *Spirit of Place*
PC: *Prospero's Cell*	TGI: *The Greek Islands*

Preface

1 Programme for French television produced by Yves Hoffmann, 1988

Chapter 1: Shangri-la

1 BBC TV, *Spirit of Place: Lawrence Durrell's Egypt*, 9 April 1978
2 Programme for French television produced by George Hoffman, 1988
3 'Le bon plaisir de Lawrence Durrell', *France Culture*, Paris, French national radio. Michael H. Begnal (ed.), *On Miracle Ground: Essays on the Fiction of Lawrence Durrell*, Bucknell University Press, Lewisberg, 1990: 13–14, The graveyard scene also crops up in Durrell's first novel, *PPOL*
4 Rudyard Kipling, *Kim*, Macmillan, London, 1941: Chapter 2
5 Alfred Perlès, *My Friend Lawrence Durrell*, Scorpion Press, London, 1961: 18
6 Gerald Durrell, *The Garden of the Gods*, Collins, London, 1978: 113
7 Durrell to Henry Miller, [c. 27 January 1937], Ltrs: 50
8 Richard Pine, *Lawrence Durrell: The Mindscape*, Macmillan, London, 1995: 27
9 BBC TV, *Intimations*, interview with Malcolm Muggeridge, 19 October 1965
10 *PPOL*: Chapter 7
11 Margaret Durrell, *Whatever Happened to Margo?*, André Deutsch, London, 1995: 18
12 'Down the Styx', *SOP*: 417–22, A Letter to Aunt Prudence
13 Gerald Durrell, *My Family and Other Animals*, Hart-Davis, London, 1959, and Margaret Durrell, *Whatever Happened to Margo?*
14 *Radio Times*, 13–19 March 1976: 4
15 BBC TV, *Intimations*
16 Gerald Durrell, *My Family and Other Animals*
17 BBC TV, *Intimations*
18 Sappho Durrell, 'Journals and Letters', *Granta*, Autumn 1991: 71
19 Begnal (ed.), *On Miracle Ground*: 16
20 Durrell to Henry Miller [mid-December 1957], Ltrs: 300–2
21 *PPOL*: 142–3
22 BBC TV, *Intimations*
23 *PPOL*: Book I
24 'From the Elephant's Back', *Fiction Magazine*, Winter 1983: 59
25 BBC TV, *Intimations*
26 Christopher Martin-Jenkins (ed.), *Quick Singles: Memories of Summer's Days*, Dent, London, 1986: 18

27 Daniel H. Minassian, 'Portrait of Lawrence Durrell,' *Architectural Digest*, 1 August 1991: 30
28 *SITME*: 33–4
29 *Ibid.*: 35
30 'From the Elephant's Back': 59
31 *Ibid.*
32 BBC TV, *Intimations*
33 *PPOL*: 115–16
34 Begnal (ed.), *On Miracle Ground*: 13
35 *A Century Observed* (Souvenir of St. Joseph's College, North Point, Darjeeling, 1888–1988), St. Joseph's College, Darjeeling: 71
36 *SOP*: 15
37 'Constellation', MS (SIU)
38 *Mountolive*: 89

Chapter 2: Torn Up by the Roots

1 *PPOL*: 157
2 *QF*
3 'Asylum in the Snow', *SOP*: 258–85
4 Martin Seymour-Smith, *Rudyard Kipling*, Papermac, London, 1990: 7
5 BBC TV, *Intimations*, interview with Malcolm Muggeridge, 19 October 1965
6 'Françoise Kestsman La Flamme de Durrell', *Elle*, 26 October 1992: 56
7 BBC TV, *Intimations*
8 E. M. Forster, 'Notes on the English Character', *Abinger Harvest*, Edward Arnold, London, 1936
9 BBC World Service, *Meridian*, interview with Edward Blishen, May 1985
10 *SITME*: 19
11 BBC TV, *Intimations*
12 Christopher Martin-Jenkins (ed.), *Quick Singles: Memories of Summer's Days*, Dent, London, 1986: 18
13 *Ibid.*
14 School Report, St Olave's and St Saviour's Grammar School, 19 December 1924
15 *Ibid*, 9 April 1925
16 Guy Wilkinson to GB, 9 May 1994
17 *Ibid.*
18 Guy Wilkinson to GB, 27 April 1994
19 Michael Dibdin, 'One Man's Retreat from Pudding Island', *Independent on Sunday*, 11 November 1990: 27

20 Guy Wilkinson to GB, 27 April 1994

21 *Olavian*, November 1925

22 *Ibid.*, December 1925

23 *Mountolive*: 87

24 *Livia*: 80

25 *Livia*: 53

26 Durrell to G. S. Fraser, 19 May 1965

27 Martin-Jenkins (ed.), *Quick Singles*: 18

28 Marc Alyn, *The Big Supposer*, Abelard-Schuman, London, 1973: 29

29 *Livia*: 184

30 BBC TV, *Intimations*

31 Durrell to J. V. Tyson, Headmaster of St Edmunds, 19 May 1988 (St Edmund's School)

32 A. T. P. Seabrook to J. J. Astbury-Bailey, 27 April 1993 (J. J. Astbury-Bailey)

33 There is no record of Lawrence Samuel sailing to or from London that year, but the 1927 *Kelly's Street Directory* names him as resident of 43 Alleyn Park suggesting that he was in residence there at the end of 1926

34 'Lawrence Durrell en dix mouvements', *Magazine Littéraire*, September 1984: 78–85

35 Durrell to Henry Miller [January 1937], in George Wickes (ed.), *Lawrence Durrell and Henry Miller: A Private Correspondence*, Faber & Faber, London, 1963: 47–9

36 Interview with D. G. Bridson, BBC Third Programme, 27 January 1963

37 *Ibid.*

38 'Constellation', MS (SIU)

39 Alyn, *The Big Supposer*: 30

40 *Ibid.*: 29

41 George Plimpton (ed.), *Writers at Work*, 2nd Series, Penguin, Harmondsworth, 1982: 261

42 *Ibid.*

43 BBC Radio 4, *Woman's Hour* 3 June 1985

44 *QF*; and *CP*: 18

45 *CVG*: 27

46 *CP*: 180

47 Durrell to Alan Thomas, [1935] *SOP*: 36

48 BBC Radio 4, *Woman's Hour* 3 June 1985

49 Alyn, *The Big Supposer*: 26

50 *Ibid.*: 30

51 Robin Livio, *Bulletin of Cannes International Film Festival*, 11 May 1973: 1–2

52 Robin Fedden, *Private Landscape*, Turrett Press, London, 1966
53 Gerald Durrell, *My Family and Other Animals*, Hart-Davis, London, 1959: 15–16
54 'Constellation', MS (SIU)
55 Gerald Durrell, 'Happy with Larry', *Sunday Telegraph*, 21 April 1991

Chapter 3: Pudding Island and the English Death

1 Durrell, 'Mr. Ought & Mrs. Should', *Man About Town*, January 1961: 44
2 *SOP*: 417–22
3 *Livia*: 23, 45
4 Beatrice R. Moore and Kathleen Giencke, *Lawrence Durrell: An Illustrated Checklist*, SIU Press, Carbondale, 1983: 1
5 Roger Green, 'Lawrence Durrell: The Spirit of Winged Words', *Aegean Review*, Fall/Winter 1987: 23
6 *SOP*: 25
7 *Livia*: 104
8 *PS*: Chapter 9
9 *SOP*: 17–25
10 John Heath-Stubbs, *Hindsights*, Hodder & Stoughton, London, 1993: 263–8
11 Guy Wilkinson to GB, 18 July 1994
12 Dylan Thomas to Henry Treece, 6/7 July 1938, Ltrs: 311
13 Guy Wilkinson to GB, 18 July 1994
14 John Gawsworth, *Book Collecting & Library Monthly*, July 1969: 81
15 *Livia*: 140
16 Richard Pine, *Lawrence Durrell: The Mindscape*, Macmillan, London, 1995: 394 (n. 52)
17 *Times Literary Supplement*, 9 February 1933: 95
18 *KTMP*: Chapter 10
19 See early collections of poems, *Ten Poems*, The Caduceus Press, London, 1932; and *Transition: Poems*, The Caduceus Press, London, 1934; and *CP*: 25–42
20 *CP*: 36
21 George Plimpton (ed.), *Writers at Work*, 2nd Series, Penguin, Harmondsworth, 1982: 274
22 Durrell to Alan Thomas, c. June 1936, *SOP*: 49–50
23 *SOP*: 24
24 Alan Thomas, 'Some Uncollected Authors: XXIII: Lawrence Durrell', *Book Collector* Spring 1960: 56–63
25 Plimpton, *Writers at Work*: 274

26 Interview with D.G. Bridson, BBC Third Programme, 27 January 1963

27 *Times Literary Supplement*, 6 December 1934: 878–9

28 Durrell to George Wilkinson, 1934 (Iowa)

29 *Ibid.*

30 Durrell to George Wilkinson, Christmas 1934 (Iowa)

31 *SOP*: 26

32 Marc Alyn, *The Big Supposer*, Abelard-Schuman, London, 1973: 37–8

Chapter 4: In Prospero's Cell

1 Durrell to Alan Thomas, [postmark 14 March 1935], *SOP*: 30

2 *TGI*: 16

3 *PC*: 11

4 Marc Alyn, *The Big Supposer*, Abelard-Schuman, London, 1973: 38

5 *SOP*: 31

6 Theodore Stephanides, 'First Meeting with Lawrence Durrell and the House at Kalami', *Deus Loci*, September 1977–June 1978: 2–7

7 CBC TV, *The Search for Ulysses*, [n. d.]

8 Gerald Durrell, *My Island Tutors*, BBC Home Service, 9 December 1952

9 Gerald Durrell, *My Family and Other Animals*, Hart-Davis, London, 1959

10 Durrell to Alan Thomas, 4 June 1935 (quoted in Ian MacNiven, 'Lawrence Durrell Discovers Greece', *Journal of the Literary Imagination*, Spring 1991: 89)

11 See Derek Stanford, *The Freedom of Poetry*, The Falcon Press, London, 1948: 123–35 where Durrell is dubbed 'the Gauguin of modern poetry'

12 Gerald Durrell, *Birds, Beasts and Relatives*, Collins, London, 1969: 74

13 Durrell to Alan Thomas, [1936], *SOP*: 49

14 Henry Miller, *Tropic of Cancer*, John Calder, London, 1963: 275

15 Durrell to Henry Miller, [August 1935], Ltrs: 2

16 Alyn, *The Big Supposer*: 45

17 BBC TV, *Intimations*, interview with Malcolm Muggeridge, 19 October, 1965

18 *Mountolive*: 56

19 BBC TV, *Intimations*

20 Stephanides, 'First Meeting': 3

21 Henry Miller to Durrell, 1 September 1935, Ltrs: 3

22 Durrell to Henry Miller, [September? 1935], Ltrs: 3–4

23 Alyn, *The Big Supposer*: 65

24 *Times Literary Supplement*, 9 November 1935

25 [John Mair], 'Among New Books', review of *PPOL*, *Janus*, No 1, January 1935

26 Alan Thomas, 'Some Uncollected Authors: XXIII: Lawrence Durrell', *Book Collector*, 9 Spring 1960: 56

27 Durrell to Henry Miller, [early 1936], Ltrs: 11

28 Interview with D. G. Bridson, BBC Third Programme, 27 January 1963

29 'Mr. Ought and Mrs. Should', *Man About Town*, January 1961: 44

30 Durrell to Alan Thomas, [1936], SOP: 40

31 *PS*: 91

32 *PS*: 110

33 Durrell to Alan Thomas, [1936], SOP: 38

34 Durrell to Henry Miller, [early 1936], Ltrs: 11

35 *Ibid.*: Ltrs: 8–12

36 George Orwell, review of *Tropic of Cancer, New English Weekly*, 14 November 1935; *Collected Essays*, vol. 1, Penguin, Harmondsworth, 1970: 179

37 Durrell to Alan Thomas, [1936], SOP: 38–40

38 Introduction to reprint of *BB*, Olympia Press, Paris, 1959: 8

39 Durrell to Alan Thomas, [1936], SOP: 38–40

40 Durrell to Henry Miller [early 1936], Ltrs: 11

41 Durrell to John Gawsworth [1936], SOP: 42

42 One short story, 'The Cherries', was published in the *Daily Express*, probably with the help of Gawsworth's Barbara, who worked for the paper.

43 Durrell to Alan Thomas, [1936?], SOP: 46

44 *Ibid.*: 47

45 *Ibid.*: 48

46 Henry Miller to Durrell, [June 1936], Ltrs: 15–17

47 Durrell to Henry Miller, [c. August 1936], Ltrs: 17–20

48 Durrell to Henry Miller, September 1936, Wickes: 23–4

49 Durrell to Henry Miller, [early November] 1936, Ltrs: 22–3

50 *Ibid.*: 22

51 *PC*: 22

52 Durrell to Henry Miller, [c. 12 December 1936], Ltrs: 29–30

53 *Ibid.*: 30

54 Durrell to Richard Aldington, [1 December 1959], Ltrs: 107

55 *KTMP*: 5

56 *Twentieth Century*, Fall 1987: 375

57 G. S. Fraser, *Lawrence Durrell: A Study*, Faber & Faber, London, 1968: 49

58 George Orwell, *Down and Out in Paris and London*, Gollancz, London, 1933

59 George Orwell, 'Inside the Whale', *New Directions in Prose and Poetry, 1940; Collected Essays*, vol. 1, Penguin, Harmondsworth, 1970: 540–78

60 Durrell to Henry Miller, [end December 1936), Ltrs: 38

61 In *SOP* it is dedicated to Anaïs Nin, but this was a retrospective dedication.

Chapter 5: Up and Running in Paris and London

1 *SOP*: 258–72

2 Henry Miller to Durrell, 3 January 1937, Ltrs: 39–41

3 Anaïs Nin to Durrell, 3 January 1937 (SIU)

4 Durrell to Henry Miller, 6/7 January 1937, George Wickes (ed.), *Lawrence Durrell and Henry Miller: A Private Correspondence*, Faber & Faber, London, 1963: 47–9

5 Durrell to Henry Miller, [mid-January 1937], Ltrs: 42–6. (This letter was later published as 'Hamlet, Prince of Denmark', in *Delta*, Christmas 1938.)

6 'The Prince and *Hamlet*', *New English Weekly*, 14 January 1937: 271–3

7 Conrad Moricand, 'Astrological Portrait of Lawrence Durrell', Appendix to Marc Alyn, *The Big Supposer*, Abelard-Schuman, London, 1973: 153–7

8 Durrell to Henry Miller, [February? 1937], Ltrs: 54–5

9 *CP*: 111

10 In *SOP*, 'Asylum in the Snow' (258) is dedicated to Nin and 'Zero' (245) to Miller – the other way around

11 Henry Miller to Durrell, 8 March 1937, Ltrs: 55–7

12 Durrell to Henry Miller, [March 1937], Wickes: 70–1

13 Anaïs Nin, 15 March 1937, 'Notes on the Black Book' (SIU)

14 Durrell to Henry Miller, [late March 1937], Ltrs: 63–5

15 Theodore Stephanides, 'Days in Paleocastrizza', *Deus Loci*, June 1983: 10

16 Henry Miller to Durrell, 5 April 1937, Ltrs: 68

17 Alan Thomas Diary, *Deus Loci*, 1993: 13–35

18 T. S. Eliot to Durrell, 28 June 1937 (SIU)

19 Henry Miller to Durrell, 15 July 1937: Ltrs: 79–80

20 Durrell to Henry Miller and Anaïs Nin, 21 July 1937, Ltrs: 81–3

21 Henry Miller to Durrell, 29 July 1937 Ltrs: 84–7

22 Alfred Perlès, *My Friend Lawrence Durrell*, Scorpion Press, London, 1961: 10–14

23 *The Diary of Anaïs Nin*, vol. 2 (1934–1939), Harcourt Brace, San Diego, 1967: 223

24 *Ibid.*: 237

25 Anaïs Nin to Durrell, [c. November] 1938 (SIU)

26 *The Diary of Anaïs Nin*, vol. 2: 233

27 Henry Miller to Claude Forde, 8 January 1958 (SIU)

28 *The Diary of Anaïs Nin*, vol. 2: 238

29 *Booster*, September 1937

30 *Ibid.*

31 *The Diary of Anaïs Nin*, vol. 2: 244

32 *Labrys*, July 1979: 47

33 Durrell to Henry Miller, [1 September 1937], Ltrs: 92–3

34 T. S. Eliot to Durrell, 9 September 1937 (SIU)

35 Henry Miller, *Order and Chaos Chez Hans Reichel*, Loujon Press, Tucson, Arizona, 1966: Introduction

36 George Bernard Shaw to Durrell, 9 September 1937 (SIU)

37 Cecily Mackworth to GB, 26 June 1994

38 David Gascoyne to Durrell, 18 October 1937, in Gascoyne's *Collected Journals, 1936–42*, Skoob Books, London, 1991: 139–40

39 Cecily Mackworth to GB, 26 June 1994

40 *The Diary of Anaïs Nin*, vol. 2: 264

41 Anaïs Nin to Durrell, September 1937 (SIU)

42 *The Diary of Anaïs Nin*, vol. 2: 253

43 Henry Miller, 'A Boost for *The Black Book*', *Booster*, October 1937: 14

44 George Orwell, 'Back to the Twenties', review of the *Booster, New English Weekly*, 21 October 1937: 30–1

45 'The Booster', *New English Weekly*, 4 November 1937: 78–9

46 George Orwell, 'The Booster', *New English Weekly*, 11 November 1937: 100

47 *The Diary of Anaïs Nin*, vol. 2: 231–9

48 T. S. Eliot to Durrell, 5 November 1937 (SIU)

49 Jay Martin, *Always Merry and Bright*, Capra Press, Santa Barbara, 1978: 329–30

50 CP: 43

51 Buffie Johnson, 'Personal Reminiscence of Lawrence Durrell', *Twentieth Century*, Fall 1987: 288–9

52 Dylan Thomas to Durrell, [December 1937] Ltrs: 265–6

53 Durrell to Henry Miller, [after 25 December 1937], Ltrs: 97

54 Henry Miller to Durrell, 16 December 1937 (SIU)

55 Henry Miller to Durrell, 30 December 1937 (SIU)

56 Anaïs Nin to Durrell, early March 1938 (SIU)

57 Anaïs Nin to Durrell, [c. April 1938] (SIU)

58 Gascoyne, *Collected Journals, 1936–42*: 149
59 Anaïs Nin to Durrell, [c. June 1938] (SIU)
60 Durrell to Henry Miller, [May 1938], Wickes: 124

Chapter 6: The End of the Idyll

1 Durrell to Henry Miller, [May 1938], George Wickes (ed.), *Lawrence Durrell and Henry Miller: A Private Correspondence*, Faber & Faber, London, 1963: 124
2 Anaïs Nin to Durrell, [c. June 1938] (SIU)
3 Audrey Beecham to Durrell, 17 June 1938 (Bodleian)
4 Henry Miller to Durrell, 24 June 1938 (SIU)
5 Durrell to Henry Miller, [July 1938], Wickes: 125–6
6 Durrell to Alan Thomas, [1938], *SOP*: 52–3
7 Durrell to Henry Miller, [August 1938], Wickes: 129–31
8 Jack Kahane, *Memoirs of a Booklegger*, Michael Joseph, London, 1939: 276
9 Henry Miller to Anaïs Nin, 24 August 1938: Ltrs: 173–4
10 Hugh Gordon Porteus, review of *The Black Book*, *New English Weekly*, 15 September 1938: 341–2
11 Henry Miller to Durrell, 25 September 1938, Ltrs: 100–1
12 Henry Miller to Anaïs Nin, [29 September 1938], Ltrs: 176
13 Henry Miller to Anaïs Nin, [30 September 1938], Ltrs: 177
14 Henry Miller to Durrell, 11 [October 1938], Ltrs: 102–3
15 Durrell to Henry Miller [mid October 1938], Ltrs: 103–4
16 Durrell to Desmond Hawkins, October 1938 (Hawkins)
17 Henry Miller to Durrell, 25 October 1938, Ltrs: 104–6
18 Henry Miller to Durrell, 15 November 1938 (SIU)
19 Henry Miller to Durrell, 16 November 1938 (SIU)
20 'Books: Dithyrambic Sex', *Time*, 21 November 1938: 69–70
21 Durrell to T. S. Eliot, December 1938, *Twentieth Century*, Fall 1987: 351–2
22 *CP*: 56
23 Thames TV, *The World at War*, 3: 'France Falls', 14 November 1973
24 Alfred Perlès: *My Friend Lawrence Durrell*, Scorpion Press, London, 1961: 14
25 Durrell to T. S. Eliot, [21 January 1939]: 352
26 'Poets under the Bed', *Sunday Times*, 26 June 1983: 43
27 Dylan Thomas to Vernon Watkins, postmark 8 January 1939, Ltrs: 351
28 Henry Miller to Durrell, 11 January 1939 (SIU)
29 Durrell to Henry Miller, 19 January 1939 (SIU)
30 Desmond Hawkins, 'Books of the Quarter', *Criterion*, 18 January 1939: 316–8

31 Anne Ridler, 'Recollections of Lawrence Durrell', *Twentieth Century*, Fall 1987: 293–5
32 *The Diary of Anaïs Nin*, vol. 2: 332
33 Durrell to Henry Miller, [c. 28 January 1939]: 113–15
34 *The Diary of Anaïs Nin*, vol. 2: 333
35 Dylan Thomas to Durrell, [?February 1939], Ltrs: 355
36 Durrell to Henry Miller, [mid-February 1939], Ltrs: 115–16
37 Dylan Thomas to Tambimuttu, 5 March 1939, Ltrs: 361–2
38 *New English Weekly*, 2 March 1939: 316
39 Henry Miller to Durrell, 4 March 1939, Ltrs: 116–19
40 *Ibid.*
41 Durrell to Henry Miller, [after 4 March 1939], Ltrs: 119–20
42 T. S. Eliot to Durrell, 26 March 1939 (SIU)
43 'Shades of Dylan Thomas', *Encounter* IX, December 1957: 59
44 Dylan Thomas to Durrell, March 1939: Ltrs: 368–9
45 Henry Miller to Durrell, 13 March 1939: Ltrs: 128–9
46 Robin Fedden (ed.), *Personal Landscape*, Editions Poetry, London, 1945: 13
47 Henry Miller to Durrell, 21 November 1942: Ltrs: 158
48 Henry Miller to Anaïs Nin, 9 September 1939: Ltrs: 211
49 Henry Miller, *Colossus of Maroussi*, Minerva, London, 1991: 21
50 *Ibid*: 27
51 George Plimpton (ed.), *Writers at Work*, 4th Series, Penguin, Harmondsworth, 1977: 164
52 Miller, *Colossus of Maroussi*: 36–7
53 Peter Parker, *Ackerley: A Life*, Constable, London, 1989: 114
54 Xan Fielding to Durrell, 28 April 1959 (SIU)
55 Robin Fedden, *Private Landscape*, Turrett Press, London, 1966
56 *Ibid.*
57 *Twentieth Century*, Fall 1987: 303–4
58 Robin Fedden, *Private Landscape*
59 *Ibid.*
60 The poem about the black bidet is unpublished, as far as I can tell.
61 Durrell to Anne Ridler, [late October 1939] SOP: 61–3
62 'Mysticism: The Yellow Peril', *New English Weekly*, 25 January 1940: 208–9
63 Durrell to Elizabeth Smart, November 1939 (NLC)
64 Durrell to Elizabeth Smart, [early February 1940] (NLC)
65 CP: 87
66 CP: 88
67 CP: 97
68 CP: 86

69 Nigel Dennis, 'New Four-Star King of Novelists', *Life*, 21 November 1960: 104
70 *CP*: 85–6
71 *CP*: 89–90
72 *CP*: 112
73 Durrell to Anaïs Nin, [mid January 1940] (SIU)
74 Henry Miller to Anaïs Nin, 12 January, 1940, Ltrs: 219–20
75 John de St Jorre, *The Good Ship Venus*, Hutchinson, London, 1994: 28
76 Durrell to Anaïs Nin, [early February, 1940] (SIU)
77 *Ibid.*
78 Anne Ridler to George Barker, 19 February, 1940 (NLC)
79 Durrell to Henry Miller, [after 18 June 1940], Ltrs: 137–9
80 Durrell to Henry Miller, [c. July 1940], Ltrs: 139–42
81 Durrell to Anne Ridler [early June 1940], *SOP*: 64–6
82 *CP*: 92
83 Durrell to Henry Miller, 10 November [1940], Ltrs: 144
84 Durrell to Henry Miller, [before 13 February 1941]: Ltrs: 145
85 Durrell to Henry Miller, 13 February 1941, Ltrs: 145–6
86 Henry Miller to Durrell, 1 March 1941, Ltrs: 146
87 Artemis Cooper, *Cairo in the War 1939–45*, Hamish Hamilton, London, 1989: 78–9
88 Interview with D. G. Bridson, BBC Third Programme, 27 January 1963
89 Marc Alyn, *The Big Supposer*, Abelard-Schuman, London, 1973: 55
90 Cooper, *Cairo in the War*: 79
91 BBC TV, *Spirit of Place: Lawrence Durrell's Egypt*, 9 April 1978

Chapter 7: The Great Cultural Hinge

1 BBC TV, *Spirit of Place: Lawrence Durrell's Egypt*, 9 April 1978
2 Durrell to Anne Ridler, [1942?], *SOP*: 75; Artemis Cooper, *Cairo in the War 1939–45*, Hamish Hamilton, London, 1989: 79–80
3 Sir Bernard Burrows to GB, 14 September 1995
4 Robin Fedden, *Private Landscape*, Turret Press, London, 1966
5 *Ibid.*
6 Interview with D. G. Bridson, BBC Third Programme, 27 January 1963
7 John Lehmann, *In My Own Time: Memoirs of Literary Life*, Little Brown, Boston, 1969: 339
8 Durrell to T. S. Eliot, 13 February 1942 (SIU)
9 Patrick Leigh Fermor, 'Observations on a Marine Vulcan', *Twentieth Century*, Fall 1987: 305
10 See T. S. Eliot to Durrell, 13 February 1942 (SIU)

11 'Bernard Spencer', *London Magazine*, January 1964: 44
12 BBC TV, *Spirit of Place: Lawrence Durrell's Egypt*, 9 April 1978
13 CP: 99
14 Cooper, *Cairo in the War*: 196
15 Thames TV, *The World at War*, 8: 'The Desert War', 19 December 1973
16 'Propaganda and Impropaganda' in *BT*; Cooper, *Cairo in the War*: 194
17 Cooper, *Cairo in the War*: 201
18 *Ibid.*: 150
19 Sappho Durrell, 'Journals and Letters', *Granta*, Autumn, 1991: 62
20 Fedden, *Private Landscape*
21 *Personal Landscape*, vol. 1, Pt 4, 1942: 7–8
22 Interview with D. G. Bridson, BBC Third Programme, 27 January 1963
23 BBC TV, *Spirit of Place: Lawrence Durrell's Egypt*, 9 April 1978
24 George Lassalle to GB, 1 September 1995
25 Durrell to Henry Miller, 23 May [1944]: Ltrs: 171–3
26 Durrell to Miller, [mid-May, continued late May, 1944], Ltrs: 167–70
27 *Ibid*
28 CP: 119
29 Durrell to Robin Fedden, [early March] 1944 (SIU)
30 *Times Literary Supplement*, 28 August 1943: 417
31 *Poetry Review*, September/December, 1943: 199–200
32 John Bayliss, *Poetry Quarterly*, Winter, 1943: 117–8
33 Alex Comfort to Durrell, 1 November 1943 (UCL)
34 T. S. Eliot to Durrell, 21 September 1943 (SIU)
35 Anne Ridler to Durrell, 21 October 1943 (SIU)
36 Cooper, *Cairo in the War*: 255–6
37 Durrell to Henry Miller, spring 1944, Ltrs: 169
38 Gwyn Williams, *Twentieth Century*, Fall 1987: 299
39 T. S. Eliot to Durrell, 2 October 1943 (SIU)
40 Gwyn Williams, *Flyting in Egypt: The Story of a Verse War 1943–45*, Alun Books, Port Talbot, 1991
41 Galina Vromen, 'Lawrence Durrell Takes Stock', *International Herald Tribune*, 17 November 1978
42 Durrell to Henry Miller, [c. 25 December 1943], Ltrs: 159
43 Durrell to Robin Fedden [late January 1944] (SIU)
44 CP: 123
45 CP: 120
46 CP: 113
47 'Mr. Ought & Mrs. Should', *Man About Town*, January 1961: 44

48 Diana Gould, 'Lawrence Durrell in Alexandria and Sommières', *Twentieth Century*, Fall 1987: 310
49 T. S. Eliot to Durrell, 1 April 1944
50 Durrell to Henry Miller, [c. 25 December 1943], Ltrs: 159
51 Durrell to Henry Miller, 8 February 1944, Ltrs: 159–60
52 Henry Miller to Durrell, 7 April 1944, Ltrs: 161–3
53 Xan Fielding, *Hide and Seek*, Secker & Warburg, London, 1954
54 Durrell to Henry Miller, [c. October 1946], Ltrs: 199–200
55 Durrell to Henry Miller, 8 February 1944, Ltrs: 159–60
56 Diana Gould to Durrell, 10 September 1944 (SIU)
57 Durrell to Henry Miller, [April 1944]: Ltrs: 164–5
58 Henry Miller to Durrell, 5 May 1944: Ltrs: 165–7
59 Durrell to Henry Miller, [mid-May, continued late May, 1944], Ltrs: 167–70
60 Durrell to Henry Miller, [September 1944], Ltrs: 176
61 G. S. Fraser, *A Stranger and Afraid*, Carcanet Press, Manchester, 1983: 124
62 Olivia Manning, 'Poets in Exile', *Horizon*, October 1944: 277
63 'Airgraph on Refugee Poets in Africa', *Poetry London* (New Poets Number), December 1944: 212–5
64 Tambimuttu, 'Dear Fraser', *Poetry London* (New Poets Number), December 1944: 219
65 Anne Ridler to Durrell, 13 October 1944 (SIU)
66 Henry Miller to Durrell, 18 February 1945: Ltrs: 177–9
67 Durrell to Henry Miller, [Spring 1945], George Wickes (ed.), *Lawrence Durrell and Henry Miller: A Private Correspondence*, Faber & Faber, London, 1963: 202
68 Durrell to Henry Miller, 5 March, 1971: Ltrs: 446–8
69 T. S. Eliot to Durrell, 5 April 1944 (SIU)
70 Gwyn Williams, *Twentieth Century*, Fall 1987: 299
71 CP: 154–5

Chapter 8: Return to Greece: Reflections on a Marine Venus

1 Durrell to Henry Miller, 22 June 1945, Ltrs: 181–2
2 Durrell to Gwyn Williams, [1945], SOP: 78–9
3 *Times Literary Supplement*, 7 July, 1945: 320
4 Durrell to T. S. Eliot, [early summer] 1945, *Twentieth Century*, Fall 1987: 355
5 T. S. Eliot to Durrell, 2 September 1945 (SIU)
6 G. W. Stonier, 'The Enchanted Island', *New Statesman*, 24 November 1945: 357–8
7 Durrell to George Leite, 1 December 1946 (SIU)
8 Durrell to Anne Ridler, 15 June [1946], SOP: 84–6

9 Christopher Martin-Jenkins (ed.), *Quick Singles: Memories of Summer's Days*, Dent, London, 1986: Preface

10 Durrell to T. S. Eliot, 17 November 1945, *Twentieth Century*, Fall 1987: 357

11 Durrell to Robin Fedden, January/February 1946 (SIU)

12 *Ibid.*

13 *Ibid.*

14 Mary Mollo, 'Larry, My Friend', *Deus Loci*, December 1983: 1–13; *Twentieth Century*, Fall, 1987: 317–28

15 *Ibid.*

16 Hugh Gordon Porteus, 'Poetic Equations', *Time and Tide*, 15 June 1946: 570

17 Durrell to T. S. Eliot, [April 1946], *SOP*: 82–4

18 Sir Patrick Reilly to Foreign Office, 6 June 1946 (PRO)

19 Durrell to Anne Ridler, 15 June [1946], *SOP*: 84–6

20 Raymond Mills, 'With Lawrence Durrell on Rhodes', *Twentieth Century*, Fall, 1987: 312–16

21 Durrell to Henry Miller, 25 September 1946, Ltrs: 198–9

22 *Ibid.*

23 Xan Fielding to Durrell, 29 April 1959 (SIU)

24 Durrell to T. S. Eliot, 20 October 1946, *SOP*: 86–7

25 Henry Miller to Durrell, 7 October 1946 (SIU)

26 *CP*: 176–80

27 Durrell to John Lehmann, [November 1946] (Iowa)

28 Durrell said he went there in 1948, but this is impossible as he was in South America for the whole of that year

29 Preface to *Pope Joan*, André Deutsch, London, 1960

30 H. P. Croom Johnson (Foreign Office) to Montagu Pollack (British Council), 9 December 1946 (PRO)

31 Miss Aitken (Foreign Office) to Sir Patrick Reilly, 20 December 1946 (PRO)

32 Durrell to Henry Miller, 20 January '1946' [i.e. 1947], Ltrs: 200–1

33 Marc Alyn, *The Big Supposer*, Abelard-Schuman, London, 1973: 63

34 Durrell to Henry Miller, 9 July [1947], Ltrs: 211–13

35 M. D. Edwards (Foreign Office) to Miss K. Graham (BIS Middle East, Cairo), 1 March 1947 (PRO)

36 Interview with D. G. Bridson, BBC Third Programme, 27 January 1963

37 Artemis Cooper, *Cairo in the War 1939–45*, Hamish Hamilton, London, 1989: 258

38 Durrell to George Leite, April 1947 (SIU)

39 Interview with D. G. Bridson, BBC Third Programme, 27 January 1963

40 Durrell to Henry Miller, [June 1947], Ltrs: 208–10
41 Carl Jung to Durrell, 15 December 1947 (SIU)

Chapter 9: In the Wilderness: Argentina and Yugoslavia

 1 Durrell to Anne Ridler, [autumn 1947], *SOP*: 92–4
 2 Durrell to Henry Miller, [c. end of November 1947], Ltrs: 218–19
 3 British Council letter, 23 December 1947 (PRO)
 4 Durrell to Richard Aldington, 26 March 1957, Ltrs: 17–18
 5 T. S. Eliot to Durrell, 27 January 1948 (SIU)
 6 Durrell to Mary Hadkinson, 7 February 1948, *SOP*: 94–5
 7 Jorge 'Monono' Ferreyra, 'Durrell in Córdoba', *Twentieth Century*, Fall 1987: 330
 8 Durrell to Lawrence Clark Powell, [mid-April 1948]: *SOP*: 95–6
 9 Durrell to Mary Hadkinson, [May 1948] (Sommières)
10 P. G. Wodehouse to Durrell, 19 May 1948 (SIU)
11 Ian MacNiven (ed.), *The Miller–Durrell Letters, 1935–80*, Faber & Faber, London, 1988: 207
12 T. S. Eliot, 'Burnt Norton', *The Four Quartets*, Faber & Faber, London, 1944: 11
13 *KTMP*
14 T. S. Eliot to Durrell, 11 July 1948 (SIU)
15 T. S. Eliot to Durrell, 4 March 1949 (SIU)
16 See T. S. Eliot to Durrell, 11 August 1948 (SIU)
17 Raúl Victor Peláez, 'Larry's Long Siesta of 1948', *Twentieth Century*, Fall 1987: 333
18 'Aegean Background', *Times Literary Supplement*, 16 October 1948: 585
19 Alfredo Olivera, 'The Trajectory of a Shooting-Star: Lawrence Durrell', *La Nación*, 17 January 1965
20 Margaret Durrell, *Whatever Happened to Margo?*, André Deutsch, London, 1995: 19
21 Durrell to Henry Miller, 22 January [1949], Ltrs: 227
22 *Mountolive*: 83
23 Durrell to Theodore Stephanides, [July 1949], *SOP*: 100
24 Durrell to Theodore Stephanides [1949], *SOP*: 100–1
25 Durrell to George Orwell, [June/July 1949]) (UCL)
26 'Henry Miller – Man of Genius', *Horizon*, 20 July 1949
27 Henry Miller to Durrell, 14 March 1949, Ltrs: 228–31
28 Durrell to Henry Miller, 5 September 1949, Ltrs: 232–3
29 Durrell to Henry Miller, 10 September 1949, Ltrs: 233
30 Durrell to Maurice Girodias, September 1949 [referred to in MacNiven (ed.), 1988: 238–9]
31 Durrell to Henry Miller, [early October? 1949], Ltrs: 238–9

32 Henry Miller to Durrell, 28 September 1949 (SIU)
33 Interview with Eugene Lyons and Harry T. Antrim, 22 March 1970, *Shenandoah*, Winter 1971
34 Henry Miller to Durrell, 3 October 1949, Ltrs: 237–8
35 Durrell to Henry Miller, [early October 1949], Ltrs: 238–40
36 Durrell to Anne Ridler, [c. 12 October 1949], *SOP*: 103–4
37 Durrell to Henry Miller, 27 October 1949, Ltrs: 243
38 Durrell to Henry Miller, [early March? 1950], Ltrs: 247–8
39 Durrell to Henry Miller, [March/April 1950] Ltrs: 248
40 Durrell to Theodore Stephanides, 10 May 1950, *SOP*: 104
41 Durrell to Anne Ridler, [June 1950], *SOP*: 104–5
42 Peter Russell, 'Sappho', *Time and Tide*, 12 August 1950
43 Margaret Rawlings to Durrell, 23 August 1950 (SIU)
44 John Gawsworth to Durrell, 3 November 1950 (SIU)
45 Margaret Rawlings to Durrell, 8 November 1950 (SIU)
46 Durrell to Theodore Stephanides [winter 1950/51], *SOP*: 107–8
47 *CP*: 213, 218, 219
48 *Times Literary Supplement*, 26 January 1951, 46; *CP*: 224–5
49 Durrell to Anne Ridler, 15 February 1951, *SOP*: 108–9
50 Sappho Durrell, 'Journals and Letters', *Granta*, Autumn 1991: 62
51 Durrell to Henry Miller, [early September, 1951], Ltrs: 255
52 'Mr Lawrence Durrell's "Sappho" ', *The Times*, 22 January 1952: 7
53 Henry Miller to Durrell, 10 March 1952, Ltrs: 259–60
54 Alfred Perlès to Durrell, March 1952 (SIU)
55 Henry Miller to Durrell, 27 April 1952, Ltrs: 261
56 Durrell to Anne Ridler, [May 1952], *SOP*: 110–11
57 Durrell to Henry Miller, [May 1952], Ltrs: 261–2
58 'Voyage of Ideas', *Times Literary Supplement*, 23 May 1952: 339
59 'Shorter Reviews', *New Statesman*, 28 June 1952: 782
60 Durrell to Anne Ridler, 17 August [1952], *SOP*: 111–12
61 Durrell to Henry Miller [c. October 1952]: Ltrs: 263
62 Sappho Durrell, 'Journals and Letters': 62–3

Chapter 10: The Bitter Lemons of Cyprus

1 *BL*: 40
2 Durrell to Henry Miller [May? 1953], Ltrs: 269–70
3 Henry Miller to Durrell, 3 May 1953, Ltrs: 268–9
4 Harold Nicholson 'Dodecanese', *Observer*, 23 August 1953
5 Anne Ridler to Durrell, 23 August 1953 (SIU)
6 Durrell to Theodore Stephanides, 30 October 1953, *SOP*: 119–20
7 Durrell to Henry Miller, [postmark 24 October 1953], Ltrs: 272
8 *Ibid.*
9 Shelley Cox 'The Road Not Taken: Lawrence Durrell's Unpublished

Novel "The Village of the Turtle-Doves" ', *Studies of the Literary Imagination*, Spring 1991: 19–27

10 Durrell to Henry Miller, 20 November 1953, Ltrs: 273–4
11 Durrell to Alan Thomas, [1953] *SOP*: 120–1
12 Durrell to Henry Miller, [c. April 1954], Ltrs: 276–7
13 *Ibid.*
14 Sappho Durrell, 'Journals and Letters', *Granta*, Autumn, 1991: 64
15 Durrell to T. S. Eliot, [1954], *SOP*: 126
16 Penelope Tremayne to GB, 22 January 1993
17 Durrell to Freya Stark, 1 June [1954], *SOP*: 124–5
18 Durrell to Freya Stark, [December 1954], *SOP*: 127
19 *Ibid.*
20 Gerald Durrell to Lawrence Durrell, 20 October 1954 (SIU)
21 Gerald Durrell to Lawrence Durrell, 14 December 1954 (SIU)
22 Anne Ridler to Durrell, 10 October 1954 (SIU)
23 Charles Foley, *Island in Revolt*, Longmans, London, 1962: 11
24 Gerald Durrell, 'My Brother Larry', *Twentieth Century*, Fall, 1987: 264
25 Patrick Leigh Fermor to Durrell, 15 June 1955 (SIU)
26 Foley, *Island in Revolt*: 29
27 Sappho Durrell, 'Journals and Letters': 62
28 Durrell to Freya Stark, [1955] *SOP*: 128–9
29 Lord Scarborough to GB, 8 November 1994
30 Durrell to Henry Miller, [c. November 1955], Ltrs: 278–9
31 Kingsley Martin, 'Paradise Lost', *New Statesman*, 27 July 1957: 120
32 Diana Gould (Menuhin) to Durrell, 29 January 1956 (SIU)
33 Durrell to Henry Miller, [c. January? 1956], Ltrs: 279–80
34 George Plimpton (ed.), *Writers At Work*, 2nd Series, Penguin, Harmondsworth, 1977: 267
35 *Justine*: 217
36 Lord Scarborough to GB, 8 November 1994
37 *Ibid.*
38 Diana Gould (Menuhin) to Durrell, 11 April 1956 (SIU)
39 Penelope Tremayne to GB, 22 January 1993
40 *Ibid.*
41 Penelope Tremayne, *Below the Tide*, Hutchinson, London, 1958: 13ff
42 *BL*: 243
43 Laurence Olivier to Durrell, 25 July 1956 (SIU)
44 Henry Miller to Durrell, 3 August 1956 (SIU)
45 Henry Miller to Durrell, 18 September 1956 (SIU)
46 Memo from Sir Robert Stanley to P. H. Newby, 13 September 1956 (BBC Written Archives)

47 Cecily Macworth to GB, 26 June 1994
48 Durrell to Richard Aldington, 26 March 1957, Ltrs: 17–18
49 G. S. Fraser, 'Matter and Art', *New Statesman*, 13 October 1956: 459
50 *The Times*: 3 January 1956
51 *Times Literary Supplement*, 12 October 1956: 599
52 *BL*: 251
53 Henry Miller to Durrell, 12 December 1956 (SIU)

Chapter 11: Variations on a Theme of Love

1 'A Poet Shocks with Truth and Beauty', *Books and Bookmen*, February 1957: 22–3
2 Durrell to Henry Miller, [late April? 1957], Ltrs: 287
3 Durrell to Terence Tiller, 16 January 1957 (BBC Written Archives)
4 Richard Aldington to Durrell, 1 February 1957: Ltrs: 4–5
5 Richard Aldington to Durrell, February 1957, Ltrs: 6
6 Henry Miller to Gerald Robitaille, 25 February 1957
7 Durrell to Alan Thomas: [14–17 February 1957) *SOP*: 136
8 Freya Stark to Durrell, 5 February 1957 (SIU)
9 Henry Miller to Durrell, 13 February 1957, Ltrs: 284
10 Diana Gould (Menuhin) to Durrell, 22 March 1957 (SIU)
11 *Sunday Times*, 9 February 1957
12 Durrell to Jean Fanchette, [early 1958] (SIU)
13 Christopher Middleton, *The Heraldic Universe*, BBC Third Programme, 23 April 1957
14 Durrell to Henry Miller, [late February 1957], Ltrs: 285
15 Penelope Tremayne, *Below the Tide*, Hutchinson, London, 1958: 104
16 Durrell to Richard Aldington [c. 18–20 March 1957], Ltrs: 11–13
17 Richard Aldington to Durrell, 18 March 1957 (SIU)
18 Durrell to Ella and Alan Thomas [postmark 4 April 1957] *SOP*: 138–9
19 ' "Prometheus Bound" and "Sappho" ', *The Times*, 26 March 1957: 3
20 Roy Walker, 'Radio Drama', The *Listener*, 4 April 1957: 575
21 Durrell to Richard Aldington [26 March 1957], Ltrs: 17–18
22 Durrell to Ella and Alan Thomas [postmark 4 April 1957] *SOP*: 138–9
23 'Poet's Kingdom', *New Statesman*, 4 May 1957: 583
24 Durrell to Henry Miller, [end April 1957], Ltrs: 288–9
25 Gerald Sykes to Durrell, 20 June 1957 (SIU)
26 Durrell to Henry Miller, [June 1957], Ltrs: 290–1
27 Robert Stock: 'Loneliness in the Isles of Greece', *Poetry*, March 1958: 396–9

28 Richard Aldington to Durrell, 24 June 1957, Ltrs: 24

29 Originally called *Bitter Lemons of Cyprus*, a title revived for the reissued paperback and the cassette version for the 1990s travel market

30 Kingsley Martin, 'Paradise Lost', *New Statesman*, 27 July 1957: 120–1

31 'The Tragedy of Cyprus', *Times Literary Supplement*, 23 August 1957: 502

32 'Book Reviews', Bernard Spencer, *London Magazine*, October 1957: 57–8

33 Hugh Gordon Porteus to Durrell, 30 July 1957 (SIU)

34 Durrell to Alan Thomas, [received 3 July 1957], *SOP*: 142–3

35 Durrell to Henry Miller, [mid July 1957], Ltrs: 293–4

36 Henry Miller to Durrell, 31 July 1957, Ltrs: 294–5

37 Henry Miller to Durrell, 9 August 1957 (SIU)

38 Sir John Harding to Durrell, 12 August 1957 (SIU)

39 Gerald Sykes, 'It Happened in Alexandria', *New York Times Book Review*, 25 August 1957: 4

40 'Eros in Alexandria', *Time*, 26 August 1957: 84

41 Phoebe Adams, *Atlantic*, September 1957: 86

42 Diana Gould (Menuhin) to Durrell, 25 September 1957 (SIU)

43 Durrell to Alfred Perlès, [October 1957] (Victoria)

44 Alfred Perlès to Durrell, [October 1957] (SIU)

45 Durrell to Henry Miller, [before 20 January 1957], Ltrs: 305–6

46 Claude Forde to Henry Miller, 18 December 1957: Ltrs: 303–4

47 'People in the News', *Sunday Times*, 15 December 1957

48 Claude Forde to Henry Miller, 18 December 1957, Ltrs: 303–4

49 Durrell to Henry Miller, [before 20? January 1958], Ltrs: 306

50 Sir Bernard Burrows to GB, 14 September 1995

51 Richard Aldington to Durrell, 1 December 1957, Ltrs: 35–6

52 R. W. Flint, 'A Major Novelist', *Commentary*, April 1959: 354

53 Richard Aldington to Durrell, 13 December 1957, Ltrs: 37–8

54 'Roman Étrangers', Jacques Howlett, *Les Lettres Nouvelle*, February 1958 290–2

55 'Note', Dominique Aury, *Nouvelle Revue Française*, March 1958

56 'A la recherche de l'amour moderne', *L'Express*, 10 March 1958

57 Jean Fanchette to Durrell, 18 March 1958 (SIU)

58 Durrell to Henry Miller, [late February 1958], Ltrs: 307

59 *New York Times Book Review*, 2 March 1958: 6

60 George Steiner, 'On the Scene', *Yale Review* June 1958: 600–4

61 Gordon Merrick, 'Will Lawrence Durrell Spoil America?', *New Republic*, 26 May 1958: 20–1

62 Anaïs Nin to Durrell, 22 April 1958 (SIU)

63 *The Journals of Anaïs Nin*, vol. 6 (1955-1966), Peter Owen, London, 1976: 162–4
64 *Ibid.*: 190
65 Anaïs Nin to Durrell [c. October 1957] (SIU)
66 Durrell to Henry Miller, [early July? 1958]: Ltrs: 320–1
67 Durrell to Theodore Stephanides, [1958], *SOP*: 146
68 Durrell to Henry Miller, [mid August 1958], Ltrs: 320–1
69 Gerald Sykes to Durrell, 21 July 1958
70 Durrell to Gerald Sykes, [29 July 1958]
71 Gerald Sykes, 'Alexandria Revisited', *New York Times*, 24 August 1958: 4
72 'Cabal and Kaleidoscope', *Time*, 25 August 1958: 80
73 Paul Bowles, 'A Dimension of Love', *Saturday Review*, 23 August 1958: 16
74 Charles Rollo, 'Fiction Chronicle', *Atlantic Monthly*, September 1958: 80–1
75 Durrell to Richard Aldington, [c. 4–14 August 1958], Ltrs: 50–1
76 *Ibid*: 53–5
77 Richard Aldington to Durrell, 24 September 1958, Ltrs: 56–7
78 Durrell to Jean Fanchette, [12 September 1958], Ltrs: 38–9

Chapter 12: Living with Fame

1 Jean Fanchette to Durrell, 3 October 1958 (SIU)
2 Durrell to Richard Aldington [c. 23–26 November 1958], Ltrs: 67–8
3 Frank Kermode, 'Romantic Agonies', *London Magazine*, February 1959: 51–55
4 Pamela Hansford Johnson, 'New Novels', *New Statesman*, 25 October 1958: 567
5 *The Journals of Anaïs Nin*, vol. 6 (1955–1966), Peter Owen, London, 1976: 182–3
6 Henry Miller to Durrell, 19 November 1958, Ltrs: 336–7
7 Anaïs Nin to Durrell, [before 8 November 1958] (SIU)
8 Richard Aldington to Durrell, [c. 20–22 November 1958], Ltrs: 64–5
9 Anaïs Nin to Durrell, [c. December 1958] (SIU)
10 *The Journals of Anaïs Nin*, vol. 6: 182–3
11 Diana Gould (Menuhin) to Durrell, 4 December 1958 (SIU)
12 Harry T. Moore (ed.), *The World of Lawrence Durrell*, SIU Press, Carbondale, 1962: 156
13 *Ibid.*: 157
14 *Ibid.*: 159–60. Originally in *Two Cities*, 15 April 1959: 25–28
15 Durrell to Richard Aldington, [26 January – 1 February, 1959], Ltrs: 75–7
16 Durrell to Richard Aldington, [after 1 February 1959], Ltrs: 80–1

17 *Ibid.*: 81
18 Arthur Luce Klein, interview with Lawrence Durrell, August 1961
19 Donald Barr, 'Intrigue is the Way of Life', *New York Times Book Review*, 22 March 1959: 4
20 Rod Nordell, 'Relativity in the Novel', *Christian Science Monitor*, 26 March 1959: 11
21 Charles Rollo, 'Reader's Choice', *Atlantic*, April 1959: 134
22 Richard Aldington to Durrell, April 1959, Ltrs: 88–9
23 Edwin Mullins, *Reunion in Paris*, BBC Third Programme, 2 July 1961
24 Durrell to Gerald Sykes, [after 13 May 1959] (SIU)
25 Jean Cau, 'Prix', *L'Express*: 7 May 1959: 29–30
26 Mary Hadkinson to Durrell, 14 November 1959 (SIU)
27 Gerald Durrell, 'Happy with Larry', *Sunday Telegraph*, 21 April 1991 (partly-unpublished draft) (Sommières)
28 Alan Pringle to Durrell, 13 May 1959 (SIU)
29 Mai Zetterling to Durrell, 13 May 1960 (SIU)
30 Nigel Dennis, 'New Four-Star King of Novelists', *Life*, 21 November 1960: 104
31 Henry Miller to Durrell, 9 July 1959, Ltrs: 344–7
32 David Holloway, 'Why Mr Durrell Can't Afford to Write Poetry' *News Chronicle*, 9 September 1959
33 Henry Miller to Durrell, 10 September 1959
34 Anne Leslie, 'This Infuriating Man', *Daily Express*, 8 December 1964
35 Jean Blanzat, *Figaro Littéraire*: 12 December 1959: 14
36 'The River Rhône', *Holiday*, January 1960
37 Thomas Morgan 'The Autumn Arrival of Lawrence Durrell', *Esquire* September 1960: 108–111

Chapter 13: Après le Déluge: After the Quartet

1 Jean Fanchette to Durrell, 8 February 1960 (SIU)
2 Richard Aldington to Durrell, 10 February 1960 (SIU)
3 Despidena Learmouth to Durrell, 18 February 1960 (SIU)
4 Jean Fanchette to Durrell, 9 March 1960 (SIU)
5 'The Carnal Jigsaw', *Time*, 4 April 1960: 94
6 Granville Hicks, 'Crown for a Majestic Work', *Saturday Review*, 2 April 1960: 15
7 Frank J. Warnke, 'The May Costumes of Love', *The New Republic*, 9 May 1960: 20–2
8 Walter Wanger, *My Life with Cleopatra*, Transworld, London, 1963
9 Jean Blanzat, *Figaro Littéraire*, 21 May 1960: 11
10 Jacques Vallette, 'Note on *Clea*', *Cahiers du Sud*, July 1960

11 Mai Zetterling, *All Those Tomorrows*, Cape, London, 1985: 173
12 Jay Martin, *Always Merry and Bright*, Capra Press, Santa Barbara, 1979: 453
13 Henry Miller to Durrell, 17 July 1960 (SIU)
14 George Steiner, 'The Baroque Novel', *Yale Review*, June 1960: 488–95
15 Martin Green, 'A Minority Report', *The Yale Review*, June 1960: 496–508
16 'No Clue to Living', *Times Literary Supplement*, 27 May 1960: 339
17 'Landscape with Literary Figures', *New York Times Book Review*, 12 June 1960: 1, 26, 30
18 John C Kelley, 'Lawrence Durrell: *The Alexandria Quartet*', *An Irish Quarterly Review*, 52, 1963: 52–68
19 Jean Fanchette to Durrell, 23 June 1960 (SIU)
20 Alan Clodd to Durrell, 30 June 1960 (SIU)
21 Nigel Dennis to Durrell, 8 July 1960 (SIU)
22 Beatrice Dennis to GB, 21 August 1994
23 *Ibid.*
24 Freya Stark, 'The Greeks Still Have a Word for It – Xaĩpe' *New York Times Book Review*, 6 November 1960: 7
25 Kimon Friar, 'In the Shadow of the Parthenon', *Saturday Review*, 12 November 1960: 35
26 Durrell to Nigel Dennis, 13 December 1960 (Beatrice Dennis)
27 'Sappho and After', *Labrys*, July 1979: 31–3
28 Jean Fanchette to Durrell, 21 December, 1960 (SIU)
29 Durrell to Richard Aldington, [before 24 January 1961]: Lits: 169–70
30 BBC TV, *Talking of Films*, Peter Duval Smith talking to Lawrence Durrell, 8 March 1961
31 W. J. Weatherby, 'The Durrell Brothers', *Guardian*, 6 May 1961: 4
32 Beatrice Dennis to GB, 21 August 1994
33 Jean Fanchette to Durrell, 5 April 1961
34 'Women of the Mediterranean', *Réalités*, June 1961
35 Denis de Rougemont, *Passion and Society*, Faber & Faber, London, 1956
36 Alfred Perlès to Durrell, 22 July 1961 (SIU)
37 Henry Woolf to GB, 26 February 1995
38 Peter Lewis, 'The Epic Leaves Ends Trailing' *Scottish Daily Mail*, 22 August 1961
39 Harold Hobson, 'The Quick and the Dead', *Sunday Times*, 27 August 1961: 26
40 Kenneth Tynan, 'Durrell in Three Dimensions', *Observer*, 27 August 1961: 10

41 Alan Thomas to Durrell, [August] 1961 (SIU)

42 Curtis Cate, 'Lawrence Durrell', *Atlantic*, December 1961: 63–9

Chapter 14: Incubating

1 Richard Aldington to Claude Durrell, 30 January 1962 (SIU)

2 George Seferis, 'Poets Reading No 6, *Lawrence Durrell: Greek Poems*', Jupiter Records, April 1962

3 'Thinking about "Smartie" ', *SOP*: 71–3

4 Richard Aldington to Durrell, 13 June 1962 (SIU)

5 Stephen Spender, *Journals 1939–1983*, Faber & Faber, London, 1985: 251

6 *Ibid*.: 252

7 'Durrell Returns to "Magic Greece" ', *Icones* (Athens), 9 November 1962: 24–5

8 'British Museum Bill' Letter to *The Times*, 19 December 1962: 9

9 *Newsweek*: 18 February 1963: 60

10 Gerald Sykes, *New York Times Book Review*, 7 April 1963: 16

11 'Quick Guide to Latest Reading', *The Times*, 9 May 1963: 15

12 D. J. Enright, 'Public Faeces', *Encounter*, August 1963: 84–6

13 Robin Fedden to Durrell, 9 January 1963 (SIU)

14 Durrell to Henry Miller, 1 May [1963], Ltrs: 395

15 *CP*: 271; 'Durrell at Delphi', *Realités*, November 1964: 64–9

16 *Icones* (Athens), 19 July 1963 32–3

17 'Bernard Spencer', *London Magazine*, January 1964: 42–7

18 Henry Miller to Durrell, 30 October 1963, Ltrs: 397–8

19 *Time*, 3 January 1964: 56

20 *The Times*, 7 January, 1964: 11

21 *Times Literary Supplement*, 5 December 1963: 1011

22 Durrell to Wallace Southam, [11 January 1964] (SIU)

23 'Cyprus', *The Times*, 22 May 1964: 13

24 'Lawrence Durrell: Vive L'Epfsistentialisme', *Le Quotidien*, 14 November 1974: 11

25 Alfred Perlès to Durrell, 7 April 1964 (SIU)

26 'Oil for the Saint; Return to Corfu', *Holiday* (Philadelphia), October 1966; *SOP*: 286–303

27 *Bedales Chronicle*, summer 1965: 15

28 Durrell to Alan Warren Friedman, 18 October 1964 (SIU)

29 Anne Leslie, 'This Infuriating Man', *Daily Express*, 8 December 1964

30 'Tse-lio-t', *Preuves*, April, 1965; 'The Other T. S. Eliot', *Atlantic*, May 1965: 60–4

31 Ghislaine de Boysson to GB, 6 May 1995

32 John Gawsworth to Durrell, 20 October 1965 (SIU)

33 John Gawsworth to Durrell, 1 November 1965 (SIU)
34 BBC TV, *Intimations*
35 Durrell to Audrey Beecham, [reply to letter of 24 May 1966] (Bodleian)
36 Anaïs Nin to Durrell, 5 December 1966 (SIU)
37 *SITME*: 33
38 Durrell to Audrey Beecham, [reply to letter of 24 May 1966] (Bodleian)

Chapter 15: Back to Women and Fiction in a World of Sad Ghosts

1 Sappho Durrell, 'Journals and Letters', *Granta*, Autumn 1991: 61
2 Ève, Sappho, Ghislaine and Françoise experienced being put into his novels as characters.
3 'Pooter', *The Times*: 9 March 1968: 21
4 Peter Collier, 'A Talk with Lawrence Durrell', *New York Times Book Review*, 14 April 1968: 15
5 BBC TV, *The Arts This Week*, 25 March 1970
6 John Gawsworth to Durrell, 7 October 1967
7 Durrell to Henry Miller, 20 November 1967, Ltrs: 422–3
8 Durrell to Henry Miller, 2 December [1967], Ltrs: 423–4
9 Roy Perrot, 'Lawrence Durrell: An Author in his Setting', *Observer Magazine*, 31 March 1968: 37, 38, 40, 42
10 Durrell to G. S. Fraser, 27 November 1967 (NLS)
11 Alan Thomas to Durrell, 7 January 1968 (SIU)
12 'Pooter', *The Times*, 9 March 1968: 21
13 Hiroko Tokuda (Hoki) to Durrell, quoted by John Windsor in 'Love Letters of a Sexual Revolutionary', *The Independent*, 15 July 1988
14 John Unterecker to 'Mr. G.', 5 May 1968 (SIU)
15 'Abel is the Novel, Merlin is the Firm', *Time*, 5 April 1968: 64
16 Gerald Sykes, 'Durrell's 1984', *New York Times Book Review*, 14 April 1968: 4, 14
17 Kenneth Rexroth, 'A Steady Note of Mockery', *The Nation*, 10 May 1968: 674
18 G. S. Fraser, 'By Courtesy of the Firm', *New Statesman*, 12 April 1968: 483–4
19 Robert Pitman, 'Has Mr Durrell Cast His Strange Spell Over YOU?', *Sunday Express*, 28 April 1968: 6
20 Durrell to G.S. Fraser, [mid-May 1968] (NLS)
21 Conrad Moricand 'Astrological Portrait of Lawrence Durrell', Appendix in Marc Alyn, *The Big Supposer*, Abelard-Schuman, London, 1973: 156.

22 *CVG*: 27
23 Hiroko Tokuda (Hoki) to Durrell, quoted by John Windsor in, 'Love Letters of a Sexual Revolutionary'
24 Diana Gould (Menuhin) to Durrell, 7 July 1968 (SIU)
25 Gerald Durrell to Lawrence Durrell, 26 June 1968 (SIU)
26 Alan Thomas to Durrell, 10 May 1969 (SIU)
27 Larry Marcus-Durrell, [August 1969] (Sommières)
28 Beverly Grey, 'Justine Qui Confond', *UCLA Daily Bruin*, 25 July 1969: 5–6
29 Penelope Gilliat, 'The Current Cinema', *The New Yorker*, 9 August 1969: 67–9
30 Dan Wakefield, 'New Styles of Storytelling', *Atlantic Monthly*, November 1969: 170–2
31 Henry Miller to Durrell, 3 September 1969, Ltrs: 434–5
32 Henry Miller to Durrell, 27 February 1970, Ltrs: 438–9
33 BBC TV, *The Arts This Week*, 25 March 1970
34 BBC TV, *The Lonely Roads*, 21 March 1970
35 'The Long Arm of the Firm', *Times Literary Supplement*, 26 March 1970: 325
36 Richard Holmes, 'The Technological Iolanthe', *The Times*, 21 March 1970: V
37 Christopher Ricks, 'Female and Other Impersonators', *New York Review of Books*, 23 July 1970: 8
38 Richard Boston, 'Nunquam', *New York Times Book Review*, 29 March 1970: 4, 20
39 Eugene Lyons and Harry T. Antrim, 'An Interview with Lawrence Durrell', *Shanandoah*: Winter 1971: 42–58
40 'Osric Allen Talks to Lawrence Durrell', *Nouse*, 28 May 1970: 4
41 'The Kneller Tape', in Harry T. Moore (ed.), *The World of Lawrence Durrell*, SIU Press, Carbondale, 1962: 168
42 'Writer Durrell Makes a Splash as a Painter', Reuters for *Los Angeles Times*, 1 January 1971
43 Durrell to Henry Miller, 28 January 1971, Ltrs: 443
44 *Ibid.*: 443
45 Durrell to Henry Miller, 19 February 1971, Ltrs: 444–6
46 Henry Miller to Durrell, 12 February 1971, Ltrs: 444
47 Durrell to Henry Miller, 5 March 1971, Ltrs: 446–8
48 Robert Nye, 'Magic is Not Enough', *The Times*, 12 August 1971: 8
49 Diana Gould (Menuhin) to Durrell, 14 July 1971 (SIU)
50 Durrell to Henry Miller, 11 August 1971, Ltrs: 450–2

Chapter 16: The Prince of Darkness or the Devil at Large

1 Jacques Lacarrière, *The Gnostics*, Gallimard, Paris, 1973; City Lights Press, San Francisco, 1989

2 Richard Pine, *Lawrence Durrell: The Mindscape*, Macmillan, London, 1995

3 'Duffy's Dublin', *Vogue*, May 1975: 70–3

4 Durrell to Henry Miller, 12 February, 1972, Ltrs: 454–6

5 *The Plant Magic Man*, Capra Press, Santa Barbara, 1973

6 Mary (Mollo) Hadkinson to GB, interview, 16 April 1993

7 Henry Miller to Durrell, 20 September 1972, Ltrs: 456

8 *Ibid.*

9 Durrell to Henry Miller, 11 December 1972, Ltrs: 460–1

10 Henry Miller to Durrell, 31 March 1973, Ltrs: 464–5

11 Philip Howard, 'The Wall Comes Tumbling Down', *The Times*, 28 April 1973: 14

12 Atticus, *Sunday Times*, 29 April 1973: 32

13 Howard, 'The Wall Comes Tumbling Down': 14

14 Paul Theroux, 'A Savage Charcoal Sketch', *The Times*, 26 April 1973: 10

15 Philip Howard, 'The Wall Comes Tumbling Down': 14

16 Robin Livio, 'Who are You, Lawrence Durrell?', *Bulletin of the Festival International de Cannes*, 11 May 1973

17 Durrell's Notebook for c. 1972–73 (Sommières)

18 Ghislaine de Boysson to GB, 6 May 1995

19 *Ibid.*

20 *Ibid.*

21 Anaïs Nin to Durrell, 19 November 1973 (SIU)

22 Ghislaine de Boysson to GB, 6 May 1995

23 BT

24 Lacarrière, *The Gnostics*: 17

25 Henry Miller to Durrell, 19 September 1974, Ltrs: 474–5

26 Ghislaine de Boysson to GB, 6 May 1995

27 *Ibid.*

28 BBC Radio 4, *Kaleidoscope*, 14 October 1974

29 'Hugh Herbert Interviews Lawrence Durrell', *Guardian*, 18 October 1974

30 Christopher Wordsworth, 'Lampreys on a Lordly Dish', *Guardian*, 17 October 1974

31 Paul Hordequin, 'Dr Larry et Mister Epfs', *Le Quotidien*, 14 November 1974

32 Diana Gould (Menuhin) to Durrell, April 1975 (SIU)

33 Durrell to Henry Miller, 28 March, 1975, Ltrs: 477–8

34 Ian McNiven, 'Lawrence Durrell and the Nightingales of Sommières',

in Lawrence W. Markert and Carol Peirce, *On Miracle Ground II*,
SIU Press, Carbondale, 1984: 236
35 'Mandrake', 'Lawrence Durrell on the Point of Avignon', *Sunday
Telegraph*, 26 May 1985
36 Ghislaine de Boysson to GB, 6 May 1995
37 BBC TV, *Spirit of Place: Lawrence Durrell's Greece*, 13 March 1976
38 Durrell to Henry Miller, 3 November 1975, Ltrs: 479–81
39 'Up for Air', *The Times*, 21 November 1975: 16
40 Ghislaine de Boysson to GB, 6 May 1995

Chapter 17: The Avignon Quintet: *Cruel Fiction*

1 *SITME*: 23
2 Jolan Chang to Durrell, 10 January 1976 (Ghislaine de Boysson)
3 Peter Adam, *Not Drowning But Waving*, André Deutsch, London,
1995: 332
4 James Heilpern, 'Portrait of the Artist as Expatriate', *Radio Times*,
13–19 March 1976: 4–5
5 Anaïs Nin to Durrell, 12 April 1976 (SIU)
6 Durrell to Cecily Mackworth, [April/May] 1976 (Mackworth)
7 Justine Picardie, 'A Father's Shadow', *Independent Magazine*, 28
September 1991, 29
8 'Lawrence Durrell Takes Stock', *International Herald Tribune*, 17
November 1978: 13
9 Deirdre Bair, *Anaïs Nin: A Biography*, Bloomsbury, London 1995:
514
10 Rupert Pole to Durrell, 2 March 1977 (SIU)
11 Durrell to Henry Miller, 28 April 1977, Ltrs: 484–5
12 Diana Gould (Menuhin) to Durrell, 6 May 1977 (SIU)
13 Durrell to Henry Miller, 7 August 1977, Ltrs: 497–8
14 Adam, *Not Drowning But Waving*: 369
15 The account of this trip to Egypt has been gleaned from *ibid.*:
363–9
16 'Poetry', *The Times*: 27 October 1977: 3
17 Durrell to Henry Miller, 30 May 1978, Ltrs: 494–5
18 Durrell to Henry Miller, 4 June 1978, Ltrs: 495–6
19 Richard Holmes, 'Autumn Fiction II', *The Times*, 21 September
1978: 12
20 Julian Barnes, 'Trick or Treat', *New Statesman*, 22 September 1978:
378
21 Keith Brown, 'X en Provence', *Times Literary Supplement*, 13
October 1978: 1140
22 Durrell to Henry Miller, 16 October 1978, Ltrs: 497–8
23 Henry Miller to Durrell, 23 [October 1978], Ltrs: 498–9

24 Picardie, 'A Father's Shadow': 28

25 Ghislaine de Boysson to GB, 6 May 1995

26 'Lawrence Durrell Takes Stock', *International Herald Tribune*, 17 November, 1978: 13

27 Durrell to Henry Miller, 6 January 1979, Ltrs: 501–3

28 Henry Miller to Durrell, Christmas, 1978, Ltrs: 499–500

29 Durrell to Henry Miller, 10 January 1979, Ltrs: 503–4

30 Durrell to Henry Miller, 29 March 1979, Ltrs: 504–5

31 Alfred Perlès to Durrell, 9 April 1979 (SIU)

32 Picardie, 'A Father's Shadow': 28

33 Alistair Forbes, 'Dwarves Abounding in Provence', *New York Times Book Review*, 22 April 1979: 14

34 Sappho Durrell, 'Journals and Letters', *Granta*, Autumn 1991: 70

35 *Ibid.*: 74

36 *Ibid.*: 75–8

37 *Ibid.*: 79–81

38 Durrell to Henry Miller, 14 December 1979, Ltrs: 507–8

39 Sappho Durrell, 'Journals and Letters': 83

40 Durrell to Henry Miller, 28 December 1979, Ltrs: 508–9

41 Henry Miller to Durrell, 9 January 1980, Ltrs: 509–10

Chapter 18: The Avignon Quintet: *The Mystery of the Quincunx*

1 Sappho Durrell, 'Journals and Letters', *Granta*, Autumn 1991: 84–5

2 *Ibid.*: 86

3 Andrew Sanger, 'A Life in the Day', *Sunday Times Magazine*, 14 September 1980: 127

4 Justinc Picardie, 'A Father's Shadow', *Independent Magazine*, 28 September 1991: 28

5 Ian McNiven and Harry T. Moore, *Literary Lifelines*, The Viking Press, New York, 1981

6 Charles Champlin, 'Letters Charting the Literary Tides', *Los Angeles Times*, 5 May 1981

7 'Books Briefly Noted', the *New Yorker*, 18 May 1981: 169

8 John Carey, 'Richard Aldington's Septic Psyche', *Sunday Times*, 12 July 1981: 43

9 George Hill, 'The Prince of Literary Lions', *The Times*, 16 July 1981: 10

10 Ghislaine de Boysson to GB, 6 May 1995

11 Sappho Durrell, 'Journals and Letters': 88–9

12 *Ibid.*: 89

13 *Ibid.*

14 *Ibid.*
15 Eric Ollivier, 'Lawrence Durrell: Un Européen Bien Tranquille', *L'Express*, 27 August 1981
16 David Pryce-Jones, 'In Praise of People, Places and Ideas', *Sunday Telegraph*, 17 October 1982
17 'The Snare That Trapped Mrs Durrell', *The Times*, 8 December 1981: 10
18 Alfred Perlès to Durrell, 9 March 1982 (Victoria)
19 Alfred Perlès to Durrell, 20 September 1982 (Victoria)
20 Durrell's Notebook c. 1982 (Sommières)
21 Sappho's Diary, 10 July 1982: Sappho Durrell, 'Journals and Letters'
22 Ciaran Carty, 'The Second Childhood of Lawrence Durrell', *Independent on Sunday*, 9 June 1985: 13
23 Michel Braudeau, 'Apres ça j'aurai tout dit', *L'Egoïste*, August 1984
24 David Pryce-Jones, 'In Praise of People, Places and Ideas'
25 Claire Tomalin, 'A Reader's Guide to the Booker', *Sunday Times*, 3 October 1982: 43
26 Justine Picardie, 'A Father's Shadow': 30
27 Ghislaine de Boysson to GB, 6 May 1995
28 Michel Braudeau, 'Apres çạ j'aurai tout dit'
29 Jean Montalbetti, 'Lawrence Durrell en Dix Mouvements', *Magazine Littéraire*, September 1984: 78–85
30 Justine Picardie, 'A Father's Shadow': 30
31 Robert Briatte, 'Un portrait inachevé', *Dolines*, October/November 1984: 13–17
32 'Durrell: The Magic of the Avignon Quintet', *Le Republicain Lorraine*, October, 1984
33 Françoise Erval, 'Un torent d'images de mots et d'idées', *France Soir*, 26 January 1985
34 Bruno de Cessole, 'Lawrence Durrell existe, je l'a rencontré', *Magazine Hebdo*, 23 November 1984
35 David Gascoyne to Durrell [September 1984] (SIU)

Chapter 19: Out of Breath

1 *Le Monde*, 26 April 1985
2 Ciaran Carty, 'The Second Childhood of Lawrence Durrell', *Independent on Sunday*, 9 June 1985: 13
3 Allan Massie, 'Stately Progress of the Imagination', *Scotsman*, 24 May 1985
4 'Mandrake', 'Lawrence Durrell on the Point of Avignon', *Sunday Telegraph*, 26 May 1985
5 Desmond Christy, 'The Devil and Mr Durrell', *The Guardian*, 28 May 1985

6 Lord Scarborough to GB, 8 November 1994
7 Andrew Morgan, 'Durrell the Great, Weaving his Sensuous Spells and Basking in Praise', *Liverpool Daily Post*, 20 May 1985
8 BBC Radio 4, *Woman's Hour*, 3 June 1985
9 Interview with Edward Blishen, BBC World Service, *Meridian*, May 1985
10 Edward Blishen to GB, 25 February 1995
11 Helen Simpson, 'The Mellowing of Lawrence Durrell', *Vogue*, June 1985: 234, 237, 283
12 Patrick Parrinder, 'The Naming of Parts', *London Review of Books*, 6 June 1985: 22–3
13 Ciaran Carty, 'The Second Childhood of Lawrence Durrell': 13
14 Cécile Wajsbrot, 'Lawrence Durrell', *Les Nouvelles Littéraire* (Paris) April 1986
15 David Lida, 'Lawrence Durrell: The Romantic Renegade', *W* (New York), 5–12 May 1986: 18
16 Charles E. Claffey, 'Lawrence Durrell: British Author of the Exotic is still Dazzling his Critics', *Boston Globe*, 25 April 1986: B3–4
17 Michael H. Begnal (ed.), *On Miracle Ground: Essays on the Fiction of Lawrence Durrell*, Bucknell University Press, Lewisberg, 1990: 18
18 Lida, 'Lawrence Durrell'
19 Elizabeth Kastor, 'Lawrence Durrell's Odyssey of the Mind: The Evolutionary Travels of the Author of *The Alexandria Quartet*', *Washington Post*, 29 May 1986
20 Gilles Costaz, 'Lawrence Durrell Under the Verandah', *Le Matin*, 6 June 1986
21 Durrell to Cecily Mackworth, [before 27 February 1987] (Mackworth)
22 Philippe Delaroche, 'Lawrence Durrell, 'Je suis un philosophe, c'est plus pénible, parce que je vois; a réalité', *Le Matin*, 24 August 1987
23 *Lawrence Durrell Herald*, 9: 1987/88: 10
24 'Le diable aux Célestins', *Le Figaro*, 10 November 1987: 44
25 *Ibid.*: 47
26 Andrew Harvey and Mark Matousek, *Interview*, March 1988: 119–20
27 John Windsor, 'Love Letters of a Sexual Revolutionary', *Independent*, 15 July 1988
28 Geraldine Norman, 'Buyers Are Backwards in Coming Forward', *Independent*, 23 July 1988
29 Vivian Gornick, 'Masters of Self-Congratulation', *New York Times Book Review*, 20 November 1988: 2
30 Anthony Burgess, 'Dear Henry, Yours Larry', *Observer*, 28 August 1988

31 Television film by George Hoffman for French television, 1988
32 National Public Radio's *Week End Edition*, 18 January 1989
33 'Le Vieux Sage', *Le Figaro*, 12 August 1989
34 Alfred Perlès to Durrell, [September 1989] (SIU)
35 David Gascoyne, 'Lawrence Durrell', *Independent*, 10 November 1990
36 *Bookseller*, 3 November 1989
37 Michael Dibdin, 'One Man's Retreat from Pudding Island', *Independent on Sunday*, 11 November 1990: 27

Chapter 20: The Bubble Reputation

1 David Gascoyne, 'Lawrence Durrell', *Independent*, 10 November 1990
2 Patrick Leigh Fermor, 'Durrell', *Spectator*, 17 November 1990: 28–30
3 Erica Jong, 'Durrell Had a Rare Courage', *New York Observer*, 10 December 1990
4 Anthony Burgess, 'The Rich Appetites of an Englishman Abroad', *Independent*, 9 November 1990: 21
5 Kenneth McLeish, 'Scarifying the Stodge', *Sunday Times*, 11 November 1990, section 8: 6
6 Philip Howard, 'Modernism's Better Half', *The Times*, 9 November 1990: 14
7 David Hughes, 'Durrell's Last Words Endure', *Mail on Sunday*, 11 January 1991
8 Roger Clarke, 'Scenes from Provençal Life', *Sunday Times*, 25 November 1990: 4
9 Susan Spano Wells, 'In the Footsteps of the Gods', *New York Newsday*, 9 December 1990
10 Nicholas Delbanco, 'Tribute to South of France Explores Time and Terrain', *Detroit Free Press*, 16 December 1990
11 Nicholas Shakespeare, 'Durrell Affair with Suicide Daughter Sappho', *Sunday Telegraph*, 26 May 1991: 1
12 Lois Rogers and Stewart Payne, 'The Truth about a Literary Legend, Incest and the Woman Who Loved her Father to Death', *Evening Standard*, 31 May 1991: 18–19
13 'Françoise Kestsman La Flamme de Durrell', Elle, 26 October 1992: 56
14 G. S. Fraser, *Lawrence Durrell: A Study*, Faber & Faber, 1968: 28
15 CP: 322, 336

Index